STUDIES IN SOUTH ASIAN LINGUISTICS

Studies in South Asian Linguistics

Sinhala and Other South Asian Languages

JAMES W. GAIR

SELECTED AND EDITED BY BARBARA C. LUST

New York   Oxford
OXFORD UNIVERSITY PRESS
1998

Oxford University Press

Oxford   New York
Athens   Auckland   Bangkok   Bogota   Bombay   Buenos Aires
Calcutta   Cape Town   Dar es Salaam   Delhi   Florence   Hong Kong
Istanbul   Karachi   Kuala Lumpur   Madras   Madrid   Melbourne
Mexico City   Nairobi   Paris   Singapore   Taipei   Tokyo   Toronto   Warsaw

and associated companies in
Berlin   Ibadan

Library of Congress Cataloging-in-Publication Data
Gair, James W.
    Studies in South Asian linguistics : Sinhala and other South Asian
languages / James W. Gair ; selected and edited by Barbara C. Lust.
        p.   cm.
    ISBN 0-19-509521-9
    1. Sri Lanka—Languages—History   2. Sinhalese language—Grammar.
    3. Tamil language—Dialects—Sri Lanka—Jaffna District—Grammar.
    4. Sri Lanka—Languages—Political aspects.   I. Title.
    PK2808.G35   1998
    491'.485—dc20   95-46071

9 8 7 6 5 4 3 2 1

Printed in the United States of America
on acid-free paper

Acknowledgments

The following chapters appearing in this volume are based on previous publications as listed below. Permission to reprint has been granted by the publishers of the original articles and is gratefully acknowledged.

Sinhala, an Indo-Aryan Isolate. 1982. *South Asian Review* 6(3): 51–64.

Colloquial Sinhalese Inflectional Categories and Parts of Speech. 1967. *Indian Linguistics* 27: 32–45.

Action Involvement Categories in Colloquial Sinhalese. 1971. In M. Zamora, J. Michael Mahar, and H. Orenstein (eds.), *Themes in Culture: Essays in Honor of Morris E. Opler*, pp. 238–256. Manila: Kayumanggi Publishers.

Subjects, Case and INFL in Sinhala. 1991. In M. Verma and K. P. Mohanan (eds.), *Experiencer Subjects in South Asian Languages*, pp. 13–41. Palo Alto, Calif.: Center for the Study of Language and Information.

Sinhala Non-verbal Sentences and Argument Structure (with John Paolillo). 1989. In V. Srivastav, J. Gair, and K. Wali (eds.), *Cornell Working Papers in Linguistics* 8 (Special issue on South Asian Linguistics), pp. 39–77. Ithaca, N.Y.: Cornell University.

Discourse and Situational Deixis in Sinhala. 1991. In Lakshmi Bai Balachandran and B. Ramakrishna Reddy (eds.), *Studies in Dravidian and General Linguistics: A Festschrift for Bh. Krishnamurti*, pp. 448–467 (Publications in Linguistics 6). Hyderabad, India: Osmania University.

On Distinguishing AGR from agr: Evidence from South Asia (with Kashi Wali). 1988. In D. Brentari, G. Larson, and L. MacLeod (eds.), *Papers from the Parasession on Agreement in Linguistic Theory*. CLS 24 (2): 87–104. Chicago Linguistic Society.

Sinhala Focused Sentences: Naturalization of a Calque. 1985. In Bh. Krishnamurti, C. Masica, and A. Sinha (eds.), *South Asian Languages: Structure, Convergence and Diglossia*, pp. 147–164. Delhi: Motilal Banarsidass.

Some Aspects of the Jaffna Tamil Verbal System (with S. Suseendiraraiah). 1981. *International Journal of Dravidian Linguistics* 10(2): 370–384.

Review of F. Southworth and M. Apte (1974), Contact and Convergence in South Asian Languages. 1978. (Selections) *Language* 54: 461–465.

How Dravidianized Was Sinhala Phonology: Some Conclusions and Cautions. 1985. In R. L. Leed and V. Acson (eds.), *Festschrift for Gordon H. Fairbanks*, pp. 37–55. Honolulu: Oceanic Linguistics, University of Hawaii.

The Verb in Sinhala with Some Preliminary Remarks on Dravidianization. 1976. (Selections) *International Journal of Dravidian Linguistics* 5(2): 259–273.

Sinhalese Diglossia. 1968. *Anthropological Linguistics* 10(4): 1–15.

Sinhala Diglossia Revisited or Diglossia Dies Hard. 1985. In Bh. Krishnamurti, C. Masica, and A. Sinha (eds.), *South Asian Languages: Structure, Convergence, and Diglossia*, pp. 322–336. Delhi: Motilal Banarsidass.

Acquisition of Null Subjects and Control in Some Sinhala Adverbial Clauses (with B. Lust, L. Sumangala, and M. Rodrigo). 1989. In *Papers and Reports on Child Language Development [Stanford]* 28: 97–106.

Children's Acquisition of Hindi Anaphora in 'jab' Clauses: A Parameter Setting Paradox (with B. Lust, T. Bhatia, V. Sharma, and J. Khare). 1995. In Vijay Gambhir (ed.), *Teaching and Acquisition of South Asian Languages*, pp. 172–189. Philadelphia: University of Pennsylvania Press.

TO

W. S. Karunatillake

student, scholar, colleague, friend, and constant source of
both information and insight,

and

to all of the others in South Asia, too many to name, who have
made my work not only possible but a joy, and granted me
the inestimable privilege of entry into their languages and culture.

sace labetha nipakaṃ sahāyaṃ
   saddhiṃcaraṃ sādhuvihāridhiraṃ
abhibhuyya sabbāni parissayāni
   careyya ten' attamano satimā.

PREFACE

This volume contains representative papers spanning most of my professional career, making this a welcome opportunity to indulge in some personal acknowledgments, some of which have not previously appeared publicly and are thus long overdue.

I was privileged to have been encouraged to persist in academia at several points by those I respected as teachers. Several members of the English faculty of the University of Buffalo fall into that category, particularly my tutor, Professor Harold Boner, Professor Henry Ten Eyck Perry, and, more directly related to linguistics, Professor Elda Baumann, who, in her courses that we would now call philological, taught me the value of precision in both search and statement in language studies and alerted me to the ACLS summer linguistics fellowship that started me on my way.

I was also lucky enough to learn from many masters in linguistics, among whom I might mention Henry Lee Smith, who first inspired me to enter the field in a lecture that revealed, to my surprise, that language was susceptible to precise, economical, and formal analysis and statement. In the many hours that I was able to spend with him since, I also learned that the interplay of data, especially new data, and principled analysis was exciting and fun. Many others—including but not limited to W. Freeman Twaddell, Martin Joos, Jim Downer, William Moulton, and George L. Trager—contributed to my studies, but I must especially single out Charles F. Hockett, whose insights into language and its structure (not omitting the distinction between deep and surface structure and other concepts that were daring and even revolutionary at the time), as well as his range of interests encompassing language and culture, never ceased to amaze me.

Many if not all of those whom I just mentioned would disapprove, I am sure, of the theoretical directions that I subsequently followed, but their lessons stay with me and form the indispensable foundation for whatever followed.

Among my gurus in linguistics, I must, finally, single out Gordon H. Fairbanks, who more than anyone else was responsible for my commitment to South Asian linguistics, as I point out in the introductory note to the paper from his Festschrift included here, which I would also rededicate at this time. Gordon remained, for me, "an incomparable field of merit" in the field.

I would also be remiss if I did not mention John Roberts and Morris Opler, whose very different approaches to anthropology formed a crucial part of my background in that discipline.

Other acknowledgments appear in the notes or text of many papers in this volume, but I would be remiss if I did not express here my debt and affection for the many friends and colleagues in South Asia whom I have been privileged to know over the years. There are too many to catalogue here, but I would like to single out my departed colleague M. W. S. (Sugath) De Silva, with whom I first worked on Sinhala and who is cited numerous times in papers here, and W. S Karunatillake, who is featured in the dedication to this volume.

Finally, thanks are due to L. Sumangala, for help in assembling the papers included in this volume; and to John Paolillo and Alice Davison, Kashi Wali, and K. Subbarao, for both critical comments and valuable assistance in its organization at various points. Steve Bonta provided invaluable help in assembling the index. Above all, Barbara Lust is owed unbounded gratitude for the great amount of effort, patience, and persistence that she invested in the organization of this volume, without which it would not exist, as well as for brightening my life in innumerable ways.

Ithaca, New York   J. W. G
August 1997

CONTENTS

A NOTE ON TRANSCRIPTION

AND TERMINOLOGY

The transcription used for examples in the chapters in this volume follows in general the familiar conventions used for South Asian languages and is largely self-explanatory. However, there are some differences across the essays that reflect variations in the manner of presentation of their original form, often in response to different publication requirements, limitations of available fonts, and intended audience. It was felt that it was simplest to retain the transcriptions in their original form, since they involved only variant notational representations not significantly different analyses, and it became clear that to attempt standardization would bring other complications into play. In some chapters, where transcription differences or conventions for a particular language are relevant, the necessary information will be given in the notes.

A few points are worth noting here, however.

Vowel length is generally indicated by doubling the vowel symbol. In some cases, however a macron is used, so that the word for 'uncooked rice' in Sinhala is generally represented as *haal*, but could also be represented as *hāl*. In a few articles, especially those relating to Sinhala diglossia, both transcriptions are used and the distinction is systematic, with the former system being used for spoken forms and the latter employed in transliterating written forms in the Literary variety, as well as for forms in the classical languages Sanskrit and Pali.

Similarly, retroflex consonants may be represented by either capitalization or underdot. Thus the Sinhala form for 'mouth' may be *maṭə* or *maTə*.

Some specific characteristics of Sinhala phonology and transcription should also be noted in this connection. The Sinhala prenasalized stops, or "half-nasals," are represented as *m̆b*, *n̆d*, *n̆ḍ* (*n̆D*), and *n̆g*, and they contrast with nasal+voiced stop clusters *mb, nd, ṇḍ* (*nD*), and *ng*. Sinhala has a three-way contrast between *a, aa,* and *ə*. The distributions of *ə* and *a*, however, are largely predictable, and the two are in near complementation, with the contrast hinging on a few lexical items. In the written language, only a two-way difference is represented, between *a* and *ā*, and transliterations here, as opposed to representations of spoken examples, reflect this. In Colloquial Sinhala, all final nasals are generally neutralized to the velar nasal [ŋ], and that is reflected in many examples in this book in which these forms are so written. In several chapters, however, following the system that was used in Gair 1970, *n* is taken as the unmarked nasal, surfacing as [ŋ] finally. In other instances, however, the underlying nasals *m, n,* and *ŋ*, which surface for some speakers in at least some forms, are represented in examples.

Forms represented as ending in *-yi* in some chapters are given as ending in *-y* in others. This does not reflect a phonetic difference, but only different analyses, reflecting an as yet unresolved indeterminacy in Sinhala phonology. In some chapters the difference in representation is systematic: the very frequent predication marker *yi* is represented as such in citation, but in examples it is given in its generally occurring surface form *-y*.

The essays here do not deal directly with phonology, so that the differences across chapters in transcription do not affect the conclusions and analyses in them. For one general description of Sinhala phonology, see J. B. Disanayaka, *The Structure of Spoken Sinhala*, Vol. 1, *Sounds and Their Patterns* (National Institute of Education, Sri Lanka, 1991). A recent Cornell doctoral dissertation by Rebecca Letterman (Letterman 1996) presents a more technical analysis with an account of earlier work and an extensive bibliography.

Most terminology in this volume is standard within linguistics or is defined within the specific chapter. However, there are some differences in the nomenclature for categories, representing to some extent the result of analyses as they understandably progressed over time. The crucial categories are defined within the chapters and thus should cause no difficulty.

In some cases, the designation of the same element was changed as work progressed because another term seemed more accurately to capture its nature. The most important case of this is probably the change from "emphatic" to "focused" or "cleft" for an important Sinhala sentence type, accompanied by a shift in the designation of the associated verbal affix from "emphatic" (EMPH) to "focus" (FOC), especially as it appears in the glosses. A similar consideration applies to the case designation "nominative" which replaced "direct" in some later papers and to "nonpast" which in some papers appears as "present." Other such changes over time are dealt with in the various notes.

The designation for the language with which most of this book is concerned also varied over time, as well as that for the country of its location. In the 1960s, the names "Sinhalese" and "Ceylon" were current. Subsequently, the name of the country was officially changed to Sri Lanka. Also, the officially preferred name for the language in English (*sinhala* has always been used in Sinhala itself) gained increasing, though not universal, currency. In some of the earlier articles, such as the " Sinhala Diglossia" chapter, the original usage, which included the title, was designedly retained, since it appeared to better locate the article in the appropriate time frame and in the proper temporal relation to the later efforts on the topic.

INTRODUCTION

The papers and extracts here represent a selection from work in the linguistics of South Asian languages that spans just over thirty years. Although some of them appear in print for the first time in this volume, most of them have been published elsewhere. Many of the latter, however, appeared in Festschrifts, memorial volumes, or other sources that are difficult to access. Also, although the range of topics is wide, the papers here taken together inform each other and the developing general paradigm of cross-linguistic investigation in which they are set. It thus appeared advisable to have this collection appear in one volume.

If there is any one theme that runs through the material collected here, in addition to the concentration on South Asian languages, it is the interaction and interrelation between linguistic theory and actual language data. Throughout, these writings reflect a particular approach to cross-linguistic research; that is, on the one hand, an attention to the abstract concerns for fundamental principles embodied in current linguistic theory and, on the other, fidelity and depth in the treatment of specific languages. The research collected here has attempted to maintain an awareness that languages, despite their adherence to universal principles, have an internal system, an architectonics of their own. This fact, which is one of the fundamental insights of linguistic theory since Saussure, has often been overlooked in current cross-linguistic research, in which the search for universal principles, however admirable and exciting, has often been pursued to the exclusion of language-specific principles and internal systems, Throughout, the papers collected in this volume have attempted to maintain a dual responsibility: on the one hand, to the structure inherent in a language, reflected largely here in studies of Sinhala, as well as of other South Asian languages, and, on the other, to linguistics as a science with its own principles and procedures, concerned with the fundamental nature of the human language capability.

Concern for these interrelations has remained constant in this work even as linguistic theory has changed continually over time. The earliest of them, "Colloquial Sinhalese Inflectional Categories and Parts of Speech" (1967, but written several years earlier), represents a straight neo-Bloomfieldian descriptivist treatment of one set of phenomena within the structure of Sinhala (then commonly called Sinhalese). At the time, however, it represented a pioneering attempt to provide a principled description of that language by approaching it as a system of forms defined fundamentally by formal contrasts. Along with the work of my colleague the late M. W. S. De Silva (including his joint work with William Coates, also unfortunately deceased), it formed the beginnings of published work on Sinhala in terms of modern linguistics, and it seemed a revolutionary step to those who had operated within the framework of traditional or meaning-based grammar.

As the attention shifted to syntax, the inadequacies of the strict descriptivist approach in even arriving at a satisfactory description of the language became apparent, and that awareness resulted in the early transformational probings reflected in the monograph *Colloquial Sinhalese Clause Structures*. Publication of that work was unfortunately delayed until 1970, though it was largely a revised version of my 1962 Ph.D. dissertation and submitted much earlier. Its theoretical sources were thus in fact largely restricted to Chomsky's 1957 *Syntactic Structures* and Robert Lees's 1960 *The Grammar of English Nominalizations*, along with the work of Zellig Harris and a few other sources that appear in its bibliography. It thus preceded (at least in composition) the important theoretical developments in Chomsky's 1965 *Aspects*, as well as other intervening work.

However, the attempt to apply the available transformational–generative armament to the extensive description of a language of a quite different type from English revealed both the power of that approach taken as a descriptive device and its limitations, as it was then formulated, in dealing with a very different kind of language. In particular, that tension between theory and data revealed and illustrated a number of problems that generative grammar would have to face and that still pertain today to a considerable extent, though in a different guise, and thus often couched in different terms. Among them was (to use now-current terms somewhat anachronistically) the determination of constituent structure in a language that combined free word order ("nonconfigurationality") with a fundamentally strongly left-branching schema and apparently quite free deletion of subjects and other constituents (which might now be referred to as "super pro drop").

These characteristics forced one to face a number of problems, such as the difficulty of defining just what constitutes an argument, the necessity of distinguishing between different kinds of empty categories (represented there as "discourse deletion" versus "zeroing"), the necessity of dealing with something like theta roles in determining argument structure, and the need to incorporate lexical information somewhere in the grammar in order to deal with limitations and irregularities in the relationship between apparently related structures (expressed there as "quasitransformations" along with a rudimentary lexicon relating to them). The very frequent employment of focusing (clefting) in Sinhala, its special morphological marking, and especially its pervasiveness in the grammar across apparently radically different types of sentences including both verbal and nonverbal exemplars posed the problem of expressing a relationship of that kind with sufficient generality to capture the cross-type parallels while retaining a sufficient degree of explicitness and precision. The description of *Colloquial Sinhalese Clause Structures* included here elaborates further on those concerns as they then appeared in relation to some crucial characteristics of Sinhala. As several of the later papers, along with even a casual perusal of the relevant present-day literature, will reveal, those issues are far from settled even at the time of this writing, despite the considerable progress in theory and cross-linguistic work in the meantime, and the data as such remain relevant.

Much of the subsequent work represented here in the section on syntactic and morphosyntactic studies continued and expanded those concerns, although in different terms as the theory of transformational-generative grammar and then the modern theory of Universal Grammar (UG) developed. For example, the 1967 "Action Involvement Categories" paper, which preceded the rise of "case grammar" (e.g., Fillmore, 1968), essentially dealt with the interaction of case assignment and theta role. The 1976 paper "Is Sinhala a Subject Language?" once more addressed the problem of defining constituents and (in current terms) finding the proper linkage among syntactic position, grammatical relations, case marking, and theta roles, in that instance within a typological framework. That paper has not been included here, largely because essentially the same concerns were addressed in the later (1991) paper "Subjects, Case and INFL in Sinhala," cast basically in the more recent Government and Binding framework. In that paper, the lexicon once more assumed a central importance, as was foreshadowed in *Colloquial Sinhalese Clause Structures* in dealing with some of the same phenomena, so that the "quasi transformations" of that volume reemerged in the later paper transmuted to lexical specifications and processes.

The concern with INFL, agreement, and their interaction with case assignment also informs the paper "On Distinguishing AGR from agr: Evidence from South Asia," done jointly with Kashi Wali and incorporating materials and analyses from other more detailed papers on Hindi and Marathi by the same authors listed in the bibliography. Again, this is couched within a framework of typology and Universal Grammar.

The concern with anaphora, empty categories, and their interaction with both sentence structure and discourse is continued in the paper on deictic categories, "Discourse and Situational Deixis in Sinhala," and in the paper "Pronouns, Reflexives and Antianaphora in Sinhala," which related the relevant language-specific phenomena to the general theory of binding domains and types of anaphoric expressions.

Other interactions are also reflected in these papers. They involve those among history, description, and more abstract principles of linguistic theory—that is, interactions between synchronic and diachronic analyses (For example, the papers on linguistic area and on historical phonology.) These papers assume that any current linguistic theory must be compatible with linguistic change. This concern is analagous to the concern for cross-linguistic analyses, and in some cases, this linkage becomes explicit, as in the 1986 paper "Sinhala Focused Sentences: Naturalization of a Calque," in which the point of view is historical and areal, but where there is also a clear linkage with the synchronic and theoretically based analyses of that construction. The topic of cross-language influence, linguistic area, and the methodology for dealing with it is also addressed in three other papers in that section, as are grammaticization ("Some Aspects of the Jaffna Tamil Verbal System") and the interaction of typology and borrowing.

The diglossia papers reveal another set of interactions, in this case that between language structure and its social use. In these, a historical dimension is also involved, as well as more abstract principles of general linguistic theory. These are almost always centered on the attempt to define varieties in terms of the relationship between their structural properties—for example, agreement—and the parameters of their use. In the 1986 paper "Sinhala Diglossia Revisited or Diglossia Dies Hard," the central concern is for the dynamics of change (retention or loss) linked to the social and functional setting, but in the other diglossia papers included here, the concern is to correlate fundamental functional differences with structural ones. Once more, however, there is an evident movement from the basically descriptive to linkage with the developing theory of UG as a source of explanation.

Thus, in addition to attempting to arrive at and systematically express the structure of specific language subsystems, the research represented here, taken as a whole, reveals the tension that exists among specific language data, the language-specific system that underlies it, and the more abstract linguistic theory of UG as formulated in a particular theoretical paradigm at any one time. The results of these cross-linguistic studies thus force us to confront the interface between language universals and systematic language specifics. For example, current theory of UG proposes to eliminate phrase-structure rules based on labeled lexical categories and incorporates a more abstract X-bar theory. It replaces particular movement transformations with a general "move alpha" rule constrained by hypothesized universal principles of structure dependence that constrain "landing site," as well as direction, locality, and content of movement. The grammar of the Sinhala focus construction, however, must somehow capture the fact that the focus of a Sinhala cleft may appear in various positions in the linear structure, including an *in situ* one, but also that its basic position appears to be to the right of the verb. This problem is illustrated not only in the early *Colloquial Sinhalese Clause Structures* treatment and in the papers on the history of the construction, but it is presented more elaborately with greater explicit justification in the paper on nonconfigurationality and focus.[1] This rightward location and variability is distinct from a preverbal position, possibly involving adjunction to verb, as has been claimed, for example, for Hungarian. There is evidence that both types crucially involve movement, but the cross-linguistic distinction must be captured somehow, if not in the lexical definition of phrase structure and a lexically specific language-specific set of movement rules, then in some manner in the mapping from the more abstract UG to the language-specific grammar.

This issue has an obvious counterpart in the study of first-language acquisition: namely, if the child is innately guided only by the abstract principles of UG, then the acquisition task lies in mapping these UG principles to the language-specific grammar of the language that it is acquiring. This area of study is instantiated in two papers in this volume on the acquisition of some participial constructions in Sinhala and of anaphora in Hindi *jab* clauses in which UG-based linguistic analysis and experimental acquisition data illuminate each other.

Because of the interrelations within and across these papers, it has often proved difficult to segregate the papers into single headings, and those given here are far from watertight, but they have been provided to indicate both the general range of topics dealt with and the emphases of specific papers within the sections.

Finally, the papers reflect the interaction between the languages of South Asia and their relation to wider principles of linguistics, which characterizes the whole set, at least tangentially. It is sincerely hoped that they may also convey in some way the love for South Asia and its languages and their speakers that is the fundamental cause of the markedly regional orientation of the exemplars of the practice of linguistics as represented in this volume.

I

BACKGROUND AND DESCRIPTION OF BASIC CATEGORIES

Sinhala, an Indo-Aryan Isolate

This chapter originally was a paper delivered at a panel surveying South Asian Languages at the MLA meeting in 1981; it later appeared in a special issue of the South Asian Review, *which contained the papers from the panel. It was intended for an audience of largely non–South Asian specialists, so that it has a general and introductory character. It serves as a general introduction to Sinhala and its history, and it touches on a number of the problems that are dealt with in much greater depth in other chapters in this volume. It thus seemed suitable for inclusion here as part of a general introductory section. The paper bore an introductory note dedicating it to M. W. S Sugathapala De Silva (Sugath), who had passed away shortly before it was given, as a "respected colleague, and a pioneer in the application of the insights of modern linguistics and sociolinguistics to the study of Sinhala," adding that he was "taken away at the height of his productive powers, [and] his potential contributions, like his ready wit, will be sorely missed."*

Sinhala (Sinhalese), the majority language of Sri Lanka (formerly Ceylon) has a number of features that make it especially interesting to the scholar of South Asian languages and the South Asian linguistic area.[1] It is the southernmost Indo-Aryan language (along with the closely related Divehi of the Maldive islands). For over two millennia it has been isolated from its sister languages of the north by both its island location and the intervening Dravidian languages of South India, with which it has been in contact, often close, throughout that time. Most important in that connection has been Tamil, although it might be more accurate to say Tamil–Malayalam or "southern south Dravidian languages," since much of the contact predates the split of the latter two languages.

Sinhala tradition has it that the group that brought the languages with them arrived on the date of the *parinibbāna* (final passing away) of the Buddha, traditionally 544–543 B.C. As a matter of fact, somewhere around that time does appear to be a reasonable date, since we have inscriptions in old Sinhala dating from the early second or late third centuries B.C., and by that time the language had already undergone important changes that made it distinct from any of the Indo-Aryan languages of North India.

It has long been disputed whether Sinhala originated as a western or eastern Indo-Aryan language. One reason for the uncertainty is clearly that the language left India before most of the major sound changes took place that ultimately distinguished the subgroups of Indo-Aryan languages. This, too, makes a date somewhere around the sixth century B.C. seem reasonable. Competent scholars have argued for both eastern and western origins on both linguistic and cultural–historical grounds (see the summary in De Silva 1979: 14–17), but some recent work on the history of Sinhala phonology has provided some evidence for a generally eastern origin (Karunatillake 1969, 1977).

In his classic 1956 paper "India as a Linguistic Area," Murray Emeneau suggested a number of features that characterized South Asian languages and cut across language families, a list that has since been expanded by him and others (see the useful summary in Masica 1976:187–90). Sinhala clearly belongs in that area, and in many ways it belongs to the southern part of it. As I stated in an earlier paper:

> No one who has worked on Sinhala, Tamil, and on some Northern Indo-Aryan language such as Hindi can fail to get some global feeling of similarities shared by the first two in contradistinction to the latter. There is a danger, however, in drawing too ready conclusions about massive Dravidianization of Sinhala, since it is easy to overlook similarities and differences in the opposite direction and ignore the less exciting question of the extent to which Sinhala has remained distinctively Indo-Aryan. (Gair 1976b: 260)

Indeed, Sinhala has retained its Indo-Aryan identity despite the constant contact with Dravidian languages, a persistence that I referred to in the same paper as "a minor miracle of linguistic and cultural history" (Gair 1976b: 259). It has emerged as a language with a unique character within the South Asian linguistic area, a result of its Indo-Aryan origins, Dravidian influence, and independent internal changes. There were other influences as well, some of them from the languages of successive colonizers, but it is often overlooked in this regard that there was clearly some other, apparently non-Dravidian, language (or languages) spoken on the island before the advent of Sinhala. This is shown not only by the existence of the aboriginal Veddas (whose language is now essentially a dialect of Sinhala) but also by the existence of a number of items in the Sinhala vocabulary that cannot be traced to either Indo-Aryan or Dravidian languages (see Hettiaratchi 1959, 1974; De Silva 1979: 16). The role that some indigenous languages, or language, played in the formation of Sinhala has not really been investigated, but it may well have been more than is generally recognized.

The task of sorting out all of this in the history of Sinhala, and particularly identifying the external influences and internal developments and their interactions, has barely begun, though a start has been made (as for example, Silva 1961; Hettiaratchi 1974; Ratanajoti 1975; De Silva 1979, esp. ch. 1 and ch. 2; Gair 1976b, 1986b). In this paper I will attempt a brief summary of some of that work and will briefly illustrate some of these strands in the history of the language as they relate to different levels of structure.

The Lexicon

The presence of items in the Sinhala vocabulary that apparently come from an indigenous source was mentioned earlier, and this was recognized as early as the thirteenth-century classical Sinhala grammar *Sidatsaṅgarā*, which listed forms like *naraṁba* 'see' and *koḷoṁba* 'ford, harbor' (interestingly enough, the source of the name of the present capital). The vocabulary of Sinhala remains fundamentally Indo-Aryan, but there is a large component of borrowings from Dravidian languages, including some very basic terms (see the list in Gunasekara 1891: 356–68 for examples). A number of common household and culinary terms are from Dravidian languages, many of them of sufficiently long standing to have undergone quite early Sinhala sound changes such as *kættə* (pl. *kæti*) 'chopper', from Tamil *katti*. Even some kin terms, such as *massinaa* 'cousin', *akka* 'older sister', *appocci* 'father (dialectal)' are of Dravidian origin, and the kinship system itself is generally recognized to be South Indian in nature. Especially striking are mixed Sinhala–Tamil compounds such as *balaaporottu* 'expectation' from Sinhala *balaa* 'looking' and the parallel Tamil form *poruttu* 'having been patient, having endured'.

There are, of course, a number of words from the colonial languages Portuguese, Dutch, and English, and there are some from Malay and other languages (see the lists in Gunasekara 1891: 368–82), with which we need not concern ourselves here.

The Phonology

Influence of Dravidian languages on the phonology of Sinhala has been suggested by various scholars, with perhaps the strongest claims being made by Elizarenkova (1972). On balance, however, it appears that phonology is not one of the areas of strongest Dravidian influence. A detailed examination of the claims for such influence has been made elsewhere (Gair 1985; Chap. 14 in this volume); only a general summary can be made here.

The consonant systems of Middle Indo-Aryan, Tamil–Malayalam, and Sinhala are given in table 1–1. For Middle Indo-Aryan I have used essentially Old Sinhala (about 3rd century B.C.) with the aspirate consonants (*ph, bh*, etc.) restored; it can be taken as a plausible representation of the immediate ancestor of Old Sinhala. For Tamil–Malayalam, I have used Jaffna (Sri Lanka) Tamil with loanwords eliminated, but I have retained /L/ even though it is not distinguished from /l/ in spoken Jaffna Tamil, since it was characteristic of early Tamil. The result very closely approximates the older Tamil system as reflected in the orthography. Sinhala is represented by Modern Colloquial Sinhala, which agrees almost completely with the system represented in classical thirteenth-century grammar and literary works. The symbols *ṁb, ṅḍ, ṅ̆ḍ, ṅg* represent prenasalized stops, the so-called half-nasals. These represent a distinctive Sinhala development, setting it off from both the Dravidian and the Indo-Aryan languages,[2] and they present a number of interesting problems for the phonologist (see Coates and De Silva 1960; Gair 1970: 24; Feinstein 1979).

Otherwise, the system very closely resembles the Middle-Indo-Aryan one except for the lack of a voiced and voiceless aspirated stop series contrasting with the unaspirated ones. This is a peculiarly Sinhala feature with respect to Indo-Aryan, since in languages of that family within India itself none has lost that feature completely.[3] This dramatic change occurred before the earliest inscriptions, and it is probably the strongest candidate for substratum phonological influence from the Dravidian fam-

Table 1–1 Consonant Systems

Middle Indo-Aryan (Pre-OS)

Lab.	Dent.	Retro.	Pal.	Vel.
p	t	ṭ	c	k
ph	th	ṭh	ch	kh
b	d	ḍ	j	g
bh	dh	ḍh	jh	gh
m	n	ṇ	(ñ)	
v		y		
		r		
		l		
	s			h

Tamil (Jaffna)ᵃ

Lab.	Dent.	Alv.	Retro.	Pal.	Vel.
p	t	ṯ	ṭ	c	k
m	n		ṇ	ñ	
v		y	r		
		l	(L)		
			ḷ		

Sinhala (13th c. and modern)ᵇ

Lab.	Dent.	Retro.	Pal.	Vel.
p	t	ṭ	c	k
b	d	ḍ	j	g
m̆b	n̆d	n̆ḍ		ŋ̆g
m	n		ñ	ŋ
w		y		
		r		
		l		
	s			h

ᵃIn Jaffna Tamil, r is a trilled retroflex, L is a voiced frictionless lateral continuant, and c is s intervocally.
ᵇNote that m̆b, n̆d, etc. are prenasalized stops (the "half-nasals").

ily, which, it will be noted, also lacks aspirates. On the other hand, the possibility that some other, indigenous, language was responsible cannot be neglected (see Gair 1985b for discussion). The Sinhala vowel system is given in table 1–2.

The development of a three-way contrast among ə (schwa, a vowel like that at the end of English *sofa), a,* and *aa* is uncharacteristic of either Dravidian or Indo-Aryan languages. However, the contrast between ə and *a* is limited, and it is based largely on the occurrence of ə in the first syllable of a few items, especially the forms of the very frequent verb *karə* 'do' (contrast *karə* 'shoulder'). Otherwise, though frequent in occurrence, ə could be considered a positional variant of *a*. Long əə occurs only in loanwords like *šəət* 'shirt'. The thoroughgoing contrast in length of vowels resembles Dravidian more than Indo-Aryan, which has generally been conservative in not developing such a contrast for *e* and *o* (as in Sanskrit and in Middle Indic languages, like Pali, which lack it, as well as in modern languages like Hindi). It has thus been suggested as another possible Dravidian influence. On the other hand, Sinhala did at one time lose all vowel length, which is most un-Dravidian, and the present contrast is a result of internal developments, particularly the loss of some consonants between vowels and word-finally (Karunatillake 1969: 101ff.), a change that cannot easily be reconciled with Dravidian influence (see Gair 1982 for details) The vowels *æ* and *ææ* (similar to those in English *hat* and *bad*) are, like the prenasalized stops, a distinctive characteristic of Sinhala within the area and arose through the assimilation of long *aa* to a following *i*, as part of a general process of umlaut (see Geiger 1938: 18ff., Karunatillake 1969: 77ff.).

In summary, Sinhala phonology shows some features, such as the merging of the aspirates with their unaspirated counterparts, that suggest the influence of other languages, possibly Dravidian. However, it also retains much of its Indo-Aryan character and exhibits several unique developments that set it off clearly within the general area.

The Morphology

Morphological comparison of Sinhala with the other languages entails too many specific features to be attempted here. Here I will simply observe that Sinhala shares a number of South Asian morphological characteristics with both Indo-Aryan and Dravidian but that it also exhibits some distinct characteristics that set it off from the others, and I shall content myself with pointing out a few of the latter.

Table 1–2 Sinhala Vowels

	Short			*Long*		
	Front	*Central*	*Back*	*Front*	*Central*	*Back*
High	I		u	ii		uu
Mid	e	ə	o	ee	əə	oo
Low	æ		a	ææ		aa

In verb morphology, Sinhala has a number of characteristic features, such as the development of three main conjugations of verbs, the third of which constitutes largely involitive verbs, which are commonly derivable from verbs of the other classes and associated with particular sentence types (see Geiger 1938: 138ff, De Silva 1960, Gair 1970: 261ff). Examples of such verbs contrasted with others, are:

> *man atin   wiiduruwə biñduna.*
> I   Agent glass   got-broken
> 'I broke the glass (accidentally).'

Compare:

> *mamə wiiduruwə binda.*
> I   glass   broke
> 'I broke the glass (on purpose).'

And :

> *maṭə   eekə kiyawuna.*
> I-DAT that   got-said
> 'I blurted that out/misspoke.'

Compare:

> *mamə eekə kiwwa*
> I   that said
> 'I said that.'

Although the origin of such verbs may lie in the passive stems of Middle Indo-Aryan (Geiger 1938: 138), they have been greatly extended and developed within Sinhala and they greatly contribute to the distinctive "feel" of the language. (For details and a summary of the syntactic constructions, see Gair 1970: 72–89 and the more extended treatment in Gunasinghe 1978.)

Sinhala gender categories provide another interesting example of its distinctive character. Sinhala has given up the Indo-Aryan grammatical gender for natural gender (i.e., gender that accords with meaning rather than being the often arbitrary property of a lexical item). Dravidian languages also have natural gender, but the Sinhala categories are different. The major distinction is between ANIMATE and INANIMATE. Within animate, there is a HUMAN versus NONHUMAN distinction, which is reflected in numbers and in pronouns such as *eyaa* 'he/she', *eeka/uu* 'it, that animal' (compare *eekə* 'it, that thing').

Crosscutting these gender distinctions in colloquial Sinhala is another sex-based one: GENERAL versus FEMININE. The general category, as in *eeka* 'that animal' and *eyaa* 'that human', is used freely with both masculine and feminine reference. The feminine—as exemplified by *ææ* 'that woman', *eeki* 'that female animal'—is used to clearly specify that the designee is female.[4] Thus, the division is as in table 1–3. In

Table 1–3 Sinhala Pronominal Gender

	General		*Feminine*
Animate			
Human	*eyaa*		*ææ*
Nonhuman	*eeka*		*eeki*
Inanimate		*eekə*	

Literary Sinhala, however, there is a distinction between masculine and feminine much like that in English (or present-day Tamil): *hetema* 'he', *ōtomō* 'she'.

Sinhala pronouns and demonstratives also show an interesting four-way deictic contrast relating to the relative position of speaker and that which is referred to, as for example (using the demonstrative adjective and inanimate pronoun): *mee* 'this', *meekə* 'this one' (near speaker); *oyə* 'that', *ookə* 'that one' (near hearer); *arə* 'that', *arəkə* 'that one' (away from both, but in sight); *ee* 'that', *eekə* 'that one' (which has been referred to earlier). This resembles a Tamil distinction, lost in most dialects but retained in Sri Lanka Jaffna Tamil, with roots *i-* 'this, by speaker', *u-* 'that, by hearer', and *a-* 'that, but Tamil *a-* is an equivalent for both Sinhala *ara-* and *ee-*. The latter distinction is thus a special feature of Sinhala, and the entire system may constitute another example of areal influence modified by independent development. Only a careful tracing of the history of these forms will tell.

Another feature worth noting is the development of an INDEFINITE–DEFINITE distinction in Sinhala, marked by noun suffixes that reflect the animate–inanimate distinction in their form, as shown in table 1–4: In Literary Sinhala, these affixes also reflect the masculine–feminine distinction: *minisaku/miniseku* 'a man (accusative)', *kāntāwaka* 'a woman (accusative)'.

The Syntax

Syntactic comparison of Sinhala with the other languages also involves a number of features, but lends itself more readily to general characterizations based on BRANCHING DIRECTION. Simply, if somewhat imprecisely, put: LEFT-BRANCHING structures are those in which a modifier or complement precedes its head (that which is modified or complemented); RIGHT-BRANCHING structures have the opposite order. Thus, French *(un) pauvre homme* 'poor man' (showing pity) is left-branching, whereas *(un) homme pauvre* 'poor man' (referring to a man who is poor) is right-branching. Though many

Table 1–4 Definiteness in Sinhala

	Inanimate	*Animate*
Definite	*potə* 'the book'	*gonaa* 'the bull', *miniha* ' the man'
Indefinite	*potak* 'a book'	*gonek* ' a bull', *minihek* ' a man'

languages, perhaps the majority, are mixed in that they include both right- and left-branching structures, some are relatively consistent in favoring one or the other. One characteristic of South Asian languages in general is that they include a number of left-branching structures. For example, they have, among other things, postpositions rather than prepositions (Sinhala *gaha laŋgə* 'tree near' = 'near the tree'), auxiliary verbs that follow their main verbs (Sinhala *gihilla tiyenəwa* 'gone is' = 'has gone'), and objects that precede their verbs: ([*mamə*] *ee potə siriṭa dunna* '[I] that book Siri-DAT gave' = 'I gave that book to Siri'). (See Masica 1976, especially chapter 2, for a clear summary with further examples.) However, as Masica states:

> It would be incorrect to say that Indian languages as such are left branching. Only Dravidian languages—and not all of them—are consistently and exclusively left-branching. The crux of the matter is the complex sentence. . . . Only Dravidian . . . forces nominal object clauses to precede their verb and adjectival ("relative") clauses to precede the noun they qualify; in Hindi, Bengali and Santali [a language of the Munda family] they normally follow. The typical Indo-Aryan device of a relative marker preceding the noun, with the main body of the clause . . . following the noun but preceding a correlative in the main clause, may be considered a compromise as far as relative clauses are concerned. (1976: 25)

Now, the interesting aspect of Sinhala in this regard is that it is consistently left-branching like the southern Dravidian languages. This is particularly striking with regard to clausal objects (of verbs of saying, etc.) and relative clauses. Note, for example, the contrast between the Hindi and Sinhala sentences below, both meaning 'I say that Sunil went yesterday', in terms of the position of the quotative clause (bracketed) in relation to the verb of saying:

HINDI: *māĩ kahtaa hũu* [*ki sunil kal   gayaa*].
          I   say   aux that Sunil yesterday went

SINHALA: (*mamə*) [*Sunil iiye   giyaa kiyəla*] *kiyənəwa*
          (I)   Sunil yesterday went that   say

Similarly, in forming relative clauses, Hindi, like many Indo-Aryan languages, uses both correlative structures and structures with a relative clause following its head (as in English), as illustrated by the following, with essentially the same sense:

[*jo   admii is   dukaan mẽ kaam kartaa   hai*], [[*vo*]   *kal   gayaa*].
   which(REL) man this shop   in work does AUX, he   (CORR) yesterday went
or:

[(*vo*) *aadmi* [*jo   is   dukaan mẽ kaam kartaa hai*]] *kal   gayaa*
(that) man   who (REL) this shop   in work does   AUX yesterday went
'The man who works in this shop went yesterday.'

In Sinhala, however, the relative clause structure is always left-branching, formed by adding a special affix to the verb and placing the whole clause before its head.[5] Thus the Sinhala translation of the Hindi above is:

[[*mee kadee   wæḍə kərənə*]   *miniha*] *iiye   giyaa*
this   shop-LOC work do-AFFIX man   yesterday went
'The man who works in this shop went yesterday.'

Thus, Sinhala is a thoroughgoing left-branching language like Tamil (or Japanese, to take an example outside the area), a type that has also been called a "consistent OV language" (Lehmann 1978, ch. 1). One possible exception, depending upon how we analyze it, is the noun phrase with a numeral or some other quantifier, in which the noun precedes the quantifier: *pot tunak* 'books three-a' = 'three books', *pot kiipeyak* 'books several' = 'several books'. It should be noticed that this is the regular Sinhala construction, but it is also an option in Tamil in some circumstances, as in Jaffna Tamil *vaattimaar naaluupeer* 'teachers four-persons' as an alternate for *naalu vaattimaar* 'four teachers'.

Given the overall close resemblances between Sinhala and the south Dravidian languages in regard to branching direction, Dravidian influence as a factor in Sinhala's acquisition of its present syntactic character does appear probable, indeed.

One particular syntactic structure is worth mentioning here. Sinhala has a sentence type called a FOCUSED or CLEFT SENTENCE, in which a special affix appears on the verb, and some constituent of the sentence (which often appears to the right of the verb) is emphasized or foregrounded, with a semantic effect much like English "It is *that* book that I haven't read." As an example:

mee bas-ekə yanne   kalutərəṭə
this bus   go-present-affix Kalutara-DAT
'It is to Kalutara that this bus is going.'

Such sentences bear a strong resemblance to sentences in south Dravidian languages, such as the following from Jaffna Tamil, in which the verb appears in a verbal noun form:

inta bas poratu   yaaḷpaaṇattukku
this bus go-pres-nominal Jaffna-DAT
'It is to Jaffna that this bus is going.'

Since no construction of a similar form seems to occur in any of the northern Indo-Aryan languages, Dravidian influence appears likely here, too. However, as I have argued at some length elsewhere (Gair 1980, 1986b), even if the construction was formed initially under such influence, Sinhala has made it its own, elaborating and expanding it so as to make it an important part of its syntax, and one that interacts in an exceedingly complex way with other phenomena. Thus, the Sinhala focused sentence offers by itself a striking example of the unique character of the language, arising from a history in which it built on an Indo-Aryan base, underwent influences from Dravidian, and finally, through internal, independent developments, fashioned its own character within the South Asian area. As noted earlier, Dravidian influence operated more strongly in syntax than in phonology, in which Sinhala retains a more strongly Indo-Aryan character than has sometimes been claimed. Closer investigation of the differential influence at different levels of structure, taken in conjunction with material from cultural and political history, may help to cast new light on the texture of intercultural relations in the history of Sri Lanka. In 1935 Wilhelm Geiger and D. B. Jayatilaka remarked:

> It is, no doubt, a splendid proof of the proud national feeling of the Sinhalese people that they were able to preserve the Aryan character of their language in spite of their geographical isolation. And indeed, the structure of Sinhala itself appears to parallel the position of Sinhala culture and society within the South Asian culture area: Clearly part of the region, and influenced in many ways by its South Indian neighbors, as well as by other nations and communities that have entered its history, but always retaining and developing its own special character throughout the over two millenia of its existence on the island of Sri Lanka. (xvi)

Subsequent research has, I believe, shown that statement to have been insightful, indeed.[6]

Colloquial Sinhala Inflectional Categories and Parts of Speech

This paper appeared in Indian Linguistics *27: 32–45. It represented largely a revision of the analysis that was included as a preliminary to my syntactic analysis in* Clause Structures in Spoken Colloquial Sinhalese *(1963) and in a revised form in* Colloquial Sinhalese Clause Structures *(1970). It is cast in the descriptive mode of the time—that is, American structural and descriptive linguistics, of which it can serve as an illustration—but it still appears to be a useful overview of the forms in question and is thus included here with minor changes in format and references, with a few added notes where updating appeared clearly called for, for the sake of accuracy.*

This chapter is an attempt to present a survey of the inflectional categories of colloquial Sinhala and a part-of-speech classification such that these categories might be useful in making typological comparisons with other related or nonrelated languages or as a preliminary to the description of syntax.

It is important to note that Sinhala presents a virtually classic case of diglossia, with written and colloquial varieties that are sharply divergent on every level of structure.[1] The analysis presented here applies only to current Colloquial Sinhala as spoken generally by everyone, educated and uneducated alike, for all purposes of everyday communication. None of the varieties that are customarily written are taken into account; these require a different analysis.

Inflectional Categories

Sinhala stems showing inflection fall into three main classes:

1. *Substantives* inflect for CASE. This constitutes the largest class of inflected stems and is an open class.
2. *Verbs* inflect for TENSE. The class of verb stems is much smaller than that of substantives (probably not more than a few hundred stems) and is closed or nearly so.

3. *Quasiverbs* inflect for neither case nor tense, but they show paradigms of a few forms having some resemblance to inflected forms of verbs. This class is small, generally of from three to five stems depending on dialect.

Other stems show no inflection, or in a few cases they show marginal inflection to be noted.

Substantive Inflection

Case

For substantives in general there are four cases: DIRECT, as in *potə* 'the book', *miniha* 'the man'; DATIVE, as in *potəṭə, minihaṭə*; GENITIVE, as in *potee, minihage*; and IN-STRUMENTAL, as in *poten, minihagen*. Most substantives show only these four cases, but some show two more: ACCUSATIVE, as in *minihawə*, and VOCATIVE, as in *miniho*. Examples of other substantives are *dekə* 'two', *mokə* 'what', *uḍə* 'above', *laṅgə* 'near', and *keriimə, kerilla* 'doing'.

The accusative case occurs only with animate nouns and pronouns (discussed later) and poses a problem in morphology versus syntax. It occurs only in specifi-able syntactic positions, for example, with objects of a transitive verb: *mamə minihawə dækka* 'I man-accusative saw' = 'I saw the man.' However, its occurrence in those positions is always optional—that is, the same noun could occur in the same position in the direct case: *mamə miniha dækka*. The regularity with which it appears varies, apparently, from dialect to dialect and perhaps from speaker to speaker. Earlier, the *wə* of the accusative was treated as a separate particle, (the accusative marker) rather than as a case inflection. Either way, certain difficulties arise, but it now seems simplest to treat it as an inflection.[2] The class of nouns with which it appears produces plural nondirect case forms by adding a nasal before the case inflections, hence *miniha* (direct singular), *minihaṭə* (dative singular), *minissu* (direct plural), *minissunṭə* (dative plural). This nasal may also appear before the -*wə*: *minissunwə*. Hence, if we take *wə* as a particle, we must have a nasal-final oblique case form in the plural that occurs independently of other cases, but it would so appear, in colloquial Sinhala, only preceding the *wə*. The morphophonemics are thus simplified by treating *wə* as a case affix.

A few other forms do, however, have an OBLIQUE case form that occurs indepen-dent of other case inflections. The only such forms in my data are the first person pronoun *mamə* and the demonstratives *mee* 'this' and *ee* 'that', with oblique forms *maa, mii*, and *ii*, respectively. These occur, other than before case affixes, in a very few positions, most noticeably before the postposition *laṅgə: maa laṅgə, mii laṅgə, ii laṅgə*. (The recognition of this marginal case for these forms does not simplify mat-ters for the nouns just discussed, however, or force the recognition of an independently occurring oblique case there, since the ranges of distribution are not the same; for the nouns, it is the direct case form that occurs before *laṅgə*.)

Number

All forms that inflect for number are substantives, but by no means do all substan-tives so inflect. There are two numbers, SINGULAR and PLURAL: *potə* 'the book', *pot* 'books'; *miniha* 'the man', *minissu* 'men'.

Definiteness

Definiteness subsumes two specific categories, DEFINITE and INDEFINITE: *potə* 'the book', *potak* 'a book'; *miniha* 'the man', *minihek* 'a man'. If a form inflects for both definiteness and number, it will show definiteness only in the singular. However, there are forms, such as numerals, that show definiteness but not number: *dekə* 'two', *dekak* '(a) two'.

    In general, definiteness is confined to substantives, but there is at least one exception: *witərə* 'about' does not take case but appears in the indefinite as *witərak* 'only'. Interestingly, *witərə* has other peculiarities that make it a class of one. Thus it is the only form in my data that occurs in the indefinite following another indefinite form with which it is not in a coordinate or alternative relationship:

    pot   tunak   witərak
    books three-indef witərə-indef
    'only three books'.

Compare the different construction

    pot   dekak   tunak
    books two-indef three-indef
    'two or three books'.

Gender

Some substantives, primarily numerals, have ANIMATE and INANIMATE gender forms: *dekə* 'two (inanimate)', *denna* 'two (animate)'. The animate forms from three up are, internally, compounds with the form *denaa* 'animate beings' (grammatically singular); hence *tunə* 'three (inanimate)', *tundenaa* 'three (animate)'. Despite their compound nature, these may most simply be considered phrasal inflection,[3] since they not only parallel the noncompound animate *two* form, but they also belong in a set with the noncompound inanimate numerals since they function like them except for agreement: *pot dekə* 'two books', *pot tunə* 'three books'; *minissu denna* 'two men', *minissu tundenaa* 'three men'.

    The numeral *one* shows a more elaborate set of gender categories. It has, within the animate form, separate HUMAN and ANIMAL-DEROGATORY forms, and within the latter it has a further distinction between GENERAL, which may be used for a referent of any sex, and FEMININE, used only with a female referent: *ekə* 'one (inanimate)', *ekkenaa* 'one (human)', *ekaa* 'one (animate, animal-derogatory, general)', *ekii* 'one' (animate, animal-derogatory, feminine)'. Some pronouns also show these further gender categories.

    There is also a set of numeral forms for a marginal RESPECTFUL gender, used primarily for clergy: *haamuduruwəru tunnamə* 'three monks'. These are also compound forms, based on *namə* 'name'.

Stem forms

Some substantives have an occurrent stem form that appears as the first member of compounds. This form is neutral as to case, but it may resemble the direct singular, the direct plural (most commonly for inanimate nouns), or neither. Hence *gee* 'the house', whose stem form is also *gee* and whose plural is *gewal; potə* 'the book', whose stem form and plural both are *pot; miniha* 'the man', whose stem form is *minis* and plural form is *minissu*.

Verbs

From a verb stem (which may include derivational affixes in addition to a root), PAST and NONPAST tense themes are created, and forms in these tenses are built on those themes. There is also a PARTICIPIAL theme (for some verbs, this is identical to the nonpast tense theme), which serves as the basis for several participial forms.[4] In addition, there are separately formed VERBAL NOMINALS.[5] The nature of the resultant paradigm, which includes twenty-five forms, may be grasped from the array shown in table 2–1, which represents the greater part of it. (A few forms, particularly imperatives of various grades, are not included). The verbs *kərənəwa* 'do', *adinəwa* 'pull', and *teerenəwa* 'understand' serve to represent the three main regular morphophonemic classes. For the first, the nonpast and participial themes are identical; for the other two they are not. The forms in table 2–1 may show some slight variation from dialect to dialect, but the basic pattern appears to remain the same, based on available data. It is worth noting that verbs in Colloquial Sinhala do not show person or number agreement in the usual sense with their subjects, but the differences in form within the paradigm, other than reflecting semantic differences, relate primarily to use in different types of clauses.[6]

One stem, *dannəwa* 'know', lacks past tense forms, but it has the characteristic present tense paradigm and participial form and is thus most simply included in the inflectional verb class.[7]

Quasiverbs

A small group of stems, including *nææ* 'not', *æti* 'might be', and *bææ* 'impossible, can't' show very limited paradigms whose forms resemble verb forms either in the clause types in which they occur, in their shape, or in both. The maximum overt differentiation is six forms, shown only by *nææ*. The paradigms are given in table 2–2.

Some of these forms—namely, the emphatic, conditional, and concessive forms of *nææ* and *æti*—clearly share inflectional morphemes with the similarly named inflectional forms of verbs, but they lack tense. The remainder are named after the verb forms they most closely resemble in distribution.

For some dialects, other forms must be included. For the south, we must include *æhæki* 'possible, can', and for some Kandyan speech we must include *oone* 'necessary, want' and *puluan* 'possible, can'.

Verb–Substantive Relationships

Some forms within the verbal paradigm inflect for case and thus are substantives. This includes not only the verbal nominal forms but also the basic forms, both

Table 2–1   Verb Forms

	kərənəwa 'do'	adinəwa 'pull'	teerenəwa 'understand'
Tense Forms (built on tense themes)			
Basic			
nonpast	kərənəwa	adinəwa	teerenəwa
past	kerua	ædda	teeruna
Emphatic			
nonpast	kəranne	adinne	teerenne
past	kerue	ædde	teerune
Conditional			
nonpast:	kərətot	aditot	teeretot
past	keruot	æddot	teerunot
Concessive			
nonpast	kərətat	aditat	teeretat
past:	keruat	æddat	teerunat
Adjectival			
nonpast	kərənə	adinə	teerenə
past:	keruə, keruu	æddə	teerunə
No past counterparts			
Hortative			
nonpast[a]	kərəmu	adimu	(no form)
Volitive Optative			
nonpast[a]	kərannan	adinnan	(no form)
Involitive Optative			
nonpast[a]	kəraawi, kəray	adiiwi, adii	teereewi, teerey
Contemporaneous			
nonpast[a]	kəraddi	adiddi	teereddi
Infinitive			
nonpast[a]	kərannə	adinnə	teerennə
Present Participle			
nonpast[a]	kərətə	aditə	teeretə
No nonpast counterparts			
Prior temporal			
past[b]	keruaama	æddaama	teerunaama
Permissive			
past[b]	keruaawe	æddaawe	teerunaawe
Participle Forms (built on the participial theme)			
Base Form	karə	ædə	teeri
Perfect Participle	kərəla	ædəla	teerilaa
Reduplicated	kərə kərə	ædə ædə	teeri teeri
Adjectival	kərapu	ædəpu	teericcə
Perfective	kərapi	ædapi	teericci
Verbal Nominals (gerunds)			
	keriimə, kerilla	ædiima, ædilla	teeriimə teerilla

[a]This form has no past counterpart.
[b]This form has no nonpast counterpart.

Table 2–2   Quasiverbs

	næ̃æ̃ 'not'	æti 'might be'	bæ̃æ̃ 'impossible'
Basic	næ̃æ̃ ⎤		bæ̃æ̃
	⎟	æti ⎤	
Adjectival	næti ⎦	⎟	
		⎟	bæri
Emphatic	nætte	ætte ⎦	
Participial	nætuə	ætuə	bæruə
Conditional	nætot	ætot	—[a]
Concessive	nætat	ætat	bæruat

[a]Not attested in my data.

nonpast and past, which inflect for dative and instrumental. Hence, dative *yanəwatə* 'for going' and instrumental *yanəwayin* 'from/by going'; dative *giyaatə* 'for having gone' and instrumental *giyaayin* 'from/by having gone'. In independent clauses, however, the basic forms not only do not inflect but also are mutually substitutable with nonsubstantive forms.

Other Stems

Stems that do not belong to one of the three categories of substantives, verbs, or quasiverbs above generally do not show inflection and may be classed together as PARTICLES. One marginal exception, *witərə,* has been noted under the discussion on substantives; other exceptions will be stated for certain adjectives later.

Part-of-Speech Classification

While the strictly inflectional classification is revealing and typologically interesting, it may be rendered still more so by adding the perspective of a classification that also takes into account similarities in syntactic behavior. Also, as a preliminary to syntactic description, the inflectional classes given are both too general and too few, but remaining within the classification and continuing to subclassify on inflectional grounds alone will not sufficiently increase its utility for that purpose. Forms in Sinhala with different inflectional paradigms may share important syntactic characteristics, suggesting that we might classify them together rather than with forms with more similar paradigms. For example, *gamə* 'village' and *mokə* 'what' both inflect for definiteness as well as case, while *kauru* 'who' and *lankaawə* 'Ceylon' show case but not definiteness. Yet *gamə* and *lankaawə*, on the one hand, and *mokə* and *kauru* on the other, share syntactic similarities that make it useful to classify them together at some stage in the grammar. Thus I shall now attempt a part-of-speech classification using combined inflectional and syntactic criteria. The approach is essentially that outlined by Hockett,[8] by whom a part of speech is defined as "a form-class of stems which show similar behavior in inflection, in syntax, or both" so that "the PART OF SPEECH SYSTEM OF A LANGUAGE is the classification of all its stems on the basis of similarities and differences of inflectional and syntactic behavior."

Retaining the inflectional classification of the first part of this chapter as background and point of reference, I shall now give preference to syntactic rather than inflectional criteria when the two are not in agreement and order the classes primarily on the basis of large-scale syntactic similarities. On this basis, the following classification is proposed.

Nouns

Nouns are substantives and commonly show a paradigm including inflection for definiteness and number: *potə* 'the book', *potak* 'a book,' *pot* 'books'; *miniha* 'the man', *minihek* 'a man', *minissu* 'men'. Most nouns inflect for the four cases indicated earlier for substantives in general; some, like *miniha,* have two more. The latter are generally animate in gender on the basis of numeral agreement, which will be discussed later in this chapter.

Syntactically, nouns are characterized by privilege of occurrence as heads in attributive constructions that may have a demonstrative (*mee* 'this', *oyə, arə, ee* 'that') as first member and may include adjectives (to be defined later) as attributes: *ee lamea* 'that child', *alut paarə* 'the new road', *arə puraanə pansələ* 'that ancient temple'. These phrases, or the noun alone, in turn have a characteristic range of occurrence, not stated here, that helps to define them.

Forms that show both these sets of characteristics are NOUNS. In addition, some substantive forms that do not share the full inflectional paradigm may conveniently be included on syntactic grounds, as, for example, place nouns like *koləmbə* 'Colombo', which do not generally appear in the plural or indefinite, and collective nouns such as *wii* 'paddy', and *kiri* 'milk', which occur only in the plural. An especially interesting group of forms occurs unaccompanied only in the plural, but they form a periphrastic singular with *eka* 'one' so that the plural and the *ekə* forms together fill out the entire noun paradigm: *bas* 'buses', *bas ekə* 'the bus', *bas ekak* 'a bus'. It is simplest to treat the *ekə* forms as phrasal inflections—that is, as single units parallel to the singular forms of other nouns—so that *bas ekə* 'the bus' is to *potə* 'the book' as *bas* 'buses' is to *pot* 'books'.

Verbs

Verbs were defined earlier as an inflectional class, and that class is carried over unchanged here. Verbs characteristically occur as predicators in clauses: *mamə yanəwa* 'I am going', *ee minissu iiye eekə kerua* 'those men did that yesterday'. As mentioned earlier, the class of verbs proper is much smaller than that of substantives, and this is true even if we consider only the noun subclass of the latter. The class of verb stems is augmented, however, by PHRASAL VERBS of various kinds composed of a verb stem bearing the main inflection preceded by another form that may or may not be verbal. Examples are *wædə kəranawa* 'work', (noun stem plus verb), *hitaa gannəwa* 'decide' (verb stem plus verb), *hambə wenəwa* 'meet' (indeterminate stem, occurring only in phrasal verbs, plus verb), *teerun gannəwa* 'grasp, understand' (verbally based derived noun stem plus verb), *saarə wenəwa* 'become fertile' (adjective plus verb), and so on. These by no means exhaust the possibilities.

Adjectives

Adjectives are particles, defined by their characteristic range of syntactic distribution. They occur as attributes preceding nouns and may in turn be preceded by a demonstrative: *arə loku gewal* 'those big houses', *ee alut potə* 'that new book'. They may also function as predicators in clauses: *arə gewal lokuy* 'those houses are big', *mee potə alut* 'this book is new'. There are three main classes of adjectives: descriptive adjectives, quantifying adjectives, and modal adjectives.

The DESCRIPTIVE ADJECTIVES constitute the largest subclass. Examples are *hoňdə* 'good', *alut* 'new', *matəkə* 'remembered', *narəkə* 'bad'. Vowel-final descriptive adjectives are obligatorily marked, when they function as predicators in clauses to which no transformations have been applied,[9] with a form of shape *-y*, the ASSERTION MARKER, which will be described later in this chapter. Hence we find cases such as the example with *lokuy*, above, or *mee potə prasidday* 'this book is famous'. Consonant-final descriptive adjectives are not so marked, as with *alut*, above, or *mee potə prəyoojanəwat* 'this book is useful'.

Descriptive adjectives may be subclassed as direct, impersonal, or common. The DIRECT form occurs with a direct case subject as in the last two examples. The IMPERSONAL form occurs with a dative case noun or other substantive but not with a (direct case) subject: *lameaṭa ṭikak asəniipay* 'the child is a bit sick'. The COMMON form occurs in both types of construction: *miniha hoňday* 'the man is good', *minihaṭə hoňday* 'the man is well'.

The QUANTIFYING ADJECTIVES—*madi* 'too little', *æti* 'enough', *wæḍi* 'too much'— in addition to sharing the general syntactic characteristics of adjectives, have a special (and defining) privilege of occurrence following descriptive adjectives to form quantifying adjective phrases that have a range of occurrence like that of the descriptive adjective alone: *hoňda madi* 'not good enough', *loku wæḍi* 'too big', *barə æti* 'heavy enough'. The occurrence of the *-y* form is optional with these quantifying adjectives.

The MODAL ADJECTIVES are *oonə* (*oone, oonæ*) 'wanted, needed', *puluan* 'possible', and *epaa* 'don't want'. The rule for the occurrence of the *-y* form on these is the virtual reverse of that for descriptive adjectives: In the relevant position, it occurs (optionally) on consonant-final *puluan* but not on vowel-final *oonə* or *epaa*. These adjectives have special syntactic characteristics, most notably free occurrence in clauses such as *maṭa yannə puluani* 'I can go', that stand in a regular relationship to verbal clauses like *mama yanəwa* 'I am going'. In some dialects, as noted earlier, *oonə* (*oone, oonæ*) and *puluan* may be quasiverbs.

Adjective–Substantive Relationships

Many adjectives are morphologically related to substantives, commonly nouns, in that they share a common root: *prəyoojanəwat* 'useful', *prəyoojanee* 'the use, function'; *digə* 'long', *digə* 'length', *alut* 'new', *alutə* 'newness'. Various kinds of derivational relationships and identities are involved among adjective, substantive, and substantive stem.

At least two descriptive adjectives—*narəkə* 'bad' and *matəkə* 'remembered'— are exceptional in that they have, as adjectives, two-form paradigms, with full forms,

as cited, and distinct stem forms *narak* and *matak*, which occur when they are verbalized with *wenəwa* 'be, become' or *kərənəwa* 'make': for example, *matak wenəwa*
'remember', *matak kərənəwa* 'remind'. Compare the related *amatəkə* 'forgotten',
which, like other adjectives, shows no such distinction: *amatəkə wenəwa* 'forget'.
The distinct stem forms, however, are also the stem forms of substantives that are
homonymous with the adjectives. (A possible alternative to homonymy here would,
of course, be to set up a separate class of adjective substantives, but this would
complicate the analysis in a different direction.)

All of these adjective–substantive relationships require investigation in detail,
particularly since they appear to be involved in transformational relationships and
thus have syntactic as well as morphological implications.

Major and Minor Parts of Speech

The three part-of-speech classes just described—nouns, verbs, and adjectives—are
large, and together they include by far the majority of stems in colloquial Sinhala.
Members of each of these classes commonly serve as predicators in clauses. For
example:

ADJECTIVE: *meekə   hoňday.*
this-one good-y
'This one is good.'

NOUN: *meeka   potak.*
this-one book-Indef
'This one is a book.'

VERB: *meekə   dæn yanəwa.*
this-one now go-Nonpast
'This one is going now.'

All of them also serve as nuclei for still larger syntactic classes, including
multistem constitutes of various kinds, that may substitute for them. These three
parts of speech may thus be called MAJOR. The remaining parts-of-speech classes
are MINOR. They are numerous and generally small in membership, though they are
by no means unimportant. Often they involve overlapping membership such that a
single form may belong to more than one of them or may even be a member of one
of the major classes, as well. Furthermore, some of them present special problems of
definition, since they are defined on the basis of specific syntactic patterns and are
thus difficult to define in any meaningful way before those patterns are described.
Thus, I make no attempt at a fine-grained or exhaustive presentation here but offer
only those classes that seem to be most important and necessary if one is to talk
about Colloquial Sinhala grammar even in relatively general terms.

Some Minor Parts of Speech

QUASIVERBS were described earlier as an inflectional class. Though they differ from
one another in the details of their syntactic behavior so that they show themselves

quite early in the analysis to be classes of a single member each, they share the characteristic that they are commonly introduced in transformations as auxiliaries. Since they do occur as predicators of clauses, however, they are quasiverbal in this respect, as well as in some of their inflectional characteristics.

NUMERATIVES are substantives defined by their privilege of occurrence following direct case plural nouns to form numerative phrases, in which position they carry any case inflection correlated with the occurrence of the phrase in larger forms: *pot huñgak* 'many books', *minissu dennatə* '(to) the two men'. NUMERALS, one important subclass, are characterized by their appearance in separate gender forms and an ordinal form: *dekə* 'two-inanimate', *denna* 'two animate', *deweni* 'second'. Gender inflection was described earlier. The gender forms inflect for case and definiteness but not number: definite direct *deka* 'two (inanimate)', *denna* 'two (animate)'; definite dative *dekatə, dennatə;* indefinite direct *dekak, dennek;* indefinite dative *dekəkətə, dennekutə;* and so on. Numerals have the unique characteristic of entering into a special type of compound with each other to form a (presumably) infinite series: *dekə* 'two', *wisi dekə* 'twenty-two', *de siya wisi dekə* 'two hundred and twenty two', and so on.

Occurrence with the animate or inanimate forms of numerals serves as a basis for classifying nouns by gender as ANIMATE or INANIMATE, for example: animate *minissu denna* 'two men', inanimate *pot dekə* 'two books'. This classification is then found to correlate largely with the shapes of the inflectional affixes of nouns. For example, nouns with a genitive in *-ge* are overwhelmingly animate in gender, and only such nouns show accusative and vocative case forms. Nonnumeral numeratives include *kiipe* 'several', *huñgə* 'many', *ṭika* 'few', and *saməharə* 'some'. These differ from each other in the extent to which they share the inflectional and agreement characteristics of numerals.

ADVERBS are particles that occur as attributes to predicators in clauses or to clauses as a whole. This class includes *aayee, aayet,* and *ayime* 'again', *aapəhu* 'back', *yantan* 'barely', *namut* 'but, however', *itin* 'so', *dæn* 'now', *nitərə* 'steadily, always'. The class of adverbs is quite small. Much larger is the syntactic (not part-of-speech) class of ADVERBIALS, forms that have privileges of occurrence like those of adverbs. This syntactic class includes a great many case-inflected forms of substantives along with other types of forms.

POSTPOSITIONS are of two kinds: POSTPOSITIONAL PARTICLES and SUBSTANTIVE POSTPOSITIONS: POSTPOSITIONAL PARTICLES are particles that follow substantives, whose case they govern, to form postpositional phrases like *gænə* in *ee potə gænə* 'about that book'. Other examples are *issərə* 'before', *tisse* 'throughout', *iñdəla* 'from', *kiəla* 'by (agent)', *lawaa, lawwa = kiəla* 'by (causee)'. SUBSTANTIVE POSTPOSITIONS, like postpositional particles, follow substantives, whose case they govern, to form phrases, but they themselves may inflect for case in that position. Thus *lañgə* in *kaḍee lañgə* 'near the boutique' and *kaḍee lañgəta* 'to near the boutique'. Among others are *pahalə* or *palleha* 'below', *ihəla* 'above, up', *digə* 'alone', *kiṭṭuwə* 'near, vicinity of', *gaawə = lañgə*. This class in particular shows a great deal of overlap with other classes, including the major classes of nouns and adjectives. Thus, *digə is* also a noun 'length' and an adjective 'long', as indicated before, and *lañgə is* also an adjective, as in *ee kaḍee lañgay* 'that boutique is nearby'.

Demonstratives and other deictics also occur in Sinhala. The DEMONSTRATIVES *mee* 'this' and *oyə, arə, ee* 'that' occur in the characteristic position in noun phrases, in which they may precede adjectives. They are substantives, but they do not inflect for case in that position. Demonstratives also occur adverbially as well as pronominally in a limited number of environments. The pronominal demonstratives occur notably as objects of certain postpositions: *miiṭa issərə* 'before this—dative'. They also occur as subjects in clauses with a noun or noun phrase as predicator: *mee magee pot* 'these are my books'.

The demonstratives show, as a set, a four-way deictic distinction. They may be classified accordingly as FIRST PROXIMAL *mee* (proximity to speaker), SECOND PROXIMAL *oyə* (proximity to hearer), DISTAL *arə* (away from both speaker and hearer), and ANAPHORIC *ee* (reference to something preceding in the discourse). Forms classifiable according to this distinction may be called DEICTICS, and Sinhala has a number of deictic sets. Among them are the DEMONSTRATIVE PRONOUNS, which may substitute for nouns and noun phrases and are classifiable by gender categories like those for the numeral *one*. Thus we find (only first proximal forms are given as examples) *meekə* 'this one, it (inanimate)', *meyaa* 'he, she (human)', *meeka* or *muu* 'this one, he, she, it (animate, animal-derogatory, general)', *meeki* 'she (animate, animal-derogatory, general)'. At least some speakers have a human feminine anaphoric form *ææ*, and others have a first proximal *mææ*, as well. Thus the general/feminine distinction operates here within human as well as animal-derogatory categories.

Other deictic sets (again represented by the first proximal form) include PROADVERBS *mehee* 'here', *metənə* 'here, this spot', *mehaa* 'this way', *mehemə* 'thus, this way/manner'; DEICTIC PARTICLES[10] *mennə*, 'voici'; and DEICTIC QUANTIFIERS *meccərə*, 'this much'.

PERSONAL PRONOUNS are substantives classifiable by PERSON and inflectable for, or classifiable by, NUMBER. The first person pronouns are *mamə* 'I' and *api* 'we'. There are numerous second person pronouns implying various degrees of respect and differential status,[11] among them *too, uṁbə, tamuse, ohee, obə,* and *tamunnanse*. Forms used as third person pronouns are generally deictics, and they thus belong to other classes, primarily the class of demonstrative pronouns.

INTERROGATIVES are substitutes that appear in interrogative clauses, and their presence helps to mark those clauses as interrogative. Most interrogatives correspond to some set of deictics, which they resemble in privileges of occurrence and commonly in form, as well. They include, among others, *koy* 'which', *mona* 'what', *kookə* 'which one (inanimate)', *kooka* 'which one (animal)', and *kawuru* 'who'.

The assertion marker and the question marker, minor parts of speech with which I conclude this part-of-speech presentation, are classes of one member each. The ASSERTION MARKER has been previously mentioned as the *-y* that occurs obligatorily or optionally on different classes of adjectives in certain syntactic positions. It may also occur optionally on forms of other classes under similar syntactic conditions, but these are not simply statable until the relevant portions of the syntax have been given, and they are thus not specified further here. The assertion marker appears as *-i* when affixed to *puluan,* otherwise it appears as *-y* after vowels and *-uy* after consonants: *puluani, hoñday, potuy* (the *a ~ ə* alternation in *puluan* is part of a generally statable one in Sinhala and is not restricted to these forms). The QUESTION MARKER *də* occurs in and marks interrogative clauses, both with and without interrogatives: *eyaa adə enəwa də* 'Is he coming today?', *eyaa kohaaṭə də yanne* 'Where is he going?'

Summary

The minor part-of-speech classes that have been listed are by no means exhaustive. There are numerous other classes, most of them defined on the basis of occurrence in specific syntactic patterns and thus most easily presented along with those patterns in a later portion of the grammar. I have attempted to give what appears to be a minimal list for the purpose of embarking on a description of colloquial Sinhalese syntax. In the entire presentation, I have attempted to illustrate an approach to the classification of inflection and parts of speech for that language that appears to me to be productive and, hopefully, to reveal at the same time a few distinctive features of its grammar. Above all, I have attempted to render my classificatory criteria both formal and explicit while remaining true to the genius of the colloquial variety of Sinhala as a linguistic entity fully worthy of study in its own right and not simply as the shadow of another variety.

Action Involvement Categories in Colloquial Sinhala

This paper was written for the Morris Opler Festschrift, Themes in Culture (*Zamora et al. 1971*). *It related to that scholar's interests in both South Asia and themes in culture since it dealt with a South Asian language and attempted to present some broad categories of a kind that appeared to be the closest analogue within language to themes in culture as a whole and the relevant meaning–form relations. Since that time, there has been a considerable amount of work on such linguistic aspects as agentivity, volitivity, and control, including work on involitivity in Sinhala (for example, Gunasinghe 1978, 1985, and most recently Inman 1993 and references therein). The paper here was, as far as I know, the first systematic attempt to point out and describe that important aspect of Sinhala, and it appears to me still to represent a useful summary description of the relevant aspects of the language and so to be worthy of inclusion here.*

There appear to be in the speech behavior of Sinhala speakers some definite, observable correlations between the quality of a participant's involvement or potential involvement in an action or state[1] and the grammatical devices employed in its expression. This paper is an initial attempt to tease out some of these correlations, specifically by examining some grammatically important contrasts in verb morphology and sentence type from that point of view and also by attempting to relate the two broad action-involvement categories that emerge to still other grammatical phenomena.

Put differently, the object of investigation is the meaning of certain grammatical features. The view of language accepted here as basic to such an investigation is one essentially in the Bloomfieldian tradition. It is expressed neatly by Chafe:

> When people speak or when they listen to speech, they make use of a very complex set of habits that enable them to relate EXPERIENCE to SOUND. I am using these terms as Edward Sapir used them when he wrote that "The essence of language consists in the assigning of conventional, voluntarily articulated sounds, or of their equivalents, to the diverse elements of experience." . . . Either a person attempts to communicate a part of his own experience to others by making sounds, or he perceives sounds and from them modifies his own experience to accord in some way

and to some degree with the experience which the producer of the sounds wished to communicate. The habits underlying this kind of behavior generally and fruitfully are assumed to involve the imposition of "structure" on both the universe of experience and the union of sound. (1965: 23)

Chafe further used the term SEMOLOGY to refer to "the complex of linguistic habits that involve the structuring of experience," a usage generally in accord with that of a number of other investigators. In this sense, the categories to be sought here are semological. Such an attempt involves numerous and notorious pitfalls, not the least of which is the possibility of oversubjectivity. As far as I can, I shall attempt to minimize this possibility by using as a point of departure formal contrasts between sets of utterances. Nevertheless, a number of intuitive judgments will be required, and here the dilemma arises, with familiar counterparts in the study of other aspects of culture, that investigators for whom a language is not their mother tongue are unlikely to have the deep grasp of it necessary to ensure that their judgments are well founded, while mother-tongue speakers have difficulty in achieving the necessary distance from their own language. However, I agree with those who, like Chafe (and Hockett in his *State of the Art* [1968]), feel that "meaning is in every way as important as sound in our approach to an understanding of language as a whole" (Chafe 1965: 23). Thus, an attempt at uncovering some semological categories in another language, even as an exploratory first step, would seem to be not only justified but also required.

Verb Type and Sentence Type

I shall first, as background, make a brief excursion into one aspect of verb morphology followed by a brief sketch of sentence types. A verb stem in Sinhalese may contain, in addition to a root, one of two morphemes {P} and {C}. Verbs containing these morphemes may be referred to as a "P verb" or a "C verb," respectively. A verb containing neither of these is an "A verb". The basic pattern is a set of three verbs, an A, a P, and a C, sharing a common root,[2] such as *kapənawa* 'cut' (A), *kæpenawa* 'get cut' (P), and *kapawanawa* or *kappanawa* 'cause to cut' (C). There may be, as here, alternate C verbs with no difference in meaning or distribution. There are also defective sets and sets of more than three, but this is unimportant for our present purpose and may without too much difficulty be accommodated within the general scheme given. The three verbs in a set inflect in parallel fashion, each having essentially the same paradigm, including past and nonpast tenses and perfect participial forms. Thus, for example, we see the past tense forms *kæpuwa* 'cut', *kæpuna* 'got cut', and *kæppuwa* 'caused to cut' and the perfect participles *kapəla* 'has cut', *kæpila* 'has gotten cut' and *kappala* 'has caused to cut'. One important point is that the type of verb—that is, whether it is an A, P, or C verb—is usually clearly recognizable throughout the paradigm. In particular, any given form of a P verb is virtually always immediately recognizable as such by its shape as distinct from the corresponding forms of an A or C verb.

The correlation between verb type and occurrence in sentence type is neither one-to-one nor complete, but there is a definite high-frequency pattern to which remaining examples can be related. In giving sentence examples, each will be followed by an item-by-item gloss and then a translation equivalent. The cases of nouns or pronouns are indicated with -d for dative, -g for genitive, -a for accusative, and -i for instrumental. The remaining case that concerns us, the direct, is unmarked. Verbal categories, other than the A, P, and C already discussed, are not symbolized but are merely indicated in translation, except for the two affixes -*wi* and -*nnan*, which roughly translate as 'might' and 'will'; these will be important to the discussion later. In schematic formulae for sentence types, N stands for nominal (i.e., noun, pronoun, or noun phrase), V for verb and A for adjective. Parentheses indicate optionality, usually constituents present in some but not all examples of a type.

In general, P verbs occur in three types of sentence, though not every such verb will occur in all three. These are, with schematic formulae and examples:

Involitive Sentences [N-d (N) V]
a. *maTə kiyəwuna.*[3]
   I-d   got-spoken (P)
   'I spoke involuntarily.'

b. *maTə pansələ peenəwa.*
   I-d   temple see (P)
   'I see the temple.'

Inactive Sentences [N(-a)V]
a. *minihawa bimə   wæTuna.*
   man-a   ground fall (P)
   'He fell down.'

b. *huləñgəTə gaha wæTuna.*
   wind-d   tree fell (P)
   'The tree fell from the wind.'

Passive Sentences [N atin N(-a)V][4]
a. *miniha atin laməyawə wæTeewi.*
   man   by   child-a   get-dropped-*wi* (P)
   'The child might be dropped by that man.'

b. *banDa atin pol   siiyak   witərə kæDenəwa.*
   Banda by coconuts a-hundred about get-picked (P)
   'About a hundred coconuts can be picked by Banda!'

There are some minor subtypes not adequately accounted for by the formulae, but what is said for the types given can be extended to them, and they are thus given no special consideration here.

A full statement of these sentence types and the diagnostic criteria for them has been given in detail elsewhere (Gair 1970). Here I need say only that they are distinguished in three main ways. First, they are distinguished by the occurrence of a P verb, though this is not an invariable indication or even a necessary one, as we shall see. Second, they are distinguished by the constituents other than the verb that may occur in them—in particular, the dative case nominals in the involitive ones, the possible occurrence of an agentive constituent with *atin* 'by' in the passive ones, and the accusative case nominals in the inactive ones. The accusative, however, applies only to animate nominals, and its occurrence even there varies from speaker to speaker, presumably with dialect. For some speakers, it is seldom if ever employed in Colloquial Sinhala, but others employ it more regularly. We have indicated in constructions where it can appear for the latter, since it furnishes a clear and simple criterion for distinguishing sentence types that are otherwise distinguishable only by more complicated criteria difficult to state briefly.

The two types of criteria given so far are overt; the third is covert: the existence of a possible contrasting sentence (or sentences), of a different type, usually one subsumed under the formulae for transitive sentences and intransitive sentences (given later in this chapter) with an A or C verb, and bearing a statable, recurrent (for other similar pairs), formal resemblance to the one at hand. Thus, for the second passive example above, there is another possible sentence in Sinhala:

> *banDa pol   siiyak   witərə kaDənəwa.*
> Banda coconuts a-hundred about pick (A)
> 'Banda picks about a hundred coconuts.'

This, of course, suggests a transformational type of relationship. I note its existence but will not attempt to specify it formally here.

A and C verbs can be treated together. They generally occur in sentences of two types: transitive and intransitive. C verbs occur in both causative and noncausative transitive sentences but not in intransitive sentences, while A verbs do not occur in causative sentences:

Transitive Sentences
1. Noncausative [N N(-a)V]
   a. *mamə minihawə dækka.*
      I   man-a   saw (A)
      'I saw the man.'

   b. *laməya duwəwə   waTTənəwa.*
      child   daughter-a drop (C)
      'The child drops the daughter.'

2. Causative [N N-d *kiyəla* N V] or [N N *lawaa* N V]
   a. *mamə BanDaTə kiyəla gas   kæppuwa.*
      I   Banda-d *kiyəla* trees caused-to-cut (C)
      'I got Banda to cut the trees.'

   b. *mahattəya lameya lawaa pol   kaDəwənəwa.*
      gentleman boy   *lawaa* coconuts cause-to-pick (C)
      'The gentleman gets the boy to pick the coconuts.'

Intransitive Sentences [N V]
    a. *balla burənəwa.*
       dog   bark (A)
       'The dog barks.'

    b. *nœTTuwo hoñdəTə   naTənəwa.*
       dancers   well   dance (A)
       'The dancers dance well.'

Again, diagnostic criteria for these types have been given in detail elsewhere (Gair 1970), but we should note that they are parallel to those for involitive, passive, and inactive sentences. First, in verb selection, they are related with high frequency to morphological type. Second, there is the possible occurrence of other specific types of constituents, particularly the occurrence of a subject in the direct case, (which is true of both transitive and intransitive sentences and distinguishes them both from the first three types) and the permitted occurrence or nonoccurrence of a direct object in the accusative case distinguishing transitive from intransitive sentences. Third, there are covert relationships to sentences of other types so that, for example, the first causative example can be related to a noncausative transitive clause:

    banDa gas   kœpuwa.
    Banda trees cut (A)
    'Banda cut the trees.'

Causative sentences may be considered a special type of transitive that it is not important to distinguish for present purposes. We can simplify our presentation by setting them aside henceforth and ignoring the distinction between A and C verbs, thus restricting ourselves to examples with the A and P verbs, with the understanding that what is said of the former will also apply for C verbs and causative sentences.

Structurally, involitive, inactive, and passive sentences fall into an IMPERSONAL group, as against transitive and intransitive, which fall into another, ACTIVE, group primarily on the basis of the possible occurrence in the latter of a direct-case subject involving certain affix restrictions on the verb (which will be considered later).

Semological Correlates

We may now turn to look for semological correlates of our formally determined types. It would obviously be too much to expect to find some single simply statable "type meaning" that will apply both exhaustively and exclusively to every one of the potentially countless sentences subsumed within a type, but it is possible to state some highly generalized meanings that are likely to be associated with sentences of one type as against another. These relate primarily to the quality of participant involvement in the action expressed. Active sentences, either transitive or intransitive, with animate nominals as subjects, commonly express conscious and/or voluntary participation in the action of the sentence; that is, the sentence implies action involving choice and control so that one could conceivably decide to do it or not. Sentences of impersonal types, however, commonly express actions or states in which the individual does not participate with that degree of volition. The speaker is likely to be as much undergoer as participant, and the same potentialities for choice and control are lacking.

Within this general characterization of impersonal sentences there are further differences in meaning associated with the formally distinguished subtypes, though they are not as marked as that between impersonal as a group and active. Thus, involitive sentences commonly suggest forces operating within the individual so that the action is habitual, automatic, or despite oneself. For example, take the "spoke involuntarily" sense of the first involitive above, or:

maTə næTenəwa.	*mee dawaswələ maTə wæDə kerenəwa.*
I-d get-dancing (P)	These days-g I-d work get-done (P)
'I automatically dance (when I hear music).'	'These days–just work (habitually).'

There is a recognizable involitive subtype illustrated by the first of the earlier examples with *peenawa* 'see' that involves perception or understanding, in other words, automatic or passive reaction to an impinging stimulus. Other examples are the following:

laməyaTə eekə æhuna.	*maTə ee potə teerenəwa.*
child-d that heard (P)	I-d that book understand (P)
'The child heard that.'	'I understand that book.'

The "see" and "hear" examples may be compared with the following active sentences with different verbs, implying more voluntary participation:

mama perəhærə bæluwa.	*laməya kataawə æhuwa.*
I procession looked (A)	Child story listened (A)
'I saw (watched) the procession.'	'The child listened to the story.'

The "listen/hear" verbs are A and P verbs sharing the same root and thus exemplify the morphological relationships described earlier. The "look/see" verbs, however, while also A and P respectively, are unrelated morphologically. The important point to be made concerning these particular active/impersonal differences is not that concepts like "look" versus "see" and "listen" versus "hear" are expressed by distinct verbs, since this is common enough in English and elsewhere, but that they are associated with differently marked syntactic types and partially with morphological relationships so as to be an integral part of a more general pattern.

As compared with involitive sentences, those of the inactive type commonly imply external forces acting on an individual, so that he or she is not as "internally powered"; in other words, there is a lack of even potential control:

maawə lissenəwa.[5]	*minihawə wæTuna.*
I-a slip (P)	man-a fall (P)
'I'm slipping.'	'The man fell.'[6]

Of the three impersonal types, the passive is the most difficult to characterize in these terms. In general, sentences of this type involve focus on the action rather than on the performer, but this cannot be equated with the English "was hit" passive, for which the most common Sinhala equivalent is, rather, an active sentence without an expressed subject. Special connotations are involved such as that something could or might happen if the situation were left undisturbed, that some voluntary action on someone's part might have involuntary, unwanted consequences, or that the action was accidental and one is not really responsible. For example, if a man finds his car dented and uses the active interrogative sentence:

> *magee kaar-ekee hæppuwe mokədə?*
> my   car-g   hit (A)   why
> 'Why did you hit my car?'

he is imputing volition to the hearer. He thus is more likely to use something like the passive interrogative sentence:

> *magee kaar-ekee hæppunee kohomə də?*
> my   car-g   hit (P)   how
> 'How did my car get hit?'

Similarly, when I noted one day that the lid on the office coffeepot was broken, saying in English. "We broke the lid," a Sinhala speaker who had just entered asked for clarification:

> *api kæDuwa də,   api atin kæDuna   də?*
> we break (A) question, we atin get-broken (P) question
> 'Did we break it on purpose (active), or did we break it by accident (passive)?'

Thus, the passive shares with the other impersonal types the implication of a lack of control or volition or both, which is particularly highlighted by the contrast with the alternative active in the last example.

In summary so far, there is, for the grammatical distinction between active and impersonal sentences, an associated semological distinction implying the presence or absence of control, choice, or volition. It will prove useful to have a term to refer to these semological categories as distinct from the grammatical active/impersonal distinction with which they have so far been congruent. We will use PURPOSIVE/ REACTIVE for them.

Sinhala has animate/inanimate gender categories, which are marked by different patterns of substantive inflection and numeral agreement. There is almost complete congruence between these grammatical gender categories and the difference in type of referent implied by their names. Humans and animals are designated by ANIMATE nominals, plants and nonliving things are designated by INANIMATE nominals. The intersection of the gender categories with the grammatical and semological categories discussed earlier is interesting. Examples of sentence types given so far have largely involved animate nominals. With relatively rare exceptions, inanimate nominals do not occur as subjects of active sentences, as objects in the dative case nominal in involitive sentences, or as the agent in passive sentences (all representing the participant). Not surprisingly, they occur as objects of transitive sentences and as the object of the action in passive sentences, but they also occur in inactive sentences. The latter are common equivalents for English intransitive sentences with inanimate subjects:

awwəTə   lii   pipirenəwa.   wæssəTə wii   temenəwa.
sunshine-d wood burst (P)   rain-d   paddy get-wet (P)
'The wood splits from the sunshine.'   'The paddy gets wet from the rain.'

Though inanimate nominals do not have a marked accusative case, such sentences can be analyzed as inactive on other grounds, such as the P verbs and the occurrence of other constituents.[7] Thus, on the whole, inanimate nominals are treated in Sinhala as incapable of volition or action, and this is reflected in their occurrence in sentence types.

Linking Pattern and Reality

The pattern of morphological, syntactic, and associated semantic relationships presented so far appears to be a live one to the extent that speakers seem able to coin and understand large numbers of utterances that fit it. However, it is also an idealized one, in that the signaling in actual discourse of the syntactic and semantic categories involved is a much more complicated matter than it would suggest. Our main concern should be ultimately to contribute to the understanding of the actual linguistic behavior of speakers, and when we attempt to characterize the relationship between the pattern as presented and actual recorded utterances, two main sources of complexity emerge.

The first discrepancy between pattern and reality involves a general characteristic of Sinhala discourse. For the syntactic pattern discussed (and others as well), those constituents that serve for the analyst as the clearest marks of different sentence types are commonly omitted from sentences in actual discourse. In terms of the pattern above, this means that sentence type may be signaled by the verb alone, as in the conjoined active and impersonal sentences in:

kæDuwe   næœ, kæDuna.
broke (A) not,   got broken (P)
'(I) didn't break it on purpose; it just broke.'

or by way of contrast:

kæDune   næœ, kæDuwa.
got-broken (P) not,   broke (A)
'It didn't just break; (he) broke it on purpose.'

The pattern as presented, however, was in terms of "full" sentences. The truncated examples just given could be expanded into such full ones, but the result would be most uncharacteristic of Sinhala discourse.

The second source of disparity between pattern and reality is more limited to the pattern at issue, and it further complicates the signaling by verb alone that may result from the previous one. The morphological type of the verb, though generally easily recognizable, is not a sure signal of sentence type, since the correlation between them is not complete. While all P verbs seem to occur in at least one impersonal type, some occur in active ones as well. For example, *hærenəwa* 'turn' occurs in both active transitive and inactive sentences:

mamə ee handiyen hæruna.	*maawə ibeemə hæruna.*
I that corner-i turned (P)	I-a automatically turned (P)
'I turned at that corner.'	'I turned involuntarily.'

This is true also of *wæTenəwa* 'fall' and many others.

The implied transformational relationships between sentences with related verbs are also not as neat as presented, partly because there is semantic specialization of single members of some sets of verbs, with the result that sentences containing them do not fit into transformationally related sets. For example, given the A verb *gahanəwa* 'hit', we would expect a P verb *gæhenəwa*. It does in fact exist and occurs in impersonal sentences, but it most commonly occurs in inactive ones with the special sense 'shiver, start(le)', and such sentences are isolated—they do not form part of a set of transformationally related sentences.[8] Despite the complexities in representing the categories with which we have been concerned in actual discourse, however, they may be established clearly enough by contrasting pairs of utterances as has been done, and I may now attempt to extend them by considering other grammatical and lexical features.

Sinhala has nonverbal sentences; that is, those in which the predicator (i.e., nuclear constituent) is a form such as an adjective or nominal. There are two major types:[9]

Equational Sentences [N Predicator]
1. With Nominal as Predicator [N . . . N]:
   a. *eekə gunəseenage alutmə   potə.*
      that Gunasena-g   new-EMPH   book
      'That is Gunasena's latest book.'

   b. *ee   pansələ bohomə prəsiddə ekak.*
      that temple   very   famous   a-one
      'That temple is a very famous one.'

2. With Adjective as Predicator [N . . . A(-Y)] (the -Y represents a form—the assertion marker—that occurs obligatorily on vowel-final adjectives in this position):
   a. *ee   mahattəya bohomə prəsidday.*
      That gentleman very   famous-Y
      'That gentleman is very famous.'

   b. *minihage potə huñgak hoñday.*
      Man's   book much   good
      'The man's book is very good.'

Impersonal Sentences [N-d Predicator]
1. With Nominal as Predicator:
   a. *eyaaTə adə   hariyəTə unə.*
      he -d   today really   fever
      'He has a real fever today.'

   b. *mee   dawaswələ eaaTə huñgak karədərə.*
      These days   he-d   much   trouble
      'He has a lot of worry these days.'

2. With Adjective as Predicator [N A(-Y)]
   a. *laməyaTə dæn hoñday.*
      child-d   now good-Y
      'The child is well now.'

   b. *eyaaTə dæn sumaanəyak witərə asəniipay.*
      he-d   now a-month   about ill-Y
      'He has been sick for about a month now.'

Formally, the impersonal sentences, with their dative case nominals, bear an immediately perceivable resemblance to verbal sentences of the involitive type. Semantically, they commonly express states and situations over which people have no control and/or into which they did not enter by choice, as a partial listing of adjectivals and nominals entering into them will show. (The sense given here is for impersonal sentences; some of these forms also occur in equational sentences, usually with a different meaning). Adjectives that can be used in this way include *hoñdə* 'well', *asəniipə* 'ill', *saniipə* 'healthy', *pissu* 'mad', *keentiy* 'angry', and *tuwaalə* 'injured'. Nouns that can be used in this way include *hembirissaawə 'cold', mæle-eriyaawə 'malaria', kahawunə* 'yellow fever', *unə 'fever', niwaaDu* 'vacation,' and *karədərə* 'trouble'.

Thus, taken as a group, impersonal and nonverbal sentences bear a resemblance in their semantic correlates to impersonal verbal ones as a group, though not specifically only to the involitive subtype of the latter, to which they bear the closest formal resemblance. Thus they, like those verbal sentences, reflect the reactive category on the purposive–reactive dimension.

On the other hand, it cannot be said that equational sentences as a group resemble active verbal sentences and thus reflect the purposive category of that dimension. There are many adjectives and nouns that occur in equational sentences that cannot be seen to imply states any less involitive than those expressed by involitive sentences. As only one example, there is no reason to think that *miniha pissek* 'he a-crazy-person' = 'he is a crazy fellow' is any less involitive than *minihəTə pissuy* 'he-d crazy-Y' = 'He is mad.' Similarly, *tuwaalə* 'injured' occurs in both equational and involitive sentences, but the semantic difference is 'the whole versus a part' rather than volition versus nonvolition:

miniha tuwaalay.	*minihaTə tuwaalay.*
he injured-Y	he-d injured-Y
'He is injured (generally, or the whole).'	'He is injured (a part).'

To summarize, while impersonal sentences furnish further expressions of the reactive category, equational sentences as a group do not similarly relate to the purposive category. Some express voluntary, some involuntary states, and because there are no formal signals within the type to correlate with such meaning differences, one can only say that the type as a whole is neutral to the distinction. There is an interesting possibility that specific equational sentences bear a latent relation to one or the other of those categories on the basis of the type of verbal sentence emerging when they are verbalized by the addition of certain verbs, but this is a line of investigation remaining to be pursued and involves an area of Sinhala grammar to be touched on later, but as yet very little understood.

More on Categories of Verbs

The relationships examined so far between grammatical sentence type and meaning category may be summarized thus:

SEMANTIC CATEGORY:	Purposive	Reactive	Neutral
SENTENCE TYPE:	Active	Impersonal	Equational
	↑Verbal ↑	↑ Non-Verbal ↑	

Some verbs involve special problems in placement on the grammatical or semological dimensions above. Three such in particular—*tiyenəwa* 'be (inanimate)', *innəwa* 'be (animate), stay, remain', *wenəwa* 'be, become, happen'—are particularly important in the grammar. The verbs *tiyenəwa* and *innəwa* occur with inanimate and animate nominals respectively: *potak tiyenəwa* 'There is a book' but *putek innəwa* 'There is a son'. In form, *tiyenəwa* is a P verb, and this taken together with its occurrence with inanimate nominals suggests classification as an impersonal, specifically inactive verb. Apparently *innəwa* is an A verb ("apparently" because it has unique morphophonemic characteristics making it difficult to classify as either A or P), and when it occurs in the sense 'stay, remain' it is an active intransitive (and semantically purposive) verb. However, *innəwa* and *tiyenəwa* as 'be' fall naturally into a set in which they are complementary and show a unique kind of agreement in gender with nominals. In this "be" function, they do not classify neatly as grammatically active or impersonal as a set but may be put into a special STATIVE category, reflecting a similar neutral status on the purposive–reactive semantic dimension, simply asserting existence or a state without necessary implication of purposiveness or its absence.[10] And *wenəwa* 'be, become, happen' occurs frequently as a component in phrasal verbs, commonly verbalizations of nonverbal forms such as adjectives; in this situation, it occurs in both impersonal and active sentences. (These will be considered shortly.) In occurrences by itself, however, it falls into the same stative category as *innəwa* and *tiyenəwa*. Like them, it is neutral as to the purposive–reactive dimension, though it implies a change of state rather than a continuing state.

Allocative and Similar Sentences

There are sentences of a special type, the ALLOCATIVE, that have verbal and nonverbal varieties. Allocative sentences bear formal resemblances to both impersonal and active or equational sentences, and they thus pose special problems in grammatical classification. However, these problems are clarified when considered in the light of the grammatical–semological analysis accomplished so far, and they are thus of particular interest here. Allocative sentences involve a dative case nominal, an allocative constituent, in construction with a remainder analyzable as an intransitive or an adjectival equational sentence. They are thus of the general form [N-d . . . N . . . verb] or [N-d . . . N . . . A(-Y)]. Three of the four verbs occurring in the verbal type are *tiyenəwa*, *innəwa* and *wenəwa*. The fourth is the phrasal verb *hambə wenəwa* 'meet, find, obtain, be available':

maTə potak tiyenəwa.
I-d   a-book be(inan.)
'I have a book.'

eyaaTə putek innəwa.
he/she-d a-son be (anim.)
'She has a son.'

minihəTə dæn salli   hambə wenəwa.
man-d   now money get
'He's getting money now.'

maTə mahattəya hambə unaa.
I-d   gentleman meet
'I met the gentleman (unarranged).'

mahattəyaTə aeksiDanT-ekak unaa.
gentleman-d an accident   became
'The gentleman had an accident.'

Such sentences with *innəwa/tiyenəwa* involve gender restriction relating to the direct case nominal (not to the allocative constituent) as the examples show, and they imply possession that is generally of a longer-term or inalienable type.

Allocative *wenawa* sentences generally imply something happening to the referent of the allocative constituent. Those with *hambə wenəwa* involve finding or receiving (as wages or gifts) or encountering someone. In the "find/receive" sense, the latter contrasts neatly with transitive sentences with the phrasal verb *hambə kərənəwa* 'earn' (*kərənəwa* 'do, make'), and in the "encounter" sense it contrasts with sentences in which *hambə wenəwa* is an active transitive verb with the sense 'meet (on purpose or by arrangement). Thus, compare the above with the following sentences, which have direct case subjects:

miniha dæn salli hambə kərənəwa.
'The fellow is making money now.'

mamə mahattəyawə hambə unaa.
'I meet the master (on purpose).'

In earlier analyses (Gair 1963 and 1970), the special grammatical peculiarities of *innəwa*, *wenəwa*, and *tiyenəwa* were recognized, and they were included in a special subclass of stative verbs, but this was considered a subclass of intransitive active verbs, primarily because the animate/inanimate agreement of *innəwa* and *tiyenəwa* suggested the subject–verb relationship that is a characteristic of active rather than impersonal sentences. *Wenəwa* was included because it falls most naturally into a group with them, though it lacks the same agreement characteristics. Allocative sentences with these verbs, because they are apparently built on intransitive sentences with them by the addition of an allocative constituent, were included under the same general heading, despite the resemblance of the allocative constituent to the dative case constituent in impersonal sentences, and this analysis was extended to allocative *hambə wenawa* sentences. However, stative verb sentences were even more sharply segregated from both impersonal and active ones, and they made an independent category on that dimension largely as a result of attempting to relate them to semological categories arrived at from other types.

This change by itself automatically leads to a change in the analysis of allocative sentences containing those stative verbs, and when we attempt to relate allocative sentences as wholes to those semological categories, an even more basic shift in classification is suggested, affording an even clearer example of the possible usefulness of a semological analysis based on clear cases in deciding doubtful points of grammar.

The resemblance of the allocative constituent to the dative case nominals in some impersonal types has already been noted. When we now look at the meanings of the allocative sentences, other resemblances appear. The *hambə wenəwa* ones are clearly reactive in view of their contrast with the active transitive (and clearly purposive) sentences with the same verb or *hambə kərənəwa*. Allocative sentences with *wenəwa* with their "happen to" sense also seem clearly reactive, though no such neat contrast can be adduced for them. Those with *innəwa* and *tiyenəwa* are not so clearly reactive, but they certainly lack the choice–volition sense characteristic of the purposive category and are, if not reactive, at most neutral to the distinction.

Before drawing any grammatical conclusions, it is necessary to include some allocative sentences with *tiyenəwa, wenəwa*, and *hambə wenəwa* of a slightly different form. These have verbal forms, infinitives, in place of the direct case nominals of those above and are thus of the shape [N-d . . . Verb-inf. . . . Verb]. Their general senses may be gathered from the following examples:

maTə yannə tiyenəwa.
I-d   to-go   be
'I am (supposed to) go.'

eyaaTə yannə unaa.
he-d   to-go   became
'He had to go.'

maTə dæn Sinhələ kataa karannə hambə wenəwa.
I-d   now Sinhala to-talk obtain
'I get a chance to speak Sinhala now.'

For all of these, the action of the infinitive is made necessary or possible by something else external to it. This is particularly clear for the *wenəwa* ones, imply-

ing that the situation requiring some action has come about quite without any volition on the actor's part. The *tiyenəwa* ones imply necessity or obligation, possibly
by prearrangement. Similarly, the *hambə wenəwa* ones suggest a situation such that
one has the opportunity to do something, and though action itself is probably voluntary, the enabling situation is external to the speaker and furnishes a limiting or
enabling frame for those actions. Thus all of these, including the ones with *tiyenəwa,*
quite clearly furnish another reflection of the reactive category.

When all of the verbal allocative sentences (with both nominals and infinitives)
are considered as a group in terms of both their form and meaning in relation to the
semological categories that have been uncovered, it seems that the earlier classification of them as active should be revised. Though they may be built on intransitive (more precisely stative) sentences, the latter have combined with dative case
nominals in a constructional relationship like that in some types of impersonal sentences. The entire sentences resulting are thus of an impersonal type. It is possible
that "have" sentences with *innəwa* and *tiyenəwa* and nominals should be segregated
as a special, neutral subtype, but since we lack clear indications of this, it is simplest
at present to include them with the rest. In sum, given formal resemblances in two
directions such as those shown by allocative sentences, we have used the semological
categories established in clear cases as evidence in making a decision on their grammatical classification.

There are sentences with the (P) verb *hædenəwa* 'get made' that resemble verbal allocative sentences, such as:

> *maTə unə   hædenawa.*
> I-d   fever get-made
> 'I'll get a fever.'

They generally involve names of diseases also occurring as predicators of nonverbal
impersonal clauses (compare the earlier example with *unə*). Grammatically they are
impersonal, and in meaning, clearly reactive. In Sinhala, such states as disease
are, as a group, generally expressed in impersonal sentences, whether verbal or
nonverbal.

There are also nonverbal allocative sentences, analyzable as allocative constituents in construction with adjectival equational sentences, and these should be briefly
considered. As with verbal allocative sentences, the included sentences may have
either a direct case nominal or an infinitive as subject. Examples, with *hoňdə* 'good',
purudu 'accustomed', are:

> *maTə mee kææmə hoňday.*
> I-d   this food   good-Y
> 'This food is good for me.'

> *maTə mee kææmə kannə hoňday.*
> I-d   this food   to eat good-Y
> 'It's good for me to eat this food.'

> *maTə mee kææmə puruduy.*
> I-d   this food   accustomed-Y
> 'I'm used to this food.'

> *maTə mee kææmə kannə puruduy.*
> 'I-d   this food   to eat accustomed-Y'
> 'I'm accustomed to eating this food.'

Various adjectives appear in such sentences, though not necessarily with both types of subjects. Among them are *aasa* 'feel like', *æti* 'enough', *madi* 'too little', *higə* 'scarce, short of', *puluwan* 'can, possible', and *oonə* 'want, must'. The latter two share special grammatical characteristics leading to their segregation as "modal adjectives." Setting them aside for the moment, it is not yet clear how nonverbal allocative sentences as a group relate to the purposive–reactive dimension. Some, like those with *hoňdə*, *higə*, *æti*, and *madi*, have apparently reactive senses; for others like *purudu* and *aasa*, it is not clear that such is the case. There are also some special as-yet-unsettled questions of grammatical analysis involved with this type, and it is probably safest to consider them, as a group, to be neutral, like equational sentences, at least pending closer grammatical and semological investigation of them.

For *puluwan* and *oonə*, however, the situation is different. In sentences resembling allocative ones, they have the senses "can" and "want," respectively, with either direct case nominals or infinitives:

maTə ee wæDə puluwani.	*maTə mee kææmə kannə puluwani.*
I-d that work possible-Y	I-d this food to-eat possible-Y
'I can do that work.'	'I can eat this food.'
maTə mee potə oonə.	*maTə eekə kannə oonə.*
I-d this book want.	I-d that to-eat want.
'I want this book!	'I want to eat that.'

There are also sentences that have these forms but are of a quite different type, analyzable as equational sentences with an infinitive attribute to *puluwan* and *oonə* and having the senses "might (it might be that)" and "must (have to)" respectively:

mamə eekə kannə puluwəni.	*mamə mee kææmə kannə oonə.*
I that to-eat possible	I this food to eat necessary
'I might eat that.'	'I must eat this food.'

These contrast in both form and sense with the allocative type above. They contrast particularly neatly with sentences with infinitives, from which they differ in external form only by having direct rather than dative case nominals. The contrast in sense between 'can/might' (for *puluwan*) and 'want/ must' (for *oonə*) very nicely reflects the purposive–reactive distinction. However, the particular way it is signaled is just the opposite of that for verbal sentences: The direct case ones are reactive, the dative case ones are purposive. In this respect, *oonə* and *puluwan* are quite special.[11] Interestingly, they are in a sense archetypal to the purposive category, summarizing in themselves the two major notions of control or capability and choice or volition inherent in it.

The difference in case marking relevant to semological category where *puluwan* and *oonə* are involved points up the possible complexities in the actual signaling of such categories. In searching out such categories, one cannot expect them necessarily to be signaled in some straightforward manner. They are established initially on the basis of sets of formal contrasts associated with recurrent differences of meaning, then linked and extended on the basis of similarity of meaning. The fact that the latter may be associated with different, apparently even opposing—formal signals is not any more important or startling here than in any other kind of linguistic analysis as long as the conditions for these differences, as in this case the presence of *puluwan* and *oonə* as against other predicators, can be clearly specified. It only underlines the arbitrariness and complexity of form–meaning relationships, and it does not argue against the validity of the categories proposed.

There are other ways that purposive and reactive action involvement are signaled in Sinhala, though they are not entirely independent of the sentence type distinctions already treated. It remains to survey them briefly.

Adverbials and Action Involvement

There are in Sinhala two main types of adverbials with a broadly instrumental sense: instrumental case nominals and dative case nominals. The difference between them correlates with the purposive–reactive distinction, since the instrumental case nominals generally express an instrument or agency that is consciously or purposively employed, while the dative case nominals commonly refer to something outside one's control. Compare, for example:

> *mamə mee attə   pihiyen kæpuwa.*
> I   this branch knife-i cut (A)
> 'I cut this branch with the knife (purposively).'

> *atə   pihiyaTə kæpuna.*
> hand knife-d   cut (P)
> '(My) hand got cut by the knife (accidentally).'

Not surprisingly, such instrumental case adverbials commonly appear in active sentences and the dative case ones in impersonal sentences, though the correlation is not complete.

Verbalizers Signaling Action Involvement

There are in Sinhala several verbs that occur as "verbalizers" with nonverbal forms such as nouns or adjectives so as to make phrasal verbs. Usually, there are two or more of them that occur with the same nonverbal elements, thus forming a set of phrasal verbs. The most common ones are probably *wenəwa* 'be, become' and *kərənəwa* 'do, make', and such pairs as the following with *pissu* 'crazy' might lead us to seek a correlation between these verbalizers and the purposive/ reactive distinction:

> *maawə pissu weewi.*   *miniha maawat pissu keruwa.*
> I-a   crazy become-wi   man   I-a-too crazy made
> 'I might go crazy.' (impersonal inactive)   'The man drove me crazy, too.' (active, transitive)

But the correlation is not so simple and direct. Phrasal verbs with *kərənəwa* are indeed active, usually transitive, and purposive in meaning, but not all phrasal verbs with *wenawa* are impersonal and reactive. Thus, to take only one example of many, *taraha kərənəwa* 'make (someone) angry' is clearly active and purposive in sense, but *taraha wenəwa* 'become angry, take offense' is active intransitive, not impersonal, and it is fundamentally purposive, not reactive. Take for example:

> *taraha wennə epaa.*
> angry become don't
> 'Don't become angry.'

where the implication of potential control is clear. Thus *kərənəwa/wenəwa* verbalization is congruent with purposive–reactive only with some nonverbal forms and not with others.

But there is more, for *taraha* also occurs with other verbs, forming phrasal verbs also with *gannəwa* 'take,' *yanəwa* 'go', and *enəwa* 'come'. With *gannəwa*, the result is like that with *wenawa*, though more transient anger may be implied:

> *taraha gannə epaa.*
> anger take don't
> 'Don't get angry.'

However, *yanəwa* and *enəwa* appear to be free alternates here, and the resulting phrasal verb is grammatically impersonal (of the involitive type). It implies involuntary anger and is thus reactive:

> *mahattəyaTə eekəTə hariyəTə taraha giyaa.*
> gentleman-d that-d really anger went

> *mahattəyaTa eekaTa hariyəTa taraha aawa.*
> gentleman-d that-d really anger came
> 'The master really got angry at that.'

Thus with *taraha*, there is actually a larger set of verbalizers of which *kərənəwa* and *wenəwa* form a part, and together with *gannəwa* they form a subset of active, purposive phrasal verbs contrasting with the impersonal, reactive ones formed with *yanəwa* and *enawa* (which are not per se impersonal, but they are active as main verbs). In addition, *keenti* 'anger' appears with the same set of verbalizers, and there are probably others. Finally, *hinaha* 'laughter' occurs with *wenəwa* and *yanəwa* in parallel constructions, with the senses 'laugh' and 'laugh involuntarily', but it does not apparently occur with *kərənəwa*.

There are at least two sets of verbalizers that clearly reflect the purposive–reactive distinction and do not include *wenəwa* and *kərənəwa*. These are:

> *arinawa* 'open' (purposive) versus *yanəwa* 'go' (reactive): as in (*kiṁbuhun arinəwa* 'sneeze', *haccin arinəwa* 'sneeze', *æænun arinəwa* 'yawn', all voluntary (or at least controllable); as opposed to *kiṁbuhun yanəwa, haccin yanəwa, æænun yanəwa*, in the same senses, but involitive.

daanɔwa 'put' (purposive) versus *wæTenɔwa* 'fall' (reactive):   as in *hæti*
daanɔwa 'pant, breathe heavily', *maañcu daanɔwa* 'handcuff', *agul daanɔwa*
'lock, close'; as opposed to *hæti wæTenɔwa* 'pant (uncontrollably),' *maañcu*
wæTenawa 'get handcuffed', *agul wæTenawa* 'get locked, closed'.

Both of these sets show a neat congruence with the purposive–reactive distinction,
and for both this accompanies the grammatical distinction between occurrence in
active and impersonal clauses. Thus, here the selection of a verb from a lexical set is
on the same functional plane as the selection from morphologically related sets treated
earlier. There are probably other sets of verbalizers that we have not yet encountered,
and it would not be surprising if those above were still further expandable by the
addition of further nonverbal forms or even additional verbalizers.

Inflectional Verb Morphology

For a last reflection of the different kinds of action involvement, we return to verb
morphology, this time to inflection. Within the colloquial Sinhala verb paradigm,
there are two endings, *-nnan* and *-wi* (in some dialects *-y*), that indicate action that
has not yet occurred. These are in large part restricted to first and nonfirst person,
respectively: *mamɔ yannan* 'I'll go', *eyaa yaawi* '(s)he might go'. Thus the difference between them might be viewed primarily as one of person. They also imply
another distinction, however, as the translations above suggest. Furthermore, there
is a correlation with occurrence in different sentence types, for the restriction in person as stated applies only to active sentences. In impersonal clauses, *-nnan* does not
appear, only-*wi,* regardless of the person of any nominals in the sentence:

maawa lisseewi.	*minihawa lisseewi.*
I-a slip-wi	man-a slip-wi
'I might slip.'	'The man might slip.'

Thus these affixes commonly imply not only a difference in person but also a difference in the character of involvement in the action. *-nnan* implies that the action will
be undertaken voluntarily, by choice and under the control of the speaker, who is
also the participant. *-wi*, however, implies, from the point of view of the speaker, an
action not under his control. In impersonal sentences, where only *-wi* (and not *-nnan*)
is possible, this may be because the action is of a kind that does not allow such control, whether or not the speaker is also participant, as in the two "slip" examples just
above. In active sentences, where the action is of a purposive kind, it is under someone else's control, not the speaker's, as in:

mahattɔya aTɔTɔ witɔrɔ eewi.
gentleman eight-d about come-wi
'The gentleman might come at about eight.'

Thus at least one component of the distinction between these affixes is a distinction
in sense reflecting the broader purposive–reactive one.[12]

Summary

I have attempted to extract, from various aspects of Sinhala structure, two semological categories relating to action involvement, one implying choice–volition and/or controllability, the other implying involition and/or lack of control. These are very broad and involve numerous subcategories, but they seem to be important and pervasive in the language, at least to the extent that they are connected in part with some fundamental grammatical features. Pervasive, however, does not mean exhaustive. That is, these categories can be linked to important grammatical classes subsuming large numbers of forms, but there are also classes on the same level and large numbers of utterances that are neutral to these categories or to which they are irrelevant. In this sense, they resemble themes, which, however important and widely manifested, do not apply to each and every aspect of a culture.

These categories, if they prove valid, are in a fundamental sense an important aspect of the cognitive style of Sinhala speakers, but no claim has been made that they reflect the nonlinguistic perceptions of those speakers or that they relate to any other aspects of culture. Rather, I have been attempting to characterize some aspects of the linguistic behavior of Sinhala speakers with respect to the machinery that the language appears to make available to express one kind of difference between events. It is also not necessary that these categories have relevance only to Sinhala. It might be possible to discover them, or similar ones, in other languages both in and out of South Asia, and it would be interesting to compare the level of linguistic structure on which they are expressed and the manner of their expression.

II

SYNTAX: CONFIGURATION, ORDER, AND GRAMMATICAL FUNCTION

About *Colloquial Sinhalese*
Clause Structures

Colloquial Sinhalese Clause Structures (CSCS) began as my Ph.D. dissertation, essentially completed in 1962. At the time of writing, it was the first treatment of the language in the then-still-young framework of transformational grammar and the first extended general treatment of Sinhala syntax. At the time that it was written, there were few models for such a treatment of a language other than English—and none on that scale for any South Asian one. It did not reach publication, in a revised form, until 1970. Thus, a number of important works in that framework, including Chomsky's *Aspects of the Theory of Syntax*, appeared in the meantime, so that much of CSCS already had a somewhat old-fashioned quality in theoretical terms within the rapidly developing theory of generative grammar. However, it remained the most complete principled treatment of Sinhala syntax, and it still retains much of that character, despite subsequent work done on the language in that general framework. Furthermore, many of the problems that it raised, both language specific and general, have still not found conclusive treatment, and they underlie much work in current generative linguistics. From the standpoint of this volume and the chapter in this section. the relevance of CSCS is that it set the stage for much of that subsequent work by raising several important questions regarding the structure of the language in relation to general linguistic theory, and it thus formed a kind of foundation and blueprint for that later work. In essence, these issues were forced upon the researcher by unavoidable aspects of the structure of the language, for which previous generative work, based largely on English, provided no models.

One question that immediately confronted the researcher could be described in the most general and theory-neutral terms as the existence of different argument structures, syntactic and semantic, correlated with verbal morphology. The Sinhala version of this, while sharing a number of features with other languages of the area, such as the existence of causatives applying to both transitive and intransitive structures, has a somewhat special character within that area, most notable of which is the existence of a well-developed system involving a morpheme associated especially with both involitivity and differences in syntactic patterns. Thus, as described in other chapters within this volume, Sinhala verbs may be classified as A, C, and P verbs, with the latter two including, respectively, the Causative ({C}) and Involitive ({P}) morphemes respectively.[1] These are linked to a set of case arrays allowing all Sinhala cases but one, along with some postpositional phrases, to occur in matrix or embedded subject position, as largely described in chapter 6, "Subjects, Case, and INFL in Sinhala."

Furthermore, the system associated with these morphemes involves a number of complex interactions, including successive occurrence and recursion, and among other things, it led to difficulties in establishing the facts relating to the range of usage in and obtaining clear judgments of grammaticality. The main problem posed by these structures in regard to linking description and theory in terms of the version of the theory underlying the work was that the association of different, definable grammatical structures with the verb morphology was not one to one, and there were a number of exceptions and apparent loose ends, idiomatic and otherwise, Under the theoretical assumptions employed at the time of writing CSCS. transformations should apply straightforwardly wherever their structural definitions were met, but it appeared impossible to associate sets of possible sentences with a set of structural descriptions such that this requirement could be satisfied. I could note here that while that might in retrospect appear to he primitive and naive when so put, the fundamental problem has not disappeared, and it raises its head in other forms in current work in what is now termed termed the "morphology–syntax interface." Another, complementary, question that arose was the manner of assignment of structure to the output of transformations, which did prove to be a serious one as the theory progressed,[2] as well as the related question of the "baseless" transformation, that is, the existence of sentences that clearly fit the description of types from transformations but for which no underlying sources could be found.

Now, of course, many of these problems would be relegated to the lexicon, but given the syntactic armament at hand at the time, the general approach that was adopted in CSCS was to borrow from Harris (1957) the notion of a separate type of operation, the QUASITRANSFORMATION, which, while having the basic character of a transformation, allowed exceptions. In Sinhala, many morphosyntactic operations of that kind represented relations between identifiable sentence types that were clearly productive but not thoroughgoing and exceptionless enough to be considered "true" transformations. They were thus presented as a special subtype of INTERTYPE TRANSFORMATIONS. However, since characterizing the possibilities and exceptions inevitably led to the lexicon, a logical step appeared to be to account for them in those terms. As a result, the last part of chapter 5 of CSCS suggests such a move and sketches the form that the relevant part of a lexicon might take. At the time, the lexicon was not a prominent element of the theory as understood. Thus, that suggestion was presented as a classification of verbs, but it did foreshadow subsequent work and was carried out in later theoretical terms in this specific context in the "Subjects, Case, and INFL in Sinhala chapter.

Another problem for the investigator was the existence in Sinhala not only of both verbal and non verbal clauses but also of numerous subtypes of each, which were duly classified in CSCS. Although there has been subsequent work on nonverbal clauses (see Gair and Paolillo, chapter 7, in this volume, and Sumangala 1992), no equally comprehensive account of the numerous types of nonverbal clauses in Sinhala has yet appeared to my knowledge, so that those interested in such phenomena may find the remainder of that chapter still worth consulting.

One other point remains to be noted: Since Sinhala, unlike English, was not only SOV but had the character later referred to as "nonconfigurational" along with the common use of null arguments (also noted in chapter 4 of CSCS), it was no simple matter to state structural descriptions in terms of the trees and bracketing in the models (primarily Chomsky's *Syntactic Structures*) then available. Actually, though it was never made fully explicit in the work as it appeared, a flat structure was consciously assumed for Sinhala clause types because of the apparent mobility of constituents and the across-the-board accessibility of constituents to processes such as clefting. The solution in CSCS was thus to assume—instead of the standard NP–VP structure—a flat structure occupied by MAJOR CONSTITUENTS expressed in combined categorical and functional terms, which were then available to the transformational process (such as clefting) and could appear in variant constituent orders. Those descriptions were couched in terms that resembled what would later be called grammatical relations or grammatical functions, and they thus foreshadowed, even if in a primitive way, some later theoretical developments such as case grammar and relational grammar. Chapter 5 here, "Nonconfigurationality, Movement, and Sinhala Focus," was an attempt to reconcile the tree-configurational and nonconfigurational approaches by following up on a suggestion by Chomsky (1981) that essentially incorporated both into a single analysis by invoking a dual representation. The specific approach in that paper was subsequently superseded by an analysis involving the later concepts of functional categories, head-to-head movement, and specifier–head agreement (Gair and Sumangala 1991; Foley and Gair 1993). That later work is not reproduced here, but the earlier paper is included as a clear description of the problem and is still the fullest account of the relevant data.[3]

In sum, CSCS stands as an example of an early attempt to deal with the syntax of a language of a different type from that generally represented in the literature of the time within early transformational–generative grammar. Thus, taken together with the later work represented here and other work still emerging, it demonstrates how far we have progressed with theory (as well as the extent to which some problems are both fundamental and persistent). It can also serve as a still essentially accurate account of the Sinhala phenomena involved, and the interested reader is referred to it for such. In effect, it constitutes a rich and extended introduction to the later work embodied in the chapters in this section, though it is hoped that they will stand on their own.[4]

Nonconfigurationality, Movement, and Sinhala Focus

This paper was delivered at the Linguistic Society of Great Britain in March 1983 and was couched in theoretical terms current at that time. Since then, there have been numerous significant developments that would affect the argumentation here. The α/β pairings suggested in Chomsky 1982, which play a central role here, did not find general acceptance, and different versions of nonconfigurationality were presented as in Hale's 1983 paper "Warlpiri and the Grammar of Non-configurational Languages," which was not available when this was written. Subsequently, also, nonconfigurationality has generally been reduced to scrambling, which has generated a great deal of discussion. However, both the data and the description here have held up, and the account here seems still to be the clearest and the most complete, concise statement of the relevant data. Also, the general approach to the movement view of Sinhala focus still appears to me to be fundamentally intuitively correct, and no completely satisfactory solution to the problems of the construction at issue has yet appeared in my opinion. The reader's attention is also directed to Gair and Sumangala 1991, which attempts to account for a set of the relevant phenomena in a later theoretical framework. I thus felt it worthwhile to make both of the papers available, not only to provide an account of the Sinhala phenomena in a principled way but also in hopes of contributing to a better and more complete account in the future, within whatever theoretical framework makes that possible.

It has been claimed that nonconfigurational languages (W* or X*) do not involve syntactic movement and, further, that the absence of movement in these languages follows in fact from fundamental properties of nonconfigurationality (Hale 1978 et seq; Chomsky 1981: 128). The absence of movement in these languages causes a problem for their incorporation into a theory such as the Revised Extended Standard Theory in its Government and Binding (GB) version, which treats processes such as WH-question formation, relativization, passivization, and causativization in terms of movement (Chomsky 1981: passim). Even if such processes are treated as not involving movement (e.g., Chomsky's "assume GF" treatment for passive and causative in Japanese), there is still a problem if these processes appear to be subject to constraints that within the theory are characterized as constraints on syntactic movement—for example, subjacency.[1]

Sinhala, an Indo-Aryan language and the majority language of Sri Lanka, exemplifies this problem: It is a nonconfigurational language. At the same time, it has a focused sentence construction that exhibits features associated with movement, and that construction has thus been accounted for in earlier treatments in terms of movement (Gair 1970; Fernando 1973; DeAbrew 1980).

In this chapter, I will first briefly characterize Sinhala as a nonconfigurational language and describe the relevant features of the focus construction. I will then argue that these two features of the language can be reconciled within the general framework of standard theory by extending a proposal advanced by Chomsky (1982: 132) with regard to nonconfigurational languages. This extension will lead to a principled characterization of the parametric distinction between configurational and nonconfigurational languages.[2]

Sinhala as a Nonconfigurational Language

In unmarked order, Sinhala is basically a thoroughgoing left-branching language in which modifiers and complements, including relative clauses, are generally to the left of their heads. Nevertheless, it exhibits all of the characteristics attributed to nonconfigurational languages by Hale (1978, 1981) and Chomsky (1981: 127–35).

Word Order

Although Sinhala does have a favored SOV order, as shown in (1), in root sentences, all of the variant orders are possible, as in (2):[3]

(1) *gunəpaalə aliyekwə*   *dækka.*
     Gunapala elephant-INDEF-ACC saw
     'Gunapala saw an elephant.'

(2) a. *gunəpaalə dækka aliyekwə.*
     b. *aliyekwə dækka gunəpaalə.*
     c. *aliyekwə gunəpaalə dækka.*
     d. *dækka gunəpaalə aliyekwə.*
     e. *dækka aliyekwə gunəpaalə.*

Constituent Separation

Sinhala also allows constituents to occur outside of and nonadjacent to the maximal projection to which they clearly belong at some level of representation. For example, not only, as in (3), can constituents of embedded Ss move beyond S' but, as in (4) and (5), constituents of NPs, such as relative clauses or genitive attributes, can occur separated from their heads. Example (5) shows multiple dislocations, with a relative clause rightmost and a genitive phrase occurring to the right of its head:

(3) *yanəwa nan man kiyannan [ee pættəṭə].*
     go   if   I   will-tell that place-DAT
     'I will tell (you) if I go to that place.'

(4) *bas   hoňdə næœ [ee paare yanə].*
     busses good not that road go-PRES-REL
     'The buses that go on that road aren't good.'

(5) *æœy, danne næddə [ban]   [miniha] [arə liliige]   [harak maranə].*
     what know-E not-Q fellow(you) man   that Lily-GEN cattle kill-REL
     'What, you (impolite) don't know that man of Lily's that kills cattle?'

The Sinhala Focused Sentence Construction

General Description

The Sinhala focused sentence construction (sometimes called a cleft, pseudocleft, or emphatic construction) involves a special marking of the tensed verb. Sentences (6) and (7) are focused sentences of this type, to be compared with (8), their "neutral" counterpart. The usual phonological form of the focusing affix is *is -nne* in the present and *-e* in the past. It will be indicated as -E in glosses, as in (5) and (6). Here and in subsequent examples, superscripting with *f* will be used to indicate the association of the focus and the focus-marked verb:

(6) *lankaawe   ayə kanne^f   bat^f.*
     Sri Lanka-LOC people eat-NONPAST-E rice
     'It is rice that Sri Lankans eat.'

(7) *bat kanne^f   lankaawe   ayə^f.*
     rice eat-NONPAST-E Sri Lanka-LOC people
     'It is Sri Lankans that eat rice.'

(8) *lankaawe   ayə bat kanəwa^f.*
     Sri Lanka-LOC people rice eat-NONPAST
     'Sri Lankans eat rice.'

Essentially, the -E affix indicates that the focus is external to the verb—that is, that the focus does not include the verb. Thus, if focus is taken to be a constituent at some level of representation, a neutral sentence will have a representation like (9); a focused sentence will have one like (10).[4] As (9) and (10) show, in neutral sentences, focus includes the verb but is not limited to it, and in focused sentences, focus is external to the verb and applies only to tensed (±/-PAST) sentences:

(9) neutral: [S ... [Foc ... V]]   (... may be null)

(10) focused: [S ... [Foc ^A]^f ...   V^f]   (... may be null, A may not be)
                        + tns

Focus-marking forms, commonly clitics or particles, include *də* 'question', *-yi* emphasis or limitation, *tamay* 'certainly, forsooth', *lu* 'reportative', *nan* 'if', and *nee/ ne* 'n'est ce pas'. They are restricted to occurrence immediately following the focus of a sentence. They thus occur following the verb of a neutral sentence or the focus of a focused sentence, and their occurrence on any constituent other than the verb requires the presence of the -E affix.

The *də* particle is used in forming yes/no questions, either neutral as in (11) or focused as in (12) and (13), with *də* following the questioned constituent. Questioning of any constituent (other than the verb) with *də* will require focusing of that constituent and thus the appropriate verb marking with -E:[5]

(11) ee   miniha heṭə   yanəwa   də?
      that man   tomorrow go-NONPAST Q
      'Is that man going tomorrow?'

(12) ee   miniha yanne^f heṭə^f də?
      that man   go-NONPAST-E tomorrow Q
      'Is it tomorrow that that man is going?'

(13) heṭə   yanne^f ee   miniha^f də?
      tomorrow go-NONPAST-E that man   Q
      'Is it that man who is going tomorrow?'

WH-questions also require *də*, co-occurring with a WH-form (or more precisely a K-M–form, since that is their phonological form in Sinhala). Examples are *mokak* 'what (sg. indef.)', *monəwa* 'what (pl.)', *kau(ru)* 'who', *kookə* 'which', *koy* 'which (det.)', among others. In root sentences (in the sense of Emonds 1976), the focusing of WH-constituents is virtually obligatory. WH-forms plus *də* commonly form a unit such as *mokakdə* and *kaudə*, as in examples (14) and (15), and in fact they are so listed in some dictionaries. Sentence (16), with a WH-form but no cooccurring *də*, and sentences (17a) and (17b), with the focus marker *də* not following the focused WH-form, are ungrammatical:

(14) gunəpaalə kəranne^f mokak^f də?
      Gunapala do-NONPAST-E what   Q
      'What is Gunapala doing?'

(15) eekə hædue^f kau^f də?
      that make-PAST-E who Q
      'Who made that?'

(16) *gunəpaalə mokak kərənəwa/kəranne?
      Gunapala   what   do-NONPAST/do-NONPAST-E

(17) a. *eekə kauru hædua   də?
         that   who   make-PAST Q

      b. *eekə kauru hædue   də?
         that   who   make-PAST-E Q

Actually, some qualification is necessary concerning the ungrammaticality of (17a), since there are instances in which a WH-form is not focused and hence is not adjacent to *də,* particularly in some types of embedded sentences. Although (17a), with the non -E form *hædua* as a straightforward question, will generally be rejected by a native speaker, it is in fact possible as an embedded sentence, particularly as complement of a verb expressing doubt concerning the whole proposition, as in (18):

(18) *eekə kauru hædua də danne nææ.*
      that who   did   Q know not
      '(I) don't know who could have done that.'

And, in fact, with the proper intonation, (18) is possible even as an independent sentence in context of strong doubt, as in "I wonder who on earth could have done (a thing like) that?" Such examples show clearly that WH questioning and focus are independent, though linked, phenomena. It is for that reason that focusing on WH-forms was described as having a "virtually obligatory" character, and the conditions on it are clearly pragmatic, not grammatical. If focused, however, WH-forms are immediately followed by *də.* Thus, example (17b) with *hædue,* the -E form, is ungrammatical in any context.

Focus and Rightward Movement

Note that all examples of focused sentences so far, with or without WH-forms, have exhibited rightward placement of the focused constituent. This is not an uncommon order, and rightward movement and verb marking have been taken together to constitute a focusing transformation in previous treatments (e.g., Gair 1970; Fernando 1973; DeAbrew 1980). For example, Fernando, who worked within the *Aspects* framework, formulated her "Pseudo Cleft" transformation in as in (19) (1973: 237). Her "incomplete" form is our -E; *-yi* is the focus-marking form listed earlier:

(19) PSEUDO CLEFT:
      SD: [X–Y–X   V   ]S ===> OPT
                        Pred
      1 2 3 4
      SC: 1 0 3   [4incomplete] 2 + *yi*

There is a problem, however, in taking rightward movement to be a crucial aspect of focusing, given the nonconfigurational character of Sinhala. Specifically, there is a problem because a focused constituent need not be placed rightward but can occur in its "original" position—in other words, *in situ.* This is shown by example (20a), in which the focus occurs in the same linear position as its counterpart in the neutral sentence (8) above, repeated here as (20b) to make comparison easier. The focus marker *-yi* makes the focused status of *bat* 'rice' clear:

(20) a. *lankaawe   ayə   batuy[f] kanne[f].*
          Sri Lanka-LOC people rice-yi eat-NONPAST-E
          'It is (only) rice that Sri Lankans eat.'

    b. *lankaawe   ayə   bat kanəwa.*
       Sri Lanka-LOC people rice eat-NONPAST
       'Sri Lankans eat rice.'

Furthermore, as with neutral sentences, in keeping with the non-configurationality of Sinhala, other orderings are also possible for this sentence as in (21) through (25):[6]

(21) *batuy^f kanne^f lankaawe ayə.*

(22) *kanne^f batuy^f lankaawe ayə.*

(23) *lankaawe ayə batuy^f kanne^f.*

(24) *batuy^f lankaawe ayə kanne^f.*

(25) *kanne^f lankaawe ayə batuy^f.*

Example (26) offers a particularly compelling example of the independence of focusing and rightward placement; it was used in proffering coffee. Here, not only is the focus leftward but also the elements of the presupposition are out of order, with the verb not occurring rightmost:

(26) *meeke^f   tiyenne^f   siini.*
     this-one-LOC be-NONPAST-E sugar
     'The sugar is in this one.'
     (i.e., 'It is in this one that the sugar is')

It is thus obviously clear that Sinhala focus cannot be accounted for simply by converting previous movement analyses to instances of "move α" between configurational representations of D and S structures.

Sinhala Focus Not Clause-Bound

Up to now, we have restricted our attention to focus within single root sentences. Thus the focused element has always been sentence-internal and the possibility that focusing could be subject to bounding constraints related to movement, specifically subjacency, has not arisen.

Sinhala focus, however, is not clause-bound.[7] Sinhala has a number of complementizers, all rightwards in accordance with the general left-branching nature of the language. These include verbal affixes, as for example, *-la,* the past participial or gerundive affix, and *-aamə,* the prior temporal affix, which are affixed to verbs. They also include others such as *koTə* 'when', *kan* 'until', and *hinda* or *nisaa* 'because', which are particles that require specific affixes on the verbs that precede them. Other complementizers, such as *kiyəla* 'that, (quotative)' and *nan* 'if', occur following sentences with root characteristics and allow processes like focusing to occur within them (we will return to these later). None of these complementizers, however, induce opacity to focusing from a lower to a higher S.

Examples (27) and (28) illustrate focusing into lower clauses with two kinds of complementizers. The (a) and (b) examples illustrate variants with and without rightward placement. (The null symbol Ø in these and subsequent examples should be taken, at least for the present, as only a convenient device for showing the "original" position of the focused element, i.e., its position in the (a) variants or neutral sentences.) Example (27) has a WH-form and the question marker. Example (28) has an embedded quotative clause:

(27) a. *kohee dǝʃ gihilla   mehaaṭǝ enneʃ?*
     where Q gone-COMP here-DAT come-NONPAST-E
         [+ppl]

  b. *Øʃ gihilla   mehaaṭǝ enneʃ   kohee   dǝʃ?*
     gone-COMP here-DAT come-NONPAST-E where-DAT Q
         [+ppl]
     'Where did you come here having gone?'

(28) a. *siripaalǝ eekǝ gunǝpaalǝṭayʃ   dunna   kiyǝla man kiwweʃ.*
     Siripala that Gunapala-DAT-EMPH give-PAST COMP I   say-PAST-E

  b. *siripaalǝ eekǝ Øʃ dunna   kiyǝla man kiwweʃ   gunǝpaalǝṭayʃ.*
     Siripala that   give-PAST COMP I   say-PAST-E Gunapala-DAT-EMPH
     'It was to Gunapala that I said that Siripala gave that.'

Example (28) exhibits two important features. The lower verb is not marked for focus, even though it is a tensed finite form that is susceptible to such marking, but the upper verb is marked for focus. Also, the focused element bears the case marking appropriate to the lower clause, regardless of placement of the focused element. That is, in this example, the focus, *gunǝpaalǝṭǝ*, is dative as indirect object of *dunna* 'gave.' The focus thus stands in a case (and θ-role) relation to the lower verb but in a focus relation to the higher one. Examples (29) through (32) illustrate that unbounded focusing is possible out of clauses with other complementizers as well as the quotative one:

(29) a. *Øʃ hituaamǝ   oluwǝ kakiyanneʃ   monǝwa dǝʃ?*
     think-PAST Comp head ache-NONPAST-E what   Q
     '?What is it that your head aches when you have thought it?'

(30) a. *ee waeDǝ tamayʃ kǝrǝnǝ koṭǝ   mamǝ satuṭu wenneʃ.*
     that work EMPH do-REL COMP I   happy become-NONPAST-E

  b. *Øʃ kǝrǝnǝ   koṭǝ   mamǝ satutu wenneʃ   ee waeDǝ tamayʃ.*
     do-REL COMP I   happy become-NONPAST-E that work EMPH
     '?It's that work that I become happy when I do.'

(31) a. *kauʃ dǝ enǝ   kan   oyaa mehemǝ inneʃ.*
     who Q come-REL COMP you like-this stay-NONPAST-E

  b. *Øʃ enǝ   kan   oyaa mehemǝ inneʃ   kauʃ dǝ?*
     come-REL COMP you like-this stay-NONPAST-E who Q
     '?Who is it that you are waiting like this until (they) come?'

(32) *Øꜝ kaapu   hinda   lameage   baḍə   ridenneꜝ   monəwa dəꜝ?*
      eat-ppl-REL   COMP child-Gen stomach ache-NONPAST-E what   Q
      '?What did the child's stomach ache because he ate?'

Focus is unbounded to greater depths, as seen in sentence (33a), bracketed in (33b), which shows focusing to three clauses below the highest:

(33) a. *Øꜝ ee   baḍu   horəkankəlaa kiyəla siripaalə kiwwa   kiyəla sunil*
        that goods steal-PAST   COMP Siripala say-PAST COMP Sunil
        dannəwa   kiyəla oyaa kiwweꜝ   gunəpaaləꜝ də?
        know-NONPAST COMP you say-PAST-E Gunapala   Q
        'Was it Gunapala who you said that Sunil knows that Siripala said stole the merchandise?'

       b. [s4[s3[s2[s1 *Øꜝ ee baḍu horəkankəlaa kiyəla*] *siripaalə kiwwa kiiyəla*] *sunil dannəwa kiyəla*] *oyaa kiwwe gunəpaaləꜝ də*]

In all such instances, the case of the focused element is that appropriate to its "original" position in the lowest clause, as subsequent examples will also show.

Focus is also unbounded in that neither WH nor questioning in a lower clause, nor focusing within a lower clause, acts as a barrier to focusing. Examples (34) and (35) show focus out of a questioned lower clause; example (35) is bracketed in (36):

(34) *Siripaalə eeka Øꜝ dunna   də kiyəla eyaa aehueꜝ   gunəpaaləṭəꜝ   də?*
      Siripala that   give-PAST Q COMP he   ask-PAST-E Gunapala-DAT Q
      '?Was it to Gunapala that he asked whether Siripala had given that to?'

(35) *Siripaalə mokak Øꜝ dunna   də kiyəla eyaa aehueꜝ   gunəpaaləṭəꜝ   də?*
      Siripala what   give-PAST Q COMP he   ask-PAST-E Gunapala-DAT Q
      '?Was it to Gunapala that he asked whether Siripala had given what to?'

(36) [*siripaalə mokak Øꜝ dunna də kiyəla*] *eyaa aehueꜝ gunəpaaləṭəꜝ də*

Example (37) shows focusing out of a focused lower clause (capital and lower-case superscripts relate focus to the appropriate verbs):

(37) [*mamə Øꜝ mokak dəꟳ dunneꟳ   kiyəla*] *oyaa aehueꜝ   siripaaləṭəꜝ də*
      I   what Q give-PAST-E COMP you ask-PAST-E Siripala-DAT Q
      '?Was it to Siripala that you asked what it was that I gave?'

Note that in this example, both the higher and lower Ss are focused. Again, however, the case of the higher focus is appropriate to the lower verb.

It also appears that double focusing of a lower clause element—that is, by its own verb and the verb of a higher sentence—is possible, as examples (35) through (37) suggest. Note, for example, that in (38), the case of the higher focus is appropriate to the lower S; in other words, dative as required by *gahanəwa* 'hit' is subcategorized for a dative object:[8]

(38) a. (Focused declarative)

gunəpaalə Ø^f gæhue^f kiyəla karu kiwwe^f sirspaalətə^f də?
Gunapala   hit-PAST-E COMP Karu say-PAST-E Siripala-DAT Q
'?It was Siripala that Karu said that it was he who was hit by Gunapala.'

b. (Focused question)

gunəpaalə Ø^f gæhue^f kiyəla karu kiwwe^F siripaalətə^{f,F} də?
Gunapala   hit-PAST-E COMP Karu say-PAST-E Siripala-DAT Q
'?Was it Siripala that Karu said that it was he who was hit by Gunapala?'

(39) eyaa Ø^f bonne^f kiyəla man kiwwe^{f,F} arakku tamay (kasippu nemey)^{f,F}.
he   drink-PRES-E COMP I   say-PAST arrack EMPH (moonshine not)
'It is arrack that I know that it is he that drinks (not moonshine).'

(40) miniha Ø^f ænne^f kiyəla man danne^{f,F} mee pihiyen^{f,F}.
man   stab-PAST-E COMP I   know-PAST-E this knife-INST
'I know that it is with this knife that it was he that stabbed (someone).'

Statement of Constraint

The above facts show that not only is Sinhala focus unbounded, but there is no WH-island constraint on focusing in Sinhala, whether WH is focused or not. The rules for WH, in fact, are simply subcases of those for other constituents in relation to focusing. That is, given the semiobligatory focusing characteristic of WH forms, the rest follows automatically, and there is no separate WH movement.[9]

Focusing does, however, observe the complex noun phrase constraint (CNPC) with regard to relative clauses. This is shown by the ungrammaticality of examples (41) and (42). Example (41) involves a focused WH-form marked by də, and (42) contains a non–WH-form marked by the focus marker tamay:

(41) a. *Ø^f horəkankərəpu minihekwə   hoyanne^f mokak də^f?
         stole-COMP   man-INDEF-ACC seek-NONPAST-E what   Q

b. *mokak də horəkankərəpu minihekwə   hoyanne?
   what   Q stole-COMP   man-INDEF-ACC seek-NONPAST-E
   'What are you looking for a man who stole?'

(42) a. *Ø^f kiewwə   lameawə   guruwərea prasansaakerue^f ee potə
         read-PAST-COMP child-ACC teacher   praise-PAST-E that book
   tamay^f.
   EMPH

b. *ee pota tamay^f kiewwə   lameawə   guruwərea pransansaakerue^f.
   that book EMPH read-PAST-COMP child-ACC teacher   praise-PAST-E
   'It was that book that the teacher praised the child who read.'

The CNPC has been, since Chomsky 1973, subsumed under SUBJACENCY, which is defined as a constraint on movement in syntax (See Chomsky 1973; Huang 1982; and others). In fact, the constructions in examples (37) through (39), which involve Ss that are not opaque to focusing, also involve S' which includes COMP. On the other hand, the Ss within NP in examples (41) and (42) involve a COMP-less structure, NP. The obvious implication is that COMP-to-COMP movement is allowed in the one set but blocked in the other.

Statement of the Problem

We are now faced with the following problem. Sinhala focus is subject to a constraint associated with movement. Specifically, it is subject to subjacency in the form of the CNPC. Yet there is no necessary surface reflection of movement in Sinhala focus. The focused element may remain in situ (i.e., in its unmarked position); or even if not located in situ, it may still not be located outside the relevant bounding domain. That is, even if we do derive some surface orders in Sinhala focus by movement, that movement has no clear or necessary relation to the relevant constraint on this process, namely, subjacency.

Note that this problem would remain even if subjacency were considered to be a constraint on representations rather than on movement (as in Koster 1978 and in Freidin 1978). We would still have to invoke a level of representation where the empty categories and their antecedents were properly located for subjacency to apply.

One obvious approach to this problem is to look for a level of representation in Sinhala that has the necessary configurational characteristics, whether or not movement is assumed. What could be the proper level of representation?

LF is an obvious candidate. However, this can quickly be ruled out, since subjacency does not apply here in general.[10] More specifically, consider sentence (41b). Here, syntactic focusing to a WH-form in a relative clause is blocked, so that the question marker cannot directly follow it. However, sentence (43a) is possible, with the entire NP containing the relative clause focused, as shown by the position of the question marker: the relevant bracketing is given in (43b):

(43) a. *mokak kərəpu   minihekwə   də hoyanne?*
         what   stole-COMP man-INDEF-ACC seek-NON-PAST-E

   b. [[NP[S*mokak kərəpu*] *minihekwə*]*də*]*ᶠ hoyanneᶠ*

The interpretation of (43), given in (44), is in fact the desired one for the ungrammatical (41b). This requires the movement of *mokak* 'what', together with Q, in LF. That is, with the *mokak də* bracketed outside of S, and with the proper variable supplied, the syntactically blocked (41b) becomes a reasonable LF representation, as in (44). This shows conclusively that the constraints on focus extraction in Sinhala apply in syntax, not in LF.

(44) [*mokak$_i$ də*] [*e$_i$ horəkankkərəpu minihekwə hoyanne*]$_s$

Resolution of the Problem

In order to account for nonconfigurational languages, Chomsky (1982) proposes, that both D-structure and S-structure can each be considered a pair (α, β) such that:

(45) α is a formal syntactic structure and β is a representation of associated GF's (Grammatical functions). . . . For English, β is derived from α by abstraction from order, etc. For Japanese, [and by extension, for Sinhala, JWG] α is a "flat" structure formed by the base rule [$_{X\text{-bar}}$ W*X] and β is essentially the same as the corresponding element in English. Case and binding theory crucially consider the element β of the pair (α, β) in both types of language, but we need not make the distinction in English, since β is a simple abstraction from α. (1982: 132)

Chomsky then calls his β structure a "representation of GF's" that are "associated" with a "formal syntactic structure" (i.e., α) through random assignment of GFs to the constituents of α structure, thus accounting for the variable word order. On p. 131, for example, he refers to the structure shown in (46) for Japanese as a "convenient shorthand for a list of GF's" associated with that part of the formal syntactic structure (a) of (47), which includes NP_2, NP_3, and the verb of (46):

(46) [$_{S1}$$NP_2$, [$_{VP1}$ NP_3, [$_{V1}$ *tabe*]]] (for the "NP_2 eat NP_3" part of 47)

(47) $NP_1NP_2NP_3$[$_V$tabe-sase]
   (NP_1 causes NP_2 to eat NP_3)

However, this β structure does have a configurational character.[11] Chomsky refers to the GFs as [NP, VP], [S, VP], [NP, S].[12] In order for the θ-criterion and case filter, as well as the binding theory, to apply properly, β structure must have the configurational properties[13] that this notation implies. I will thus assume that structure is configurational and subject to X-bar theory.[14] The association of elements in α with those in β is, however, still random, as in Chomsky, subject to some qualifications to be made later.

We thus consider that for each α structure, as reflected in the surface, there is a β representation at both D- and S-structure. This β structure provides the necessary configurational properties so that focusing can be treated as an instance of D→S movement within β structure. That is, the movement is from β D-structure to β S-structure. This movement is not necessarily reflected in the (α β) matching and thus need not be apparent on the surface. This proposal is schematized in figure 5–1.

Accepting a dual matching structure of this kind will allow us to capture the intuitions reflected in the "classical" transformational treatments of Sinhala focus (Gair 1970; Fernando 1973; deAbrew 1980). At the same time, it accommodates the problem of the varied surface orders discussed above, since the movement is only in

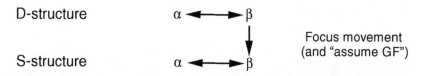

Figure 5–1 Schema describing the role of movement in nonconfigurational languages.

β structure. Note that since the (α, β) pairings are not one to one, there will be one β structure for a set of α structures such as in examples (1) and (2) or (21) through (25) above.

To be justifiable in terms of GB theory, however, the proposed movement should leave a trace and be moved to some well-defined landing site, with relevant constraints applying in an independently motivated fashion.

The general location of the landing site is determined if we make the quite natural assumption that the rightward position (on which earlier treatments in all frameworks agree) is the unmarked one and if we note that the focused element usually occurs preceding overt complementizers in surface orders.[15] In the base schema of β Sinhala, there are two likely candidates for the position of the focus node that meet these conditions. These are shown in the trees in (48) and (49). The focus node may either occur directly under S-bar as in (49) or be adjoined to COMP as an optional expansion, as in (48).

(48)

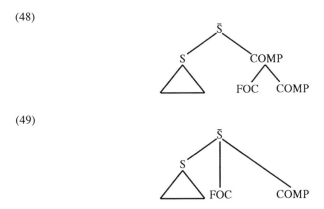

(49)

Although each of these representations has its advantages and disadvantages, the position under COMP involves familiar problems of c-command by elements of a branching COMP (see Chomsky 1982: 52ff.). Thus I adopt the representation in (49) here.[16]

Given the representation (49) for Sinhala structure, the facts of Sinhala focusing that I outlined above are easily accommodated. Focus within a single S-bar proceeds by movement of the focused element to the focus position in β structure, as in (50).

(50)

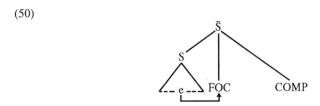

The trace left is a variable (at LF) properly bound by a c-commanding Ā antecedent. Forms such as *də* 'question', *yi* 'emphatic', and others listed earlier with focus-marking properties are base generated in FOC.[17] The condition on the occurrence of the -E verbal affix is simply that the FOC position of its own sentence is occupied (and external to it). Unbounded focusing can proceed by COMP-to-COMP movement, with the focused element ending up in FOC of the higher S.[18] Two routes are possible. The moved form can move directly to its own COMP and then onward, as in (51), or it could move first to the FOC position of its own S, as in (52), and thence to COMP and onward.

(51)

(52)

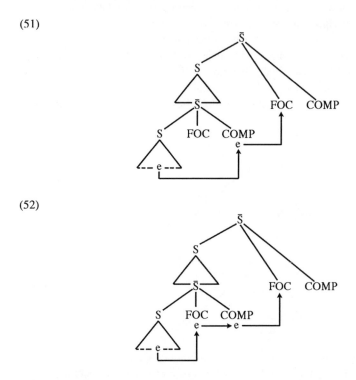

The first path, in (51), accounts for those sentences in which the focused element, which originates in a lower clause, is in a focus relation to a higher verb and not its own. The second path in (52) accounts for the multiple focus cases in which it bears a focus relation to its own and a higher verb. The -E affix appears on the proper verbs in each case if we extend the condition on its appearance to include trace as well as phonetically realized forms in FOC. For simplicity, I have restricted the trees to two-S depth, but deeper unbounded focusing is possible as stated earlier, and appears to require no further provisions.

Focus extraction from relative clauses is blocked by subjacency, thus accounting for the CNPC effects, since movement to any FOC position passes at least two bounding nodes, NP and another that I take to be S-bar for reasons that go beyond this chapter.[19]

There is, however, another possible structure that has not been accounted for so far and should be dealt with for completeness. Recall that certain complementizers, such as *kiyəla* 'quotative' and *nan* 'if', followed clauses with root characteristics, allowing focusing to occur within them. The difference between these and other complementizers is largely accounted for by the fact that they are not themselves verbal affixes, unlike the other ones, and they do not require specific verbal affixes, which block focusing, since they cannot cooccur with the focus (-E) affix. Internal focusing in *kiyəla* and *nan* clauses is illustrated in (53) and (54):

(53) *miniha giyee   koləṁbəṭə   kiyəla mamə dannəwa.*
     man   go-PAST-E Colombo-DAT COMP I   know
     'I know that it was to Colombo that he went.'

(54) *oyaa enne   koləṁbəṭə   nan maṭə kiyannə.*
     you come-PRES-E Colombo-DAT I-DAT   tell-INF
     'If it's to Colombo that you come, tell me.'

These complementizers do, however, differ from each other: *kiyəla* does not require the focus of its clause to immediately precede it, and it also allows focus-marking forms to occur, as in (55):

(55) *giyee   koləṁbəṭə   də kiyəla mamə danne   næœ.*
     go-PAST-E Colombo-DAT Q COMP I   know-E not
     'I don't know if it was to Colombo that (someone) went.'

However, *nan* is itself a focus-marking form and thus requires that the focus of its clause immediately precede it. This difference may be accounted for if we assume that *kiyəla* is inserted directly into COMP, thus allowing FOC to be filled by movement while *nan* is inserted into FOC, thus occupying that position, as do other focus-marking forms, when movement of another constituent there takes place. One detail that remains to be worked out is that *kiyəla* does not block movement of other constituents through COMP, but the answer there would apparently be the same as for English *that*.

Conclusion

Essentially, it has been argued here that even in nonconfigurational languages, it is necessary to refer to configurational structures to adequately account for such phenomena as Sinhala focusing, and that regarding S and D structures as α and β pairings makes the necessary structures available, once we recognize the essentially configurational nature of β structure in all languages. This approach is generally convergent with recent work by others, such as Mohanan's (1983b) argument that some principles of the binding theory apply in LS ("lexical structure," essentially equivalent to β structure) and some work by Katagiri (1983) accounting for scope properties of Japanese "floated" quantifiers in terms of β structures. Sinhala focusing is particularly interesting, since it gives evidence for movement in β structure, and it cannot be reexpressed in terms of grammatical functions, as could some of the others and Chomsky's "assume a GF." It is essentially independent of both grammatical function and θ role, referring only to constituency, since a wide range of constituents are subject to focusing.

This approach also has interesting implications for the nature of the configurationality parameter (Chomsky 1982; Hale 1981) that can only be touched on here. It allows that parameter to be reduced to identity or lack of it in α, β structure matching at all syntactic levels of representation. A fully configurational language can thus be defined as one exhibiting such identity. As is well known, nonconfigurational languages commonly exhibit "preferred orders" (Hale 1978 et seq.; Chomsky 1981: 127) and exhibit various degrees of constituent order freedom. This could be regarded as a function of constraints, both language specific and category specific, permitted on the divergence of α and β structure matchings, in effect allowing for degrees of configurationality with differences in detail across languages. As one example, both Sinhala and Japanese allow order freedom to prenominal modifiers, including adjectives, determiners, and relative clauses. The freedom with which they can occur separated from their heads in Sinhala, however, does not appear to be replicated in Japanese. Similarly, the negative *nai* in Japanese appears restricted to the immediately postverbal position. Its closest Sinhala counterpart *næœ*, however, is not so restricted, though that is clearly its "unmarked" (i.e., structure) position, but it can occur in other positions throughout the sentence, including sentence-intial. The crucial constraint is that if it does appear postverbally, no other form may intervene (see DeAbrew 1980). Such differences are statable in a principled way in terms of α and β structure pairings,[20] allowing us to capture a range of language-specific and typological facts.

Most importantly, the proposal made here, together with work along similar lines mentioned earlier, has the theoretically desirable consequence of reducing the typological gap between configurational and nonconfigurational languages, allowing all of them to be more clearly subject to the set of basic principles that are the goal of linguistic theory.

Subjects, Case, and INFL in Sinhala

This paper was given at the conference on experiencer subjects held at the University of Wisconsin in 1988, and it appeared in the volume Experiencer Subjects in South Asian Languages, *edited by Manindra K. Verma and K. P. Mohanan (CSLI, Stanford 1990). It is in an essential way a quarter-century-later approach to the same general phenomena in Sinhala that were treated as requiring "quasi transformations" in* Colloquial Sinhalese Clause Structures, *and to a great extent it is an extension of the conclusion at least broached there that accounting for those phenomena required appeal to the lexicon. It is also an object lesson in the way the interaction of linguistic theory and specific language data changes in form while in some fundamental way it remains constant. It also illustrates in at least two ways the rapidity with which current linguistic theory develops and changes: first, through the differences between the treatment here and the earlier one and, second, even more by the extent to which some aspects of the theory reflected here have changed since 1988. For example, the suggestion here that the Specified Subject Constraint (SSC) could perhaps be invoked in accounting for which argument moves where would, if retained, undoubtedly be cast in terms of minimality of one sort or another. Similarly, much recent work has fractionated INFL, with accompanying differences in the way case is assigned.*

These developments could be accommodated fairly straightforwardly in this chapter, but also, as this introductory note is being written, minimalist and bare phrase-structure hypotheses have appeared, and if the data here were considered in those terms, the paper would have a quite different appearance. Nevertheless, however radical such changes might appear, they still represent at base a continuity with earlier generative theory, and they have to stand the same test of adequacy in accounting for phenomena such as that here, so that one should welcome the challenge.

It is also of specific interest that those latest theories are, as I understand them, increasingly lexically (and morphologically) driven. Thus they are in a real sense consonant with the general approach here, however different they might be in execution, and the same fundamental questions concerning the partial lack of congruity between morphology (such as the A, P, and C morphological elements here) and syntactic (and semantic) behavior remain to be dealt with. Thus, I feel that this chapter is still fundamentally correct in its general approach and worth including here, since it still serves as a principled description of the Sinhala phenomena and may contribute to the discussion of such phenomena in newer theoretical terms.

Sinhala subjects appear in several cases, in both intransitive (I) and transitive (T) sentences as illustrated in (1):

(1)   a. (I) *miniha   duwənəwa.*
           man-NOM run-PRES
           'The man runs.'

        (T) *siri adə apətə ballekwə dunna.*
            Siri-NOM today us-DAT dog-INDEF-ACC give-PAST
            'Siri gave us a dog today.'

      b. (I) *minihaṭə   diwenəwa.*
           man-DAT run-INVOL-PRES
           'The man runs (involuntarily).'

        (T) *maṭə dæ̃ aliyawə   peenəwa.*
            I-DAT now elephant-ACC see-PRES
            'I see the elephant now.'

      c. (I) *minihawə gaṅgəṭə   wæṭeewi.*
           man-ACC river-DAT fall-OPT
           'The man might fall into the river.'

      d. (I) *ehee poliisiyeŋ   innəwa.*
           there police-INSTR be(Animate)
           'There are police there.'

        (T) *aanḍuweŋ   eekətə   aadaarə   denəwa.*
            government-INSTR that-DAT support-PL give-PRES
            'The government gives support for that.'

Note that nominative, dative, and instrumental subjects occur with intransitive (I) as well as transitive (T) predicates, as shown in (1a) and (1b). However, accusative subjects occur only with intransitive predicates, as in (1c), and dative subject verbs may take their objects in the accusative, as shown in the transitive sentence in (1b). These latter features differentiate Sinhala from so-called QUIRKY CASE languages such as Icelandic and such related North Indian Indo-Aryan languages as Hindi and Marathi (Andrews 1982; Cowper 1988; Gair and Wali 1987, 1988, and references therein), although there are also obvious similarities. The subject properties of these external NPs have been dealt with to some extent elsewhere (Gair 1971, 1976a; Inman 1988, 1993). In this paper I will be concerned with their case assignment aspects, particularly as they relate to the content of INFL on the one hand and the lexicon on the other. In doing this, I will refer, where necessary, to OBLIQUE SUBJECTS, using this term in the sense common in Indic linguistics to mean "cases other than nominative (or direct) case."

The instrumental case–marked subjects as in (1d) are limited to instances where the NP designates a collectivity or institution, and they are always singular in form.[1] From the transitive example in (1d), one might assume that this follows from their being a source together with the fact that instrumental case in Sinhala functions as an ablative–instrumental. However, there are sentences for which this would be hard to sustain, as in the intransitive example in (1d) or in (2):

(2) poolisiyeŋ   gunəpaaləṭə   hariyəṭa   gæhuwa.
     police-INSTR Gunapala-DAT really   hit-PAST
     'The police really beat Gunapala.'

Given the restriction to subjects with specific semantic properties, one would expect such sentences to have counterparts with other cases, as indeed they have, with subjects in the nominative, as in (3a), (3b), and (3c). Compare these examples with (1d) and (2):

(3)   a. *ee iskoole*   *apee lamay*   *innəwa.*
        that school-LOC our   children   be-PRES
        'Our children are in that school.'

      b. *loku mahattəya*   *eekəṭə*   *aadaarə denəwa.*
        big   gentleman-NOM that-DAT   support   give-PRES
        'The boss gives support for that.'

      c. *siriseenə*   *gunəpaaləṭə*   *hariyəṭa gæhuwa.*
        Sirisena-NOM Gunapala-DAT really   hit-PAST
        'Sirisena really beat Gunapala.'

Thus, instrumental case subjects clearly represent alternants of nominative case subjects that may surface under specific semantic conditions.[2] For the purposes of this chapter, they may thus be subsumed under nominative, and I will not deal further with them here, though they obviously raise interesting questions.

The accusative case also requires some specific attention as background for what follows. The accusative affix *-wə,* not surprisingly, appears on direct objects as well as on subjects, as in (1a) and (1b) above. In all positions, it is restricted to animate nouns or animate pronouns,[3] and the extent to which it is employed differs with dialect. There are some dialects that employ it rarely if at all,[4] and others use it with pronouns but rarely if at all with full nouns. This chapter represents the "*wə*-full" dialect, since the relative case assignment is more visible there. The distinctions between the types of sentences hold, however, in the absence of *-wə,* though they have to be inferred from behavioral rather than coding properties.

We must also note here that Sinhala is DIGLOSSIC, with sharply distinct written and spoken varieties. In SPOKEN SINHALA, which includes the varieties used for virtually all situations in which the medium is primarily oral, agreement of any type is lacking, both of verbs and within NPs. This is not true of the written variety, referred to as LITERARY SINHALA. That variety has strong verbal agreement, and in that respect and in a number of associated features, it is typologically quite distinct from the spoken language.[5] It has been argued elsewhere (Gair and Wali 1988; also see chapter 18) that this relates to differences in the content of INFL, particularly relating to the AGR element. This point will become important later in this chapter, which deals only with COLLOQUIAL SPOKEN SINHALA. This term subsumes the varieties of the language most commonly used for virtually all daily conversation. The other main variety of Spoken Sinhala, FORMAL SPOKEN SINHALA includes the subvarieties used in formal situations, such as lectures, public speeches, sermons, etc. In common with Colloquial Sinhala, it lacks agreement, but it differs from it lexically and in some grammatical features (Gair 1968; also see chapter 16 on diglossia and INFL, this volume).

As further background, we require a brief account of some aspects of Sinhala verb morphology. Though Colloquial Sinhala lacks verb agreement, there are a number of finite and nonfinite affixes (see De Silva 1960; Gair 1967). These are added to verb stems, which may in turn be morphologically complex. On the basis of their internal constituency, verb stems fall into three major classes, which are associated with conjugation types. These have been designated as A, P, and C verbs, respectively. A VERBS (the designation came originally from "active") are generally morphologically simple, but in any case they lack the stem-formative morphemes that define the other two classes. Examples are cited in a finite form ending in *-nəwa*, often referred to in the literature as the BASIC or SIMPLE FORM. These include: *yanəwa* 'go', *kərənəwa* 'do', and *hadənawa* 'make'. C VERBS (for "causative") include a causative morpheme, of which the usual allomorph is -(ə)wə-, such as *yawənəwa* 'send', *kərəwənəwa* 'cause to do', and *hadəwənəwa* 'cause to make, get made'. Causatives of intransitive roots are transitive, those from transitives are causatives, as is common in modern Indo-Aryan languages. We will not deal further with causatives here, except to note that what we say of transitives will generally extend to them.[6] "Of special interest here are the P VERBS. (The P designation was originally given arbitrarily in Gair 1963 because they had been called "passive" in some earlier literature. Though they are not passive in any true sense, as will become apparent shortly, it is simplest to keep the designation.) There is a close association between P verbs and oblique subjects in that such subjects occur overwhelmingly (though not exclusively) with P verbs, whereas nominative subjects are similarly associated with A or C verbs. Here it is useful as a starting point to view P verbs as being involved in the set of processes or intersentential relations, including especially those illustrated in (4) through (6), in which the (a) members have A verbs and the (b) members have P verbs:

(4)   DETRANSITIVIZATION:
    a. *laməya*   *wælikandak*   *hæduwa.*
       child-NOM sand-hill-INDEF make-PAST
       'The child makes a sandpile.'

    b. *(hulaŋgeŋ)*   *wælikandak*   *hæduna.*
       (wind-INSTR) sand-hill-INDEF make–P-PAST
       'A sandpile formed (because of the wind).'

(5)   INVOLITIVIZATION OF INTRANSITIVE (yielding a dative or accusative subject):
    a. *mamə*   *naṭənəwa.*
       I-NOM dance-PRES
       'I dance.'

    b1. *maṭa*   *næṭuna.*
       I-DAT dance-P-PAST
       'I danced (by impulse).'

b2. *maawə nǽṭuna.*
    I-ACC dance-P-PAST
    'I danced (for some external reason).'

(6)   INVOLITIVIZATION OF TRANSITIVE (yielding a dative subject):
    a. *mamə ee wacane kiwwa.*
       I-NOM that word   say-PAST
       'I said that word.'

    b. *maṭə ee wacəne kiyəwuna.*
       I-DAT that word   say-P-PAST
       'I blurted that word out.'

However, by no means all instances of P verbs, even where they occur in one of the (b) type sentences in (4 through 6), are linked to corresponding active sentences or even active (A) verbs. For example, the PERCEPTION VERBS *teerenəwa* 'understand' and *peenəwa* 'see, be visible' do not have such counterparts (at least synchronically),[7] but they do take dative subjects as in (7). Note once more that the object may be in the accusative, a point to which we will return later:

(7)   *maṭə   horaawə   penuna.*
    I-DAT thief-ACC see-P-PAST
    'I saw the thief.'

Similarly, there are intransitive P verbs that have no A counterparts, such as *wǽṭenəwa* 'fall' and *hǽrenəwa* 'turn'. These may appear with nonnominative subjects, as illustrated in (8a) and (8b). There is some variability across speakers, but in general, *wǽṭenəwa* takes an accusative subject; *hǽrenəwa* may occur with dative or accusative, as in (8a):[8]

(8)   a. *minihawə tamaŋge pokune   wǽtuna.*
       man-ACC self-GEN pond-GEN(LOC) fall-P-PAST
       'The fellow fell in his own pond.'

    b. *(saddəyak   ǽhila)*   maawə/maṭə   hǽruna.
       (sound-INDEF hear-ABS) I-ACC/I-DAT turn-P-PAST
       '(Hearing a sound) I turned (involuntarily).'

Interestingly, some of these P-ONLY VERBS may also appear without morphological change with agentive, or at least volitive, subjects in the nominative, as in (9):

(9)   *mamə arə handiyəṭə   gihiŋ   waməṭə   hǽrennaŋ.*
    I-NOM that corner-DAT having-gone right-DAT turn-VOL-OPT
    'I will go to that corner and turn right.'

No alternation with an accusative subject is possible in (9) in the appropriate, volitive sense. (The VOLITIVE-OPTATIVE verbal affix shown, which is largely limited to (first-person) volitive actors in the nominative, could also not appear with an oblique subject here—see below).

Clearly, all of these P-only verbs[9] have the P morpheme entered along with the root in the lexicon. It is equally clear, however, that the processes described in (4 through 6) are also lexical, since they involve changes in the number or nature of θ-roles. If they were syntactic, they would violate the theta criterion and projection principle, which are central to the general theoretical framework within which we are working here (Chomsky 1981 and much subsequent work).

A word needs to be said at this point concerning the case of objects. As noted earlier, direct objects, if animate, are marked for accusative case, and that case is limited to either that position or the subject of single-argument verbs. With inanimate objects, one cannot tell whether they are nominative or accusative, but it is reasonable to assume that inanimate objects are also in the accusative, despite the lack of specific marking.

Not surprisingly, there are indirect objects in the dative, which precede the direct object in the unmarked order, as in the transitive sentence in (1a). However, Sinhala also has a number of verbs, such as *gæhenawa* 'hit', that require dative direct objects, as illustrated in (2) and (3c). Clearly, this is a lexically specified feature of such verbs.

The occurrence of accusative marking on both objects and intransitive subjects has led Gunasinghe (1978, 1985) to claim that Colloquial Sinhala is fundamentally an ERGATIVE language. It is true that one could isolate an ergative subsystem with some transitive–intransitive verb pairs, but this ignores the existence of both active intransitive sentences with nominative subjects, as in (1a), (5a), and (9), and involitive ones with dative subjects, as in (1b) and (5b1). One could equally well isolate an ACTIVE subsystem (Mallinson and Blake 1981: 52, following Klimov) for intransitive verbs, with case dependent on the agent or patient status of the subject. However, the ergative analysis does embody an important insight into the structure of Sinhala that should be captured. I will claim that it falls out of a general pattern that, hopefully, will emerge in the present analysis.

An important—in fact crucial—point to note in this respect is that such lexical processes in Sinhala as those in (4) through (6) appear to affect only the subject, or at least the outermost, argument in unmarked sentence order. Other arguments within VP are unaffected with regard to case or θ-role. In an intuitive sense, the VP is inviolate, and this holds true whatever the case of the object(s). It holds for all of the appropriate pairs in (4) through (6), and it shows up especially clearly in sentence pairs such as (10) and (11), which have different subject cases in their (a) and (b) members but an animate object marked accusative in (10) and dative in (11) throughout:

(10) a. *mamə   aswəyawə   elewwa.*
    I-NOM horse-ACC chase-PAST
    'I chased the horse.'

   b. *matə   aswəyawə   elewunaa.*
    I-DAT horse-ACC chase-P-PAST
    'I involuntarily (on impulse) chased the horse.'

(11) a. *mamə laməyaṭə   bænna.*
      I   child-DAT scold-PAST
      'I scolded the child.'

    b. *maṭə   laməyaṭə   bænuna.*
      I-DAT child-DAT scold-P-PAST
      'I (involuntarily /on impulse) scolded the child.'

It follows that none of the processes shown in (4) through (6) are like passive in English or similar languages since they involve no difference in object case assignment. Colloquial Sinhala appears, in fact, to lack a true passive, periphrastic or otherwise, in contradistinction to Literary Sinhala, which has one, a point that has been argued in several places in the literature (see Gair and Wali 1988; Gunasinghe 1978, 1985, and chapter 4, note 23). There are, however, two constructions in addition to the sentence types illustrated in (4) through (11) that bear a superficial resemblance to passives as found in other languages. The first of these generally involves a P verb, and it allows an argument corresponding to the agent of an active transitive sentence to appear in a postpositional phrase with the postposition *atiŋ*. A pair of this type is illustrated in (12). The sense is that the action was accidental, without volitive participation of the actant in the *atiŋ* phrase:

(12) a. *laməya   wiiduruwə binda.*
      child-NOM glass   break-PAST
      'The child broke the glass (on purpose).'

    b. *laməya atiŋ wiiduruwə biňduna.*
      child   atiŋ glass   break-P-PAST
      'The child broke the glass (by accident).'

The second of the passive-like constructions has completely escaped notice in the literature, as far as I am aware, and it in fact came to my attention only recently, thanks to W. S. Karunatillake and Lelwala Sumangala, in whose dialects, at any rate, it is clearly productive. This construction, illustrated in (13), resembles the *atiŋ* one, but the relevant argument is in the instrumental case. The sense is commonly capabilitative or habitual, as in (13a), or, in the negative, disinclination or refusal, as in (13b):

(13) a. *ammageŋ   sinhala kææmə hoňdəṭə hædenəwa*
      mother-INSTR Sinhala food   well   make-P-PRES
      'Mother (always) makes Sinhala food well.'

    b. *mageŋ   ewwage wædə kerenne   næœ.*
      I-INSTR that-kind work do-P-PRES not
      'I don't do that kind of work.'

These constructions present a number of still not fully resolved problems of analysis that require separate treatment. For example, the degree to which the *atiŋ* and instrumental constituents show subject properties is not clear, nor is it easy to determine due to a number of factors such as the general paucity of subject-oriented structures in Sinhala and the difficulty of combining volitive and involitive sentences.[10] Furthermore, the relation to active sentences is not straightforward, since there are sentences of the types under consideration with verbs that lack straightforward A-verb equivalents, and there is a degree of idiomaticity as well.[11] Earlier, I called the *atiŋ* sentences "passives" (1970) simply as a terminological convenience, which evoked some misunderstanding and discussion, though I clearly indicated their involitive character (see, for example, Gunasinghe 1985). In the present context, it is sufficient to note that neither type appears to be a true passive and that both types exhibit features that invite treatment along with the oblique argument sentence types illustrated in (4) through (11), including, most obviously, the common association with P verbal morphology. The inviolability of the verb phrase holds in these as well, and there is no case changing or other evidence for promotion of the object. They do require underlyingly transitive verbs (or at least a second argument where there is no direct A-verb counterpart), but they are also theta-sensitive, in Williams and Travis's (1982) sense. In fact, they may participate in interesting contrasts in volitionality and/ or control (used here in the semantic sense of potential control of action) with the transitive dative subject types in (1b), (7), (10b), and (11b) as illustrated by the three-way set in (14), which includes (6b) repeated as (14a). The semantic differences are hard to capture, but they are real, and they are roughly indicated in the translations:[12]

(14) a. *maṭə   ee   wacəne kiyəwuna.*
         I-DAT that word   say-P-PAST
         'I blurted that word out (on impulse).'

     b. *maŋ atiŋ ee   wacəne kiyəwuna.*
         I   atiŋ that word   say-P-PAST
         'I accidentally said that word (unthinkingly).'

     c. *mageŋ   ewwage wacəne kiyəwenne   næœ.*
         I-INSTR that   word   say-P-PRES not
         'I never say that kind of word.'

As we might expect, it is difficult to find many full three-way sets such as those in (14), given theta-sensitivity and the special senses involved. For example, the A verb *dannəwa* is transitive and has a P counterpart *dænenəwa*, but the latter allows only a dative oblique argument, has the special sense 'experience, feel (a sensation)', and does not appear with *atiŋ* or instrumental arguments. This limitation is at least in part a result of the verb root lacking the volitivity or potential control component necessary to license either of the latter two.

Under current assumptions, it is amply clear that the two constructions under discussion are not passives but form a set with the others described earlier, and like them, they involve θ-role and case marking differences on the EXTERNAL ARGUMENT in the sense of Williams (1980, 1981) and Williams and Travis (1982), leaving the object case unaffected. It is equally clear that theta-sensitivity and the lack of straightforward morphosyntactic relationships[13] make a straightforward syntactic derivation, such as that generally assumed for the passive in current theory, difficult here as well, and they incline one toward assuming a lexical derivation.

From the above description, it is clear that what we need to provide is explanations for the following:

1. Sinhala allows subjects in any one of several cases.
2. Subject case is linked, though not in a strict one-to-one fashion, with verb morphology.
3. There are both intransitive and transitive oblique-subject sentences.
4. Accusative-subject sentences are always intransitive, but those with nominative or dative subjects can be either transitive or intransitive.
5. The processes that produce relations between sentences such as those in (4) through (6) appear to affect only subjects, or external arguments.

It is also clear from the examples so far that Sinhala case marking bears an intimate connection with θ-roles as lexically specified, although I have not attempted to specify the content of those roles here. This, together with the variety of cases appearing in argument positions and the resistance of Sinhala case to change under syntactic processes, might lead us to conclude that case is also fully specified in the lexicon. We can call this view the STRONG LEXICAL CASE-ASSIGNMENT HYPOTHESIS. In the remainder of this paper, I will attempt to show how such a hypothesis for Sinhala might be executed.

I will assume, in approaching these questions, that the basic tree structure for Sinhala is, as for other languages, of the kind proposed in Chomsky 1986, as in (15):

(15)

However, I will also propose that V′ is iterable and that all arguments of the sentence are initially generated in D structure under VP and assigned case there. This clearly owes much to Fukui (1986, 1987) and Fukui and Speas (1986) and is the analysis adopted by Cowper (1988) to account for quirky case in Icelandic. However, I will not assume, as does Fukui for the typologically very similar language Japanese, that Sinhala lacks functional categories projecting phrases such as IP (or if it has an INFL, it is a "weak" one that does not project a specifier). On the contrary, it will be part of the analysis here that the externalization of arguments resulting in surface subjects is a result of the movement of the appropriate argument to SPEC of INFL but that the content of INFL differs from that of languages like English on the one hand and North Indian languages like Hindi and Marathi on the other.

There are numerous reasons for assuming that Sinhala has an INFL node, and though we cannot deal with these reasons in detail here, some may be sketched out. One very general and fundamental one is the desire to make as few perturbations to X-bar Theory as we can, so that languages share as many common features relating to UG as possible rather than falling into major radically different types on the basis of aspects of their phrase structure that are even more basic than such features as directionality of head, government, or theta assignment. As in Japanese, tense and verb affixes are postverbal and verb adjacent, so that INFL serves as a holder for them. This is the same reason that Fukui (1986) gives for assuming an INFL node in Japanese, even if it did not project a specifier.

In Sinhala, though, there are good reasons for assuming that INFL is SPEC-projecting. One is that we have to allow for the occurrence of adverbial forms and, even more importantly, participial forms requiring subject control in a position between subject and VP in unmarked order. SPEC INFL is the obvious landing site for externalization of NPs to the left of those forms. Also, although I have said that Sinhala lacks agreement, there are in fact some agreement-like relations between subjects and elements that would be naturally thought of as appearing in INFL. These will be described later, but they are obviously best accounted for as instances of some kind of coindexing between SPEC INFL and INFL. We should note here also that Sinhala, unlike Japanese, does not allow multiple subjects, which have been advanced as partial evidence for the absence of SPEC INFL in Japanese (Fukui 1986).

I will also make use of the now familiar notion that verbs are associated in the lexicon with a theta-grid and that particular cases may be specified as being associated with particular elements in that grid (Ostler 1979; Stowell 1981; Fukui 1986; Marantz 1984; Chomsky 1986, among others). This is particularly compelling in Sinhala, since, as we have noted, it is a "strong case marking" language, in which case marking of arguments is intimately linked to θ-roles. Specifying the content of those roles presents problems, as is often the case, but assuming that dative subjects are experiencers and that accusative subjects are themes (or patients), the entries for verbs such as *naṭənəwa* 'dance', *hadənəwa* 'make', *baninəwa* 'scold', and their P-verb counterparts, along with *wæṭenəwa* 'fall' and *teerenəwa* 'understand', would, as a first approximation, include the partial entries in table 6–1. I have indicated linking by "/").

Clearly, the links between the corresponding A and P verbs would be shown either by incorporating lexical rules or by consolidating entries. There are also some redundancies regarding case assignment that I will address shortly, but the general pattern is clear. All arguments are assigned inherent case by the verb within VP in D-structure, and a strong form of the uniformity condition (Chomsky 1986) obtains. Arguments would then be associated with case–theta linkages in a "bottom up" fashion proceeding from V (Fukui 1986). As examples, the VP subtrees of the D-structure trees for (1), (6), and (11), would thus be as in (16) (adverbs have been eliminated for simplicity).

(16)

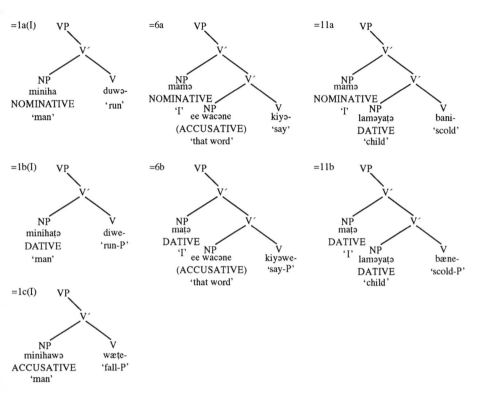

One of the arguments under VP must then externalize, moving to subject (SPEC IP) position. We will return later to the problem of selecting the proper NP and motivating the movement. In what follows, I will also use the terms "subject" and "external argument" or the related "externalize" as referentially interchangeable, depending on which aspect of them is at issue; in other words, I will use "subject" where the position itself is central and "external argument" where externality to VP

Table 6–1   Linking of Arguments and θ-Roles

Verb	Role	Gloss
naṭə-	[AG/NOM--]	'dance'
næṭə-	(P) [EXP/DAT--]	'dance (involuntarily)'
hadə-	[AG/NOM TH/ACC--]	'make'
hæde-	(P) [TH/ACC--]	'be made'
bani-	[AG/NOM TH/DAT--]	'scold'
bæne-	(P) [EXP/DAT TH/DAT--]	'scold (involuntarily)'
wæṭe-	(P) [TH/ACC--]	'fall'
teere-	(P) [EXP-DAT TH/ACC--]	'understand'

or movement to that status is involved. This differs from the usage in Williams (1981) and particularly Williams and Travis (1982), in which the first is a lexical and the second is a syntactic process (though not under that name). Under the view I am presenting here, however, there is no need to differentiate these in Sinhala, since they will be linked in a congruent fashion, and this usage will allow me to focus on the movement itself or on the landing site as appropriate.

Under the strong lexical case assignment hypothesis, it will be necessary to specify the order of arguments within the theta grid, since that sequence maps directly onto their order within VP in D-structure. The order within the theta/case grid is thus significant. Given the nonarbitrary nature of the link between θ-role and case marking, it is, of course a possibility that some way could be found to derive case marking from θ-role given a rich enough theory of θ-role content (i.e. theta-case mappings like the "realization rules" in Williams 1981),[14] and that, in turn, the order could be derived through some sort of theta hierarchy (as in Belletti and Rizzi 1988 and the earlier works cited therein). It does, in fact, appear to be the case that for Sinhala, the hierarchy agent–experiencer–theme–others does give the correct order for verbal sentences, but the case is not so clear for nonverbal sentences, which will be touched on below.

Thus for the present, I will simply assume that order does not follow from (surface) case marking in any obvious and automatic way, so that order must be specified along with both case and θ-role (see Fukui 1986 for a similarly unexecuted suggestion in regard to Japanese). Under this proposal, the order of arguments in lexical entries will, in fact, give us the unmarked surface order of Sinhala sentences, since the mapping of arguments onto VP in D-structure will in turn map, in a straightforward way by move α into S-structure. In fact, surface constituent order in Sinhala is very free, and it was, in fact, claimed at one time to be a "nonconfigurational" or X* language (Gair 1983b; chapter 5 in this volume). How we should account for this variability is a problem, but whether we do so by the matching of dual representations (as in Gair 1983b) or by scrambling, there must be some representation embodying the order here to account for case-assignment and structure-dependent operations such as focus movement (as in Gair 1983b). There are also a number of other arguments involving the binding theory that can be adduced for clause-internal configurational structure in Sinhala, as set out in Sumangala 1988.

We have now dealt with the first three problems of the five posed earlier. Let us now turn to the fourth; that is, why accusative-subject sentences are always intransitive, while those with nominative or dative subjects can be either transitive or intransitive. Under the strong lexical case assignment hypothesis, there is no problem about the latter two; it is the restriction on accusative that requires explanation. Recall that accusative subjects occur only when they are the single argument of the verb and that accusative case appears otherwise only on the direct object. What these positions have in common is that they are both adjacent to V in D-structure. This suggests that accusative is assigned only under conditions of such adjacency, externalizing only when it is the single, and hence outermost, argument. It thus surfaces only on arguments that are D-structure objects. Under the strong lexical case assignment hypothesis, however, it is still an inherent case. This explains why there are no accusative subjects of transitive Ss. In transitive sentences with accusative objects, there will always be an argument in some other case to the left of them, and that is the one that will externalize. This also explains the "ergative" properties that have been claimed for Sinhala.

Although case and order have to be specified, we can nevertheless attempt some steps toward underspecification. We could, for example, given the accusative adjacency we have observed, consider leaving that case unspecified in the theta grid, allowing it to be assigned under the appropriate conditions, namely, adjacency to V. This notion, however, immediately runs into problems. Under the assumptions made so far, this would lead to all intransitive subjects (except those already specified for dative) being accusative,[15] unless nominative intransitive subjects were specified for case. Conversely, if we were to leave nominative unmarked, we would have to specify accusative, at least in intransitive occurrence.

We might try to solve our problem by deriving nominative case marking from θ-role, and indeed it is the case that in Sinhala, (volitive) agents are not only unmarkedly subjects, as in other languages,[16] but are also nominative. Unfortunately, nominative case in all positions cannot be taken care of at this agent–nominative linkage. Subjects case marked for dative and accusative subjects are not "full agents" but "experiencers" (in general terms) and "patients/themes," respectively. However, there are apparent experiencers (and themes) that are in the nominative so that the agent–nominative linkage breaks down in the opposite direction. Thus, verbs like *dannəwa* 'know' and *wiňdinəwa* 'suffer' take nominative subjects, as in (17). (In fact, *dannəwa* does appear with the subject in the dative in some dialects, and it would be hard to argue that that represents a cognitive difference of some sort):[17]

(17) a. *miniha   mee   dawaswələ hariyətə duk   wiňdinəwa.*
       man-NOM these days   really   sorrow suffer-PRES
       'The fellow is really suffering these days.'

   b. *mamə   ee   mahattəyawə dannəwa.*
      I-NOM that man-ACC   know-PRES
      'I know that gentleman.'

Thus the agentive–nominative linkage is only a one-way one, and it accounts for only part of the data. We are still faced with the prospect that one or the other of nominative and accusative must be specified in the intransitive arrays under discussion here. If we turn again to markedness here, it is clear that the default, and hence the unmarked, case in Colloquial Sinhala is clearly the nominative.[18] This is clearly correct for intransitive sentences not only on intuitive grounds but also on the basis of frequency and, as we have seen, relative looseness of θ-role linkage. Thus it is necessary to specify accusative in the theta grids of the relevant intransitive verbs. Note however, that this is also the case for dative subjects as well as in the intransitive example in (1b): Both are lexically marked cases in that environment, intuitively a quite satisfactory result.

We can make a further appeal to markedness here, along with transitivity, and take the further step of leaving accusative unspecified in transitive sentences, saying that the unmarked case for an argument adjacent to V is accusative if there is another argument to the left. Thus, only dative needs to be specified for the second argument in the array $<\theta_1 \; \theta_2 \; V>$. This will generalize as well to dative-subject transitive sentences.[19]

The adjacency requirement is thus reduced to a simple D-structure restriction: Accusative case can only be assigned to an argument adjacent to V, but it is not the only case that can be so assigned. This might lead us to question the strong lexical case assignment hypothesis and wonder whether an appeal to structural case would lead to a more satisfactory solution. Though one might argue for that analysis on other grounds, it would not go far by itself toward simplifying the specific problem here. Even under the unaccusative (or "ergative") hypothesis (Perlmutter 1978; Burzio 1986) entailed by such an approach, accusative case marking under adjacency would still apply to two kinds of case—structural in transitive sentences, but "missing structural" in intransitive ones—and the morphological case marking would remain in both. It is hard to see any simplification there.

In commenting on the presented version of this paper, Margaret Speas raised a further question, which could well be added as a sixth to the five given earlier: Why does there appear to be a complementary restriction to the one on accusatives such that there appear to be no nominative objects? In point of fact, when we include sentences with nonverbal predicators, there are such objects, as we shall see subsequently. For verbal sentences, however, it does appear to hold, providing we assume as we did earlier that inanimate objects are also in the accusative despite the lack of accusative morphology on inanimate nouns. The answer here, if we maintain the strong lexical case assignment hypothesis, is that this restriction is a reflection of the unmarked status of nominative together with the widespread association of nominative not only with agentivity but also with external argument status. In this case, it is the "destined" external argument, the leftmost argument in the theta grid.[20]

Under the assumptions we have made so far, it is clear that in every sentence, some argument originating in VP must move to subject, SPEC IP.[21] Given the analysis here under which the S-structure subjects are in SPEC IP, this is simply a restatement of the Extended Projection Principle under standard GB assumptions (Chomsky 1981) together with a requirement that some argument must externalize. We must now turn to motivating the externalization of some argument from some position under a V'. We must also account for the range of subject cases and for the selection of the proper NP to be externalized. In much later work within GB theory that deals with passives, unaccusatives, and "quirky case," the motivation for movement to SPEC IP from within VP and the selection of the NP to be moved has been accounted for by interaction of Case theory and the case filter ($*_{NP}$[-case]) (Chomsky 1981; Burzio 1986; Cowper 1988; Belletti and Rizzi 1988; and many others). The general approach has been that the affected NP, lacking structural case as assigned by the verb, moves to SPEC INFL, where it can acquire structural case under government from INFL, usually from an AGReement element there.[22] In addressing the possibility of applying some form of this approach to Sinhala, something more needs to be said concerning the nature of INFL in the language.

Earlier, I stated that Sinhala has no agreement, and it has been claimed elsewhere on the basis of this and other features that it lacks AGR. However, there are two affixes that at least resemble agreeing forms.These have been called the "volitive and involitive optative" (Gair 1970) and are represented respectively by -*nnaŋ* and -*wi* (-*yi* in some dialects). They are attached directly to the stem as finite affixes (i.e., replacing tense). It is true that they do not represent AGR, since they do not impose nominative case, occurring instead with whatever subject case the verb otherwise assigns. They are illustrated in (18) and (19), which can be compared with the indicative sentences (5a) and (8a). Earlier examples were furnished in (8b) and (9):

(18) *mamə naṭannaŋ.*
    I   dance-VOL-OPT
    'I will dance (volitively).'

(19) *minihawə tamaŋge pokune   wæṭeewi.*
    man-ACC self-GEN pond-GEN(LOC) fall-VOL-OPT
    'The fellow might fall in his own pond.'

These affixes do, however, place restrictions on the θ-role of the external arguments with which they may occur. The volitive affix requires a (volitive) agent, while the involitive affix excludes it. There are also apparent restrictions as to person, since the former generally requires a first person subject and the latter occurs most often with a non–first person subject, but these restrictions are not absolute, and they can be attributed to pragmatic factors largely connected with the intersection of expressions of volitionality with person in Sinhala (see Gair 1967, 1971).[23] What we have here, then, is an agreement-like phenomenon involving θ-role. It is not true agreement, however, since the restriction is semantic or pragmatic in nature, and the affixes, in INFL, do not impose θ-roles. Rather, we have free movement of the eligible NP to SPEC INFL, as is the case with any other finite affix in INFL. If, however, there is a semantic mismatch between the θ-role of that NP and one of these affixes, the sentence is ill formed. This is still, however, most simply regarded as an instance of some kind of SPEC-head coindexing. This analysis nicely explains the fact that these affixes seem to show both agreement and nonagreement properties, which has been a problem in some previous analyses of Sinhala.

It was pointed out earlier that Sinhala has no passive or raising to subject operations, and there is also an absence of verbs of the "seem" type that fail to assign case within their complements. The nearest equivalent of "seems" in Sinhala—for example, *wagee*—takes a finite S as external argument and has no effect on its internal case marking. Compare (20a) and (20b) with (1a) and (1b):

(20) a. *miniha   duwənəwa wagee.*
       man-NOM run-PRES as-if
       'The man seems to be running.'

b. *minihaṭə   diwenəwa wagee.*
man-DAT run-INVOL-PRES
'It seems that the man is running involuntarily.'

Thus, *wagee* has a lexical entry similar to that given by Williams for English *seems* as in (21a) (Williams 1981: 85), but it is in fact more general as in (21b), since there is no restriction as to the kinds of internal θ-roles or their number. Even more important, the embedded S is finite and *wagee* does not trigger raising, so that externalization takes place within the embedded S, as in any other finite sentence:

(21) a. seems (Theme, Goal)

　　　b. (θ1 (. . . θn) *wagee.*

It has been argued elsewhere (Gair and Wali 1988; Gair 1992a, Chapter 18 in this volume) that these features follow from the content of INFL, and specifically from the lack of an AGR element (which in that work was contraposed to an anaphoric *agr* element, irrelevant here). Under the strong lexical approach taken here, it must be seen also as a function of the assignment of lexical case to all arguments of the verb and an associated lack of case-absorbing morphemes such as passive or forms that induce raising to subject, like "seems." What the "weak INFL" hypothesis does account for is the appearance of a range of cases in subject position that includes all of those that appear within VP. That is, INFL does project to SPEC IP, but the content of INFL, lacking agreement,[24] is not "strong" enough to impose nominative case. This contrasts on the one hand with languages like English and some familiar European ones, which assign structural nominative and impose morphological nominative on SPEC IP, and on the other hand with languages like Icelandic, Hindi, and Marathi, which assign structural case to SPEC IP but do not impose nominative morphological case. In such languages, surface subject NPs retain morphological case assigned in their D-structure positions (as in the analyses proposed by Gair and Wali 1988 and Cowper 1988, among others). However, languages of this second (i.e., Icelandic or Hindi) type appear to operate under a requirement that in transitive oblique subject sentences, nominative case, presumably under coindexing with some element in INFL, must be assigned somewhere, thus ending up on the object of nonnominative subject sentences.[25] This property has, of course, led to a great deal of discussion about the mechanism by which that assignment takes place (see the sources just cited along with Belletti and Rizzi 1988).The important point here is that no such requirement applies in Sinhala,[26] and this is consistent with the notion that INFL does not have a nominative case to discharge.[27]

We have seen much evidence that the verb does play a role in subject case assignment, but there is also some evidence that strongly indicates that INFL does not play a role in such assignment. This relates to the subject of nonfinite clauses.

In Sinhala, subordinate clauses with infinitives can, in several distributions, have overt, case-marked subjects. Here, I will mention only two clear cases: infinitival subjects of forms like *puluwaŋ* 'might',[28] and infinitival clauses subordinate to forms like *issella* 'before', as illustrated in (22):

(22) a. *mamə heṭə   yannə puluwani.*
      I   tomorrow go-INF might-PRED
      'I-NOM might go tomorrow.' ('It might happen that I go tomorrow.')

    b. *mamə ennə   issella miniha kaarekə vikka.*
       I-NOM come-INF before man   car   sell-PAST
       'The fellow sold the car before I came.'

In (22), the relevant nominals are nominative, and it is clear that they are indeed subjects of the embedded clauses. If the infinitive is an oblique subject verb, however, the subject of that verb will appear in the appropriate case, as shown in (23) for dative subjects:

(23) a. *lameaṭə   æhennə puluwani.*
      child-DAT hear-INF might-PRED
      'The child might hear.'

    b. *maṭə   teerennə   issella lækcərekə ivərə unaa.*
       I-DAT understand-INF before lecture   finish become-PAST
       'The lecture ended before I understood.'

Thus the subject case is clearly determined by the lexical character of the verb, and not by INFL, since it remains invariant throughout finite and nonfinite forms of the latter.

The failure of INFL, or more precisely some element within it, to assign nominative case does not necessarily rule out the possibility of some sort of purely structural, or "contentless," case.[29] One must then ask what function such a structural case would perform here, unless it accounts in part for the movement of caseless arguments to subject position so as to receive it, as structural nominative does in passives or unaccusatives in other languages. Although Sinhala lacks passives, the movement of NPs from VP to SPEC INFL does resemble unaccusative movement, abstracting away from the "uncase" aspect of the latter. Thus, given the possibility of the weak structural case that I have suggested, we can regard externalization as following from a requirement that INFL has such a feature that must be discharged under a "Saturation Principle" (Fukui 1986; Fukui and Speas 1986). What this amounts to, of course, is stating that INFL contains a +SUBJ feature. In the terms employed by Fukui and Speas this would be an instance of KASE, which includes, but is not limited to, case proper. If, then, Japanese has an INFL but fails to externalize arguments, as suggested by Fukui (1986), this simply means that it lacks this specific Kase feature.

We must now ask what motivates the selection of the correct argument for externalization, if all arguments have inherent case and there is no case absorption. The case filter cannot be invoked here, as it is in English passives, unaccusatives, and raising to subject. There is also a problem with ditransitives. The relevant subtree for the transitive sentence in example (1a) would be as in (24). All three NPs— *ballekwə, apaṭə,* and *siri*—would receive case, but only the highest, *siri,* in fact externalizes.

(24)

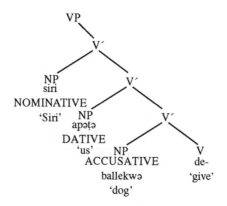

One solution, of course, would be to specify the external argument in the lexical entry of the verb, as in Williams 1981. However, this involves redundancy here, given the ordering of arguments in lexical entries that we have seen to be necessary, since it will always be the leftmost (outermost) argument that will move. We need at most, then, to specify that limitation, but it would be more satisfactory if we could derive it from independent principles. One possibility here is that we have an SSC effect[30] if that movement is to an A position and its trace is thus pronominal. The iterated Vs (with a lower limit of one) in trees such as those in Figure 6–1 can be taken to constitute a COMPLETE FUNCTIONAL COMPLEX (Chomsky 1986), so that the outermost ("uppermost" in D-structure) argument can be said to have subject properties, thus inducing the required SSC effect. While this approach is not without its problems,[31] it is promising, but it requires further investigation, particularly with regard to its interactions with other aspects of the binding theory.

Under Williams's (1981) proposals concerning predication and external arguments, there was an upper bound of one external argument, and it was specified by underlining in the lexical entry. However, there was no lower bound, so that it was possible for some predicators to have no θ-role so specified. Nevertheless, movement to subject position was possible, as in the case of passives and *seem*. This possibility has been exploited by others to account for different kinds of psych predicates, as in Belletti and Rizzi (1988), or for quirky case, as in Cowper (1988). For Sinhala, however, this is neither necessary nor possible under the analysis here. In Cowper's analysis, for example, arguments specified as external would begin in SPEC VP. In the event, these turn out to be the nominative subjects of ordinary—nonquirky —case sentences, while the nominative objects of oblique-subject sentences move into that position, thus gaining nominative case. As we have seen, obligatory nominative assignment does not apply, and there appears to be no reason for carrying the specification of external argument over into Sinhala, unless we find some properties, other than morphological nominative, of nominative subjects that would require it. The evidence so far is that active nominative subjects can be treated on a par with the others. Thus, depending on how we look at it, every sentential predication has either one external argument (in the syntax) or none (in lexical structure), and the mapping between the two is straightforward.

So far, we have dealt with the first four problems of the five posed earlier. We can now turn to the last one, namely, why do the processes that produce relations between sentences such as those in (4) through (6) appear to affect only subjects or external arguments? As stated earlier, it is clear that these processes must be lexical, not syntactic, since they affect θ-roles and may change the number of arguments. Thus the specific limitation here appears to be an instantiation of Williams's (1981: 90) general principle that a "morphological rule may affect only the external argument of its input." There is a slight difference, of course, in that no such argument is specified in the Sinhala entries, but the rule affects the outermost argument, which is designated by rule to externalize, so that the difference is trivial. Thus, the addition of the P morpheme affects the outermost argument, but note that the specific θ-role and case that results is not a function of P alone but must be assigned compositionally by Root+P,[32] since different cases and roles are possible.

Williams's rule just quoted had another half, however: "A morphological rule . . . can affect this external argument in only one of two ways: it can make one of the internal arguments into the external argument, or it can add a new external argument" (Williams 1981: 90). It is difficult to see how this part of the rule could hold for Sinhala detransitivization, as exemplified in (4a) and (4b). In terms of both morphological complexity and the phonological changes that accompany it, the P morpheme must be added, not subtracted, in relating the transitive–intransitive pairs. But its presence accompanies the absence of an argument in the relevant sentences. It is amply clear that in many such sentences, this argument is not present in any form, implicit or otherwise. While this cannot be argued fully here, an example like (25) should suffice to give a clear indication. There is clearly no implicit agent conceivable in (25b), and no purpose clause is possible, in contrast with (25a):[33]

(25) a. *(kaarekə harigassannə) baasunnæhee   plooṭarekə   ussənəwa.*
       (car   repair-INF)   mechanic-NOM float-(ACC) raise-PRES
       'The mechanic raises the (carburetor) float (to repair the car).'

      b. *(* kaarekə harigassannə) dæŋ plooṭarekə   issenəwa.*
         (* car   repair-INF)   now float-(ACC ?) rise (=raise-P)-PRES
         'The float is rising now (to repair the car).'

One could not easily argue that the P-morpheme expresses a missing (i.e., internalized) agent, for obvious semantic reasons. Furthermore, P has no such function in those processes in which it is involved where there is no change in the number of arguments, as in (5),(6), and (12).[34]

One further consequence of the proposal put forward here for Sinhala is that the language has not only no passives but also no true unaccusatives in the usual sense, since the accusative subject verbs are simply subcases of the general pattern. All argument cases are inherent, including the accusative, even though accusative case, unlike dative, is always assigned under D-structure adjacency. Accusative case subjects are thus precisely like dative ones, given the difference in θ-role and specific case linkage.

I have not mentioned nonverbal predicators, of which Sinhala has a plethora. These have been described elsewhere (see Gair 1970 and 1971; see particularly Gair and Paolillo 1988). Suffice it to say that what has been said here concerning verbal predicators can be extended in a relatively straightforward way. In the presented version of this chapter, I had stated that nonverbal predicators did not assign accusative case to subjects or objects, but this turns out to be factually incorrect. There are indeed single-argument adjectives, such as *winaasə* 'destroyed, ruined' that clearly allow accusative subjects, as in (26):

(26) *ehenaŋ maawə winaasay!*
      that-if I-ACC destroyed-PRED MARKER
      'In that case, I am ruined!'

As I stated in the presented version, there are also transitive (i.e., two-argument), nonverbal sentences (see Gair 1970; Gair and Paolillo 1988), and there the situation is more complex, or at least unclear. As stated there, they may have dative subjects and objects as in (27a) and (27b):

(27) a. *maţə kaarekə eləwannə hoňdə kenek   oonə.*
         I-DAT car   drive-INF good person-INDEF-NOM need/want
         'I want a good person to drive the car.'

      b. *mamə ee potəţə   hariyaţə kamətii.*
         I-NOM that book-DAT really   like-PRED MARKER
         'I really like that book.'

However, it is not true, as was claimed, that the objects of nonverbal predicators are never accusative but always nominative or dative. While there are speakers who resist accusative case marking on the nominative N″ in dative subject adjectival predicator sentences like (27a), for at least some speakers of "wə-full" dialects, such marking is possible, as in (28a) and this is particularly true when the N″ is a pronoun, as in (28b):[35]

(28) a. *maţə kaarekə eləwannə hoňdə kenekwə   oonə.*
         I-DAT car   drive-INF good person-INDEF-ACC need/want
         'I want a good person to drive the car.'

      b. *ammaţə   eyaawə   hoňday.*
         mother-DAT (s)he-ACC good-PRED MARKER
         'He is good for his mother.'

In fact, for such speakers an interesting contrast is possible in near-homonymous sentences. Example (29), with *eyaa* in the nominative, has a different reading from (28b), the difference roughly expressed by the difference in the English pronouns that render the dative:

(29) *ammaţə   eyaa hoňday.*
      mother-DAT (s)he good-PRED MARKER
      'He is good to his mother.'

In the reading of (29) the relevant N″ cannot be accusative marked. The explanation that suggests itself is that in (28b), case is assigned within AP (equivalent to VP in verbal sentences) by the adjectival head, whereas in (29) the dative NP is an adjunct, and the nominative NP occupies SPEC IP; that is to say, (28b) is fundamentally transitive, but (29) is intransitive. More work is needed to make this a firm conclusion, but these examples do seem to present evidence bearing on the distinction between dative subjects and dative adjuncts.

In any event, my earlier statement that nonverbal forms do not assign the accusative, which was explained as a consequence of the ability of only verbal (i.e., $-N+V$) heads to assign accusative case, together with the unmarked status of the nominative, requires amendment for at least some speakers so as to widen the class of accusative case assigners to $+V$, thus including adjectives. It apparently remains the case that nouns as predicators (i.e., $+N-V$) do not assign accusative to either subjects or objects.

It still appears to be the case, however, that there are no two argument nonverbal sentences with both arguments in the nominative or with one in the nominative and the other in the accusative. That is, there are no parallels to straight transitive verbal sentences. In two-argument nonverbal sentences, one of the arguments must be in the dative, a fact that remains to be explained. Interestingly enough, however, Sinhala has clearly nominal and nondeverbal predicators that assign an agentive θ-role. These have been treated elsewhere (Gair and Paolillo 1988), but one such is illustrated in (30):

(30) *(andǝree enǝkoṭǝ)*   *gowiyo*   *kataawǝ.*
(Andaree come-when) farmers-NOM talk(Noun)-NOM-DEF
'When Andaree came the farmers were talking intently.'

The general approach that I have taken here harmonizes with associated work on agreement phenomena presented elsewhere (Gair and Wali 1987, 1988; Gair 1992a and Chapter 18 of this volume) that appears to have promising typological implications. Differences in subject-case realization and other characteristics of subjects are associated with (possibly parameterized) differences in the content of INFL. One aspect of this situation is that languages can be seen as arraying themselves typologically along a continuum ranging from the English type through the quirky case (Icelandic and Hindi) type through the Sinhala and, assuming that Fukui is correct, on to the Japanese type, on the basis of the content of INFL, and specifically the presence or absence of $+/-$AGR, $+/-$ strong structural nominative, and $+/-$*SUBJ*. (These are not independent, but I will not pursue that point further here.)

Whether the strong lexical case assignment hypothesis should be maintained in the strong form in which I have presented it here is a question subject to further research involving not only theory-internal considerations but also a wider range of data. Reduced to the simplest terms, however, it does in fact work for the language, requiring only the stipulation that the theta grid be an ordered set together with some markedness specifications. It is also the case that ordering is required on other grounds, such as to deal with ditransitives, given the bottom-up lexical insertion, and there is moreover a not too remote possibility, touched on earlier, that it may be derivable, given a rich enough theta theory.

The second main hypothesis advanced here for Sinhala, "weak INFL," although linked to the first, is actually independent of it and could be maintained under a structural versus lexical case analysis. It does, however, connect up with other work in South Asian languages involving features such as agreement phenomena (Gair and Wali 1987, 1988, 1989; Gair in press), as well as the work by Fukui (1986) and Fukui and Speas (1986), and it receives further support therefrom.

In a real sense, this chapter represents an extension and emendation of an earlier paper (Gair 1976), which was also given at a conference on experiencer subjects at the University of Wisconsin, in which I set forth the notion of "primary NP constituent" (PNP). The basic notion there was that there is "a main NP constituent" that could vary in the number of (primarily behavioral) subject properties that it possessed and in the number of "underlying roles" (essentially θ-roles in later terminology) and cases that could be mapped onto it. The degree of "subject prominence" of a language was then a function of the degree to which both subject properties and roles were mapped onto the PNP. Subsequent developments in syntax theory outmoded that particular formulation and have shown it to be unclear in its specifics. However, this chapter retains that basic insight if we read "subject" for PNP , but it provides a principled account for that insight, in which the nature and particularly the restrictedness of the subject is a function of INFL, and its other characteristics are a function of case assignment and the structure of VP, interacting with general principles of grammar.

Sinhala Nonverbal Sentences and Argument Structure

WITH JOHN PAOLILLO

Sinhala, like other languages, has sentences with predicative phrases that are verb headed. As shown by the examples in (1), Sinhala is basically an SOV language:[1]

(1) a. *ee   mahattəya koləm̆bəṭə   yanəwa.*
     that gentleman to Colombo goes
     'That gentleman is going to Colombo.'

    b. *mamə gunəpaaləwə   dækka.*
      I   Gunapala-ACC   saw
      'I saw Gunapala.'

However, there is also a wide range of sentences lacking any overt verbal form, in which what appears to be the predicate may be headed by a member of any of the other major categories, as in (2)[2] (P in Sinhala is postpositional):

(2) AP: *ee   potə [bohomə alut].*
       that book very   new
       'That book is new'

    NP: *gunəsiri mahattəya [apee iskoole mul guruwərəya].*
       Gunasiri Gentleman our   school head teacher
       'Mr. Gunasiri is the head teacher of/in our school.'

    PP: *ee   potə [apee kaaməree tiyenə   meese uḍə].*
       that book our   room-LOC be-REL table upon
       'That book is on the table which is in our room.'

Interestingly, all of these categories may occur as predicates in English, as well. Thus, to take examples from Williams's basic (1980) analysis of predication:

(3)   AP: John made Bill *sick*.
       NP: John made Bill *a doctor*.
       PP: John kept it *near him*.
       VP: John *died*. (Williams, 1980: 206)

In English, however, only verbs may occur as predicates in independent sentences. When phrases headed by categories other than verbs occur in a main predicative relation, they do so as complements of a verb such as the copula *be*: "Bill is sick"; "Bill is a doctor"; "It is near him." In Spoken Sinhala, however, there is no obvious equivalent to the copula, and there is considerable evidence that nonverbal forms as well can be main predicators in independent sentences. (For terminological convenience, we will use the term PREDICATOR to designate the head—of whatever category—of a predicative phrase.)[3]

Here, we will first sketch in some of the fundamental properties of Sinhala verbal sentences. Then we will propose a uniform basic tree structure for both verbal and nonverbal sentences, followed by a review of the evidence for this structure, which primarily involves focus, negation, and case assignment. Finally, we will consider a type of nominal predicator sentence, the ACTION NOMINAL SENTENCE, which appears so far to be peculiar to Sinhala, and on that basis we will suggest some modifications in the specification of external arguments as presented in Williams 1981.

Verbal Predicator Sentences

Sinhala is fundamentally an SOV language, but it also exibits very free constituent order, a feature that will not concern us here.[4] Verbs in spoken Sinhala do not show agreement,[5] but they do show tense (present and past), mode, and several other categories. Among the tensed forms are two that occur as main predicators in root clauses and are of special interest here. One, the BASIC FORM (sometimes called the SIMPLE FORM), is the most "neutral" one, and it is the one that appears in the sentences in example (1). It is also the form commonly cited in dictionaries. The other, the EMPHATIC FORM (EMPH), occurs in focused, or cleft, sentences, which are very common in discourse.[6] The basic and emphatic forms of two verbs are illustrated in table 7–1.

Table 7–1   Forms of *ya*- 'go' and *kərə*- 'do'

	Present	*Past*
Basic Form	*yanəwa/kərənəwa*	*giyaa/keruwa*
Emphatic Form	*yanne/kəranne*	*giyee/keruwe*

Their endings are relatively transparent. The unmarked position for focus is rightward, as shown in (4a), as compared with its unfocused counterpart in (1). However, here, as elsewhere, order is relatively free, as shown in (4b). The focused element is in boldface:

(4)   a. *ee   mahattəya   yanne   **koləṁbəṭə** (-y)*   (SVX)
        that gentleman go-EMPH Colombo (EMPH)
        'It is Colombo that that gentleman is going to.'

    b. *ee mahattəya **koləṁbəṭay** yanne*   (SXV)
       ***koləṁbəṭay** ee mahattəya yanne*   (XSV)
       *yanne ee mahattəya **koləṁbəṭay***   (VSX)
       *yanne **koləṁbəṭay** ee mahattəya*   (VXS)
       ***koləṁbəṭay** yanne ee mahattəya*   (XVS)

    'It is Colombo that that gentleman is going to.'

Note that the verb marking remains constant. The *-y* (underlyingly *-yi*), glossed as EMPH, is a form that helps mark the focus and will be discussed shortly.

There is strong evidence for a focus position based in part on the unbounded cyclic nature of focusing as discussed in Gair 1983. The tree that was argued for there for Sinhala verbal sentences is shown in (5a), converted in (5b) to a representation more consonant with Chomsky (1986: 161). We assume here without discussion that focus movement involves Chomsky-adjunction to INFL″ (S).

(5)   a.

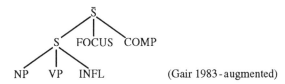

(Gair 1983 - augmented)

    b.

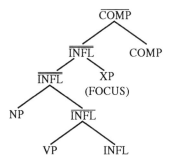

INFL does not contain AGR, since there is no agreement, but it does contain [±TNS] and probably other features that do not concern us here.[7] This is expressed in (6).

(6)   AUX   →   INFL (aux)
                [± TNS]

Nonverbal Sentences

If we assume the maximum parallelism between verbal and nonverbal sentences, which is clearly desirable theoretically, the tree in Figure 7–1 could be simply converted to the one in (7), where X is any major category.

(7)

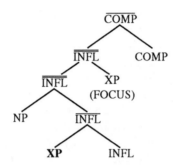

In justifying this representation for nonverbal as well as verbal sentences, several questions immediately arise:

1. What is the content of INFL?
2. Is the FOCUS node justified for nonverbal Ss?
3. Is XP in fact the (syntactic) predicative phrase, or is it the complement of a verb (such as a copula) and hence within a VP, as in English?

The last two questions in particular are interrelated, and in considering the third we will invoke evidence from focusing as well as from negation and case assignment.

Content of INFL

At present we have little to say on the content of INFL, particularly since that has not been worked out for verbal sentences, either. However, if the tree in (7) is to hold, it is clear that INFL in nonverbal sentences has a minus value for TNS, since only verbs have tense. One possible candidate for INFL will surface later in connection with adjectival predicator sentences.

Focus Marking

To make the discussion of focus clearer, we first note that a number of forms in Sinhala have the property that they are restricted in occurence to a position immediately following either a predicator of a nonfocused S or a focus of a focused S. They may thus be regarded as FOCUS-MARKING FORMS. The list includes the question marker *də*, the reportative *lu*, the conjunction *nan* 'if', and the emphatics *tamaa, tamay,* and *-yi*. (It is the latter that occurs on the focus in (4).) Examples paralleling (4), but with the question marker *də*, are given in (8); (8a) is an unfocused question, (8b) has a focused dative NP. As before, order is variable, but marking is constant, as shown in (8c). Again, the focused element is in boldface:

(8) a. *ee   mahattəya koləṁbəṭə   yanəwa də?*
        that gentleman to Colombo goes   Q
        'Is that gentleman is going to Colombo?'

     b. *ee   mahattəya yanne   **koləṁbəṭə də**?*   (SVO)
        that gentleman go-EMPH Colombo Q
        'Is it to Colombo that that gentleman is going?'

     c. *ee mahattəya **koləṁbəṭə də** yanne?*   (SOV)
        ***koləṁbəṭə də** ee mahattəya yanne?*   (OSV)
        *yanne ee mahattəya **koləṁbəṭə də**?*   (VSO)
        *yanne **koləṁbəṭə də** ee mahattəya?*   (VOS)
        ***koləṁbəṭə də** yanne ee mahattəya?*   (OVS)
        'Is it to Colombo that that gentleman is going?'

Note that the sentences in (9) are not possible. In (9a) and (9b), the focus-marking form *də* does not directly follow the focused item, which must be other than the verb as shown by the verb marking. In (9c) and (9d), *də* follows an item other than the verb, but the sentence is not focused because the verb is in the basic rather than the emphatic form:

(9) a. **ee mahattəya yanne   də   koləṁbəṭə?*
        that gentleman go-EMPH QUES Colombo

     b. **ee mahattəya koləṁbəṭə yanne də?*

     c. **ee mahattəya yanəwa koləṁbəṭə də?*

     d. **ee mahattəya koləṁbəṭə də yanəwa?*

Focus in Nonverbal Sentences

It is the case in Sinhala that nonverbal predicator sentences behave precisely like verbal ones in regard to focusing, with the single exception that since the basic and emphatic affixes are for the most part tense linked, there is commonly no change in predicator form between nonfocused and focused Ss.[8] Examples are given in (10), (11), and (12): (10) with adjectival, (11) with nominal, and (12) with postpositional predicators. The (a) members of each set are nonfocused noninterrogative, (b) are nonfocused interrogative, (c) are focused noninterrogative, and (d) are focused interrogative. Recall that *tamay* 'indeed' is, like the interrogative *də*, a focus-marking form:

(10) ADJECTIVAL PREDICATOR:

a. *mee potə alut.*
this book new
'This book is new.'

b. *mee potə alut də?*
this book new Q
'Is this book new?'

c. *mee potə tamay alut.*
this book indeed new
'It is indeed this book which is new.'

d. *mee potə də alut?*
this book Q new
'Is it this book which is new?'

(11) NOMINAL PREDICATOR:

a. *meekə   alut potə.*
this-one new book
'This is the new book.'

b. *meekə   alut potə   də?*
this-one new book-INDEF Q
'Is this the new book?'

c. *meekə   tamay alut potə.*
this-one indeed new book
or
alut potə meekə   tamay.
new book this-one indeed
'This is indeed (the one that is) the new book.'

d. *meekə   də alut potə?*
this-one Q new book
or
alut potə meekə   də?
new book this-one Q
'Is it this one that is the new book?'

(12) POSTPOSITIONAL PHRASE PREDICATOR:

a. *ee   potə   meese uḍə.*
that book table upon
'That book is on the table.'

b. *ee   potə meese uḍə də*
that book table upon Q
'Is that book on the table?'

c. *meese uḍə ee potə tamay.*
table upon that book indeed
or
ee   potə tamay meese uḍə.
that book indeed table upon
'It is indeed that book which is on the table.'

d. *meese uḍə ee potə də?*
   table upon that book Q
   or
   ee potə də meese uḍə?
   that book Q table upon
   'Is it that book which is on the table?'

A still clearer indication of the verbal–nonverbal parallel is furnished by vowel-ending adjectives, such as *hoňdə* 'good' and *rasə* 'tasty'. When these are predicators in nonfocused sentences, they appear with an affixed *-yi* (surfacing as *-y* or *-i*) referred to as the ASSERTION MARKER (ASN).[9] Examples are given in (13). The associated unfocused questions are shown in (14), with *də* following the adjective (the assertion marker usually drops before *də*):

(13) a. *mee potə hoňday.*
        this book good-ASN
        'This book is good.' (*hoňdə* 'good')

   b. *mee kææmə rasay.*
      this food   tasty-ASN
      'This food is tasty.' (*rasə* 'tasty')

(14) a. *mee potə hoňdə də?*
        this book good Q
        'Is this book good?'

   b. *mee kææmə rasə də?*
      this food   tasty Q
      'Is this food tasty?'

The focused counterparts of the sentences in (14) are shown in (15). Note that the question marker follows the focus and that the assertion marker never appears on the adjective in such focused structures:

(15) a. *hoňdə mee potə də?*
        good   this book Q
        or
        mee potə də hoňdə?
        this book Q good
        'Is it this book that is good?'

   b. *rasə mee kææmə də?*
      tasty this food   Q
      or
      mee kææmə də rasə?
      This food   Q tasty
      'Is it this food that is tasty?'

There is thus a precise parallel to the verbal forms, with the adjective plus assertion marker as the functional equivalent of the simple form and the bare adjective serving as the emphatic form. The assertion marker -*yi* is a clear candidate for INFL, but whether or not it belongs there depends in part on how we treat the verbal affixes relating to focus.

To sum up: Not only is a *focus* node justified for nonverbal sentences, as it is for verbal ones, but adjectival predicators behave like verbs with regard to visible marking. Note particularly that no copula or other verb surfaced in either the focused or the unfocused sentences.

Predicator Category and Negation

Sinhala has a number of negators, affixing and not, but only the two main nonaffixing ones, *næœ* and *nemey*, will concern us here. There are numerous dialectal variants for *nemey*, including *nevi*, *nevey*, and *nemee*.)[10]

There are two main functions for *næœ*: First, it serves as an existential negative—as the negative of the existential verbs *tiyenǝwa* 'be, exist (inanimate)' and *innǝwa* 'be, exist, stay (animate)', which it generally replaces.[11] An example is furnished in (16):

(16) a. *mehee alut pot   tiyenǝwa.*
       here   new books be
       'There are new books here.'

   b. *mehee alut pot   næœ.*
       here   new books *næœ*
       'There aren't new books here.'

Second, *næœ* serves as the "neutral" negator for nonfocused verbal sentences, and it generally follows the verb. (The verb appears with the emphatic affix, but that is irrelevant here.)[12] Examples are given in (17). Note that these are the negatives of the sentences in (1):

(17) a. *ee   mahattǝya kolǝmbǝtǝ   yanne   næœ.*
       that gentleman Colombo-DAT go-EMPH *næœ*
       'That gentleman is not going to Colombo.'

   b. *mamǝ gunǝpaalǝwǝ   dække   næœ.*
       I   Gunapala-ACC saw-EMPH *næœ*
       'I didn't see Gunapala.'

In addition, *næœ* serves the same function for adjectival predicator sentences as for verbal sentences, as shown in (18), which gives the negatives of the unfocused sentences in examples (10) and (13):

(18) a. *mee potǝ alut næœ.*
       this book new *næœ*
       'This book is not new.'

   b. *mee potǝ hoňdǝ næœ.*
       this book good *næœ*
       'This book is not good.'

c. *mee kææmə rasə næœ.*
this food   tasty *næœ*
'This food is not tasty.'

On the other hand, *nemey* serves as a focus negator for sentences with predicators of all classes. Examples are given in (19) for verbal sentences and in (20) for nonverbal sentences. Examples (20a) and (20b) are adjectival, (20c) is nominal, (20d) is postpositional. (cf. the focused nonnegative counterparts (4), (10), (15), and (11c):

(19) a. *mahattəya yanne   koləm̆bəṭə   nemey.*
gentleman go-pres-EMPH Colombo-DAT *nemey*
'It is not Colombo to which he is going.'

b. *mamə dække   gunəpaaləwə   nemey.*
I   saw-EMPH Gunəpalə-ACC *nemey*
'It wasn't Gunapala that I saw.'

(20) a. *hon̆də mee potə nemey.*
good   this book *nemey*
or
mee potə nemey hon̆də.
this book *nemey* good
'It isn't this book which is good.'

b. *rasə mee kææmə nemey.*
tasty this food   *nemey*
or
mee kææmə nemey rasə.
this food   *nemey* tasty
'It isn't this food which is tasty.'

c. *meekə nemey alut potə.*
this   *nemey* new book
or
alut potə meekə nemey.
new book this   *nemey*
'It isn't this one that is a new book.'

d. *meese uḍə   ee   potə nemey.*
table upon that book *nemey*
'It isn't that book which is on the table.'

In its function as focus negator, *nemey* may also follow the predicator of a nonfocused verbal or adjectival sentence, which would normally negate with *næœ*. That is, it behaves like focus-marking forms such as *də*. Examples are given in (21a) and (21b), which are negations of (1) and (13). Note that there is no change in predicator form, except for the usual loss of -*yi* on adjectives when another form follows:

(21) a. *ee   mahattəya koləm̆bəṭə   yanəwa nemey.*
that gentleman Colombo-DAT goes   *nemey*
'That gentleman is not going to Colombo' (but somewhere else).

mamə gunəpaaləwə   dækka nemey.
I   Gunapala-ACC saw   *nemey*
'I did *not* see Gunapala.'

b. *mee potə   hoňdə nemey.*
this book good *nemey*
'This book is *not* good.'
or
mee kæcæmə rasə   nemey.
this food   tasty-EMPH *nemey*
'It's not so that that food is tasty.'

Effectively, what is happening here is that the VP or AP or some stretch within it including the head, or possibly the entire sentence, is being focused.[13] Interestingly, in this function, *nemey* may also occur on a sentence already negated with *næcæ*, as in (22):

(22) a. *miniha aʈə   wenəkan   nægitte næcæ.*
man   eight become-until awake not
'The fellow did not awake until 8.'

b. *miniha aʈə   wenəkan   nægitte næcæ nemey.*
man   eight become-until awake not *nemey*
'It isn't the case that the fellow did not awake until eight.' (De Abrew 1981: 61)

Nominal and postpositional predicator sentences pose special problems with regard to the distribution of the two negators. For nominal predicator sentences, *nemey* is the only negator, and *næcæ* cannot appear, as shown in (23):[14]

(23) a. *meekə alut potak   nemey.*
this   new book-INDEF *nemey*
'This isn't a new book.'

*meekə alut potak   næcæ.
this   new book-INDEF *næcæ*

b. *gunəsiri mahattəya apee iskoole mul guruwərəya nemey.*
Gunasiri gentleman our school head teacher   *nemey*
'Mr. Gunasiri is not the head teacher of/in our school.'

*gunəsiri mahattəya apee iskoole mul guruwərəya næcæ.
Gunasiri gentleman our school head teacher   *næcæ*

In much previous work, this has been considered a second use of *nemey*. However, one attractive solution that allows us to unite them follows if we say that *næcæ* occurs only with forms that are [+V], assuming a common feature analysis by which verbs are [−N, +V] and adjectives [+N, +V]. Nominal sentences, which then have the features [+N, −V], have only the *nemey* negation available.[15]

Postpositional sentences appear to pose a problem for this analysis, since they are [−N, −V] but appear to negate with either *næcæ* or *nemey*, as shown in (24). The focused variant, however, occurs only with *nemey*, as expected, as shown in (25a), and *næœ* cannot appear, as shown in (25b):[16]

(24) a. *ee potə meese uḍə nemey.*
     that book table upon *nemey*
     'That book is *not* upon the table.'

   b. *ee potə meese uḍə næœ.*
     that book table upon *næœ*
     'That book is not upon the table.'

(25) a. *ee potə nemey meese uḍə.*
     that book *nemey* table upon
     'It is not that book that is upon the table.'

   b. **ee potə næœ meese uḍə.*
     that book *næœ* able upon

The problem, then, is to account for the negation of the unfocused sentences with *næœ*. There is actually a simple and straightforward explanation. Recall that *næœ* is also an existential negator. Postpositional sentences with *næœ* do have a negative existential sense, and their nonnegated counterparts have alternants with the existential verbs *innəwa* (animate) or *tiyenəwa* (inanimate), as in (26):

(26) a. *ee potə meese uḍə.*
     that book table upon
     'That book is on the table.'

   b. *ee potə meese uḍə tiyenəwa.*
     that book table upon be
     'That book is on the table.'

Thus the sentences with *næœ* in question represent it in its existential function in which it replaces those verbs. Example (24b) is thus the negative of (26b), and the negative of (26a) is (24a). Further confirmation comes from sentences with inflected adverbs as apparent predicators, which also negate with *næœ* only when they have an existential sense. Examples are given in (27) and (28):[17]

(27) a. *eekə lalitə kalaawəṭə tiyenəwa.*
     that fine art-DAT be
     'That (museum) is for fine art.'

     eekə lalitə kalaawəṭə næœ.
     that fine art-DAT *næœ*
     'That (museum) is not for fine art.'

   b. *eekə lalitə kalaawəṭə.*
     that fine art-DAT
     'That (museum) is for fine art.'

> *eekə lalitə kalaawəṭə nemey.*
> that fine art-DAT   *nemey*
> 'That (museum) is not *for fine art*.' (but for something else)

(28) a. *taatta dæŋ apee gamee innəwa.*
father now our village be (anim.)
'Father is in our village now.'

      taatta dæŋ apee gamee næœ.
father now our village *næœ*
'Father is not in our village now.'

  b. *taatta dæŋ apee gamee.*
father now our village
'Father is in our village now.'

      taatta dæŋ apee gamee nemey.
father now our village *nemey*
'Father is not *in our village* now.' (but somewhere else)

What emerges clearly from this discussion of negation is that the choice of negator is dependent on the interaction of two factors: the category of the predicator and focusing. In regard to the latter, *nemey* is the focus negator in all types of sentences, and that does not affect our argument. In regard to the former, however, it is clear that both verbal and nonverbal predicators determine negator selection on an equal basis, with the type of negation dependent on the category of the predicator, so that only adjective and verb predicators may appear with *næœ*. Note that nonverbal sentences do not sprout verbs under negation, nor do they negate like verbal ones, which might have been the case if nonverbal predicators were in fact contained in verb phrases headed by null verbs of some kind.

The "Hidden Verb" Solution

This analysis leads directly to the possibility that there is some form, say a copula, in the nonverbal sentences, which simply lacks phonological form in some tense or tense–mode categories. If this were to be identified with some existent verb—one that is spelled out phonologically elsewhere—the only reasonable candidate would be *wenəwa*, 'be, become'. But there is little reason to believe that *wenəwa* does exist in some underlying fashion here, and there are several reasons for not assuming so.

It is true that for most NP AP and NP NP sentences there is a corresponding sentence with *wenəwa*, as in (29). However, there is always a semantic loading of 'become'. Also, such sentences occur in all tenses and modes, including the present, so that one cannot say that in the verbless sentences there is a zero form of *wenəwa* that occurs in some specific tense. It would thus have to be a tenseless variant, existing only for that verb:[18]

(29) a. *miris   daanawa naŋ kæœmə rasə wenəwa.*
chillies put   if   food   tasty become-PRES
'When you put in chillies, the food becomes tasty.'

b. *gunəsiri mahattəya apee iskoole mul guruwərəya unaa.*
Gunasiri gentleman our school head teacher become-PAST
'Mr. Gunasiri became the head teacher of our school.'

If the distinction between the sentences with overt *wenəwa* and those without it could be overcome, they might be regarded as present tense variants of some sort under a "zero variant" analysis such as that proposed for "zero copula" sentences in early generative studies of other languages (such as implied for Russian, for example, in Babby 1975). In this case, however, one would expect that the verb would emerge in straightforward semantically past tense nominal or adjectival sentences, as it appears to in Russian.

In Sinhala, however, nothing of the sort happens. The verbless nominal or adjectival sentence does duty for all tenses (again, unless the 'become' sense is required). The underlying *wenəwa* solution would also not work for postpositional predicator sentences, in which that verb cannot occur unless it is strongly required by the sense. Thus (30) is extremely strange, if not downright ungrammatical:

(30) *?? ee potə meese uḍə wenawa/unaa.*
that book table upon wenawa-PRES/PAST
'That book becomes/became on the table.'

Furthermore, there are situations in which verbal sentences, with additional verb inflection, can be embedded, but nonverbal sentences cannot be, and we do not find a hidden *wenəwa* surfacing to make them possible. Instead, we find the same 'become' sense as in the independent sentences with *wenəwa*. For example, the form *kæməti* 'like' can take a complement sentence with a basic (tensed) verb marked with the dative case, as in (31a). However, nonverbal predicator sentences cannot so occur, and complement sentences with *wenəwa*, as in (31b), do not represent a way that makes it possible for them to do so, but they have a clear 'become' sense, as indicated:

(31) a. *demawpiyo duwə igenəgannəaṭa kæmətii.*
parents daughter study-PRES-DAT like-ASN
'The parents like their daughter studying.'

b. *demawpiyo putaa guruwərəyek wenawaṭa kæmətii.*
parents son teacher-INDEF become-PRES-DAT like-ASN
'The parents like their son becoming a teacher.'
(*Not* 'The parents like their son being a teacher.')

Similarly, relativization of adjectival sentences occurs in a straightforward fashion without any verb, as we might expect, as shown in (32a). However, NP NP sentences are not relativizable, as shown in (32b), which is ungrammatical without *wenə* and bad with it in the intended sense, although *wenəwa* relatives are fine as relativizations of "become" sentences like those in (29), as shown in (32c), (32d), and (32e).[19]

(32) a. *nikaŋ kannə matə rasə kææmə.*
plain eat-INF I-DAT tasty food
'Food that is tasty for me to eat plain.'

b. *guruwərəyek   (wena)   mahattəya aawa.
teacher-INDEF (become-ADJ) gentleman come-PAST
'The man who is a teacher came.'

c. miris   daanəwa nan rasə wenə   kæcæmə.
peppers put-PRES if   tasty become-ADJ food
'Food which becomes (not 'is')good when you put in chillies.'

d. guruwərəyek   wena   mahattəya.
teacher-INDEF become-ADJ gentleman
'The man who is becoming a teacher.'

e. apee iskoole mul guruwərəya unə   mahattəya.
our school head teacher   become-PAST-ADJ gentleman
'The gentleman who became (not 'is') the head teacher in our school.'

There are, however, three types of embedded clauses in which a form of *wenəwa* does not necessarily have a clear 'become' sense: namely, conditional, concessive, and "dative-although" clauses. The first two are formed with verbal affixes, the third with dative marking on the finite tensed verb (as in the *kæməti* complement clauses above). Examples for content verb clauses are in (33a), (33b), and (33c); examples for *wenəwa* clauses are in (33d, (33e), and (33f):

(33) a. ee miniha giyot   mamə yanne   næce.
that man   go-COND I   go-EMPH næce.
'If he goes I am not going.'

b. ee   miniha giyat   mamə yanne   næce.
that man   go-CONC I   go-EMPH næce
'Even if he goes I am not going.'

c. ee   miniha giyaaṭə   mamə yanne   næce.
that man   go-PAST-DAT I   go-EMPH næce
'Even though he is going I am not going.'

d. mahattəya kæməti unot   mamə yanne   næce.
gentleman like   become-COND I   go-EMPH næce
'If you like, I will not go.'

e. kæcæmə rasə unat   matə   ehen   kannə bæce.
food   tasty become-CONC I-DAT there-ABL eat-INF can't
'Even if the food is tasty, I can't eat there.'

f. kæcæmə rasə unaaṭə   matə   dæŋ kannə bæce.
food   tasty became-DAT I-DAT now eat-INF can't
'Even though the food is tasty, I can't eat now.'

Here, *wenəwa* does seem to occur so as to make embedding possible, but it is not clear that these three types justify that it is there underlyingly in all nonverbal clauses, as it only surfaces in these special circumstances. As yet, it is not entirely clear, but there is reason to assume that at least *unat* (concessive) and *unaaṭə* are not real verb forms in these usages but rather occur in COMP. First, they occur with single sentence constituents as well as with entire sentences as in (34):

(34) a. *kohee unat mamə ee   minihat   ekkə yanne   næœ!*
       where unat I   that man-ALSO with go-EMPH *næœ*
       'Wherever it is, I don't go with that guy!'

    b. *ee   unaaTə   maTə yannə puluwan.*
       that wenəwa-PAST-DAT I-DAT go-INF can
       'Nevertheless (i.e., 'even that being the case') I can go.'

They also also occur in the same way with other kinds of sentences, such as negative ones with the negator *næœ*, for which there would otherwise be no reason for supposing an underlying copula, as in (35):

(35) *ee   gamana yanne   næti unaaṭə/unat (wæḍə aḍuak   wenne   næœ.)*
    that trip   go-EMPH not *unaaṭə/unat* (work a lessening become not)
    'Even if you don't go on that trip, the work won't get less.'

The most convincing evidence is that they may occur following finite verbs, as in (36a) and (36b):

(36) a. *ee   gamənə giyaa   unat/unaaṭə (loku wæḍak unee   næœ.)*
       that trip   go-PAST *unat/unaaṭə* (usefulness become not)
       'Even though (you) took that trip, nothing useful came of it'

    b. *ee gamənə yanəwa   unat/unaaṭə (loku wæḍak wenne næœ).*
       that trip   go-PRES   *unat/unaaṭə* (usefulness become not)
       'Even if (you) take that trip, nothing useful comes of it.'

There is thus considerable reason to assume that these forms of *wenəwa* are unitary and added to the entire sentence, as they are to single constituents, rather than representing the spelling out of an underlying verb form. Though they may follow either past or present forms, as in (36), they are themselves fixed in tense, lending further support to the view that they are frozen forms. The most likely position for them would then be in COMP. In this context, we might note that the negative *næœ* takes the form *næti* before either *wenəwa* or forms in COMP, as in example (35).

Thus, *wenəwa* does not appear to be a good candidate for the hidden copula. A possible solution would be a verb with neither semantic content nor phonetic representation, but this is essentially vacuous, since there is no function that it would perform not simply attributable to INFL. Moreover, and most important, it would be transparent to negation selection and focus marking, as we have seen. The simplest solution is thus to assume that XP in (7) need not have a verb head.

Case Marking

Case marking offers further evidence for the syntactic main predicator status of at least adjectival and nominal phrases in nonverbal sentences. We will review it briefly.

Sinhala has both direct (i.e., nominative) case and dative subject verbs, both transitive and intransitive, as exemplified in (37).[20] Clearly this must involve lexical properties of the verbs:

(37) a. *maṭə   ee   kataawə teeruna.*
I-DAT that story   understand-PRES
'I understand that story.'

b. *sindu æhenəwa   naŋ laməyaṭə næṭenəwa.*
music hear-PRES if   child-DAT dance(involuntarily)-PRES
'If the child hears music, he gets to dancing.'

The important fact for our purpose here is that there are also dative subject adjectives, as shown in (38), and dative subject nouns, as shown in (39). Since that case assigment must also involve lexical properties,[21] it is another basic characteristic shared by verbal and nonverbal predicators. In nonverbal predicators, dative case assignment is clearly not mediated by verbs, null or otherwise:

(38) a. *apee laməyaaṭə   ṭikak asəniipay.*
our   child-DAT a-bit sick-ASN
'Our child is a bit ill.'

b. *minihaaṭə   hariiyəṭə keentiy.*
man-DAT really   angry-ASN
'The fellow is really angry.'

(39) a. *maṭə   mæleeriaawə.*
I-DAT malaria
'I have malaria.'

b. *maṭə   niwaaḍu.*
I-DAT vacation
'I am on vacation.'

Action Nominal Sentences

The predicative phrases in the Sinhala nonverbal sentences dealt with so far have English counterparts in terms of their predication relations with the subject, even though they may be syntactic predicates in the full sense and not complements of VPs. One type of Sinhala noun predicator sentence, however, does exhibit interesting properties that make it unusual, if not unique. These ACTION NOMINAL SENTENCES[22] are illustrated in (40). They have a noun signifying an action as predicator, which is not necessarily derived in any direct way from a verb. In fact, in most of the examples the authors have seen, they are not so derived. Both subject and predicator are in the direct case:

(40) a. *andəree enakoṭə   gowiyo kataawə.*
Andare come-when farmers talk-DEF(noun)
'When Andare came the farmers were (really) talking.'

b. *ee   særee andəree hitə   ætuleŋ   hinaha.*
that time   Andare mind inside-INST laughter
'Then Andare was really laughing with the inside of his mind.' (i.e., he was laughing to himself.)

c. *nǽwə gillunat   bǽœn   cuun.*
boat   sink-CONC band   tune
'Even if the boat sinks, the band still plays on busily.'

d. *lamay   paaḍəmə.*
children   lesson
'The children were/are busily doing their lessons.'

e. *mamə kantooruwəṭə aawaamə   okkomə minissu wǽḍə.*
I   office-DAT   come-when all   people work
'When I came to the office all the people were really working.'

These clearly differ from the more familiar type of nominal equational sentence in at least two important respects. First, there is no coreference, identity, or class inclusion relation between subject and predicate. Put simply, there is no "is" relation. Second, the interpretation is 'do' rather than 'is': "NP do the action of N."

The subjects in all examples that we have seen are animate (usually human) and in the role of Agent (or Actor, depending on what set of thematic roles we choose). The predicators seem also to have the referential characteristics of verbs rather than nouns.

There is typically an implication of intensity or repetition of the act. These sentences, to be felicitous, require a strong context of time and/or specificity, and thus they commonly include time adverbs or adverbial clauses, as most of the examples in (40) show. It is difficult to say what nouns are permitted as predicators of this type, though it appears that there must be a sufficiently strong "pragmatic" connection with the subject to allow interpretability. In our data, we have evidence for fourteen nouns used in this way; they are given in table 7–2.

An analysis of these sentences that assumes a null verb variant of some existent verb is also inappropriate here, since there is no verb with the relevant subcategorization frame and semantic interpretation. Sometimes a paraphrase is possible with a compound verb formed with *kərənəwa* 'do', as in (41a) for (40b). For (40b), however, the proper verb would be *wenəwa* 'be(come)', as in (41b). These compound verbs are existent forms, but for other nominals here there are none, and there is no basis for assuming any specific verb:

(41) a. *gowiyoo kataa kərənəwa.*
farmers talk   do-PRES
'The farmers are talking.'

b. *andaree hinəhaa unaa.*
Andare   laughter become-PAST
'Andaree laughed.'

That the predicator phrases here are true NPs is shown by the ability of at least some of them to include nominal modifiers, as in (42), where the form *tamatamange* 'each his own' is genitive. Generally, however, they occur unadorned:

(42) *eegollə   tamətamange wǽḍə.*
those-people their-own   work
'Those people were doing their own work.'

Table 7–2   Action Nominal Predicators

kataawə	'talk, story'
hinaha	'laughter'
cuun	'tune'
paaḍəma	'lesson'
wæḍə	'work'
wagaawə	'cultivation'
weləñdaamə	'trade, commerce'
raṇḍu	'fighting'
gosaawə	'noise, racket'
vinoodə	'pleasure, enjoyment'
gamənə	'trip, journey'
carikaawə	'wandering, strolling'
sakmənə, hakmənə	'promenade'
selləmə	'playing'

In English, a relation of this type is possible within NPs, as in "John's laughter," "Terry's objection to the theory," and "Mary's talk about the problem." However, when such a relation holds, the subject NP may not be the external argument of the predicator N, where external argument is defined as occurring outside the maximal projection of the predicator (Williams 1980: 81, and subsequent work). Note that this echoes in a suggestive way the syntactic difference between English and Sinhala, which we have established. That is, structures possible only as parts of sentences in English may be full sentences in Sinhala. This is an important point to which we will shortly return.

There is, however, a difference between NPs in both English and Sinhala, on the one hand, and Sinhala action nominal sentences, on the other, in the looseness or variability of the relation between subject and head. In both languages, genitive specifiers of NPs are less fixed in role than sentence subjects are, including those of the action nominal sentences. Thus in (43) or in the English translation, the relation could be possession, or even goal, whereas in the corresponding Sinhala sentence (40d), the children must be engaged in the lesson. Similarly, in (43b), the work could be the result of the activity as well as the action, but that is not possible in (40e):

(43) a. *lamayinge   paaḍəmə*
          children-GEN   lesson
          'the children's lesson'

      b. *lamainge   wæḍə*
          children-GEN   work
          'the children's work'

These sentences thus seem to require some modification in Williams's (1981) theory concerning the external arguments of nominal predicators. Here we will adopt Williams's view that the external argument of a lexical item (our "predicator") is the one that is assigned (by predication) to some NP appearing outside of the maximal projection of that lexical item:

The external argument of a lexical item is the one that corresponds to the NP in a sentence of which a phrase with that item as head is predicated. [There is set] an upper bound (of one) on the number of external arguments that a phrase can have, but no lower bound. (Williams 1981: 84)

We will also adopt Williams's convention of underlining the external argument in the representation of argument structures, for example: hit: (actor, theme); seems: (theme, goal).

For Williams, it is a "fairly clear universal" rule (1981: 85) that when verbs have both an external argument and an Actor, the Actor is the external argument. However, regarding the argument structure of nouns, he then goes on to say:

> So, if Ns have external arguments they are not Actors. But do Ns have external arguments? I believe that we want to say they do, at least when they occur as head of a phrase that is used predicatively, as in "John is a fool." We might say that *fool* had an external Theme (that is, it has the argument structure (Theme). Then we could say that when *fool* appeared as the head of a NP used predicatively, the subject of that predication corresponded to the theme of *fool*. But we can show that this will not do generally, because we can show that this would require some nouns to have both internal and external Themes. Consider the following, for example [Williams's numbering retained]:
>
> (9) I consider that [destruction of a city by evil forces]
>
> Here, "destruction of a city by evil forces" is predicated of "that". But the predicate NP has internal Theme and Actor—thus to what argument of *destruction* does *that* correspond; i.e., what is the external argument of *destruction* if not Theme or Actor? *Clearly the external argument of such a noun has no counterpart in the verbal system* [emphasis added]: suppose we invent the label *R* to name that argument of the noun which is external. Then we would assign *destruction* the argument structure (R, Actor, Theme). The label R is meant to suggest "referential", since it is this argument position R that is involved in referential uses of NPs as well. Thus, for example, if *fool* has the argument structure (R), we might assign the following logical representations for the predicative and referential uses respectively: *John* and the variable x is in the position of R:
>
> (10) John is a fool   fool (John)
>   The fool left   E!x (fool (x) & left (x))"

(Williams 1981: 84)

For subjects of Sinhala action nominal sentences, however, this analysis cannot hold, since not only are the subjects of such sentences Actors (or Agents) but their being so is a defining property of the construction. It also seems clear that the possibility of occurring in such sentences is a lexical property. However, those same nouns also have the property that they can occur in "ordinary" equational sentences as well, where the external argument is in fact Williams's *R* (or its equivalent in whatever theory of predication we choose; what counts for our purposes is the contrast between the potential roles in the same syntactic configuration). Thus *kataawə* 'talk, speech' occurs as an action predicator in the action nominal sentence in (44), but it occurs as head of subject and predicate in the equational sentence in (45):

(44) *minissu* [*NP* *kataawə*].
      people   talk-DEF
      'The people are talking.'

(45) *itaamə hoňdə kataawə* [*NP* *Gunəsiŋhəge kataawə*].
      most   good   talk-def   Gunasinha's   talk-def
      'The best talk was Gunasinha's talk.'

Thus, *kataawə* would appear to require a dual specification of argument structure such as is shown in (46). The "R" in (46a) is to allow for Williams's referential indexing, but since nouns in this use seem to have the referential properties of verbs, it is not clear that this is necessary:

(46) a. *kataawə* (<u>Actor,</u> R)   SPEECH (action)
      b. *kataawə* (<u>R,</u> Actor)   SPEECH (event/result/locus)

The internal Actor argument in (46b) is there for an obvious reason: It accounts for the actor internal to the NP in NPs like (47) or its English counterpart:

(47) *gunəpaaləge   gas   kæpiimə*
      Gunapala-Gen   trees   cutting
      'Gunapala's cutting (of) trees' (NP)

      kæpiimə (Actor, Theme, R)

Earlier, we noted that Sinhala has dative subject adjectives and nouns as well as verbs and that subject case commonly reflects subject θ-role. Thus adjectives and nouns also require specification of roles in their argument structures (in addition to that just discussed for action nouns) as in (48) and (49). Note that *hoňdə* 'good, well', like *kataawə* 'talk, speech', requires a dual representation.[23] We have no examples of adjectives with agent roles, however:[24]

(48) NOUNS: *matə   mæleeriyaawə.*
                I-DAT   malaria (Noun)
                'I have malaria.'

                matə   niwaaḍu.
                I-DAT   leave (pl.)
                'I'm on vacation.'

                mæleeriyaawə: (<u>Experiencer,</u> R)
                niwaaḍu (pl): (<u>Experiencer,</u> R)

(49) ADJECTIVES: *apee laməyatə   ṭikak asəniipay.*
                     our   child-DAT   a-bit   ill-ASN
                     'Our child is a bit sick.'

                     laməya   hoňday.
                     child   good-ASN
                     'The child is good.'

laməyaṭə   hoňday.
child-DAT   good-ASN
'The child is well/ in a good state.'

asəniipə (<u>Experiencer</u>, R)   ILL
hoňdə (Theme)   (R?)   GOOD (NATURE)
hoňdə (Experiencer)   GOOD (STATE)

Conclusions

We see, then, that Sinhala forms of nonverbal major categories (i.e., adjectives, nouns, and postpositions), as well as verbs, may serve as predicators of root sentences. Thus a common tree representation, as in Figure 7–3, is possible for all predicator categories. We also see that Sinhala nouns may have external arguments that are not simply referential (Williams's *R*) but may be, among others, perhaps, Agent and Experiencer.

We can account for the first observation in a way more linked to general predication theory by generalizing, for Sinhala, Williams's first predication environment (1980: 212), as stated in (50), to the form in (51):

(50)   1. *NP VP*
        2. *NP VP X*
        3. *NP* be *X*

        1. John died
        2. John left nude /singing/ PRO thinking he was safe.
        3. John is sick/ near Larry/ PRO to leave.

(51) 1G. *NP XP*   (where X a major category)

Notice that this automatically leads to the correct syntactic result, as well, since it allows the noncopula nonverbal sentences. This suggests a possible parameter—something like "± Restrict XP to VP in *NP XP*"—but obviously it is too early to tell whether this is valid on the basis of the languages studied. One might also ask whether Williams's third predication environment (NP be X) was then rendered unnecessary given a minus value for the environment given as 1G, but that seems not necessarily to be the case, since Sinhala does have verbs like *wenəwa* 'become' that might require it.

The suggested generalization of the first environment does not, however, account for our second observation, since if a language had the generalized version, it would not necessarily have action nominal Ss or something like them. However, it might serve to allow such a development. As one intriguing possibility along this line: Since the predication relation in NP+NP sentences is not mediated by the copula with its "is-ness," the elevation of NP (among others) to full predicate status allows a more direct projection of θ-role to the subject, without the intervening compositionality of "be NP." This then makes sentences of the action nominal kind possible. The empirical prediction is that languages with action nominal sentences will have "no copula" equational sentences, but as yet we have only the evidence of Sinhala before us.

III

DEIXIS, ANAPHORA, AND AGREEMENT

Discourse Deixis and
Situational Deixis in Sinhala

Sinhala has a four-member set of determiners that show deictic properties. These are given in table 8–1 along with a rough indication of their "core" meanings and the designations given to them in earlier work (Gair 1970: 31 ff). Reflected there are four deictic elements, generally including in their expression the phonological elements *m-*, *o-*, *a-*, and *e-* (in some forms *u-* or $\emptyset$), respectively. They occur in, and thus define, a number of sets of forms with varying functions, some of which are given in table 8–2. Note that some sets, such as *mææ* 'this woman', *ææ* 'that woman (APH)',[1] and *muu* 'this animal (or derogatorily, person)', *uu* 'that animal, person (APH)', are defective in that they lack one or more members (For a fuller listing, see Gair 1967 or 1970).

For the most part, as will be apparent from the forms that have just been given, the forms in these deictic sets are morphologically transparent. It must also be mentioned here that most of these sets have a fifth member in the form of an M- and/or K- interrogative, which are the Sinhala equivalents of WH-forms. These include *monə* 'what', *koi* 'which' (demonstratives), *kohee* 'where', *kauru* 'who', *mokə* 'what one', and *kookə* 'which one'. Together with the deictics, these form deictic–interrogative sets. We shall not, however, concern ourselves with the interrogatives here.

Lyons has defined DEIXIS as:

> the location and identification of persons, objects, events, processes and activities being talked about, or referred to, in relation to the spatio-temporal context created and sustained by the act of utterance and the participation in it, typically, of a single speaker and at least one addressee. (1977: 637)

Table 8–1   Determiners with Deictic Properties

Determiners	Core Meanings
First Proximal (1 PROX)	*mee* 'this, these': proximity to speaker, or to both speaker and hearer
Second Proximal (2 PROX)	*oyə* 'that, those (by you)': proximity to hearer
Distal (DIST)	*arə* 'that, those (over there)': distal from both speaker and hearer, generally in sight
Anaphoric (APH)	*ee* 'that, those (in question)': reference to something in the code or message, usually something preceding in the discourse

If deixis is limited to the spatio-temporal context in this way, only the proximal and distal forms of Sinhala are deictic. However, Lyons (1977, 1979) goes on to make the quite natural link between deixis and anaphora, and it is, of course, common for forms expressing spatial or speaker–hearer-related deixis to be used in "pointing" to other elements in the discourse. That is, they find use as ANAPHORA in the most general sense of that term: forms that refer to or are referentially dependent upon some element in the (usually preceding) discourse. In this context, "discourse" does not exclude the sentence in which the anaphoric form appears, though in much recent linguistic work it is common to restrict that term to forms with antecedents within that limited domain. In this chapter, however, I will use "anaphor" and its derivatives in the general sense of "discourse deixis," rather than in that restricted sense, and in fact I will not deal at all with intrasentential anaphora except for a brief mention of them at the end of this chapter. I will also use "antecedent" or "anaphoric referent" in a pretheoretical way, to designate whatever is referred back to, or resumed by, an anaphoric form, whether that referent is a concept or a linguistic element.

Three-way deictic systems resembling the first three forms of Sinhala are by no means uncommon. They are represented in South Asia at least by Jaffna Tamil: *ita* 'this', *uta* 'that (hearer related)',[2] and *ata* 'that (distal and anaphoric)'. Outside the area, they are instantiated by Japanese (*kono, sono, ano*), Spanish (*ese, este, aquel*), and numerous others (see, for example Anderson and Keenan 1985: 282 ff.). Four-member systems also occur (Anderson and Keenan 1985: 286 ff.), but the Sinhala system appears to be unusual in that it has a fourth member (APH) specialized for anaphoric use.[3] The interplay between the anaphoric element and the others may be

Table 8–2   Some Pronominal Deictic Sets

Human: *meyaa* 'this person', *oyaa, arəya, eyaa* 'that person'
Animal: *meeka,* 'this animal', *ooka, arəka, eeka* 'that animal'
Inanimate: *meekə* 'this one', *arəkə, ookə, eekə* 'that one'
Feminine (Human): *mææ* 'this woman', *ææ* 'that woman' (Defective Set)
Animal/Derogatory: *muu* 'this one', *uu* 'that one' (Defective Set)
Adverbial/Locative: *mehee* 'here', *ohee, arəhe, ehee* 'there'
Adjectival-Adverbial: *mehemə* 'this way/manner/kind', *ohomə, arəhemə, ehemə* 'that way/manner/ kind'

seen in the discourse fragments (1) and (2).[4] Note the switch to anaphoric from spatial deictic forms:

(1)   At the Corner Tobacco Stall

CUSTOMER: mehe næwikaṭ tiyenəwa də?	Do you have Navy Cuts here?
SHOPKEEPER: næwikaṭ nææ, mahattea	No Navy Cuts, Sir.
CUSTOMER: **oyə** monəwa də?	C: What are **those** (2PROX)?
SHOPKEEPER: **mee** triiroos	**These** (1PROX) are Three Roses
CUSTOMER: **eekə** hoňdə sigəræṭ jaatiyak də?	Is **that** (APH) a good brand of cigarettes?

(2)   Response to Question as to Where to Get a Taxi

PASSERBY ON STREET (pointing):

arə paarəṭə yannə.	Go to **that**(DIST) road
nættaŋ, **arə** handiyəṭə yannə.	Or else, go to **that** (DIST) corner
etənə ṭæksi tiyenəwa	There are taxis **there** (APH)
arə enne ṭæksiyak	**There** (DIST) comes a taxi.
eekeŋ yannə puluwəni	(You) can go by **that**(APH)

In each case, the anaphoric form is used only after the item or location referred to has been introduced into the discourse, and each introduction of new entities makes use of the appropriate spatial deictic. Note also that it is not required that the anaphoric form be employed exclusively after introduction. In two successive sentences (the third and fourth) of (1), spatial deictics are used with the same referent. This is appropriate since the cigarettes are located near one of the participants and are still being "pointed out" in relation to a changed point of reference. In the other examples, however, the continued use of deictic rather than anaphoric forms would be decidedly unnatural.

The relationship between distal *a-* and anaphoric *e-* forms is of particular interest. In two- or three-way systems, it is common for the distal or intermediate (2PROX) form to do double duty as a spatial deictic and the unmarked anaphoric form.[5] Thus, in English: "That's a hydrangea" as compared to "Is that what you said?" or "I said I'll go, and that's what I'll do." Similarly, in (Jaffna) Tamil: *atai taarungo* 'give me that' versus *naan atai sonnen* "I said that." In Sinhala, however, *a-* (DIST) and *e-* (APH) forms are specialized in function in a near complementary fashion. The *a-* forms are rarely used anaphorically (under circumstances to be described below) and are virtually restricted to spatial use, at least in all the data that I have collected. The *e-* forms, on the other hand, are never used in spatial terms and are restricted to anaphoric use.[6] The *m-* (1 PROX) and *o-* (2 PROX) forms, however, are not limited to spatial deixis but are very often used anaphorically as well. Still, when so used, they commonly, if not always, have some speaker–hearer linkage, as we shall see below.

In these terms, the distal (*a-*) and anaphoric (*e-*) forms do, in fact, share something as against the proximal ones. They are both in a fundamendal sense "distal," in that they are neutral with regard to the speaker and hearer axis; they differ in that their primary domains of reference are respectively space or code-message. This is reminiscent, in an interesting way, of the claim made by Kuno for the anaphoric use of forms like *ano* in Japanese—that they involve something equally known to speaker and hearer, as opposed to their spatial use, which involves distance from both speaker and hearer. Although this analysis was later modified by Kitagawa (1979) and Hinds (1973), the essential feature of "equidistance" was retained. The cross-language similarity is striking, and the major difference, aside from expected differences of detail, resides in the sharp domain specialization of the Sinhala forms. The four Sinhala deictic elements may thus be displayed in feature terms, as shown in table 8–3, using the demonstratives as examples. We thus have a situation involving markedness in a Jakobsonian sense. That is, the anaphoric forms are marked for discourse deixis, since they have a positive value for *only* that feature, and the other forms are unmarked with regard to that feature.[7]

We can now proceed to a brief characterization, with appropriate examples,[8] of the forms of all four deictic categories when they are employed with anaphoric value. In this brief treatment, I will not distinguish within each deictic category between the different functional sets (demonstrative, adjectival–adverbial, and pronominal), but I shall concentrate only on the deictic elements and their common qualities across the sets. Differences do exist between elements in different sets with the same deictic element, and a fuller treatment would require that such distinctions be made. To take a simple example, the second proximal member of the human pronominal set, *oyaa*, has found specialized use as a second person pronoun. It thus does not stand in the same relation to the other members of its set—*meyaa* (1P), *arəya* (DIST), and *eyaa* (APH), all of which function as third person human pronouns—that members of other deictic pronominal sets do to their "siblings."[9]

Forms with the anaphoric element (*e-*) are, as we have seen, essentially neutral with regard to speaker and hearer or situation, and they are thus the unmarked ones for use in simply referring back to something previously said. This has been illustrated in (1) and (2). It is shown again very clearly in the dialogue in (3), and examples could be easily multiplied:

(3)   Lalit and Nimal meet; Lalit asks Nimal to go for tea.
      LALIT: api **arə** issəraha kaḍee yamu də?   Shall we go to **that** (DIST) boutique
                                              ahead?
      NIMAL: kohomə də? **ee** kaḍee hoňdə də   Why? is **that** (APH) boutique good?

Table 8–3   Distinctive Features of Demonstratives

	mee 'this' 1PROX	*ə* 'that' 2PROX	*arə* 'that' DISTAL	*ee* ' 'that' ANAPHORIC
Speaker proximity	+	–	–	–
Hearer proximity[a]	–	+	–	–
Spatial deixis	+	+	+	–
Discourse deixis	+	+	+	+

[a]The minus value in the first column requires some qualification, since it will not allow for situations in which something is close to both speaker and hearer, where *mee* is the normal form. One natural way of handling this in line with the approach taken here is to say that in such cases the hearer is within the speaker's territory with relation to the deictic referent. Thus the first row applies and the second becomes irrelevant.

LALIT: ow, **ee** kaḍee bohomə hoṅday.	Yes, **that** (APH) boutique is very good.
ee kaḍee tee bohomə rahay.	The tea in that (APH) boutique is very tasty
NIMAL: hoṅday, ehenaŋ **ee** kaḍeeṭə yamu.	Fine. Then let's go to **that** (APH) boutique.
(lalituy, nimaluy kaḍeeṭə yanəwa.	(Lalit and Nimal go to the boutique.
kaḍee weeṭər **mee** denna laṅgəṭə	The boutique waiter approaches
enəwa. **mee** denaagen **mehemə**	**these** (1PROX) two. He asks **thus**
ahanəwa:)	(1PROX)from **these** (1PROX) two:)
WAITER: mahatteyala, monəwa də	Gentlemen, what should I bring you?
geennə?	

The use of "referring back" is relevant in characterizing the use of the Anaphoric *e*- forms, since they consistently show forward directionality in the cross-sentential uses under consideration here. That is, anaphor follows antecedent, so that they are anaphoric as opposed to cataphoric.[10] In this, they contrast sharply with the first proximal forms, which can have a CATAPHORIC—what Hinds (1973) refers to as an "anticipatory"—function, pointing forward to what will be said, as in (4), in which the use of the anaphoric forms is not possible (in the desired sense):

(4) *api mehemə kərəmu.*   'Let's do this-way.
    api meekə kərəmu.   'Let's do this.'
    **api ehemə kərəmu.*   'Let's do that-way.'
    **api eekə kərəmu.*   'Let's do that.'

When first proximal (*m-*) forms are used anaphorically, however, as opposed to cataphorically, their employment is generally optional. Thus (5) and (6) are very similar passages: Both are used to set up a discourse, and *e*- instead of *m*- forms could have been used as well in (6), except for the last, anticipatory, use of *mee* in the final line:

(5) Perera and Nilame meet in the canteen.
    pereeray, nilamey aanḍuwe depaartəmeentuwəkə lipikaaruwo dennek. **mee** denna wæḍəkəranne ekəmə depaartəmeentuwe aŋśə dekəkə. **mee** denna nitərəmə wagee munəgæhenəwa. . . . niləmeṭə pereera munəgæhenəwa kænṭimeedi. **mee** denna atəre saŋwaadey **mee**:
    Perera and Nilame are two clerks in a government department. **These** (1 PROX) two work in two sections of the same department. **These** (1PROX) two meet virtually all the time. . . . Nilame runs into Perera in the canteen. The conversation between **these** (1 PROX) two is **this** (1 PROX).

Thus the setting up and the anticipatory uses of first proximal forms must be distinguished. Though anaphoric (*e*-) forms are excluded from the latter, they are not excluded from the former, as (6) shows. Note the general use of APH forms throughout in setting up the story:

(6) soom*əwiiray raajəpaksay hoṅdə yaaluwo dennek. **ee denna** koləṁbə widyaalekə igenəgannəwa. **ee denna** dænəṭə igenəganne wíwəwidyaalə prəweéə panṭiye.

raajəpaksəṭa koləm̃bəṭə hoñdəṭə puruduy. **eyaa** poḍikaale iñdəlamə igenəgatte
koləm̃bə. soomәwiirә **ehemə** nemey. **eyaa** koləm̃baṭə aawe lañgədi. **eyaa** bohomə
æætə gaməkə lameek. **eyaa** kaliŋ igenəgatte gamee mahawidyaale. gamee
mahawidyaale igeniimə hoñdə madi nisaay **eyaa** koləm̃bəṭə aawe igenəgannə.

Somaweera and Rajapaksa are two good friends. **Those** (APH) two are studying
in a Colombo college. **Those** (APH) two are now studying in the university entrance
class. Rajapaksa is very used to Colombo. **He** (APH) has studied in Colombo from
his early youth. Somaweera is not **like-that** (APH). **He** (APH) came to Colombo
recently. **He** (APH) is a lad from a very distant village. **He** (APH) studied earlier in a
village *mahavidyalaya*. Because the education in the village *mahavidyalaya* wasn't
good, **he** (APH) came to Colombo to study.

What the use of 1PROX instead of APH forms adds is a sense of immediacy,
bringing the described situation immediately before the speaker and hearer.[11] The
relation of this to the spatial use of these forms is obvious. Illustrated here is also a
general point: When the proximal forms are used in anaphoric situations, some deictic
element of "territoriality" with regard to speaker and/or hearer is introduced, in contrast to the speaker-hearer neutral use of APH (*e-*) forms. They thus have a "double
deictic" aspect, which is simultaneously discourse deictic and situation deictic.

The use of the first proximal in foregrounding something, bringing it into the
immediate sphere of attention, is shown very clearly in (7) (*uu* is the APH member
of an animate pronoun set used for animals or, derogatorily, for humans):

(7)   One student talking to another at the university.
       kollek kæmәraawak araŋ aawa. ginipeṭṭiyak wæḍiye loku næ. **uu meekə**
wikunandə genaawe. **uu** mageŋ illuwa rupiyal desiiyak. maŋ kiwwa "tamuseṭə maŋ
onnaŋ [oonə+naŋ] rupiyal siiyak dennaŋ". **uu** kiwwa "bææ" kiyəla. maŋ kiwwa
"ehenaŋ tamuse araŋ yanəwa" kiyəla.

       A fellow came along with a camera. No bigger than a matchbox. **He** (APH-
Derogatory) brought **this** (1PROX) to sell it. **He** (APH Derogatory) asked two
hundred rupees from me. I said "If you want (will take it), I'll give you a hundred
rupees." **He** (APH Derogatory) said "(I) can't." I said "Then take (it) and go."

The sense of immediacy associated with the first proximal element also allows
it to be used to set something off against other elements in the discourse. This is shown
in (8), which is a continuation of (6) (with the new section italicized). Here, the use
of the first proximal makes the boarding house—and through it, the entire situation—
immediate with relation to the hearer/reader:

(8)   soomәwiiray raajəpaksay hoñdə yaaluwo dennek. **ee denna** koləm̃bə widyaalekə
igenəgannəwa. **ee denna** dænəṭə igenəganne wiwəwidyaalə prəweéə panṭiye.
raajəpaksəṭa koləm̃bəṭə hoñdəṭə puruduy. **eyaa** poḍikaale iñdəlamə igenəgatte
koləm̃bə. soomәwiirә **ehemə** nemey. **eyaa** koləm̃baṭə aawe lañgədi. **eyaa** bohomə
æætə gaməkə lameek. **eyaa** kaliŋ igenəgatte gamee mahawidyaale. gamee
mahawidyaale igeniimə hoñdə madi nisaay eyaa koləm̃bəṭə aawe igenəgannə.
*soomәwiiray raajəpaksay næwətila inne ekəmə booḍime. soomәwiirә **mee** booḍiməṭə
aawe giyə sumaane. itiŋ **eyaaṭə** tawəmə **mee** pæ̃ttə hoñdəṭəmə purudu næ.*

*soomawiirata londriyakata yanna oonawenawa. **eyaa** raajapaksata kiyanawa. **ee**
dennage kataaway **mee:***

Somaweera and Rajapaksa are two good friends. **Those** (APH) two are studying
in a Colombo college. **Those** (APH)two are now studying in the university entrance
class. Rajapaksa is very used to Colombo. **He** (APH) has studied in Colombo from
his early youth. Somaweera is not **like-that** (APH). **He** (APH) came to Colombo
recently. **He** (APH) is a lad from a very distant village. **He** (APH) studied earlier in a
village *mahavidyalaya*. Because the education in the village *mahavidyalaya* wasn't
good, **he** (APH) came to Colombo to study. *Somaweera and Rajapaksa are staying
in the same "boarding."* Somaweera came to **this** (*1 PROX*) *boarding just last week.
Therefore **he** (APH) is still not used to **this** (1 PROX) vicinity. Somaweera has to go
to a laundry. He tells (this) to Rajapaksa. The conversation between **those** (APH)
two is **this** (1 PROX).*

As this example suggests, the use of both anaphoric forms may also serve to
sort out elements in the discourse for the hearer/reader. This is shown also in (9),
which repeats (5) with a section omitted there restored (shown in italics):

(9)   pereeray nilamey aanduwe depaartameentuwaka lipikaruwo dennek. **mee denna**
        wædakaranne ekama depaartameentuwe anśa dekaka. **mee denna** nitarama wagee
        munagæhenawa. *pereerata giya satiye asaniipa unaa. ee nisaa **eyaa** ofis aawe næce.
        asaniipeŋ passe pereera ofis aawe aday.* nilameta pereera munagæhenawa
        kæntimeedi. **mee denna** saŋwaadey **mee.**

        Perera and Nilame are two clerks in a government department. **These** (1 PROX)
        two work in two sections of the same department. ***These** (1 PROX) two meet
        virtually all the time. Last week, Perera got sick. Therefore, **he** (APH) didn't come to
        the office. Perera came to the office the first time today after his sickness.* Nilame
        runs into Perera in the canteen. The conversation between **these** (1 PROX) two is
        this (1 PROX).

Here Perera is reintroduced into the discourse, distinct from his earlier linking with
Nilame; thus the APH *eyaa* is used in referring back to him separately. Note that there
is a shift back to the first proximal *mee* when we return to both people.

In sum, the anaphoric use of forms with the first proximal (*m-*) adds an element
of immediacy or conceptual proximity to speaker and hearer. This is, of course, perfectly consonant with their spatial use and can be seen as a straightforward extension of it.

Characterizing the anaphoric use of second proximal (*o-*) forms is more difficult, partly because the changing role interplay of speaker and hearer leads to very
complex changes in DEICTIC ANCHORING, which is the reference point for deixis. Commonly, the anaphoric use of a second proximal (*o-*) form relates the referent to the
hearer. The simplest case is one in which it bears some "natural" connection to the
hearer, as in (10), where the hearer's illness is referred to:

(10) Perera has told Nilame that he has been sick, and Nilame suggests that he go to a
       doctor.

NILAME: boræelle innəwa bohomə hoñdə doostərə kenek.	In Borella, there is a very good doctor.
unnæhege namə siilədaasə.	**His** (APH Respect) name is Siladasa.
oyaa **unnæhegeŋ** beet ṭikak gannə.	You take some medicine from **him** (APH Respect).
oyə amaaru okkomə ærey.	**That** (2PROX='your') illness will completely disappear.

Similarly, in (11), the letters are connected in a direct and obvious way with Sena:

(11) *In the post office:*

| SENA: (to Clerk) sər, **mee** liyuŋ dekə rejisṭər kərannə kiiyak yanəwa də balannə. | Sir, see how much it will take to register **these** (1 PROX) two letters. |
| CLERK: dekay panahay. liyuŋ dekəṭa **mee** muddərə aləwannə. | two-fifty. Stick **these** (2 PROX) stamps on. |

Some time later, after Sena requests some other stamps:

| CLERK: **mennə** muddərə. **oyə** rejisṭər kərənə liyuŋ dekəṭə muddərə ælewwa də? | **Here-are** (1 PROX) the stamps. Did you stick the stamps on **those** (2 PROX) letters to be registered? |

One step away from this, and into a more clearly conceptual realm, are cases in which the reference is commonly to something that has been related to the hearer in the previous discourse, as in (12) through (14). In (12), the reference of *oyə paare* 'on that (your) (2PROX) road', the reference is to the route that earlier discussion has revealed Silva to be taking. In (13) the reference of (2PROX) *ookee* is to the bus that Perera has pointed out, and the roles are switched. In (14), the reference is to a journal that Shelton, the hearer, has asked about, and that Dharmasiri knows, by Sinhala conversational convention, that he wants to examine. Note that the bus in (13) and the bookcase in (14) are first pointed out spatially by the distal forms *annə* and *arə*, respectively, and that the neutral anaphoric forms, *eeke* 'in that (loc)', and *ee* 'that' serve as bridges for a change in deictic perspective. This "bridging" use of APH is found frequently in discourse:

(12) Perera has pointed out to Silva the location of the line for his bus, which hasn't yet come, and the line is long.

SILVA: bas-ekə tawəmə æwilla næe, needə?	The bus still hasn't come, has it?
PERERA: bas-ekə tawə pæyə baagekiŋ witərə ey.	The bus will come in about another half-hour.
SILVA: matə **eeke** yannə puluwaŋ wey də kiyəla kiyannə bæe!	Whether I can go in **that** (APH) (I) can't say!
PERERA: **oyə** paare pæyə baageŋ baageṭə bas tiyenəwa. senəgə wæḍi naŋ mistə silwaṭə iilañgəṭə bas-ekeŋ yannə puluwaŋ, needə?	On **that** (2 PROX, i.e., 'your') road, the buses are every half hour. If there is too big a crowd, you (Mr. Silva) can go on the next one, can't you?
SILVA: ow, **eekə** hari.	Yes, **that** (APH) is right.

(13) Shortly after the exchange in (12), Perera points out to Silva that the bus to his destination, Gampola, has come.

PERERA: **annə**, gampələ bas-ekə æwilla!
misţə silwaţə **eekeŋ** yannə puluwaŋ, nee!

SILVA: **eekeŋ** yannə bææ wagee.
poolime hiţəpu senəgə dænətəmat **eekəţə** nægələ! itiŋ **ookee** yanəwa naŋ yanəkaŋ mə yannə wenne hiţəgənə

There (DIST), the Gampola bus has come! You (Mr. Silva) can go on **that**, can't you!

It looks as if one can't go in **that** (APH). The crowd that was in the line has now climbed into **that-one** (APH). So if (I) go in **that-one** (2 PROX), (I'll) have to stand till I get there.

(14) Dharmasiri has offered to take Shelton to meet a scholar monk later in the day. In the meantime, Shelton has asked Dharmasiri whether he has collected copies of a particular journal.

DHARMASIRI: ow. mamə mulə iňdəlamə **ee** saňgəraawə ekətukeruwa. ekə ekə awurudde saňgəraa wenə wenəmə bæňdəla tiyenəwa. **arə** pot almariye tiyenne **ee** saňgəraa tamay.

SHELTON: hoňday. haamuduruwo hambəwenḍə yanḍat tawə welaa tiyenəwa nee! mamə etəkaŋ **ee** sangəraa ţikak balannaŋ.

DHARMASIRI: hoňday. maţat poḍḍak ţawuməţə gihiŋ enḍə tiyenəwa. etəkaŋ **oyə** saňgəraa ţikə balanḍa ko.

Yes. I have collected **that** (APH) journal from the beginning. Each year's journals are separately bound. **In that** (DIST) bookcase there are **those** (APH) journals.

Fine. There is still time before we meet the Reverend monk, isn't there! Until then, I'll read **those** (APH) journals a bit.

Fine. I have to go to town for a bit, too. In the meantime, look at **that** (2 PROX, i.e., 'your') set of journals.

Very commonly, second proximal forms involve a considerable amount of inference in their linkage to the hearer and refer to something that the speaker has inferred from the hearer's previous statement, in other words, something that the speaker assumes to be true from the hearer's perspective. This shows up clearly in (15), where Nilame's question clearly implies that Perera should have stayed out longer and thus taken medical leave. Here, *occərə meḍikəl* 'that much (2PROX) medical leave' responds to that implied assertion:

(15) PERERA: næ, niləme, tawəmə niyəmə saniipeak næ. kæssat tawə ţikak tiyenəwa. æňgat hariyəţə ridenəwə.

NILAME: itiŋ æy ofis aawe?

PERERA: **occərə** meḍikəl daannə bææ, nee?

NILAME: **ehemə** kiyannə epaa.

No, Nilame, (I am) still not really well. There is still a bit of a cough. And my body really aches.

Then why did you come to the office?

(One) can't take **that-much** (2 PROX) medical leave, can one?

Don't say **like-that** (APH).

A very common use of the second proximal forms is to signal that the speaker is delivering information to the hearer, and the information is not presumably possessed by the hearer. That is, the switch to a second proximal form overtly effects the transfer and confirms the delivery, so to speak. This is illustrated clearly in (16) where the final *o-* form, winding up a series of *e-* forms, is relevant:

(16)   gamee paraña minissu huñgak ayə goviyo. **ee** minissu kammæli næ. **ee** minissu udeemə kuḿburətə yanəwa. nættaŋ govipələtə yanəwa. mulu dawəsəmə gatəkəranne kuḿbure. nættaŋ govipəlee. udee yanəkotə dawaltə kææmə arəgənə yanəwa. aapəhu gedərə enne ræ wenəkotə. **ee** enne ræætə kannay nidaagannay tamay. aayet pahuwenda udeemə kuḿburətə yanəwa. nættaŋ govipələtə yanəwa. **ee** ayəge mulu jiiwiteemə gatəwenne **ohomə** tamay.

Many of the older residents of the village are farmers. **Those** (APH) people are not lazy. **Those** (APH) people go to the paddy fields in the early morning. Otherwise they go to the fields. (They) spend the whole day in the paddy fields or the fields. When they go in the morning, they take their noon meal. They come home only when it has become late. **That** (APH) return is just to eat the night meal and sleep. Again, on the next day they go to the paddy fields in the early morning. **Those** (APH) people's entire life is spent **that-way** (2 PROX).

Passages in which there are different deictic forms with the same referent are particularly revealing, since they hold the anaphoric reference of the forms constant while varying the "territorial" deictic component. One such passage is (17):

(17)   Dharmasiri asks Shelton about his thesis topic, which Shelton has just described.

DHARMA: mahatteya kohomə də **oyə**   How did you choose **that** (2 PROX) topic?
            maatrukaawə tooragatte?

SHELTON: **eekə** tooragatte maməmə   It wasn't I who chose **that one** (APH). It
            nemey. magee mahaacaaryəwərəyay   was my professor who reminded me
            matə **mee** gænə matakkeruwe.   about **that** (1 PROX,i.e.,'this').

Dharmasiri's use of the second proximal determiner *oyə* relates the topic directly to the hearer, Shelton. Note that Shelton first uses the neutral anaphoric pronoun *eekə* and then switches to the first proximal *mee,* thus once more illustrating the use of the anaphoric form as a bridge in switching deictic perspective. Note also that in this case, the first proximal appears to relate the topic directly to the speaker, in contrast to its more common function, represented in most of the earlier examples, of rendering it immediate to speaker and hearer.

Example (18) is a particularly interesting example of the use of different forms with the same referent to associate that referent variously with the participants:

(18)   Swarna's mother and father are worried about her getting past the marriageable age and are looking into a marriage arrangement with a suitable family. Swarna prefers to keep on working as a teacher and going for further education. Her mother apprises her of the arrangements made so far, and she mentions that the prospective groom, a doctor, wants a sizable dowry: a house, a new car, and a lakh of rupees (100,000). Swarna asks how they would raise that.

MOTHER: taatta hitaŋ inne apee pol   Father is thinking of selling 25 acres of our
            idəmeŋ akkərə visipahak   coconut land, he says.
            vikunandə lu.

SWARNA: taattatə **ee** moodə wædee   Don't let Father do **that** (APH) foolish
            kərandə dendə epaa amme! maŋ   thing, Mother! Don't get into needless
            nisaa ammala apəraade amaaruwe   difficulties on my account.
            wætendə epaa.

MOTHER: **mewwa ohomə** kal damənə kaṭəyutu nemey lameyo!

These-things (1 PROX) are not duties one can put off (in) that-way (2 PROX,i.e, 'your way'), child!

koy vidiyen hari **mee** kaṭəyuttə kərandə oonæ. heetuwə, **owwage** hoňdə tanəturak darənə mahatteek soyaagannə leesi næ̃æ. **eekay**!

Somehow or other we must carry out **this** (1 PROX) responsibility. The reason is that finding **that-kind** (2 PROX) of gentleman who holds a good position is no easy matter. **That** (APH)'s why!

SWARNA: mamə naŋ kohetmə kaməti næ̃æ **ohomə** kasaadəwələṭə. maŋ wenuwəṭə naŋgi kenekuṭə **oyə** parəstaawə kataakərannə.

As for me, I don't like **those-kind** (2 PROX, i.e., 'your kind') of marriages at all. Instead of me, negotiate **that** (2 PROX, i.e., 'your') marriage proposition for a younger sister.

dæwæddə nobalənə kenek hambəunot maŋ baňdinnaŋ.

If (you) come across someone who isn't looking for a dowry, I'll get married.

Note that Mother uses 1PROX *mewwa* 'these things' and *mee kaṭəyuttə* 'this responsibility' in referring back to the immediate business at hand, whereas Swarna dissociates herself from the proposed alliance and attributes it to the mother by using 2PROX *ohomə kasaadəwələṭə* 'that kind of marriage (dative)' (*i.e.*, 'the kind you are suggesting'). Similarly, Mother's use of 2PROX *ohomə* in *ohomə kal damənə kaṭəyutu* 'things to be put off in that way' responds to a suggestion that she finds implicit in Swarna's preceding statement (and, presumably, manner).

As stated earlier, the use of distal (*arə-*) forms in anaphoric function is much less common than for the other deictics, and most examples that I have collected are from narratives, albeit narratives in Colloquial Sinhala. Thus, conclusions must be more tentative, but some things emerge clearly even from limited data.

Used anaphorically, The DIST forms share with the APH (*e-*) forms neutrality with respect to speaker-hearer linkage, and in that sense the two kinds of forms make up a set. They differ, however, in two main respects.

First, the two kinds of forms differ in specificity. They refer back to something specific in the discourse, and it appears generally that the antecedent is something linguistically expressed. APH forms may, of course, do this, but they may also have more general reference, referring, for example, to an entire situation or concept, including one that may be inferred from the discourse. The specificity of the distal forms is reflected also in their common occurrence linked with an adjectival (relative) form of the verb *kiyənəwa* 'say' to produce expressions such as *arə kiyəpu (potə)* 'that(DIST) said-REL (book)' roughly 'the aforementioned (book)'.

Second, DIST and APH forms differ in locality. DIST forms are, or can be, less local in their reference than the APH forms. Some significant distance intervenes between the DIST anaphor and its antecedent, or at the least some other entity or entitities have been introduced in the interval. The APH forms, on the other hand, are in general more local. In terms of the distinction drawn by Brown and Yule (1983: 173 ff.) between "current" and "displaced" entities, we can say that the APH forms refer to the latter. The observations above are borne out by the further observation that the pronominal forms of the distal deictic *arəkə* 'that (one)' and *arəwa* 'those (ones)' do not appear, in the data used here, at least, to occur in anaphoric use (although they do, of course, occur as situational deictics). Rather, it is the demonstrative adjective forms that are so used, accompanied by a lexical noun in the definite. This bears out Brown and Yule's observation (p. 176) that "displaced entities are regularly referred to by full lexical definite NPs." The functional basis for this seems obvious: The lexical NP is required to supply sufficient information so as to uniquely identify the antecedent over the intervening material.

Two examples, (19) and (20), may suffice to illustrate this characteristic. They are interesting in that they demonstrate an interplay of Distal *arə* with other deictics used anaphorically:

(19) This example is from a recounting of a folktale about Andare, the Sinhala jester–trickster figure. The story begins as follows:

Andaree gaməṭə alləpu gammaane wisaalə wel yaayak tibuna. **oyə** wel mædde maha wisaalə galak tibuna.

In the rural area near Andare's village there was a large stretch of paddy fields. In the middle of **those** (2PROX) fields was a large rock.

(The story goes on to say that the farmers of the area took great efforts, unsuccessfully, to dislodge and remove the rock to free the space for cultivation. One day, Andare, passing through the fields, saw a group of farmers clustered around in deep discussion, approached, and took a look.)

balənə koṭə **arə** galə waṭee iňdəgənə minissu kataawə.

When he looked (he saw) men gathered around **that** (DIST) rock in conversation.

(Andare learns the problem and offers to carry away the rock if the farmers will feed him royally for three months. The farmers eagerly agree.) The tale continues:

Andaree gedərəkə nawaattagenə tuŋmasəyakmə **arə** kiwwə hæṭiyəṭə kaṇḍə dunna.

Putting Andare up in a house for three months, they fed him in **that**-(DIST)-said manner.[12]

(20) From a description of a bus stand:

bas poolime senəgə wædiwenə koṭə **eekəṭə** kæməti pirisek innəwə. **ee** kawdə dannəwə də? **ee** tamay, welendo, hiňganno, kawikoləkaarəyo, pinuŋkaarəyo, **oyə** wagee ayə. welendo poolimə laňgəṭə enəwa baḍu wikunannə; hiňganno enəwa hiňgəmaŋ illannə; pinuŋkaarəyo pinuŋ gahanəwa poolimə laňgəṭə. **iiṭə** passe poolime senəgə laňgəṭə yanəwa salli illannə. saməharə ayə salli denəwə; saməharə ayə ahakə balaagannəwa. poolime innə koṭə ætiwenə mahansiyə huňgak durəṭə magə ærenəwa, **arə** pinuŋ balənə koṭə, tawə **oyə** waṭee piṭee siddəwenə noyek dewal dakinə koṭə.

As the crowd in the bus queue grows, there is a group that likes **that** (APH). Do you know who **they** (APH) are? **They** (APH), indeed, are vendors, beggars, poemsellers, somersault-doers [acrobats]. **That** (2PROX) kind of folk. The vendors approach the queue to sell goods; the beggars come to beg alms; the somersault-doers do somersaults near the crowd. After **that** (APH), they go near the crowd in the queue to ask money. Some people give money; some look away. When one is in the queue, the weariness you have goes away to a great extent when you see **those** (DIST) somersaults (and) seeing all the other things that are going on around in **that** (=your-2PROX) vicinity.

In both of these texts, a considerable amount of narrative intervenes between the DIST form and the antecedent. In addition, both of these show the "delivery" use of 2PROX, and in (20), this form (*oyə*) nicely sums up a chain of anaphoric *ee* (APH) forms. All of the characteristics of anaphoric *arə* that I have remarked on are quite consistent with its basic use as a spatial deictic where it is both distal and neutral with regard to speaker and hearer, so that it commonly has a "pointing" function.

It is also possible to use the DIST *arə* form where the antecedent is not in the present discourse but is something well understood to speaker and hearer from a previous one. In this usage, it is commonly coupled with an adjectival form of *kiyənəwa* 'say', as described earlier.[13] Thus, when someone arrives at my office, I may ask:

(21) *arə kiwwə potə   genaawa də?*
    that said   book-DEF brought   Q
    'Did you bring that book(we talked about before)?'

This is, of course, quite consistent with the observations that we have made about the DIST form. Here as in its other anaphoric uses, it has a sense something like "the aforesaid."[14]

We can now proceed to summarize our observations on members of the deictic sets in discourse anaphoric use.

> First, anaphoric (APH, *e-*) and distal (DIST, *a-*) forms are neutral in speaker–
> hearer orientation, generally implying (equi)distance from speaker and hearer.
> The APH forms are specialized to the anaphoric or conceptual realm, and the
> DIST ones are almost limited to the (physically) spatial one.[15] DIST forms
> do, however, have a specialized discourse anaphoric use, which complements
> that of the APH forms. The DIST and APH together form a distal set, but the
> APH forms represent the unmarked category for anaphoric use, the one that is
> used unless some special conditions obtain.[16]
>
> Second, the first proximal (1 P, *m-*) and second proximal (2PROX, *o-*) forms may
> be used anaphorically as well as spatially. In anaphoric use, they retain the
> respective speaker–hearer deictic orientations clearly observable from their
> spatial use, adding these to their anaphoric reference to the antecedent. In the
> case of the two proximal forms, it is this added element of speaker–hearer
> linkage that represents the special conditions just referred to. Although person
> deixis may be regarded as an addition—a kind of overtone—in anaphoric use,
> it is present in all uses and thus represents the constant, basic meaning of the
> forms themselves.
>
> Third, the distal forms are characteristically used with spatial reference. They do,
> however, have an anaphoric use that reflects their distal character. The
> distance is then, however, not just distance with relation to speaker–hearer

but distance within the text. As with the proximal forms, it is the fundamentally spatial, in this case distal, element that is constant across usages.

Finally, the first proximal also has an anticipatory (cataphoric) use, in referring to what will be said. Otherwise, the unmarked direction in discourse anaphora is *forward*; that is, anaphor following antecedent.

These observations are quite consonant with table 8–3, but we may now add one further dimension to it. We may capture the fundamentally spatial (speaker–hearer linked) nature of all but the APH forms by adding parentheses, signifying optionality, to their cells in the discourse deixis row, as in table 8–4, with the further understanding that when the parenthesized plus values obtain, "spatial" may refer generally to conceptual rather than physical space.

In this paper, I have dealt only with the discourse anaphoric—that is, extrasentential—uses of the deictic forms. For completeness, it should be noted that the basic intrasentential anaphor, other than null, in Colloquial Sinhala is the appropriate pronominal form of the APH deictic such as *eyaa* 'he/ she', *eekə* 'it'. This is not restricted to discourse anaphora but may also occur intrasententially—and in fact is the basic intrasentential anaphor. In this usage, however, it is generally accompanied by the emphatic clitic *mə*, as illustrated in (22). Without *mə*, the reading is strongly noncoreferential, though possible. Also, with *mə*, a noncoreferential reading is possible, though without relevant discourse context, it is the highly marked reading:

(22) a. *gunəpaalə yanəkoṭə amma nitərəmə eyaaṭə(mə)*   *salli denəwa*
Gunapala go-when mother always   he/she(APH)-DAT-EMPH money gives
'When Gunapala goes, Mother always gives him (*i.e.*, Gunapala. or someone else) money.'

b. *gunəpaalə iiye   eyaage(mə)   kaar-ekə wikka.*
Gunapala yesterday his/her-APH-EMPH car   sold
'Gunapala sold his (*i.e.*, his own or someone else's) car yesterday.'

c. *eyaa(mə)   yanəwa kiyəla gunəpaalə kiwwa.*
he/she-APH-EMPH goCOMP Gunapala   said
'Gunapala said that he (*i.e*, himself or someone else) was going.'

In this usage, which is anaphoric in a more limited sense, these forms show a number of interesting properties particularly relevant to binding theory (as in Chomsky 1981

Table 8–4 Spatial Nature of Distinctive Features of Demonstratives

	mee 'this' 1PROX	*oyə* 'that' 2PROX	*arə* 'that' DISTAL	*ee* 'that' ANAPHORIC
Speaker proximity	+	−	−	−
Hearer proximity	−	+	−	−
Spatial deixis	+	+	+	−
Discourse deixis	(+)	(+)	(+)	+

Note: Parentheses signify optionality.

and 1982 and related works by him and others). Note, for example, that in (22c), the anaphor is backward (cataphoric), though in discourse, it is always forward, as stated earlier.[17] There is also a reflexive form *taman/tanmun*, 'one's own' that may also occur in both intrasentential and cross-sentential contexts, though it occurs more commonly in the former. These issues are, however, a matter for treatment elsewhere.[18]

Pronouns, Reflexives, and Antianaphora in Sinhala

WITH W. S. KARUNATILLAKE

In current linguistic parlance, ANAPHOR is used in at least two senses. One, the most general, characterizes a form as having referential dependency—that is, having an antecedent. The other—more restrictive and technical—sense designates a form that can or must occur only under narrowly specified structural conditions that encompass both it and its antecedent. The most familiar instantiation of this is in the Binding Theory as initially embodied in three principles proposed in Chomsky 1982. It is Principle A that embodies the narrow definition of anaphor:

A. An anaphor is bound in its governing category
B. A pronominal is free in its governing category
C. An R-expression is free.[1] (p. 188)

A great deal of discussion has been devoted to the definition of GOVERNING CATEGORY; that is, the binding domain. The most commonly invoked domains, however, modulated by specific theories of phrase structure, are the minimal S (=IP), which is sometimes modulated by finiteness or agreement, and NP (=N″), though the status of the latter as a binding domain has been argued to vary in relation to specific anaphoric forms (as in Huang 1983). For the most part, here, we will be concerned with S in this regard.

The terms "bound" and "free" also have specific technical senses: A form is coindexed or not coindexed with an antecedent that commands it in some sense of "command." Various types of command have been proposed such as Command (Langacker 1969), K-Command (or Kommand) (Lasnik 1976, Kuno 1987) c-command

(Reinhart 1983) with differing definitions in Aoun and Sportiche 1983 and Chomsky 1982), and M-Command (Chomsky 1986b; essentially equivalent to the Aoun–Sportiche c-command).[2] In most recent work, however, the variant most widely invoked relevant to anaphora has been c-command, as defined in Reinhart (1983). We will adopt the following statement as sufficient for present purposes: "A c-(constituent)commands B iff the branching node that most immediately dominates A also dominates B."

In this chapter, we will be concerned with anaphora and anaphor in both senses as they relate to Sinhala. Our procedure will be first to present some Sinhala forms that are clearly anaphoric in the wider sense (i.e., referentially dependent in nature) and then examine the degree to which they are candidates for anaphor or pronominal in the narrower senses embodied in the binding theory principles above.

The three candidates that we will discuss are the lexical pronoun *eyaa* (human in reference), the reflexive *taman/tamun*, and a phonologically null element, which we will initially refer to variously as a null or phonologically unrealized pronominal or pronoun, as the context seems to require, defining and naming it more narrowly later. Subsequently, we will introduce a fourth form *anun* 'other' for the sake of comparison.

Sinhala third person overt pronouns are morphologically complex and are composed of one of four deictic elements plus a nominal element. The fourth deictic element, *ee-*, is specialized for discourse-deictic—that is, anaphoric—function, an unusual, if not unique, feature within South Asian deictic systems and, in fact, in languages in general. For example, the human set includes *meyaa* 'this person (by me)'; *oyaa* 'that person (by you)'; *arəya* 'that person (over there)'; *eyaa* '(s)he (in question)'. There are also other pronominal sets embodying this four-way deictic distinction in full and in part including inanimate, animal, derogatory, and honorific sets, but discussion and examples here will be limited to the most neutral human form *eyaa* '(s)he'. The specialization of the Sinhala *ee-* deictic element to discourse-referential dependency, where "discourse" does not necessarily imply "extra-sentential," is relevant to the present topic, since it not only contributes to the anaphoric nature of *eyaa* and similar forms but also virtually eliminates the possibility of employing *ee-* forms in direct situational deixis, for which one of the other forms must be used.[3]

Sinhala is fundamentally a strongly left-branching SOV language of the "super-pro-drop" type, allowing a null element (an empty pronominal) in all argument positions, and this is probably the most frequently occurring pronominal type. Where either an empty or phonologically realized pronominal may occur, the empty pronominal is generally preferred unless a lexical form is required by the structure (as, for example, as object of a postposition), or the entity referred to is being reintroduced or emphasized in some way, (as, for example, when focused, which requires a phonologically spelled-out form). Thus in the interchange in (1), filling in all the *eyaa*s would result in a most un-Sinhala redundancy. None, in fact, appeared in the original (adapted from Fairbanks et al., 1968, 1981, Lesson 12):[4]

(1) A: *Siri mahattəya dæn gedərə innəwa   də?*
     Siri mister   now home   be(ANIM) Q
     'Is Siri at home now?'

B: *næœ. (eyaa) taamə kantooruwe.*
no (he) still office-LOC
'No. He is still at the office.'

A: *(eyaa) kiiyəṭə də gedərə enne?*
(he) when Q home come-FOC
'What time does he come home?'

B: *kantooruwə wahanne hatərəṭə.*
Ø⁵ office   close-FOC four-DAT
'They close the office at four.'

pahaṭə witərə (eyaa) gedərə eewi.
five about (he) home come-might
'He is likely to come home at about five.'

æy, mahattəyawə hambəwennə oonə də?
why (him)   meet-INFIN want Q
'Why, do you want to see him?'

A: *ow, maṭə mahattəyawə ṭikak hambəwennə oonə.*
yes I-DAT (he-ACC) a-bit meet-INFIN want
'Yes. I want to meet (him) for a little (while).'

(eyaa) hariyəṭəmə   pahaṭə eewi   də?
(he) exactly-at-EMPH five   come-might Q
'Is he likely to come exactly at five?'

B: *kiyannə   bæœ.*
say-INFIN can't
'(I) can't say.'

saməharə dawaswələ (eyaa) enəkoṭə   ræœ wenəwa.
some   days-LOC (him) come-when night become
'Some days when he comes it's late.'

(eyaawə) hambəwennə oonə   nan ṭikak innə.
(him) meet   want-INFIN if a-little stay-INFIN
'If you want to meet him, wait a while.'

Note that in the last sentence, a null object appears in the original. Note also the pronominal use of the title *mahattəya* 'the gentleman, mister', which is common in Sinhala.

The reflexive *taman* has an alternate form *tamun* and a somewhat more formal nominative form *tamaa*. It is human, indiscriminately masculine or feminine, and generally third person in reference. Although it takes case affixes that are plural in form, it may be singular or plural in reference. The forms *tamun* and *taman* appear to be true alternates, and they certainly are alternates in the dialect we have relied on here, so that we will generally refer to them as *taman/tamun*, using one or the other in examples as they originally appeared. Also, *taman/tamun* has a use as an emphatic adjunct, and then it usually occurs with the emphatic clitic *-mə,* as in (2). This paper does not deal further with adjunct *taman(mə)/tamun(mə)*, which is clearly distinguishable from *taman/tamun* in argument positions or in its use as a possessive genitive, with which we will be concerned:[6]

(2)   *Nimal   tamammə   ee   salli   Siripaaləʈə   dunna.*
       Nimal   self-EMPH   that   money   Siripala-DAT   gave
       'Nimal$_i$ gave Siripala that money himself$_i$.'

Let us first examine the properties of these three elements with regard to the possibility of binding within the minimal S. At first glance, and as long as we restrict ourselves to that narrow domain, the situation appears straightforward and familiar. Where coreference is intended, native speakers are likely to accept (3) with *tamun* but reject (4) with *eyaa* as having coreference. (In this chapter, for the sake of exposition, we will use the notational devices of boldface for intended coreference and subscripts for possible coreference as the situation requires.)

(3)   **gunəpaalə tamunwə** *kannaaḍiyen   dækka.*
       Gunapala$_i$ self-ACC$_i$ mirror-INSTR   saw
       'Gunapala saw himself in the mirror.'

(4)   *?* **gunəpaalə eyaawə**   *kannaaḍiyen   dækka.*
       Gunapala$_i$ (s)he-ACC$_{?i/j}$ mirror-INSTR   saw
       'Gunapala saw himself in the mirror.'

Although null pronouns are perfectly possible in object position, they may not be locally bound, as example (5) shows; that is, there is no null anaphor in the narrow sense of anaphor as defined under Principle A:

(5)   * gunəpaalə$_i$ Ø,   kannaaḍiyen   dækka.*
       Gunapalai   Ø$_{*i/j}$ mirror-INSTR   saw
       'Gunapala saw himself in the mirror.'

Not surprisingly, both (4) and (5) are possible where there is extrasentential dependency—where *eyaa* and the null pronoun are free.

Where *eyaa* and *tamun* are genitives contained within a noun phrase, either may occur bound within the simplex sentence, as in (6):

(6)   **gunəpaalə$_i$** *eyaage$_{i/j}$ / tamunge$_{i/j}$ kaar-ekə vikka.*[7]
       Gunapala   his/self's   car-DEF   sold
       'Gunapala sold his(own) car.'

The problem of lack of complementarity between pronoun and reflexive in some environments, such as NPs or adjunct PPs, is familiar, with differences of detail, from other languages. Various solutions have been proposed, such as defining the binding domains for them differently in some way (Huang 1983). We need not pursue this further here, but we can simply note that the situation so far described appears to be a familiar one, with *tamun/taman* and *eyaa* obeying Principles A and B as reflexive anaphor and pronoun, respectively. There is a phonologically unrealized pronoun but no null anaphor.

The situation is actually more complex, however. Sinhala has an emphatic clitic, *mə*, which may be added to forms of virtually all categories to add emphasis. When *eyaa* is reinforced by this clitic, local binding is possible, and the complementation between it and *tamun* disappears in all the relevant environments. The reflexive interpretation becomes, in fact, the primary one out of context, and if a (linguistically) naive speaker is asked to translate an English sentence with a reflexive, this is likely to be the form given, unless the reflexive is stressed or the stimulus is "one's own," in which case *tamun* may be elicited. Nevertheless, and crucially, the emphasized pronoun retains its capability for extrasentential reference. The situation is thus as in (7) and (8). The question of possible external reference for *tamun* will be taken up later. Note that (7) and (8) are identical to (4) and (6) except for the substitution of *eyaamə*:

(7) *gunəpaalə$_i$ tamanwə$_{i/?j}$ / eyaawəmə$_{i/j}$/Ø*$*_{i/j}$ kannaaḍiyen dækka.*
     Gunapala$_i$ self$_{i/?j}$/ (s)he-ACC-EMPH$_{i/j}$/ Ø*$_{i/j}$ mirror-INSTR saw
     'Gunapala saw himself/him/her in the mirror.'

(8) *gunəpaalə$_i$ tamunge$_{i/?j}$ / eyaagemə/   kaar-ekə vikka*
     Gunapala self-GEN$_{i/?j}$ / (s)he-GEN-EMPH $_{i/j}$ car-DEF sold
     'Gunapala sold his(own)/his/her car.'

One might conclude that *eyaamə* is an anaphor, but that is scarcely convincing given the general function of *mə* and the retained possibility for external referential dependency. Furthermore, for at least some speakers, the bare pronoun may also be locally bound given a sufficiently strong discourse context. The partial complementation between *eyaa* and *taman/tamun* thus seems to be not a case of an absolute distinction between pronoun and anaphor on the basis of the binding principles but a matter of strongly preferring one interpretation over the other. The fact remains, however, that the domains within which those interpretive differences are instantiated are those that have generally been asserted as relevant for the application of the binding theory principles. In place of complementation of forms, we thus have an interpretive distinction that we might, for lack of a better term, consider to be weak application of the binding principles.

As example (9) shows, neither *taman/tamun* nor the pronoun with *mə* are necessarily subject oriented, since either NP can antecede them (a null genitive is not possible) though for at least some speakers, only the subject may antecede (Inman 1993).

(9) *taatta$_i$ putaaṭə$_j$ antiməṭə tamange$_{i/j}$/ eyaagemə$_{i/j}$ salli   dunna.*
     father-NOM son-DAT at-last   self-GEN/ (s)he-GEN-EMPH money gave
     'Father$_i$ gave the son$_j$ his(own)$_{i/j}$ money at last.'

There has been a great deal of concern with "long-distance anaphors" in South Asian languages, especially the binding of reflexive forms outside the minimal S (Davison 1990; Amritavalli 1984; Mohanan 1981b; Yadurajan 1988; and Wali 1979, among others). We may now turn to the distribution and interpretation of the forms we are dealing with in binding environments beyond the minimal S. This is obviously of particular interest for the reflexive *taman/tamun,* since we would expect the unmarked situation to be that the pronoun *eyaa,* and presumably the null pronoun as well, would be free—subject to binding outside their governing c category—under Principle B.

Examples (10) through (13) illustrate long-distance binding of the pronoun *eyaa,* the reflexive *tamun,* and phonologically unrealized pronominals into both finite and nonfinite environments. For the immediate purpose, we ignore the possibility of referential dependence outside the entire matrix sentence when assigning subscripts, but such external linking can be taken throughout to be a general property of both *eyaa* and the null pronominal, unless the subsequent discussion indicates otherwise. Minimal Ss are bracketed for clarity of exposition. The obligatorily controlled null subject of the embedded infinitive is represented as *e,* to distinguish it from the null pronoun at issue:

(10) *Nimal$_i$ Siitat$_j$*   [*e$_j$/*$_i$ tamant$_{i/j}$ eyaatem$_{i/j}$*   *tee-ekak*   *hadann$_\partial$*   *kiy$_\partial$la*]
     Nimal   Sita-DAT   [*e* self/(s)he-DAT-EMPH   tea-INDEF make-INFIN QUOT]
     kiwwa.
     said
     'Nimal$_i$ asked Sita$_j$ to make a cup of tea for self $_{i/j}$.'

(11) *lam$_\partial$ya$_i$* [*tamant$_\partial$i/ eyaat$_\partial$m$_\partial$i/ Ø$_i$*]   *d$_\partial$n*   *teeren$_\partial$wa kiy$_\partial$la*]
     child   self-DAT /(s)he-DAT-EMPH   /Ø-DAT   now   understand-PRES COMP
     kiwwa.
     said
     'The child$_i$ said that he$_i$ understood now.'

(12) [*taman$_i$ eyaam$_\partial$i / Ø iiye ræswiim$_\partial$t$_\partial$ giyaa*   *kiy$_\partial$la*]   *Siri kiwwa.*
     self /(s)he-EMPH /Ø$_i$ yesterday   meeting-DAT went QUOT Siri said
     'Siri$_i$ said that he$_i$ went to the meeting yesterday.'

(13) [*taman$_{i/j}$ /eyaam$_{i/j}$ / Ø$_{i/j}$ het$_\partial$ ræswiim$_\partial$t$_\partial$ yann$_\partial$ oon$_\partial$ kiy$_\partial$la*] *Nimal$_i$ Sirit$_\partial$j kiwwa.*
     self /(s)he-EMPH /Ø tomorrow meeting-DAT go must QUOT Nimal Siri-DAT said
     'Nimal told Siri that he (Nimal or Siri)[8] must go to the meeting tomorrow.'

In (10), the coindexing with Sita of the form in question cannot, of course, be considered a case of long-distance binding, since it is locally bound by an empty category *e$_i$* that is coindexed with *Siitat$_\partial$.* Also, it is not possible to test for the null (dative) pronoun in (10). The verb does not license it through the obligatory assignment of an NP bearing case and a θ-role, so that it is not possible to establish its existence and identify it.

Example (11) is particularly interesting, since the embedded verb requires a dative subject, and thus the location of the forms (including the null pronominal) within the tree structure is clear. Also, the lexical and pronominal forms may not be interchanged without producing a Principle C effect, as example (14) shows, thus establishing the dominance structure even more clearly. Example (14) is not possible with coreference but possible with outside reference:

(14) *tamani/ eyaai/ [lamǝyaṭǝi dæn teerenǝwa kiyǝla] kiwwa.
self /(s)he/ child-DAT now understand-PRES COMP said
*'Hei said that the childi understood now.'

Note that (13) also shows that *taman/tamun* is not necessarily subject oriented, even in long-distance binding situations.

It should also be noted that the occurrence of *eyaa* in sentences like (12) and (13), though possible, is awkward in normal Sinhala discourse, since the null pronoun is strongly preferred in intrasentential as well as extrasentential anaphora unless some reintroduction or reinforcement is involved (cf. example (1) above). This is not as true of the reflexive, which adds an increment of meaning and so does not appear redundant. Example (15), extending an example in Sumangala 1989a that illustrated only *taman*, is particularly interesting, since it illustrates both long-distance and local binding:

(15) *Kamal$_i$ kiwwa [Piyal$_j$ hituwa kiyǝla [Siri$_k$ tamanwǝ$_{i/j/k}$ /eyaawǝmǝ$_{i/j/k}$/ eyaawǝ$_{i/j/?k}$ /Ø$_{i/j/?k}$ kannaaḍiyen dækka kiyǝla]].*
Kamal said Piyal thought QUOT Siri self-ACC/ (s)he—ACC-EMPH/ (s)he-ACC/ Ø mirror-INSTR saw QUOT
'Kamal said that Piyal thought that Siri saw him(self) in the mirror.'[9]

As we would expect, and as the subscripts indicate, *eyaa*, without the reinforcement of *mǝ*, resists the local binding by *Siri*, and the null pronoun may not be bound locally but only long distance. Examples (16) and (17) show that an object null pronominal, like the other forms, can be long-distance bound by a higher subject when it is in object position in its own S.

(16) [[Ø$_{i/j}$ paare yanǝkoṭǝ] amma$_j$ tamanwǝ$_{i/?j}$/ eyaawǝmǝ$_{i/?j}$/ Ø$_{i/*j}$ dækka kiyǝla]
Banḍa$_i$ apǝṭǝ kiwwa.
Ø road-LOC go-when mother self-ACC/(s)he-ACC-EMPH Ø/ see-PAST COMP Banda we-DAT said
'Banda told us that (his) mother saw him when he (or she) was going on the road.'

(17) *gunǝpaalǝ$_i$ [poliisiyen$_j$ tamanṭǝ$_{i/?j}$ eyaaṭǝmǝ$_{i/*j}$/ Ø$_{i/*j}$ hariyǝṭǝ gæhuwa kiyǝla kiwwa.*
Gunapaala police-INSTR self-DAT/ (s)he-EMPH-DAT /Ø-DAT really hit COMP said.
'Gunapala said that the police really beat him.'

Note that in (16), the adverbial clause must also be bracketed with the complement clause unless it is taken to refer to the time of saying. Thus, in the reading in which its null subject is coindexed with Banda, it is also long-distance bound. (In the other reading, however, it is free, even if interpreted as coreferential with the mother, since there does not appear to be c-command, a situation that we will take up shortly.) The reading with the object of the complement clause coindexed with the lower subject is, of course, not possible with the null element, and coreference here is obviously unlikely on semantic grounds with the reflexive or the pronoun, even if *mə* is added. As we would expect, there are also numerous possibilities for combinations of the reflexive, pronoun, and null between the two embedded clauses, with varying degrees of naturalness, since the verb + *koṭə* 'when' combination of the adverbial clause also allows phonologically realized subjects. It is not possible or necessary to explore them here, however.

In example (17), the lower verb *gahanəwa* 'hit' requires a dative subject, Here, too, an internally reflexive reading is highly unlikely on semantic grounds and also is not possible with a singular pronoun. The subject of the lower clause could also be in the nominative case, but the instrumental is more natural with "corporate subjects" in Sinhala and does not affect the dominance structure or the coreference possibilities (see Gair 1991a for a discussion).

We have seen that all three of our anaphoric forms are subject to long-distance binding, but it is also the case that they may have non–c-commanding intersentential antecedents that thus do not bind them under the technical definition. Example (18) resembles the embedded portion of (16) and is possible with coreference between the subject NPs even if they are interchanged, as in (19), showing the lack of Principle C effects and hence of c-command[10]:

(18) [*eyaa /taman /Ø paare yanəkoṭə*] *amma Gunəpaaləwə dækka.*
     (s)he / self/ Ø road-LOC go-PRES-when mother Gunapaala-ACC saw.
     'Mother saw Gunapala when she (herself) was)going along the road.'

(19) [*amma   paare   yanəkoṭə*]   *eyaa /taman Gunəpaaləwə*ⱼ   *dækka.*
     mother   road-LOC   go-PRES-when   (s)he / self   Gunapaala-ACC   saw
     'Mother saw Gunapala when she (herself) was going along the road.'

Examples (20) and (21) are similar. They again show the anaphoric and lexical NPs interchanged, and again, the lack of principle C effects clearly shows that c-command is not involved, and the anaphoric forms are free. Note also that in (21), the case of the anaphoric forms is that required by the embedded verb *yanəwa* and not the dative assigned by the matrix predicator *oonə*, so that the location of the null pronominal can be determined as in the embedded S, as can its case. Examples (22) and (23) are interesting from another perspective, since the form *gaman* 'while', with a present tense relativizing form of the verb, requires coreference with the matrix subject, as the subscripts indicate, furnishing not only an unambiguous reading but also examples of the clear distinction between binding and obligatory coreference:

(20) [*taman*ᵢ */ eyaa*ᵢ */ Ø*ᵢ *yannə issella*] *Gunəpaaləṭə*ᵢ *kææmə kannə oonə.*
     self / (s)he / Ø go-INFIN before] Gunapaala-DAT food eat-INFIN want/need
     'Before going, Gunapala wants to eat.'

(21) [*Gunəpaalə*ᵢ   *yannə*   *issella*] *tamanṭə*ᵢ */ eyaaṭə*ᵢ */ Ø*ᵢ *kææmə kannə oonə.*
     Gunapaala-NOM go-INFIN before self-DAT/(s)he-DAT/Ø-DAT food
     eat-INFIN want/need
     'Before Gunapala goes, he wants to eat.'

(22) [taman$_{i *j}$ /eyaa$_{i *j}$ /   Ø$_{i *j}$ paare   yanə   gaman]Nimal$_i$ Siitawə$_j$
     self / (s)he /   Ø   road-LOC go-PRES-REL while Nimal Sita
     dækka.
     saw
     'Nimal$_i$ saw Sita$_j$ while he$_{i/*j}$ was going on the road.'

(23) [Nimal$_i$ paare   yanə   gaman] taman$_{i *j}$ /eyaa$_{i *j}$ /   Ø$_{i *j}$ Siitawə
     Nimal road-LOC go-PRES-REL while   self /(s)he   /Ø   Sita
     dækka.
     saw
     'While 'Nimal$_i$ was going on the road, he$_{i/*j}$ saw Sita$_j$.'

In (24), either the head or the genitive within the subject NP can antecede *taman* (*aadəree* takes a nominative subject and a dative object) though with *Taman* inter- pretation appears to be biased toward the head. As we would expect, with *eyaa* and *eyaamə*, the interpretation without *-mə* appears to be slanted toward the genitive Siri, and the null pronominal can be coindexed with the genitive but not the head:

(24) *Sirige$_i$ malli$_j$ tamuntə$_{?i/j}$ /eyaatə(mə)$_{i/j}$ / eyaatə$_{i/?j}$ /   Ø$_{i/*j}$*
     Siri-GEN   younger-brother-NOM self-DAT/(s)he-DAT(-EMPH) /   Ø-DAT
     aadəreyi.
     fond-PRED MARKER
     'Siri's younger brother is fond of him/ herself.'

In (25), the antecedent of *taman, eyaa,* or the null pronominal is within an NP that is the object of a postposition modifying a noun head that is in turn included in a postpositional phrase:

(25) [Gunəpaaləge$_i$ pawulə gænə wiswaasəyə nisaa]   taman$_i$/ eyaa$_i$ /Ø$_i$ karədəree
     Gunapala-GEN wife   about belief   because self/   (s)he/ Ø trouble-LOC
     wæṭuna.
     fell
     'Because of Gunapala's faith in his wife, he fell into trouble.'

In (26), however, the situation is reversed. *taman* and *eyaa*[11] not only occur within the NP, but they precede their antecedent, and coreference is still not only possible, but likely:

(26) [tamange$_i$/ eyaa(mə)ge$_i$ paulə gænə wiswaasəyə nisaa] Gunəpalə karədəree wæṭuna.
     self-GEN/ (s)he-GEN(-EMPH)/ wife about belief because Gunapala trouble-LOC fell
     'Because of Gunapala's faith in his wife, he fell into trouble.'

Note that in (26), the natural English translation is "his own," a point we will return to later.

In these examples without c-command, the referentially dependent forms are free by definition. However, there remains an interesting observation to be made about directionality in relation to intrasentential as opposed to intersentential discourse antecedence. Examples (12) through (21) illustrate backwards anaphora, and this is very common in subordinate structures in Sinhala, particularly with the null pronominal. However, the anaphora concerned cannot be equated with discourse anaphora, since the latter have strong, in fact virtually inviolable, forward directionality. Thus, (27) is possible, but (28) is highly unlikely at best:

(27) *gunəpaalə aawa. iiṭə passe eyaa wæḍə keruwa.*
    'Gunapala came. After that he(APH) worked.'

(28) **eyaa aawa. iiṭə passe gunəpaalə wæḍə keruwa.*

So far, we have simply assumed that the occurrences of a lexically unrealized NP, except possibly for the empty category symbolized as *e* in (10), represent the same element. For present purposes, there is no need to examine the full range of NPs in Sinhala, including traces of A movement and A-bar movement, but some discussion of control and the relation of the phonologically unrealized pronominal form(s) illustrated so far to controlled empty categories appears to be called for.

In Sinhala, overt nominals may occur as subjects of nonfinite verbal forms, such as infinitives, in a number of situations, one of which is illustrated in (29a) and (29b): The justification of the bracketing, by which the lexical NP is the subject of the lower clause, is provided by comparing (29a) with (29b) and noting that the case varies with the lower verb (*teerenəwa* 'understand' requires a dative subject):

(29) a. [*taatta heṭə   koləṁbə   iňdəla ennə*]   *puluwan.*
    father tomorrow Colombo-LOC from come-INFIN might
    'Father might come from Colombo tomorrow.'

    b. [*mee lamǝyaṭə   iiṭə   passe teerennə*]   *puluwan.*
    this child-DAT that-DAT after understand-INFIN might
    'This child might understand after that.'

Example (22) has provided an example of another situation of this kind, with an infinitival clause containing a lexical subject serving as object of the postposition *issella*.

However, when they are embedded under certain control predicates, sentences with the same nonfinite verbal forms require an empty category as subject, as in (30):

(30) *gunəpaalə*$_i$ $Ø_{i/ *j}$/*taman /*eyaa(mǝ))[12]   *hæmədaamə yannə kæmətii.*
    Gunapala-NOM$_i$ $Ø_{i/ *j}$/*self /*(s)he   every-day go-INF likes
    'Gunapala likes to go there every day.'

There thus appear to be two phonologically unrealized pronominals involved, one of which may alternate with lexical (i.e., phonologically realized) NPs and another of which may not. The first of these, with which we have been largely concerned, is a pronominal that we can henceforth designate, following common usage, as *pro*. The nature of the other is less clear. It resembles the ungoverned pronominal anaphor PRO (Chomsky 1982) that occurs controlled in nonfinite clauses in English and other languages, but the verbal forms with which it appears also allow lexical

NPs in noncontrol situations. There are several possible analyses here, such as an appeal to control theory (as in Huang 1989), so that a single phonologically null form would have different properties linked to different environments, but we need not settle the question here, since our concern is only with the "true" pronominal that may occur in governed and cased environments and hence in alternation with phonologically realized NPs.[13]

Both *pro* and *eyaa*, along with other lexical pronouns containing the discourse deictic element *ee-*, freely take extrasentential antecedents, as we would expect, as well as the intrasentential ones that have been exemplified here. We have also seen that *taman/tamun* may occur bound either locally or long distance as well as being coreferential with non–c-commanding forms within the sentence. The question then arises as to the possibility of its also having extrasentential (i.e., discourse) antecedents. It is indeed the case that when there is a possible antecedent in the sentence, whether c-commanding or not, and when the sentence is in isolation, there is an overwhelming tendency for *taman/tamun* to be linked with that antecedent in interpretation. This is particularly true in sentences in which *tamun* is locally c-commanded, as in (3) and (6), repeated here as (31) and (32), eliminating the other anaphoric forms:

(31) *gunəpaalə$_i$ tamunwə kannaaḍiyen dækka.*
Gunapala$_i$ self-ACC mirror-INSTR saw
'Gunapala saw himself in the mirror.'

(32) *gunəpaalə tamunge kaar-ekə vikka*
Gunapala self-GEN car-DEF sold
'Gunapala sold his(own) car.'

Even here, however, it is possible to force extrasentential antecedence, given a strong enough context, as for example in (33) and (34) (both of which, needless to say, have another reading):

(33) *Siita$_i$ ee kaaməreeṭə ætulunaamə hariyəṭə bayə unaa! mokədə,   horaa$_j$*
Sita that room-DAT enter-after really fright became. because(=why) thief
tamunwə$_{i/j}$ kannaaḍiyen dækka. eekay!
self-ACC mirror-INSTR saw.   That('s-why)

'Sita became really frightened when she entered the room! Because the thief saw her (specifically) in the mirror.'

(34) *taattaṭə$_i$ hoňdəṭəmə taraha giyaa! mokədə,   putaa$_j$ tamunge$_{i/j}$ kaar-ekə*
father really   anger went. because(=why), son   self-GEN car
kiyanne nætuwə vikka. eekay!
saying without sold. That('s-why)

'Dad really got mad! (His) son sold his (father's) own car without telling (him).'

It is thus clear that *taman/tamun* is not an anaphor in the narrow sense that requires that it must be bound in the local domain and not be free outside it. It is clearly different from *eyaa* in that it has a special increment of meaning that is difficult to define precisely but that ties it more closely to its antecedent. That is, it is reflexive in much the same way that English "own" in constructions like "one's own" is (though English lacks this form in argument positions), and this special sense limits the environments in which it may felicitously occur. This offers an interesting field for further study, but it clearly is very different from the structural cum coindexing relationships addressed by the binding theory.

However, *taman/tamun* has another property, commonly referred to as the "generic" use of anaphors, which is commonly associated with forms that are anaphors in the strict sense. In that usage, *taman/tamun* often appears paired, i.e., "self anteceded," as in (35):

(35) **taman** hambəkərəpu paḍi, **taman**   anunṭə   dennə   oonə næœ.
     self   earned-REL   salary self-DAT other-DAT give-INF need not
     'One does not have to give the salary one earns to others.'

However, even where not self-anteceded, *tamun* is required, or at least strongly preferred, where there is referential dependency on a generic form, as in (36). The pronoun *eyaa*, however, appears to require an antecedent to be referential in some sense yet to be precisely defined:[14] In example (36), the plural of *mangiya* 'traveler' is necessary for the generic sense. If it is read as specific, then the coreference with plural pronoun *eyaala* 'they' becomes available:

(36) *tamunge$_i$ / eyaalage(mə)$_j$ $_{?i}$ bas-ekə yanne kiiyəṭə də dænəgannə, manginṭə$_i$ booḍ-*
     ekə balannə puluwan.
     self's/ (s)he-PL bus go-FOC when QUES find-out-INF traveler-PL-DAT board-DEF
     look-INF can.
     'To find out when his bus is going, the traveler can look at the (sign)board.'

Thus the possible occurrence of these anaphoric forms is in part a function of the nature of the antecedent and the semantic nature of the linkage, not only of structure and (the form's own) category.

We may also recall here that *taman/tamun*, despite its reflexive character, is not strictly subject oriented. Thus in (37), although the first interpretation is the father, the son is also possible (and in fact, outside reference seems also to be possible, along the lines of (34) above):

(37) *taatta putaaṭə   tamange potə dunna.*
     father son-DAT self's   book gave
     'Father$_i$ gave the son$_j$ his$_{i/j}$ own book.'

Another characteristic of *taman/tamun*, which has not to our knowledge been heretofore noticed, sheds some light on its meaning vis-à-vis the other forms: namely its pairing with *anun* 'other' so as constitute a mutually defining set. The distribution of *anun* is essentially parallel to *taman/tamun*, but it is obligatorily disjoint in relation to some antecedent. This, and the mutually exclusive relation of *taman/tamun* and *anun*, was in fact illustrated in example (35). Similarly, (38a) may be compared with example (3), which is repeated here as (38b):

(38) a. ***gunəpaalə anunwə***   *kannaaḍiyen   dækka.*
Gunapalai other-ACC mirror-INSTR saw
'Gunapala saw another (i.e., someone else) in the mirror.'

b. ***gunəpaalə tamanwə*** *kannaaḍiyen   dækka.*
Gunapalai self-ACC mirror-INSTR saw
'Gunapala saw himself in the mirror.'

In (38a), the boldface does not, obviously, indicate coreference, but there is a kind of referential dependency in that *anunwə* clearly excludes Gunapala. This thus represents a kind of "inverse coindexing."

Furthermore, *anun* also functions as a generic form as in (39) and even as a self-antecedent as in (40). Note also that in (40), the two *anun*s are actually coreferential just like the two *tamun*s:

(39) *anunge   amma   dunnə   kææmə rasə næœ*
other-GEN mother give-PAST-REL food   tasty not.
'Food given by another's mother is not tasty.'

(40) ***tamunge**$_i$ deewal   **tamun**$_i$ tiyaagannə   oonə **anunge**$_{*i/j}$ deewal **anunṭə**$_{*i/j}$*
self-GEN thing-PL self   keep-INFIN must other-GEN things other-DAT
dennə oonə
give   must
'One must hold on to one's own things; one must give another's things to him (i.e., 'the other').'

These two forms are thus not only mutually exclusive in meaning but together form an exhaustive set. The contrast with *anun* suggests that the felicitous use of *taman/tamun* implies in the unmarked case the existence of other things or beings of the kind involved besides those in the scope of *taman/tamun*—in other words, that there is a complementary *anun* set, as well. This, then, helps to explain the "exclusive" sense often borne by *tamun*, as well as the stronger linkage with the antecedent implied by *tamun* in contrast with the lexical pronoun or *pro*. We might also note in passing that *anun* as a kind of antireflexive, and it shares that property with the antianaphor noted by Saxon (1984) in Dogrib. The inverse coindexing noted earlier also recalls the distinction made by Enç (1989), partly in relation to Saxon's work, between the binding and licensing of anaphoric forms. Unlike Saxon's antianaphor, however, *anun* does not behave like an anaphor with regard to binding domains but has a distribution similar to that of *tamun* with relation to the form with which it bears referential dependency. Furthermore, as we have seen, *anun* can be coindexed with itself in a strong way (i.e., it can be coreferential).

In summary, if the binding theory is looked upon as a exhaustive classification of nominal types, it has limited applicability in Sinhala. Neither the pronoun *eyaa* nor *taman/ tamun* (or *anun*) can be anaphors if that requires, under Principle A, that they not only can but *must* be bound in their local domain. On the other hand, they cannot be pronouns under principle B, since they can be bound in that domain. Of course, we could employ the device of considering *eyaa* to be a pronoun in argument positions within VP but a homonymous pronoun and anaphor when strengthened by *-mə*, but that would reduce the distinction to vacuity. It appears, however, that the overt pronoun and reflexive do not represent different nominal types defined under the binding theory but instead differ in their semantic properties, which in part make them sensitive to the referential properties of their antecedents and to the semantic content of the anaphoric linkage.

Nevertheless, it is not the case that the binding theory has no relevance here. Even under the view taken here that *eyaa* and *eyaamə* do not constitute pronoun and anaphor, respectively, their distribution in binding environments does show what we have referred to as "weak application of the binding principles."

Furthermore, the null pronoun *pro* is indeed a true pronoun under Principle B. The binding theory is thus fully applicable here if we regard it not as an exhaustive classification but as defining a set of domains relative to the possible or obligatory coindexing of anaphoric elements (in the broader sense) from which a language may choose to implement different combinations so as to evidence or not to evidence particular categories of such forms.

Sinhala lacks, then, either a lexical anaphor or an anaphor that must be bound outside of the local domain. It also lacks a lexical pronoun, if that means that it cannot be subject to local binding under principle B. It does have a phonetically unrealized pronoun *pro*. It also has an obligatorily phonologically empty element that appears under conditions involving both the verbal inflection of its own clause and the higher control predicate, though the identification of this element with PRO as usually conceived is not possible.[15] Binding theory also enters in a negative way by defining the domain in which a locally bound empty category cannot occur: the minimal S. One might say, somewhat paradoxically, that Principle A plays a role in licensing the nonoccurrence of an empty category. Thus, if the term "antianaphor" had not already been used in another way, we might use it here in a sense more in line with "antimatter," and say, somewhat paradoxically, that Sinhala, though it lacks a true anaphor, does have an "antianaphor," characterized by its nonoccurrence.

On Distinguishing AGR from *agr*: Evidence from South Asia

WITH KASHI WALI

In current linguistic theory, verb agreement has played an important role. Various interactions between agreement and other aspects of the grammar have been claimed, and agreement has been assigned crucial roles in the grammar going well beyond its traditional subject-identifying function. Within Government and Binding theory in particular (as represented in Chomsky 1982, 1986a, and 1986b), verb agreement in finite clauses has been identified with an AGR element within INFL(ection), governing and assigning case to the subject, with which it is coindexed. Thus, according to Chomsky:

> The agreement element of INFL is associated (we have assumed, co-indexed) with the subject, which it governs, since they share all maximal projections, and assigns it nominative case. (1986a: 188)

Given the crucial role played in turn by case in determining the possible occurrence of NPs and the nature and occurrence of empty categories, this function of AGR plays a central role in the grammar.

Despite the abstract nature of AGR and the properties attributed to it, there has been an implicit, if unstated, assumption in much if not all of the related literature that the relation between finite verb agreement and AGR is straightforward to the effect that finite verb agreement and AGR are congruent, with instances of verbal agreement representing AGR in a natural way. Thus, occurrences of the former could be taken without further justification to represent the latter.

However, within a single linguistic area (South Asia), and a single family within it (Indo-Aryan), agreement patterns are evidenced that call into question the easy assumption of congruence between verb agreement and AGR, particularly with regard to their role in case assignment. The languages we will be concerned with in this chapter are Hindi, Marathi, and Sinhala in its Colloquial and Literary varieties (the latter varieties differing sharply in their agreement patterns). Although these languages share a number of basic typological features, in addition to their genetic relationship, they span a wide variety of verbal agreement types in relation to both the strength of agreement and the nature of its connection with nominal arguments and their cases.

Using data from these languages, we argue that agreement is not a unitary phenomenon that can be presumed to represent the AGR element without justification but that at least one other type must be recognized: an anaphoric-type agreement that we designate as (small) *agr,* We also argue, on the basis of this evidence, that a single language may exhibit one, both, or possibly neither of these agreement types and that the existence of AGR is not necessarily linked to surface agreement. Throughout, we will assume a basic sentence tree of the kind shown in (1) as in Chomsky 1986a and 1986b, but adjusting for the verb-final character of the languages here. As far as we can determine, however, our arguments would not be seriously affected if any of the other tree structures proposed within recent theory were adopted.

(1)

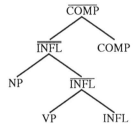

Colloquial Sinhala

Sinhala is a diglossic language with sharply distinct spoken and written varieties (Gair 1968, 1986a; De Silva 1973 and references therein). Among the features that distinguish these varieties, case marking and agreement play central roles and have been claimed to be the crucial distinguishing features (Gair 1968). From the perspective of current theory, these features become especially interesting, since these two aspects of the grammar are now linked through AGR.

Colloquial Sinhala exhibits no verbal agreement,[1] with a single verb form (within any given tense–mode combination) serving for all numbers, genders, and persons as illustrated in (2):

(2) *mamə/ oyaa/ eyaa/ api/ oyaala/ eyaala pansələtə   yanəwa.*
    I   / you/ (s)he/ we/ you-PL/ they   temple-DAT go-PRES
   'I   / you/ (s)he/ we/ you-all/   they go to the temple.'

mamə/ oyaa/ eyaa/ api/ oyaala/ eyaala pansələțə   giyɑa.
I   / you/ (s)he/ we/ you-PL/ they   temple-DAT go-PAST
'I   / you/ s)he/ we/ you-all/   they went to the temple.'

It is, in fact reasonable to claim that AGR plays no role in Sinhala, to the extent that there is no element within INFL that plays its subject case–assigning role.[2] This is currently an area of active research, but suffice it to mention here that there is a cluster of properties that can support such a conclusion. Subject case assignment is intimately linked with thematic role, and subjects, or perhaps more suitably "external arguments (Williams 1980, 1981), may be in any one of several cases, including nominative (or "direct"), accusative, and dative (see Gair 1970, 1976, 1991b for details).

Colloquial Sinhala has no passive, properly speaking. In fact there are no moving to subject (or argument externalization) operations that do not retain the original case of the moved element.

Sinhala is a language of the "super pro-drop" type—not only subjects but also objects and other arguments may be null. It also has finite transitive sentences without overt subjects but with "arbitrary agent" readings. These, as illustrated by (3a) and (3b), are true transitives in that the verbs are never used intransitively (unlike, say, English "grow" and "close"). They are the discourse-functional equivalent of passives or English "Arbitrary they" sentences, but Sinhala has no lexical equivalent of English "they" in that function. Note that they contrast with otherwise identical sentences with referential NPs or null pronouns (*pro*), as in examples (3c) and (3d):

(3)   a. *mee pætte huñgak wii wawənəwa.*
        this area   much   rice grow (TRANS)-PRES
        'A lot of rice is grown in this area.' (They grow a lot of rice in this area.)

      b. *kantooruwə wahanne   hatərəțə.*
         office   close-PRES-EMPH four-DAT
         'It's at four that they close the office.' (It's at four that the office closes.)

      c. *api/ Ø mee pætte huñgak wii wawənəwa.*
         we/ Ø this area   much   rice grow (TRANS)-PRES
         'We pro grow(s) a lot of rice in this area.'

      d. *lipikaruwo/ Ø kantooruwə wahanne   hatərəțə.*
         clerks/   Ø office   close-PRES-EMPH four-DAT
         'It's at four that the clerks/ pro close(s) the office.'

Sentences like those in examples (3a) and (3b) thus appear to afford clear instances of *pro*$_{ARB}$, since the empty categories with arbitrary reading occur in a position in which lexical NPs and referential null pronominals (*pro*) may also occur. Taken in conjunction with the other properties mentioned, a natural explanation for these instances suggests itself: the lack of AGR within INFL (or, at the least, the lack of a strong AGR with specific features to be discharged through coindexing) allows the occurrence of "featureless" governed null arguments, namely, *pro*$_{ARB}$.[3] In any event, this is a subject of current research, and we cannot not further pursue it here along with the other characteristics mentioned and the possible mechanisms by which external argument case is assigned, but we will deal with them elsewhere (Gair 1991b and the Diglossia and AGR chapter). For present purposes, we need only note that it is more than reasonable to consider that AGR plays no role in spoken Sinhala.

Literary Sinhala

Literary Sinhala, unlike Colloquial Sinhala, shows rich agreement in person, number, and gender,[4] as illustrated in example (4):

(4)   a. *mama gamaṭa   yami.*
         I   village-DAT   go PRES 1 Sg
         'I go to the village.'

     b. *hē gamaṭa   yayi.*
         he   village-DAT   go PRES 3 Sg
         'He goes to the village.'

     c. *ovuhu gamaṭa   yati.*
         they   village-DAT   go PRES 3 Pl
         'They go to the village.'

     d. *otomō gamaṭa   giyāya.*
         She   village-DAT   go PAST 3 Sg Fem
         'She went to the village.'

     e. *hē gamaṭa   giyēya.*
         he   village-DAT   go PAST 3 Sg Masc
         'He went to the village.'

Literary Sinhala nominals inflect for two numbers (singular and plural), definiteness (definite and indefinite), and six cases (nominative, accusative, dative, genitive, instrumental-ablative, and vocative). For present purposes, we need only note the nominative–accusative distinction as shown in table 10–1.

There is an intimate relation between case and AGR in Literary Sinhala, which has been formulated as the "accusative rule":

> A nominal which is in construction with an agreeing finite verb form will be in the nominative case. Otherwise, it will be in the accusative, unless it is in some other case required by the construction. (Gair 1992a: 244)

Table 10–1 Number and Definiteness in Nominative and Accusative

	Singular Definite	Singular Indefinite	Plural
Nominative	*minisā*	*minisek*	*minissu*
Accusative	*minisā*	*minisaku*	*minisun*

The sentences in example (4) have illustrated the occurrence of nominative with agreement. The occurrence of accusative on nonagreeing subjects is illustrated in (5), with past and present tense relative expressions, which are preposed in Sinhala as in (5a) and (5b), and an adverbial clause as in (5c):

(5) a. *mā   yana   gama.*
       I-ACC go-PRES-REL village
       'The village that I go to.'

     b. *mā   giya   gama.*
       I-ACC go-PAST-REL village
       'The village that I went to.'

     c. *goviyan   kumburu   væpuruvahot   (mænavī).*
       farmers-ACC   paddy-fields   sow-PAST COND   (good)
       '(It would be good) if the farmers were to sow the fields.'

Particularly interesting in this respect are Literary Sinhala focused or cleft sentences. These make use of a separate tensed form of the verb, referred to as the FO-CUSING form (FOC).[5] Although this is an independent sentence type, the FOC verb form does not show agreement, so its subject is in the accusative, as in (6).[6] Note that in (6c), both NPs are in the accusative, the first as nonagreeing subject, the second as object:

(6) a. *ovun   yannē   gamaṭa   ya.*
       they-ACC go-PRES-FOC   village-DAT AGR
       'It is to the village that they are going.'

     b. *ovun   giyē   gamaṭa   ya.*
       they-ACC go-PAST-FOC   village-DAT AGR
       'It was to the village that they went.'

     c. *kumārayan   dækkē   kumāriyan   ya.*
       princes-ACC   saw-FOC   princesses-ACC AGR
       'It was the princesses that the princes saw.'

Note that both the relative and the FOC forms of verbs *are* tensed, but neither shows agreement. This is a crucial observation, since it clearly shows the connection of nominative case assignment with agreement rather than tense.[7]

Literary Sinhala, unlike Colloquial, does have a passive, in which the subject agrees and is in the nominative case, as in (7). (The verb *læbenava* ' be obtained' serves as passive auxiliary):

(7) *(apa visin) lāŋkikayō   koṭas   kihipayakaṭa bedanu læbeti.*
     (us by)   Sri-Lankans-NOM   groups several-DAT divided Auxiliary-PRES-3PL
     'Sri Lankans are divided (by us) into several groups'.

Translated into the current frame of reference, the Literary Sinhala nominative is a structurally assigned case, assigned under government by AGR. It is also clear that the accusative, in addition to surfacing on NPs that are assigned structural accusative by the verb, serves as the default case, or the one in which the nominal must appear if it does not satisfy the agreement requirement for nominative. The phrase "case required by the construction" in the accusative rule covers lexically assigned inherent case.

In sum, in contrast to Colloquial Sinhala, Literary Sinhala exhibits "well-behaved" or "classic" AGR, in which nominative case–assigning properties and verbal agreement are intimately linked.

Hindi

Hindi exhibits quite different agreement properties The language is by now well known to exhibit a kind of aspect-conditioned "split ergativity," such that both subject case marking and agreement vary between the imperfect and the perfect. There are a number of associated complexities that we have dealt with elsewhere (Gair and Wali 1987), but here are the essential facts.

Intransitive verbs, in both the perfective and the imperfective, agree with their subject, as in (8):

(8) a. *Raam   baiṭh-taa   hai.*
         Ram   sit-IMPF   AUX
         MASC   MASC   3SG
         'Ram sits/is sitting.'

     b. *Raam   baiṭh-aa   thaa.*
         Ram   sit-PERF   AUX
         MASC   MASC   MASC
         'Ram was sitting.'

In the unmarked instance, subjects of intransitives are in a case commonly referred to as DIRECT. This is one term in a two-term inflectional case system (ignoring a vocative) in which the other term is the OBLIQUE. Oblique case is induced by postpositions, which in turn commonly mark case relations, such as *me* 'locative', *se* 'instrumental-ablative', and *ko* 'dative' or 'accusative'. Thus we find *larkaa* 'boy'(direct) but *larke ko* 'boy-DAT' (oblique + case postposition). In what follows, we will refer to all noun phrases in which the head is not in the direct case collectively as OBLIQUE NPs.

Subjects of transitive verbs in the imperfective are in the direct case, and the verb agrees with the subject as in (9a). In the perfective, however, virtually all transitive verbs take subjects with the postposition *ne*, often referred to as ERGATIVE (ERG), a usage we shall adopt here. This is exemplified in (9b):

(9) a. *Larkaa   kitaab   paṛh-taa   hai.*
         boy   book   read-IMPF AUX
         MASC   FEM   MASC, SG 3SG
         'The boy reads the book.'

b. *Larke   ne   kitaab parh-ii.*
   boy   ERG   book   read-PERF
   MASC   FEM   FEM, SG
   'The boy read the book.'

When the subject is ERG-marked, agreement depends on the case marking of the object. The object of a Hindi transitive verb may be in the direct case as in (9a) and (9b) or in the oblique case followed by the postposition *ko* as in (10a) and (10b). The occurrence of *ko* is conditioned by animacy and definiteness, under conditions that are difficult to specify, but crucially there is no aspect-linked variation in case within VP:

(10) a. *Larkaa Sitaa ko   dekh-taa   hai.*
         boy   Sitaa ko   look-IMPF AUX
         MASC   FEM   MASC SG   3SG
         'The boy looks at Sita.'

      b. *Larkiyō   ne   Sitaa ko dekh-aa.*
         Girls   ERG   Sitaa ko look-PERF
         FEM   FEM   MASC   SG
         'The girls looked at Sita.'

A verb never agrees with a *ne*-marked subject. If the subject is *ne*-marked, and thus oblique, the verb will agree with the object if it is in the direct case. If the object is *ko*-marked, and thus oblique, however, the verb takes a default form third masculine singular -(*y*)*aa*. This was exemplified in (9b) and (10b). In (9b), the subject is *ne*-marked, and the object is in direct case, so that the verb agrees with it. In (10b), however, the object is also oblique, and the verb is in the default third masculine singular.[8]

Hindi also has verbs whose subjects appear with dative *ko* as in (11). Clearly this is a lexical property of these verbs.[9] Like intransitives, dative subject sentences show no case or agreement variation with aspect as shown in (11a) and (11b). In both, the agreement is with the direct case object nominal *kitaab*:

(11) a. *Raam ko apnii kitaab acchii lagtii   hai.*
         Ram ko self's book   good   appear-IMPF AUX
                 FEM   FEM   FEM   FEM   3SG
         'Ram's book appears good to him.'

      b. *Raam ko apnii kitaab acchii lagii.*
         Ram ko self's book   good   appear-PERF
                 FEM   FEM   FEM   FEM
         'Ram's book appeared good to him'.

Thus the agreement pattern for dative subject verbs in both imperfective and perfective is similar to that of the perfective transitive verbs with *ne* subjects and direct case objects.

There are a number of additional complexities involving double-object verbs, verbs inducing special case marking, and so on that we have dealt with elsewhere (Gair and Wali 1987), but the basic points to be noted are:

1. Agreement is always with a direct case nominal within the minimal IP (=S).
2. The agreement-controlling nominal will be an argument of the verb, included in its theta-grid. However, that nominal may be the trace of an NP in an A-bar position (as, for example, in topicalization).
3. The agreement-controlling NP always c-commands the verbal forms that show agreement.[10]
4. If there is more than one c-commanding NP within IP, agreement is with the one highest NP in the tree, which we refer to as the "maximally c-commanding NP."[11]

We have thus proposed, and argued for elsewhere in some detail (Gair and Wali 1988), an agreement element *agr* for Hindi. This element occurs linked to specific verbal inflectional categories, aspect and tense (the latter a category relevant only to the auxiliary in Hindi). In Hindi, *agr* has the fundamental properties of an anaphor, in the narrow sense of that term within GB theory. That is, it is coindexed with a c-commanding antecedent within a specific domain, in this case IP. Coindexing takes place at S-structure after surface case realization.

In this context, we should also note here that agreement need not be limited to a single verb form but will apply to all forms in specifiable verbal sequences, including verb plus auxiliary sequences. This detail need not concern us here, but it is exemplified in (12) in which all verbal forms within the brackets that are susceptible to agreement agree in the relevant categories. The general rule here is that agreement will surface on all verbal forms associated with *agr,* that is, all those showing aspect or tense:

(12) *vah* [*likh-tii   cal-ii   jaa   rah-ii   hai*].
    she write   move   go   stay   AUX
          IMPF   PERF   STEM PERF   PRES
          FEM SG FEM SG   FEM SG 3SG
    'She is continuing to write.'

Note that the *agr* element cannot be AGR, since it lacks its subject-defining and case-assigning properties. Recall also that there is no variation of object case marking with aspect within VP, so that it is not the case that AGR simply shifts its case-assigning properties with aspect in some way. Also, among the properties that have been claimed for AGR is the determination of binding domains (as for example in George and Kornfilt 1981; Harbert 1987). Without assessing the validity of this claim here, we may note that there is no difference in binding domains associated with subject-controlled, object-controlled, or default *agr.* Nor is there any difference in the pro-drop properties, which have also been widely claimed to be associated with the nature of AGR.

The question then naturally arises whether Hindi does have any element within INFL that shows the case-assigning (and possibly domain-defining) properties of AGR. The answer appears to be that it does. In Hindi, ERG-marked NPs occur only as subject within finite Ss, and, as we have seen, alternate with the nominative in that position depending on transitivity and aspect. Thus, both ERG-marked and nominative NPs in that position represent structural nominative as assigned by an element within INFL. Also, the same element within INFL appears to play a role in defining binding domains (for details concerning Hindi, see Harbert and Srivastav 1988). Thus, Hindi INFL includes an element with the properties of AGR except for surfacing as agreement. Given the fundamentally abstract nature of this element, we can, without undue irony, continue to refer to it as AGR, even when it is not linked to agreement.

Marathi

Marathi affords data that is crucial in this respect, as well as to our general argument, since it shows two types of agreement. These may appear in the same sentence but under different conditions, so that the features they exhibit may diverge. One is the same sort of *agr* agreement as in Hindi, with only minor differences of detail. The other is directly related to structural case assignment, as evidenced in surface case, and thus represents AGR. Although the latter is limited in the categories it expresses, it is not significantly more so than English AGR.

In Marathi, there is agreement that varies with transitivity and aspect; that is, *agr* operates under the same conditions as in Hindi, as illustrated in (13) and (14). Examples (13a) and (13b) are imperfective and imperfective intransitive; examples (14a) and (14b) are imperfective and perfective transitive. Marathi *ni* is ERG, like Hindi *ne,* and as in the parallel Hindi sentences, (9a) and (9b), agreement is with the subject in (13a), but the object in (13b):

(13) a. *Ravi   dhaav-t-o.*
      Ravi   run-IMPF-*agr*(eement)
      MASC MASC, 3 Sg
      'Ravi runs.'

   b. *Ravi   dhaav-l-aa.*
      Ravi   ran-PERF-*agr*
      MASC MASC, 3 Sg
      'Ravi ran.'

(14) a. *Ravi   kavitaa vaac-t-o.*
      Ravi   poem   read
      MASC FEM   IMPF MASC 3Sg
      'Ravi reads a poem.'

   b. *Ravi-ni   kavitaa vaac-l-i.*
      Ravi-ERG poem   read-PERF-*agr*
      MASC   FEM   FEM 3Sg
      'Ravi read the poem.'

The Marathi equivalent of Hindi *ko* is -*la,* which occurs on objects under essentially the same conditions and, like it, is identical with the dative. In (15), the object is -*la* marked, and the agreement is default neuter singular:[12]

(15) *Ravi-ni   kavitaa vaac-l-i.*
  Ravi-ERG poem   read-PERF-*agr*
  MASC   FEM   FEM 3Sg
  'Ravi read the poem.'

Hindi and Marathi thus share *agr*-type agreement in all essential respects. Marathi, however, exhibits an additional type of agreement not found in Hindi, specifically, an agreement affix (clitic?) appearing invariantly as *-s* and restricted to second person singular. This -S element, as we shall refer to it, occurs with both the perfective and the imperfective. It always occurs at the end of the verbal complex, thus attaching itself either to the auxiliary or to the final verb if there is no auxiliary. Intransitive examples are given in (16):

(16) a. *tu   jaat   aahe-s.*
      you   go-IMPF AUX-S
      MASC   MASC SG-2Sg
      'You (Masculine Reference) are going.'

  b. *tu   jaat-o-s.*
     you   go-IMPF-*agr*-S
     MASC MASC-2Sg
     'You(Masculine Reference)go.'

  c. *tu   ge-l-aa-s.*
     you   go-PERF-*agr*-S
     MASC MASC-2Sg
     'You (Masculine Reference)went.'

In (17), a transitive imperfective sentence, both *agr* and -S agreement are, not surprisingly, subject controlled:

(17) *tu   kavitaa vaac-t-o.-s*
   you   poem   read
   MASC FEM   IMPF -*agr*-S
                   MASC-2Sg
   'You (Masculine Reference) read a poem.'

The crucial example, however, is its transitive perfective counterpart (18a). There *agr* is to the object, as expected, but the subject controlled -S still appears. Similarly, in (18b), *agr* is plural, in agreement with the object, but the singular -S agreement also appears. Thus *agr* and -S have split with regard to their controllers:

(18) a. *tu   kavitaa   vaac-l-i.-s.*
       you-ERG poem   read -*agr* -S
       MASC   FEM PERF FEM,-2Sg
                   SG
       'You(Masculine Reference) read the poem.'

b. *tu   aambe   khaall-e   aahe-s.*
   you   mangoes eat-PERF-*agr* AUX-*agr* -S
        PL   PL   PL-2Sg
   'You have eaten mangoes.'

At this point, it is necessary to consider some peculiarities of Marathi nominal morphology. In Marathi, as in Hindi, the nominative/ERG distinction is usually overtly marked. In Marathi, however, these distinctions are not spelled out phonologically in the first and second person pronouns, so that they appear as *mi* and *tu* in both categories. This has caused some misunderstanding. For example, Comrie (1984, 1985) argued that it was necessary to invoke grammatical relations rather than case marking alone in accounting for Marathi (and by extension Hindi) agreement since there was object agreement in perfective sentences with first or second person subjects even though the subject was "nominative." There is no reason to assume, however, that even surface case distinctions must universally find phonological spellout. Marathi sentences with ERG first and second person subjects have all the agreement and other characteristics of parallel sentences with subjects in other persons. The only fundamental difference between (18a) and the third person (19) is the lack of overt ERG (*-ni*) marking in (19) (and, of course, the occurrence of -S):

(19) *tyaani   kavitaa vaac-l-ii.*
     he-ERG   poˑm   read-*agr*
     MASC   FEM   PERF FEM
                       3Sg
     'He read the poem'

The simplest conclusion is that Marathi ERG and nominative forms are homonymous in the first and second person, and there is nothing more exotic about that than about English "her" vis-à-vis "him" and "his."

Note, now, that in all cases discussed, the -S agreement is with the subject—the external argument—regardless of its surface case. That is, it is with the NP that INFL would govern and assign structural nominative case under the reasonable assumption that the phrase structure for both perfective and imperfective sentences are as represented in (1). This in turn leads to the conclusion that -S agreement represents the AGR element in INFL. Surface case does not block agreement simply because the relevant condition involves nominative *structural* case, surfacing as either direct or ERG under specified conditions.

Again, as with Hindi, there are some additional complexities and problems involving passives, dative subject and ditransitive verbs, and embedded structures that we have addressed at length elsewhere (Gair and Wali 1987) and cannot deal with here, but it is clear that Marathi thus has both *agr* (on verb forms)[13] and AGR in INFL. Unlike in Hindi, however, both of these can surface as overt verbal agreement.

Marwari

At least one other Indo-Aryan language, Marwari, a dialect of Rajasthani, appears to exhibit a similar split agreement. In Marwari transitive present perfective sentences, the main (perfective) verb agrees with the object, as in Hindi and Marathi, although the accusative postposition (*ne* = Hindi *ko,* Marathi *la*) does not block agreement. The tensed present auxiliary, however, agrees with the subject. This is illustrated in (20) (from Magier 1983; transcription and gloss are converted to our pattern):

(20) *mhāī siitaa-ne dekhii   hūū*
    I   Sita-obj saw-PERF Aux-PRES
             FEM   FEM   1 SG
    'I saw Sita.'

We have not analyzed Marwari in detail, and there are a number of complications regarding case marking, tense-agreement interactions, and so on, so that we have not included it among our primary exemplary languages here. However, it does appear to represent another surfacing of AGR and *agr*, with the former clearly linked with INFL.

Conclusion

Our survey of this small sample of related languages has thus revealed an instance of verbal agreement representing "classic" AGR within INFL having case-assigning properties (Literary Sinhala). It has also found verbal agreement with anaphoric properties (*agr*) not linked to AGR coexisting with "nonagreement AGR"—an element with the functional properties of AGR but not linked to agreement (Hindi). We have also found an instance of "split" verbal agreement, with coexistent agreement patterns separately representing *agr* and AGR (Marathi), and a language in which AGR can be convincingly argued not to exist, or virtually equivalently, to lack both agreement and the functions generally attributed to AGR. The distribution of these characteristics is shown in feature form in table 10–2. This clearly suggests parameter-

Table 10–2   Agreement Patterns in Some South Asian Languages

Distribution of AGR and agr	*Hindi*	*Marathi*	*Literary Sinhala*	*Spoken Sinhala*
AGR				
+Agreement		+	+	–
–Agreement	+			
agr (always agreement)	+	+	–	–

ization, but we are hesitant to claim it at this point until we further explore the wider consequences of each setting in detail and include a wider range of languages.

The types and combinations of agreement that we have investigated here are sufficient to sustain our original statement that verbal agreement cannot be straightforwardly identified with AGR, but they certainly do not exhaust the possibilities. For example, the "anaphoric" object agreement described in Bresnan and Mchombo 1987 (where "anaphoric" has been used in a sense different from that in which we have used it in here) appears to represent still another type, and there are others to be found in the literature and undoubtedly in the field that do not fit our schema. This is a fertile area of research, with important implications for both the treatment of individual languages and the theory of Universal Grammar. We hope that our survey will make some small contribution to such an enriched and principled typology of agreement.

IV

CHANGE,
GRAMMATICIZATION,
AND LINGUISTIC AREA

Sinhala Focused Sentences:
Naturalization of a Calque

This paper was given at the Second International Conference on South Asian Languages and Linguistics held at Hyderabad in January 1980, and it appeared in Krishnamurti, Masica, and Sinha, eds. (1986), which consisted largely of papers from that conference. Subsequent work, particularly involving increased information on other languages, has shown that some of the statements made here in the historical or comparative sections required expansion or emendation, and the most important of these have been noted here in added or expanded notes and indicated as "later note." However, the description of the construction and the account of its historical development still appear to be correct in almost all particulars, and the paper also stands as an attempt at integrating principled description with internally motivated syntactic change and areal effects, so that it appeared worthy of inclusion here.

$\mathbf{S}$inhala, an Indo-Aryan language long in contact with South Dravidian languages, has a focusing construction that plays a highly visible role in its grammar.[1] Under names such as "emphatic sentences," "cleft sentences," or "focused sentences," it has been analyzed in various ways in syntactic studies (as in Gair 1970; Fernando 1973; De Abrew 1980), but its distinguishing characteristics are a special or emphatic tensed form of the verb (-EMPH),[2] commonly, though not invariably, accompanied by rightward placement of the focused constituent, as in the following:

(S1) *mamə giyee   gaməṭə.*
I   go-PAST-EMPH village-DAT
'It was to the village that I went.'

(S2) *gunəpaalə kəranne   monəwa də?*
Gunapala do-PRES-EMPH what   Q
'What does Gunapala do?'

These bear an unmistakable resemblance, in both form and meaning, to constructions in several Dravidian languages utilizing a nominal form of the verb as described for Tamil and Malayalam (Lindholm 1972), Telugu (Krishnamurti 1974), and Kannada (Schiffman 1979) and exemplified by the following from (Jaffna) Tamil:[3]

(T1) *naan poonatu*   *yaaLppaaNattukku.*
      I   go-PAST-NOM Jaffna-DAT
      'It was to Jaffna that I went.'

(T2) *cuppiramaniyam ceyyiRatu*   *enna?*
      Subramaniyam   do-PRES-NOM what
      'What is it that Subramaniyam does?'

One obvious difference between Sinhala and the others lies in the verb form. In the Dravidian languages mentioned, it is a nominal form derived from an attributive (relative-forming) participle by adding person-number endings (characteristically third person inanimate neuter), and it also functions as an action nominal in nominalized clauses (i.e., *mani pooRatu* 'Mani's going'). In current Colloquial Sinhala, however, the emphatic form has another use outside of focused sentences; it is the form regularly occurring before *næœ,* the usual negative in verbal sentences:[4]

(S3) *mamə yanne*   *næœ.*
      I   go-PRES-EMPH *næœ*
      'I don't go.'

It is difficult to subsume these two uses under any single syntactic rule, and syntactic studies have not done so as far as I know, so that we may ignore the use before *næœ* for present purposes.

The Sinhala emphatic form is thus not a clearly nominal form at present. However, though its origin is not entirely clear (contrast Paranavitana 1956: clviii with Geiger 1938: 134–35), it is probably derived from a form used as an attributive participle through the addition of a third person masculine/neuter ending. Hence the resemblance to Dravidian languages would have been even clearer at an earlier stage (and the affix does in fact retain some of that person-number character in Literary Sinhala).

The Dravidian focused sentences cannot easily be regarded as ordinary nominal equational sentences, despite the obvious resemblance, for reasons set forth clearly by Lindholm (1972). The most important distinction is the variety of kinds of constituents and case markings that can occur in focused position. The same reasoning holds for Sinhala, and since the verbal form lacks the nominal uses of the Dravidian ones, the difference is even greater. However, the resemblance between focused and nominal equational sentences does appear to play a part in the history of the construction, as we shall see.

The close resemblance of the Sinhala and Dravidian constructions, taken with the apparent lack of such forms in Indo-Aryan languages, strongly suggests a Dravidian model, or at the least Dravidian influence on Sinhala. Equally interesting, however, is the way Sinhala developed and elaborated the construction once it was acquired, so that it achieved prominence in the grammar, interacting in an intricate way with several other grammatical processes. This chapter will concern itself with the general outlines of that development, largely as they are revealed by a comparison of Sinhala with the Dravidian languages mentioned. But before I describe that development, I must characterize its end product: the current Sinhala focusing system.

Characteristics of Sinhala Focused Sentences

In recent syntactic studies, Sinhala focus has been treated either as the result of a transformation (as in Gair 1970; De Abrew 1980) or as derived from a complex deep structure plus appropriate transformations (Fernando 1973). For present purposes, however, it is sufficient to restrict ourselves to surface structure characteristics. We will also not deal with the semantics of focus, reserving that for later treatment, except to say that the focused constituent is usually a "focus of contrast" in Chafe's sense (1976: 37–38). We will thus deal with focus only as a syntactic phenomenon and initially restrict ourselves to sentences with a verbal predicator.

There are six relevant interrelated basic characteristics of Sinhala focused sentences. First, if the focus is any form other than the verb or some stretch including the verb, the verb will be marked with EMPH.[5] In the following sentences, the focus is in boldface:

(S4) *laŋkaawe   di   mamə yanne   ee   **gamətə.***
Sri Lanka-GEN while I   go-PRES-EMPH that village-DAT
'It is to that village that I go while in Sri Lanka.'

(S5) *laŋkaawe   di   ee   gamətə   yanne   **mamə.***
Sri Lanka-GEN while that village-DAT go-PRES-EMPH I
'It is I who go to that village while in Sri Lanka.'

(S6) *mamə ee   gamətə   yanne   **laŋkaawe di.***
I   that village-DAT go-PRES-EMPH Sri Lanka-GEN-while
'It is while in Sri Lanka that I go to that village.'

Second, the focused element is commonly placed after the verb (Sinhala is an SOV language), but not invariably so, as in the following examples:

(S7) *mamə ee   **gamətə**   yanne.*
I   that village-DAT go-PRES-EMPH
'It is to that village that I go.'

(S8) *kohaatə   **də yanne?***
where-DAT Q go-PRES-EMPH
'Where are you going?'

The focused element in sentences such as (S7) may be additionally marked by prominence in intonation and/or by one of the focus-marking forms to be discussed below. The factors determining whether or not rightward placement occurs are not yet clear, but they appear to include not only "information packaging" but also more purely surface considerations. For example, there appears to be a "naked verb constraint,"[6] or a reluctance to place the focused constituent rightward if the verb will be in leftmost position as a result. Thus (S8) and (S9) seem preferable to (S10), though (S10) is certainly grammatical:

(S9) *dæn yanne*   ***kohaaṭə də?***
       now go-PRES-EMPH where   Q
       'Where are you going?'

(S10) *yanne*   ***kohaaṭə   də?***
        go-PRES-EMPH where-DAT Q
        'Where are you going?'

Third, there is a set of focus-marking forms including *yi*, *tamaa*, and *tamay* (emphatics) and *lu* 'it seems, it is said' (cf. Tamil *aam*), that may only occur on the focus. It thus follows from the first characteristic that when they follow any constituent other than the verb, the verb will be marked with EMPH, as in example (S11):

(S11) ***eyaa tamay*** *gaməṭə*   *yanne.*
        he   *tamay* village-DAT go-PRES-EMPH
        'He is indeed the one who goes to the village.'

but not as in example (S12):

(S12) ****eyaa tamay*** *gaməṭə*   *yanəwa.*
        he   *tamay* village-DAT go-PRES-SIMPLE[7]

Note, however, that while these forms, when they do occur, can only occur on the focus, it is not necessary for them to occur for the sentence to be focused. See, for example, (Sl) and (S4) through (S7), in comparison with (S11) or (S13) through (S14):

(S13) *mamə yanne*   ***ee gaməṭə***   *tamay.*
        I   go-PRES-EMPH that village-DAT *tamay*
        It is to that village that I go.'

(S14) *eyaa yanne*   ***ee gaməṭə***   *lu.*
        he   go-PRES-EMPH that village-DAT it-seems
        'They say it is to that village that he goes.'

As we would expect from the second characteristic, variant orders are possible for all of these.

Thus, and most importantly, focus may be defined syntactically as the substring with which one of these forms either occurs or may occur without other structural change occurring. For example, a focus-marking form could be added to the focus in (S4) and (S5) without a change in the verb form or any other change being required.[8]

Fourth, the question marker *də* (referred to hereafter as Q), is regularly used in yes–no questions and is a focus-marking form in the sense of the third characteristic:

(S15) *gunəpaalə gaməṭə   də yanne?*
      Gunapala village-DAT Q go-PRES-EMPH
      'Is it to the village that Gunapala is going?'

(S16) *gaməṭə   yanne   gunəpaalə də?*
      village-DAT go-PRES-EMPH Gunapala Q
      'Is it Gunapala who is going to the village?'

Compare (S17), a neutral yes–no question where the focus is not on a form other than the verb:

(S17) *gunəpaalə gaməṭə   yanəva   də?*
      Gunapala village-DAT go-PRES-SIMPLE Q
      'Is Gunapala going to the village?'

This is what we would expect from the first characteristic as stated, and the other focus-marking forms may similarly occur following the verb, as in (S18):

(S18) *gunəpaalə gaməṭə   yanəva   lu.*
      Gunapala village-DAT go-PRES-SIMPLE it-seems.
      'They say Gunapala is going to the village.'

Fifth, there are two main[9] negative forms in independent sentences: *nææ,* which has been mentioned earlier as the usual negator in verbal sentences, and *nowey* (with dialectal variants that include *nemey, newi*), as exemplified in (S3), (S19), and (S20):[10]

(S19) *gunəpaalə gaməṭə   giyee   nææ.*
      Gunapala village-DAT go-PAST-EMPH *nææ*
      'Gunapala did not go to the village.'

Also, *nowey* is a focal negator, thus a focus marking form in the sense of the third characteristic:

(S20) *mamə nowey ee gaməṭə   yanne.*
      I   *nowey* that village-DAT go-PRES-EMPH
      'I am certainly not the one who goes to that village.'

(S21) *gunəpaalə giyee   gaməṭə   nowey.*
      Gunapala go-PAST-EMPH village-DAT *nowey*
      'It was not to the village that Gunapala went.'

On the other hand, *nææ,* in a verbal sentence cannot negate any constituent other than the verb or a stretch including it.[11]

    Sixth, WH-questions in Sinhala require the occurrence of both a WH-form and the question marker *də* (Q). WH-forms are characteristically focused, and it thus follows from the third and fourth characteristics that *də* will occur following the WH-form, as in examples (S2), (S8), (S10), (S22), and (S23):

(S22)   *gunəpaalə mee wæḍə keruwe*   *kohomə də?*
        Gunapala this work do-PAST-EMPH how   Q
        'How did Gunapala do this work?'

(S23)   *mokaṭə   də dæn gaməṭə   yanne?*
        what-DAT Q now village-DAT go-PRES-EMPH
        'Why (what for) are you going to the village now?'

This focusing of WH (+Q) has a semi-obligatory character.[12] Quantifier WH-forms *kiiyak* 'how many-INDEF' and *koccərə* 'how much' are exceptions, and they may occur focused or unfocused with a consequent difference in meaning:

(S24)   *miniha siini   koccərə   gatta   də?*
        man   sugar how-much get-PAST-SIMPLE Q
        'How much sugar did the fellow get?'

(S25)   *miniha siini   koccərə də gatte?*
        man   sugar how-much Q get-PAST-EMPH
        'How much sugar was it that the fellow got?'

Unfocused WH-forms also occur under two other related semantic conditions: in object complements of negated verbs such as *dannəva* 'know' and *teerenəva* 'understand' and in independent "dubious questions"—that is, these expressing general doubt—roughly with a sense like "what on earth," "can it be that":

(S26)   *miniha monəwa kərənəwa   də danne   næœ.*
        man   what-PI do-PRES-SIMPLE Q know-EMPH næœ
        '(I) don't know what he's doing.'

(S27)   *gunəpaalə monəwa kərənəwa   də?*
        Gunapala what-PL do-PRES-SIMPLE Q
        'What (on earth) is Gunapala doing?'

Compare (S2) (repeated here) with (S27).

(S2)   *gunəpaalə kəranne   monəwa də?*
        Gunapala do-PRES-EMPH what-PL Q
        'What is Gunapala doing?'

These six characteristics together constitute a clearly integrated system, and while similar individual characteristics appear in one or the other of the South Dravidian languages or Telugu, none of the latter appear to incorporate all of them, so that the total system has a distinctly Sinhala character. The precise manner in which this system developed and the exact sequence in which its separate features appeared is not yet clear and awaits a more thorough study of the relatively rich inscriptional and written documentation available as material for the history of Sinhala syntax. Also, determining the precise features that might have been borrowed would require more work in comparative Dravidian historical syntax. However, a number of suggestive points emerge from some initial explorations into older Sinhala texts and a feature-by-feature comparison with the other languages so that we can at least formulate some likely hypotheses at this time.

Characteristics of Dravidian Focused Sentences

For Dravidian comparison, I will necessarily rely mostly on Tamil, and specifically Sri Lanka Tamil, since I have a greater amount of relevant data available from that language. Otherwise, I have had to rely primarily on the sources cited earlier and on published grammars (from which it is usually difficult to extract the precise information needed). In any case, Tamil and Malayalam would seem for obvious historical reasons to be the most likely candidates for borrowing, and the initial borrowing could well have occurred at a time to make the distinction between those two languages irrelevant.

A comparison with the Dravidian languages on the basis of the available evidence reveals a number of interesting parallels and differences, particularly with regard to the focus-marking forms. Although Lindholm refers to Tamil *-aa* 'question' and *-taan* 'emphatic' as "clitics of focus" (1972: 301), they are clearly less restricted than Sinhala *də* and *tamaa* (or *tamay*) as described in the third and fourth characteristics. Nor does Tamil *-aam* 'reportative' behave like Sinhala *lu* in that regard. All of the Tamil forms may occur on forms other than the verb without obligatory clefting, as in the following:

(T3) *avaraa   naaLaykku   koLumpukku   pooRaar?*
    he-Q   tomorrow-DAT Colombo-DAT go-PRES-3 Sg-MASC
    'Is it he who is going to Colombo tomorrow?'

(T4) *avartaan   naaLaykku   koLumpukku   pooRaar.*
    he-EMPH tomorrow-DAT Colombo-DAT go-PRES-3Sg-MASC
    'He is going to Colombo tomorrow.'

(T5) *eppavaam   avar pooRaar?*
    when-it-seems he   go-PRES-3Sg-MASC
    'When did they say he is going?'

In fact, nonclefting seems to be the usual case, and since clefting is also possible, there is a possibility for contrast that is not open in Sinhala. Compare (T6), for example, with (T4):

(T6) naaLaykku   koLumpukku   pooRatu   avartaan.
    tomorrow-DAT Colombo-DAT go-NOM-PRES-3 Sg-NEUT he-EMPH
    'It is certainly he who is the one who is going to Colombo tomorrow.'

Malayalam *tanne* 'emphatic' and *-oo* 'question' also appear not to be restricted in the same way as the Sinhala forms (for *-oo*, see Lindholm 1972: 305–6; for *tanne*,

Rodney Moag, personal communication). Thus the same possibilities for contrast as in Tamil appear to exist with regard to occurrence with the focus of clefted or non-clefted sentences.[13]

Malayalam *aaNū* 'copula', also called a "clitic of focus" by Lindholm (1972: 301) is particularly interesting in that it does seem to be restricted like the Sinhala forms. In fact, Malayalam goes beyond colloquial Sinhala in requiring the occurrence of *aaNū* on the focus of a cleft sentence unless *tanne* already occurs, and this is true even if the question marker *-oo* or a WH-form appears:

(Ml) *innale   baalanaaNoo   vannatu?*
      yesterday Balan-aaNū- Q came-NOM-3Sg
      'Was it Balan who came yesterday?'

(M2) *innale   aaraaNū   vannatu?*
      yesterday who-*ana* came-NOM-3Sg
      'Who was it who came yesterday?' (Lindholm 1972: 306)

It is for that reason that Lindholm does not include Malayalam *-oo* and WH as "clitics of focus" but only *tanne* and *aaNū* (pp. 305–6). Note, however, that of the latter two, only *aaNū* is a focus marker in the sense of the Sinhala forms. Its closest equivalent is *yi*, which also has some copula functions.[14] However, *yi* does not obligatorily occur in the absence of other focus markers in colloquial Sinhala, nor does it generally occur with *də* 'question'.[15] A comparison of Malayalam with Literary Sinhala, though, reveals a much closer similarity and casts light on the probable development of Sinhala *-yi* as a focus marker when not a copula. The obligatory occurrence of *aaNū* actually appears to be part of a more general rule, covering both cleft sentences and the nominal equational sentences that they resemble in other respects. That is, Malayalam, unlike its sister languages, appears to have developed a rule requiring an overt copula even in the present tense, and *aaNū* serves that function.[16]

Literary Sinhala has a similar rule (Gair and Karunatilaka 1974: 11, 25). The copula may be a form of *wenəwā* (Sanskrit *bhū*), but the usual form (and currently the exclusive one in focused sentences) is *-yi* or one of its variants.[17] Here, as elsewhere, Literary Sinhala reflects an older stage of the language,[18] and to arrive at the present colloquial use of *-yi*, we need only to relax the obligatory nature of its occurrence as copula,[19] leaving it, then, as an optional focus-marking form as in (S28), to be compared with (S1):

(S28) *mamə yanne   gaməṭəy.*
       I   go-PRES-EMPH   village-DAT-yi
       'It is to the village that I am going.'

In verbal focused sentences with or without *-yi*, the verb retains its EMPH marking, and with the loss of the nominal character of that affix elsewhere, the resemblance between focused and nominal equational sentences is attenuated. Note, however, that while the copula rule was relaxed also in nominal equational sentences, it was not relaxed in adjectival equational sentences, where *-yi* retains its obligatory character even in Colloquial Sinhala (see (S35) below and note 15). In this respect, then, nominal equational and focused sentences were treated alike.

At present, on grounds of external history, I consider the development of an obligatory copula rule in Sinhala and Malayalam and its application to both focused and equational sentences to be a case of parallel development, but the similarity is indeed striking.[20]

Sinhala *də* and the Kannada question marker *-aa* afford another striking parallel. Unlike Tamil *-aa* and Malayalam-*oo,* the Kannada form requires obligatory clefting (Schiffman 1979: 103, 129–30).[21] Thus:

(K1)   *avnaa naaLe   uurg   hoogoodu?*
         he-Q   tomorrow town-DAT go-PRES-NOM-NEUT
         'Is it he who is going to town tomorrow?' (Schiffman 1979: 113)

On external historical grounds, of course, the likelihood of cross-language influence here is even more remote than for the Malayalam and Sinhala copula, and it must be considered a parallel development. It is interesting to speculate on the reasons for it, but that goes well beyond the scope of this paper.

The obligatory cooccurrence of *də* with WH-forms is a distinct Sinhala development and not paralleled in any of the other languages, as is the semiobligatory focusing of WH-forms given as the sixth characteristic of Sinhala focused sentences.[22] Neither, for example, apply in Tamil; compare (T7) with (S29):

(T7)   *enna taaRinkaL?*
         what give-PRES-2 Pl
         'What are you giving?'

(S29) *oyaa denne   monəwa də?*
         you give-PRES-EMPH   what   Q
         'What are you giving?'

As I shall show subsequently, the semiobligatory focusing of WH-forms and the consequent usual adjacent cooccurrence of most WH-forms and *də* in focused position are later developments than their possible cooccurrence in the same sentence, and clearly both are internal developments.

The interaction of negation and focus in Sinhala is complex, and several aspects of it have recently been treated by De Abrew (1980). The negative *nowey is* transparently from *no-* 'negative prefix' plus the third person singular of the copula *wenəwa,* and its development as a focus-marking form clearly involved the same parallel treatment of equational and focused sentences that we saw in the development of *yi.* Thus *nowey,* in addition to its function as a focus negator, also retains its functions as the regular negator of nominal (but not adjectival) equational sentences, as in (S30):

(S30) *meekə potak   nowey.*
         this-one book-INDEF   *nowey*
         'This one is not a book.'

The specialization of *nowey* to these two functions in contrast with *nææ* is a later development, like the somewhat different specialization of *yi*, since in earlier texts we may find *nowey* (or its etymon) where we would currently expect *nææ*.[23]

Two further characteristics of negation in Sinhala deserve mention here, since they show how far the system has developed. First, *nowey* may negate an entire sentence (or some stretch including the verb), but the verb appears in its usual form for nonnegative independent sentences, and the entire sentence (or that stretch) is in focus. This allows a neat possibility of contrast with parallel sentences with *nææ*. Compare, for example, (S31) with *nowey* with (S20) with *nææ*:

(S31) gunǝpaalǝ gamǝṭǝ   giyaa   nowey.
       Gunapala village-DAT go-PAST-SIMPLE *nowey*
       'It is not the case that Gunapala went to the village [he did something else].'

Second, *nææ* itself has an emphatic form, allowing it to occur as predicator in focused sentences:

(S32) gunǝpaalǝ giyee   nætte   gamǝṭǝ.
       Gunapala go-PAST-EMPH *nææ*-EMPH village-DAT
       'Where Gunapala didn't go was to the village.'

Any of the focus-marking forms may occur with the focused constituent of such *nætte* sentences, as with *dǝ* in (S33), and this includes *nowey*, as in (S34):

(S33) gunǝpaalǝ giyee   nætte   gamǝṭǝ   dǝ?
       Gunapala go-PAST-EMPH *nææ*-EMPH village-DAT Q
       'Was it to the village that Gunapala didn't go?'

(S34) gunǝpaalǝ giyee   nætte   gamǝṭǝ   nowey.
       Gunapala go-PAST-EMPH *nææ*-EMPH village-DAT *nowey*
       'It was not to the village that Gunapala didn't go.'

The semantics here, involving differential negation of presupposition and focus, are interesting but must be dealt with elsewhere.

Just as *nowey* is etymologically the negative of a copula, so *nææ* is an existential negator, still serving as the suppletive negative for *tiyenǝva* 'be, exist (inanimate)' and *innǝwa* 'be, live (animate)'. This is another striking parallel to Dravidian languages, in which the same distinction is found, as in Jaffna Tamil *illay* (=*nææ*) and *allay* (=*nowey*). Although the Sinhala morphological material is Indo-Aryan, this is another possible instance of Dravidian influence, though we must proceed with caution here because of other Indo-Aryan parallels.[24] On the other hand, we might wonder whether the Jaffna Tamil preservation of a distinction that seems to be lost in other Tamil dialects is not an instance of reciprocal influence from Sinhala.

Another set of developments, as yet unstudied in detail, has led to a further characteristic of the Sinhala focusing system not included in the previous six characteristics: its extension to nonverbal sentences.

Sinhala has a set of tenseless forms showing partial verbal inflection, including EMPH, which have accordingly been called "quasiverbs" (Gair 1970: 38). These include *nææ* as well as *æti* 'might be' and *bææ* 'cannot', and since at least the first two are clearly verb based etymologically, their inclusion in the system is not surprising.[25] However, the system has also been extended to adjectives, which do not take EMPH, but they appear in focused sentences without the *-yi* that is obligatory for them in predicate position in nonfocused sentences (cf. note 13). Compare (S35) with (S36):

(S35) *adə   mee   kehelgedi hoňday.*
       today these bananas good-*yi*
       'These bananas are good today.'

(S36) *adə   hoňdə mee   kehelgedi?*
       today good   these bananas
       'It is these bananas that are good today.'

Adjectival sentences have thus been fully integrated into the system along with verbal ones. For example, the same rules for obligatory focusing with focus markers applies as shown by (S38) in comparison with (S37) (the absence of *-yi* in (S38) is accounted for by a separate rule deleting it before *də*—cf. note 15):

(S37) *adə   mee   kehelgedi hoňdə də?*
       today these bananas good   Q
       'Are these bananas good today?'

(S38) *adə   hoňdə mee   kehelgedi də?*
       today good   these bananas Q
       'Is it these bananas that are good today?'

I have not found equivalents for this extension of focusing constructions in any of the Dravidian languages so far.

There is at least one important characteristic, which pertains to discourse rather than syntax, that differentiates Sinhala focused sentences from those in Tamil, at least among the Dravidian languages. It is difficult to define, but it might be called a "lower threshold for focus triggering." That is, the range of situations under which focusing (or clefting) is appropriate is much wider in Sinhala than in Tamil (or than in English, for that matter).[26] We might expect as much based on what has been said concerning the difference in contrast potentialities between Sinhala and Tamil in relation to some clitics and types of questions, and it stands out very clearly in passages such as the three that follow (G1), (G2), and (G3). They are taken from a recent text for Jaffna Tamil for Sinhala speakers (Gair, Suseendirarajah, and Karunatilaka 1979), and they thus keep both situation and discourse patterns as constant as possible, since they were designed to do so. Focused sentences are marked with (+FOC):

(G1) ASKING A WH-QUESTION:
     T: *yaaLpaaṇattilay atikamaay enna maram irukku?*
        Jaffna-LOC   mostly   what tree (s) be (PRES-3–Neut)

s: (+FOC) *yaapənee   wædipurə monə gas   də tiyenne?*
          Jaffna-GEN   mostly   what trees Q be-PRES-EMPH
e: 'In Jaffna, what kind of trees are there mostly?'

(G2) ANOTHER INSTANCE OF WH:

t: *avayiTTay eppa   colluvinkaL?*
    they-REF   when   say-FUT-2-PL
s: (+FOC) *eyaalaṭə   kawədaa də kiyanne?*
          they-DAT what-day Q   say-PRES-EMPH
e: 'When will you tell them?'

(G3) YES–NO QUESTION AND REPLY:

t: *yaaLpaaNattukku ovvoru naaaLum   piLeen   irukkaa?*
    Jaffna-DAT   every   day-EMPH plane(s) be-PRES-3–Neut-Q
    illay. tiŋkal,   putan,   veLLi kiLamayaLilay mattum piLeen   irukku.
    'No. Monday Wednesday Friday day-PL-LOC   only   plane (s) be-PRES-
    3–Neut

s: *yaapəneeṭə   dawasəgaane aasyaatraa tiyenəva   də?*
   Jaffna-DAT daily   plane-Pl   be-PRES-SIMPLE Q
(+FOC) *nææ, sañduda, badaada,   sikuraada witəray aasyatraa tiyenne.*
      No   Monday Wednesday Friday   only   plane-PL be-PRES-EMPH
e: 'Are there planes from here to Jaffna every day?'
   'No, there are planes only on Monday, Wednesday, and Friday.'

The foregoing comparison with Dravidian languages shows clearly that while the basic construction may have been the result of cross-language influence, a great deal of internal development took place subsequently. The exact time at which borrowing might have occurred is difficult to determine at present. We have relatively rich documentation for earlier stages of Sinhala going back to at least the second century B.C., but as yet we have nothing like a comprehensive historical study of syntax based on it. Also, the evidence prior to about 1200 A.D. is primarily inscriptional and generally not of such a nature as to include discourse conditions that would invoke the kind of construction we are examining. Such evidence as we have is often inconclusive or difficult to interpret with confidence. For example, in Sigiri graffiti as early as the eighth century (which was poetry, but often conversational in tone), sentences with nominal verb forms that are the etymons of our emphatic forms are common (Paranavitana 1956: clxiii), but it is difficult to find clear cases of declarative focused sentences. There are, however, a few examples that appear to be focused WH-forms much like modern ones:

(Sg1) *ko   ja   giye   himiya yi   (balam siṭiyuyun*
    where Q (=də) go-PAST-NOM lord   COMP (looking be-NOM-Pl-OBL
    vanno)?
    seem-NOM-Pl)
    '(They seem as if they stood (there) looking backward (wondering))
    "Where has their lord gone?"' (109, 8th century)

(SG2) *n[o] balaya yanne   kese?*
    not having looked go-PRES-NOM how
    'How does one go away without looking?' (261, 9th century)

There are also nonfocused examples with nonnominal finite verbs:

(SG3)   *sav-abaranin*   *saji*   *giri-hisa*   *siṭihi*   *kumaṭa?*
        All-ornaments-INST adorned mountain-summit-LOC be PRES-2Sg what-DAT
        'Wherefore do you, being adorned with all ornaments, stand on the summit of the
        rock?' (3, 9th century)

      Difficult as this evidence is to interpret conclusively, it does at least suggest clearly that the construction was present by the time of the graffiti (eighth through tenth centuries), thought it functioned less centrally in the grammar than at present.

      One of the earliest surviving extended prose texts, Gurulugomi's *Amāvatura*, dates from about the twelfth century. (There is, however, some still earlier commentarial material.) That text includes a number of conversational interchanges, and we find what appear to be clear examples of declarative focused sentences. The following examples are taken from the *Amāvatura*, 1967 edition, by Kodagoda Ñaṇaloka Sthavirayan Vahanse (K.Ñ.):

(SA1)   *sokaśalya*   *buduhu*   *udurāpiyannaṭa*   *nissaha yi*
        sorrow-thorns Buddha   pluck-out-NOM-DAT(= INF) suitable COMP
        sitannaṭa   *yæ*   *utsaha upanne*
        thinker-DAT COP effort born-EMPH[27]

        'It is to him who thinks "the Buddha is suitable to pluck out the thorns of sorrow"
        that effort is born.' (K.Ñ.: 282)

Though the verb form that occurs in sentences like (SA1) has been glossed here as EMPH, it clearly retains its nominal character, with both animate and inanimate uses, as shown by (SA2) and (SA3), in which it clearly occurs as subject:

(SA2)   *manah-karma mahatæ*   *yi*   *kiyanne*   *nokalakireṇu*
        mind action   important COMP say-EMPH-3Sg-Masc-Neut not backslide-adj
        nam   *ve.*
        EMPH COP-3Sg

        'The person who says that the action of the mind is (the) important (thing) will not
        backslide.' (K.Ñ. 53)

(SA3)   *ovun*   *no*   *sanhinduva badu karavuvara*   *ganne*
        them-ACC   NEG calm-PART taxes royal-revenue take-PRES-EMPH-3Sg
        daham   *noweyi*
        proper-doctrine NEG-COP-3Sg

        'Taking the royal revenue without calming them is not proper.' (K.Ñ. 103)

      Thus, sentences such as (SA4) are difficult to interpret decisively as either focused or equational, if indeed the distinction is relevant at this period:

(SA4)   *vahanse enne*   *saccaka yæ*
        Sire   come-EMPH Saccaka COP
        'Sire, Saccaka is coming.' or 'The one who is coming is Saccaka.' (K.Ñ. 171)

WH-forms are found with and without cooccurrence with *da* (= *də* = Q) as in (SA5) through (SA8). Sentences like (SA8) with *dæ* (< *da* before *yi*) occuring immediately following the WH-form appear to be the exception rather than the rule, making it clear that the modern semiobligatory focusing of WH does not apply:

(SA5) *kotaṭa   giyehi*
       where-DAT go-PAST-2Sg
       'Where did you go?' (K.Ñ. 136)

(SA6) *mohu   koyaṭa   yeti*
       these (people) where-DAT go-PRES-3Sg
       'Where are these people going?' (K.Ñ. 189)

(SA7) *dæn paeviji   væ   kumaṭa   kiyam   da?*
       now ordained been what-DAT say-PRES-1Sg Q
       'Now that I am a monk, why would I say it?' (K.Ñ. 76)

(SA8) *mese da   vaḍane kumaṭa   dæ yi   kīha.*
       thus also go   what-DAT Q   COMP say-PAST-3Pl
       '"Wherefore do you go thus?" they asked.' (K.Ñ. 145)

On the basis of this evidence, it seems clear that the construction was well established by the time of *Amāvatura* but that the modern system had not yet evolved.[28] Interestingly, except for the possible cooccurrence of WH and Q, as in (SA8), the situation reflected in these examples seems very close to that in Tamil as described earlier, with WH-forms occurring both focused and unfocused and the verb form having nominal functions outside of the focusing construction.

The evidence outlined above from Sigiri graffiti and *Amāvatura* leads to the same conclusion reached by the comparison with Dravidian languages: The complex modern Sinhala focusing subsystem is the result of a long process of internal development. The precise steps in that development remain to be worked out on the basis of much more textual study, but its general outlines are clear. The focusing construction, once established, was steadily extended in its domain. At the same time, it was, so to speak, regularized so as to subsume that increased domain under an integrated and relatively small set of rules with wide application. It also came to occupy a more central and important place in the overall syntax of the language by intersecting with an increasing number of grammatical processes. Note that one cannot describe such basic processes as yes–no question and WH-question formation, negation, or the use of emphatic particles in Sinhala without involving focusing, and at the beginning of this chapter, I used the phrase "highly visible in the grammar" with that centrality in mind.

The term "adaptation" is commonly used in historical linguistics to describe the alteration of a borrowed form so as to accord more easily with established indigenous structure. Though it is commonly used with reference to phonology, any calque or syntactic borrowing using native material involves the same general process of adaptation in principle, despite the difference in material. The fortunes of the Sinhala focusing construction, which appears to have its origin in borrowing, go far beyond adaptation, however, in that once adapted, it was extended and reinterpreted, becoming itself an important factor in further change. For this sort of process, I would suggest the term "naturalization," on the analogy of "immigration and naturalization." In these terms, the construction in Sinhala not only immigrated and changed its appearance but also went on to become a most important and influential citizen.

Some Aspects of the Jaffna Tamil Verbal System

WITH S. SUSEENDIRARAJAH

This paper appeared in the International Journal of Dravidian Linguistics *(June 1981) pp. 370–84; an earlier version was presented at the Fifth International Conference on Tamil Studies held at Madurai in January 1981. The version of the paper presented here is the same as the earlier published version except for some minor editorial changes and brief notes. However, one central aspect of that paper was a historical and descriptive account of one structural type, the pronominal verb form, seen as unique to this dialect of Tamil. That account has been challenged and a different hypothesis proposed in Steever 1988. That challenge is worth a reply, and an addendum with one has thus been added here.*

The original publication carried a note that "For unavoidable reasons, particularly the illness of one of the authors and the delays of the mail, it was not possible to send this draft to Dr. Suseendirarajah[1] in time for it to be checked and returned in time for the conference. Final responsibility for errors and omissions in this version must therefore rest with James W. Gair." This is, unfortunately, even more true of this chapter, owing to the present unhappy conditions that obtain in Jaffna, where Professor Suseendirarajah is now located, and I cannot help but be concerned for the safety and well being of a colleague for whom I have the greatest respect and affection. The addendum here is likewise my sole responsibility, though it is fully in accord with the analyses presented in Gair, Suseendirarajah, and Karunatillake 1978, and that of the original paper. I thus assume that he would concur with the conclusions presented here.

There are over two and a half million speakers of Tamil in Sri Lanka, speaking several dialects, of which Jaffna Tamil represents a major variety, with approximately 700,000 speakers at the time of writing.[2] There is also the estate Tamil largely centered in the tea-growing areas of the upcountry, which, as a result of migration in the nineteenth and earlier twentieth centuries, has more affiliation to Indian varieties. Other varieties include the east coast varieties with the population centers of Trincomalee and Batticaloa, an undetermined number of varieties of Muslim Tamil, and the Tamil still spoken in several pockets among the fishing communities of the west coast. There is, in fact, more dialect variation within Tamil in Sri Lanka than there is within the majority (Indo-Aryan) language Sinhala, spoken by 70 percent of the population, or approximately ten million at the time of writing. As yet, this variation within Sri Lanka Tamil remains largely unstudied in detail, despite some initial attempts (especially Zvelebil 1959, 1959–60, 1960, 1966; Suseendirarajah 1970, 1973a, 1973b, 1978; Thananjayarajasingham 1973).

In any event, Jaffna Tamil, located in the northernmost part of the country, notably the Jaffna peninsula, is the variety commonly thought of as the one most "characteristic" of Sri Lankan Tamil, primarily because of the preponderance of Jaffna people among Tamil professionals, civil servants, and educators in Sri Lanka. In large part, this resulted from the long, well-established, and effective educational system created in Jaffna largely through the efforts of American missionaries. In addition, Jaffna has a strong sense of cultural identity, of which the local variety of Tamil is one mark, as well as a tradition of valuing education highly, both for its own sake and as a means of professional advancement.

Jaffna Tamil has been sufficiently isolated from the Indian forms of the language for it to have developed a distinct character, so much so that Indians encountering it for the first time are likely to think that they are hearing some other Dravidian language such as Malayalam (Suseendirarajah 1967: 5). Contributing to this distinct character are a number of features of the verbal system, which it will the primary task of this chapter to present in a largely descriptive fashion. This paper may thus be considered a preliminary attempt to isolate and describe a number of characteristics of the verbal system that may be of interest to scholars of Tamil dialectology, since they represent differences from mainland varieties with which we have any familiarity, particularly from what Schiffman and others have called Standard Spoken Tamil (Schiffman 1980 and references therein). Though some individual features may be found in other dialects, the system as a whole appears to have a unique character. In any event, we would like to know the extent to which these lectures appear elsewhere, since that would in itself be of no little interest in placing Jaffna Tamil more precisely within the range of Tamil varieties.

There are dialect differences within the Tamil of the Jaffna area, but the phenomena dealt with here seem to be generally characteristic of it, at least in the language of the VēLāla community.[3] They have been found in the speech of informants from points as relatively widespread as Myliddy (Kankesanturai), Sudumalai, Point Pedro, and Chavakachcheri, and they are represented in the dramas written in Jaffna Tamil by Kanapathi Pillai.We will first briefly describe a number of features of the verbal system, some of which represent retentions of features or distinctions generally lost elsewhere, and then concentrate on one that strikes us as a particularly important innovation: the formation of a subsystem of finite, agreeing verb forms based on a combination of the verbal adjective form (often referred to as the relative participle), both present and past, with the personal pronouns. As far as we know, that subsystem as a whole, together with the corresponding negative forms, constitutes a major difference between Jaffna Tamil and the Indian varieties of the language.

Lexical Features

We will not attempt to deal with lexical differences between Jaffna Tamil and other varieties, though they exist in the verbs as elsewhere, but we will leave that for fuller dialectal study and mention only a few. One interesting fact is that Jaffna retains the distinction between the two verbs 'give', *tar-* and *kuTu-*, using the former only when either speaker or hearer is a recipient of the action. Similarly, verbs like *katai-* 'speak, converse', *paṟai-* 'say, converse', and *veLikkiTu-* 'set out' appear to be characteristic of Jaffna Tamil, and detailed comparisons with other dialects would undoubtedly unearth many more.

Person–Number Affixes

The person–number affixes of Jaffna Tamil are shown in table 12–1. In Jaffna Tamil, as in other varieties, the second person plural is used as the second person polite form. The *-iyaL* affix characteristic of Jaffna Tamil appears to be giving way to the *-iinkaL* form, perhaps under the influence of Colombo Tamil and, more indirectly, Indian Tamil. As the table shows, the second person has a further two degrees of respect in the singular. The second person intermediate-respect form also has a distinctive imperative affix *-um*; hence *niir yaarum* 'you come'. The third person has distinct affixes for two degrees of politeness, as shown, in both singular and plural. The feminine affixes *-aa* polite and *aaL* nonpolite are particularly interesting. Unlike some other dialects, Jaffna Tamil does not drop final *L* (or *l*). Thus not only are the affixes distinct, but the forms with reminiscent sandhi before clitics found in some Indian varieties—such as *avaLaa* 'is it she', *vantaaLaa* 'did she come'—would be interpreted as nonpolite forms in Jaffna Tamil, the polite forms being *avaavaa* and *vantaavaa*.

Table 12–1 Person–Number Affixes of Jaffna Tamil

Person		Singular	Plural
1		(*naan*) -*en*	(*naankaL*) -*am*
2	polite	(*niinkal*) -*iyaL, iinkaL*	
	intermediate	(*niir*) -*iir*	(*niinkal*) -*iyaL, iinkaL*
	non-polite	(*nii*) -*aay*	
3	Masculine		
	polite	(*avar*) -*aarl-ar*	(*avai*) -*inam*
	nonpolite	(*avan*) -*aan/-an*	(*avankaL*) -*aankaL / ankaL*
3	Feminine		
	polite	(*avaa*) -*aa*	(*avai*) -*inam*
	nonpolite	(*avaL*) -*aaL/-aL*	(*avaLavai*) -*aaLavai/-aLavai*
3	Nonhuman	(*atu*) -*utu*	—

Note: The forms following slashes are those used with future tense forms, where they differ from the present and past. Forms separated by commas are variants. Pronouns appropriate to the forms are given in parentheses for references.

The third person actually has three degrees of politeness like the second person, but the intermediate respect form does not have a distinct affix; the otherwise non-human in -*utu* is used for *it* for all genders and numbers. In Jaffna Tamil as in other varieties, there is no singular–plural distinction in nonhuman verb forms. Note also that the third person plural masculine -*ankal/aankal* is a nonpolite form in Jaffna Tamil, the polite form being -*inam* in both genders. This affix occurs with the inanimate stem in the present—that is, the stem without *r̄* (ṟ)—as in *paTikkir̄ankal* 'they (masc.) study' nonpolite and *paTikkinam* 'they (masc. or fem.) study' polite. Though some of these affixes appear to occur in some mainland varieties as well, the resultant system as a whole appears to be distinctive to Jaffna.

Negative

Like other dialects of Tamil, Jaffna Tamil has negatives in *illai* and a future negative in *maaTT-*. However, it also is more conservative in its negative system than the other spoken dialects with which we have any familiarity. For one thing, it retains a distinction between *illai*, which is used both existentially and to form a negative with the infinitive of other verbs, and a negative *alla* used primarily in equational sentences.[4] Thus we find *paal illai* 'there is no milk' but *itu paal alla* 'this is not milk'.

Also, Spoken Jaffna Tamil retains an inflectional negative, in finite forms, which is formed by adding the person-number affixes directly to the root of the verb, or in three forms (e.g., second person plural and the third person nonhuman and plural), following a negative affix -*aa-*. (There are, of course, some morphophonemic complications, but they do not concern us here.) Hence we find *varen* 'I won't go', *varaar* 'he won't go', *varaa* 'she won't go', *varaatu* 'it won't go, *varaayaL* 'you won't go', *varaayinam* 'they won't go', and so on. This direct negative has a generally future sense like that of the *maaTT-* negative, but it may be stronger and more definite, for example: *naan ceyya maaTTen* 'I won't do (it)' and *naan ceyyen* 'I **won't** do it.'

Causative

Jaffna Tamil resembles other dialects in having a periphrastic causative, formed with the infinitive plus any of the verbs *vai-*, *cey-*, or *paNNu*. However, it also preserves, in its spoken variety, an affixal causative in -*vi* or -*ppi*, thus, *ceyvi-* 'cause to do', *tir̄appi-* 'cause to open', and so on. Interestingly, the affixal causative appears to be the one most commonly used in Jaffna Tamil.

Pronominal Verb Forms

Perhaps the most interesting innovation within the Jaffna Tamil verbal system is the development of a subsystem of finite verb forms made by combining the verbal adjective form, (often called the relative participle), with the personal pronouns. Though sequences of the same form may occur in other dialects, they do not, as far as we are

aware, form a finite subsystem in the same way as those in Jaffna Tamil do, and with
the same uses. There are both present and past pronominal verb forms, each with its
corresponding negative. The past forms are the most clearly innovative, and we deal
with them first. In Jaffna Tamil, as in other varieties, verbal adjectives may occur
with either noun or pronoun heads to form the equivalent of relative clauses, as in
example (1):

(1)   a. *naan caappiTTa   palakaaram*
          I   eat-past-Adj food
          'the food that I ate'

       b. *ennaik- kuuppiTT(a) avar*
          I-DAT call-past   he
          'the one who called me'

In Jaffna Tamil, however, there are frequently occurring sequences of verbal
adjective plus pronoun that cannot be interpreted in that way. Note, for example, the
three examples in the following brief interchange from the opening scene of K.
Kanapathi Pillai's play *Poruḷoo Poruḷ*, (1952: 1) set in Jaffna. The forms in question
are in boldface in the accompanying phonological representation of the passage and
in the translation:

(2)   மங்கையர்க்கரசி : என்ன கமலி, என்னே நீ வரசொன்னதெண்டு
       தாமு வந்து சொன்னுன்.   எப்ப வந்தனி கொளும்பாலே ? எனக்குத்
       தெரியாது நீ வந்தது.

          கமலவேணி :   காலமைதான்   வந்தனுன்........கதைக்கிறதுக்கு
       வீட்டிலே ஒருதருமில்லை. அதுதான் உனக்கு ஆளனுப்பினனுன்.

MANKAIYARKKARACI: enna kamali, ennai nii varacconnateNTu taamu vantu connaan.
eppa **vantanii**[5] koLumpaalai? enakkut teriyaatu nii vantatu.
        KAMALAVEENI: kaalamaitaan **vantanaan** . . . kataikkiratukku viiTTilai orutarumillai.
atutaan unakku **aaLanuppinanaan**.

        MANKAIYARKKARACI: Well, Kamali? Tamu came and said that you asked me to come.
When **did you come** from Colombo? I didn't know you had come.
        KAMALAVEENI: **I came** in the morning. There is no one to talk to in the house. That's
why **I sent** someone to you.

There are several reasons for considering such verb–pronoun sequences to be
parts of verb phrases rather than noun phrases. First, it is clear that the semantic interpretation that would be required by construing these forms as verbal adjective plus
pronominal head in the usual fashion—that is, as relative clauses—would be highly
inappropriate. That is, they cannot be interpreted in context to have meanings such
as "you are the one who came from Colombo when" (even ignoring the placement
of *koLumpaalai* 'from Colombo' outside the clause),[6] "I am the one who came in the
morning" or "I am the one who sent someone to you." Rather, they are obviously
closer in meaning to the usual past finite forms found in other dialects as well as Jaffna
Tamil: *vantaay* 'you came', *vanten* 'I came', *anuppinen* 'I sent'.

Thus, in more strictly linguistic terms, it would be extremely difficult to interpret the first example as an equational sentence with the structure in (3). (We have provided the implicit subject in parentheses and placed the adverb within the clause for simplicity. Leaving it outside would, of course, make the interpretation even more difficult, since we would have to deal with an adverb extraposed from a relative clause over a noun head.) Jaffna Tamil, of course, like other varieties, has no overt copula in such sentences:

(3)   [s ([NP *nii*])   [NP[s   *eppa koLumpaalai   vanta*] [NP *nii*]]]
      [s ([NP you])   [NP[s   when Colombo-from   came] [NP you]]]
      '*you are the you who came from Colombo when?'

The adverb *eppa* 'when' poses a particular problem for such an interpretation. If we include it in the relative clause, as in the bracketing above, the required interpretation "you are the you who came from Colombo when" would seem to be highly inappropriate in context. On the other hand, if we take *eppa* to be a sentence adverb, with the entire remaining sentence in its scope and a bracketing something like:

(4)   [S ([NP *nii*]) [ADV *eppa*][NP[s *koLumpaalai vanta*][NP *nii*]]]

the required reading would seem to be something like "when were you the one who came from Colombo," which would also be inappropriate in context, though perhaps less so than the previous interpretation.

On the other hand, if we interpret the sequence *vantanii* as a finite verb with a past sense in a verb phrase, that is, in a sentence with a structure like:

(5)   [s([NP *nii*])[VP [ADV *eppa*][V *vantanii*][ADV *koLumpaalai*]]]

the natural interpretation "when did you come from Colombo" fits the context perfectly. Note also that we need not move *koLumpaalai* as we were forced to in the noun phrase interpretation so as not to leave it stranded, since there is ample precedent for such right-moved adverbials in verbal sentences. (Under the VP interpretation, it would of course be possible to interpret it as a sentence adverb rather than within the VP as we have it here, but that would be quite irrelevant to the present argument, since in either case the problems of interpretation that we encounter under the NP analysis would not occur.)

Similar arguments are easily constructed for the other examples. For instance, *atutaan* 'therefore' in the third example constitutes a problem like *eppa* in the first. Under an NP NP interpretation, if we analyze *atutaan* as occurring within a relative clause, we require a reading like "the I who sent someone therefore." If we take it to be outside a relative clause, we obtain something like "therefore (I am) the one who sent someone to you"; both are inappropriate. If, however, we interpret it as part of a verb phrase with a finite verb *anuppinanaan* '(I) sent', as in a sentence with a structure like:

(6)   [s ([NP *naan*])[VP[ADV *atutaan*][NP(Dat)*unakku*][NP *aaL*][V *anuppinanaan*]]]

parallel to a similar sentence with the ordinary past tense *anuppinen*, we obtain the appropriate reading "that is why I sent someone to you."

The possible substitutability of pronouns provides another motivation for treating these verb sequences as finite verbs rather than as nominals. In equational sentences—NP NP—with a pronoun-headed relative clause as the predicate noun phrase, we may get a pronoun agreeing with the subject in person, but we need not. We may, instead, find the third person pronoun with the appropriate gender and number. That is, both of the following are possible with essentially the same meaning:

(7) a. *(naan) kaalamaitaan vantanaan.*
         morning-EMPH   came-I

     b. *naan kaalamaitaan vantavan.*
        morning-EMPH   came-he
        'I am the one who came in the morning.'

However, it is not possible to substitute a third person pronoun in examples such as those with which we have been dealing. Thus, adjusting for the appropriate feminine gender, we could not replace the three examples with *vantavaa* 'she who came' (for *vantanii* and *vantanaan*) and *anuppinavaa* 'she who sent' in context.

In the third person, of course, pronominal verb forms of the type we are discussing will be identical in form with pronominal headed relative clauses, and we do in fact find the ambiguity we would expect to result. Thus:

(8) *capaapati kaalamai vantavar*
     Sabapathy morning   came-he

could be either 'Sabapathy came in the morning' or 'Sabapathy is the one who came in the morning'.

In Jaffna Tamil, as in other dialects, there is an action verbal nominal formed by adding the third person inanimate pronoun *atu* to the past verbal adjective: thus *vantatu* 'the having come', *paTiccatu* 'the having studied', and so on. It forms nominal clauses, such as *naan puttakattai paticcatu* 'my having studied the book'; *niinkaL koLumpukkup poona kiLamai vantatu* 'your having come to Colombo last week'.[7] These can, as in other dialects, be negated with the existential *illai as in vantatillai* (< *vantatu* + *illai*) 'The coming was not'. In Jaffna Tamil, these negatives serve as the equivalent negative to the past tense pronominal forms that we have been discussing. That is, they appear to have the same tense and aspectual implications as the verb–pronoun sequences and can thus be considered to be the negative member of a verbal subsystem with them. Thus:

(9) *niinkaL neettu   iñcai vantatu illai* (or *vantatillai*).
     you   yesterday here coming not
     'You didn't come yesterday.'

serves as the negative of

(10) *niinkaL neettu vantaniinkal.*
    you   yesterday came-ADJ you
    'You came yesterday.'

The semantic equivalence of these negatives with the pronominal verb forms might tempt us to interpret them syntactically as negated NP VP sentences parallel to their positive counterparts, something like:

(11) [$_S$[$_{NP}$ *niinkaL*][$_{VP}$ *neettu iñcai* [$_{V+NEG}$ *vantat(u) illai*]]]

However, we do not know at present of any compelling syntactic reason for not continuing to interpret them as nominalized clauses with an existential negative, as in:[8]

(12) [$_S$ [$_{NP}$ [$_{NP}$ *niinkaL*][$_{VP}$ *neettu iñcai vanta*]*atu*] [$_{V(NEG)}$ *illai*]]]

That is, we have no convincing motivation for concluding that their entering into a semantic subsystem with the pronominal verbs has led to a syntactic change by which they require rebracketing. In any event, however, they cannot be analyzed as equational sentences since the pronoun is always third person inanimate, regardless of the subject of the verb in the adjectival form. Also, Jaffna Tamil, as stated earlier, retains the distinction between negatives *illai* and *alla*, and nominal equational sentences require the latter. Hence we have contrasts such as:

(13) *naan yaaLppaaNam poonatillai.*
    Jaffna   went-NOM-NEG
    'I have not gone to Jaffna.'

versus:

(14) *naan yaaLppaanam poonavan   alla.*
    Jaffna   went-ADJ-he not
    'I am not the one who went to Jaffna.'

If the sentences under discussion were NP NP sentences, they would require *alla*, not the *illai* that in fact appears in them.

    Furthermore, Jaffna Tamil has the negative verbal adjective formed with *-aata*, such as *pookaata* 'not going' 'not having gone'. As expected, this may modify pronouns, as in:

(15) *ankai pookaatavai   (incai varuvinam).*
    there go-NEG-they (here come-they)
    'Those who didn't go there (will come here).'

Such forms, unlike those with the verbal noun plus *illai*, cannot function as the negative of the pronominal verbal forms. They may occur in the predicate but have a quite different sense, as in:

(16) *capaapati ankai pookaatavar.*
     Sabapathy there go-NEG ADJ-he
     'Sabapathy is (the) one who does not/didn't go there.'

Thus, though it is not entirely certain whether we should analyze the negation with verbal noun plus *illai* as negated noun phrase or verb phrase, an equational NP NP interpretation is not possible, so that they lend no support to an analysis of their positive counterparts as equational sentences.

There are, as we have seen, strong reasons for treating such verb–pronoun sequences as those illustrated in the quoted passage as finite verbs. They are, as the passage exemplifies, frequent in spoken Jaffna Tamil, and in our experience they clearly constitute a feature of that dialect that appears unusual, if not startling, to speakers of other dialects. While these sequences have a generally past meaning, they also clearly involve a contrast in meaning with the ordinary past inflected forms (in terms of their occurrence in other dialects) such as *vanten* (vs. *vantanaan*) and *anuppinen* (vs. *anuppinanaan*). While this meaning contrast has not yet been analyzed in sufficient detail, it is generally true that the pronominal past forms emphasize the completion of an action or the fact of its having taken place, and they have been called the "emphatic past" for that reason (Gair, Suseendirarajah, and Karunatilaka 1978: 270, 291). Actually, it appears that we are witnessing the birth of an aspectual category distinction in Jaffna Tamil, namely, a perfective/imperfective contrast. This is, incidentally, in addition to the definite/indefinite distinction based on the past participle plus inflected forms of the verb *viTu-*, which is found in Jaffna Tamil as in other dialects. In fact, the latter distinction appears to crosscut the aspectual category in question, with the categories operating independently. Thus, all of the following are possible: *paTiccen*, past 'I studied'; *paTiccuviTTen* or *paTicciTTen*, past definite; *paTiccanaan*, past perfective (or emphatic); *paTicciTTanaan* past perfective definite, leading to a very rich set of distinctions within the general category of past.

Jaffna Tamil also has present tense pronominal forms, based on the present tense verbal adjective plus personal pronouns, such as *vaara naan* 'I come', *paTikkira naan'* I study', etc. The same general considerations that lead us to interpret the past tense sequences as finite verb forms apply here as well, and we can thus deal with the present forms briefly. They do appear to imply a different semantic distinction from the past forms, however, generally having a habitual sense. Thus:

(17) a. *naankaL cooru caappiTuranaankaL.*
      we   rice   eat-PRES-ADJ-we
      'We eat rice (generally).'

     b. *appaa munti(k) kuTikkiravar.*
       father before   drink-PRES-he
       'Father used to drink.'

Note that the action described in the second example is past, and in fact completed, so that these forms convey the habitual aspect rather than present time, though they are present tense forms in terms of their inflection.

There is a corresponding negative for these forms, as well, formed by adding *illai* directly to either the present verbal adjective or to the present action verbal noun formed from the present verbal adjective plus *atu*:

(18) *avar iñca vaaṟeellai* (< *vaaṟa* + *illai*) or *vaaṟatillai* (< *vaara* + *atu* + *illai*).
     he   here come-ADJ not *or* come-VBLNOUN not
     'He doesn't come here.'

This negative formation, or at least that with the verbal noun, occurs in other dialects as well, also with the habitual sense. Jaffna Tamil, however, appears to be unique in having developed a specifically marked positive counterpart for it—that is, the non-negative habitual form with the verbal adjective and personal pronoun.

To recapitulate, what Jaffna Tamil has developed is a subsystem of finite verbal forms based on the combination of the verbal adjective with personal pronouns, each with its corresponding negative forms. With the past tense forms, this exemplifies a perfective–imperfective or emphatic–nonemphatic distinction vis-à-vis the regular inflected forms, and with present tense forms, the distinction is habitual–nonhabitual. This subsystem is summarized in table 12–2, using first person forms of *var-* 'come' and *paTi-* 'study' as examples. These forms contrast, as we have noted, with the more usual present and past tenses—that is, with *vaaren, paTikkiṟen; vanten, paTiccen,* and so on.

Further investigation of the semantic implications of these forms may reveal that a single category distinction is involved within both tenses, corresponding to the obvious morphological parallels, but this is by no means an obvious conclusion, and it will require examination of a much wider range of data exemplifying the use of these forms than we have been able to carry out as yet.

We also cannot at present offer an explanation buttressed by sufficient historical evidence for how and by what stages these pronominal verb forms came about. It would not seem unreasonable, however, that they began as relative clause formations involving an intermediate stage by which the pronoun head was permitted to have an indefinite interpretation, thus allowing it to be modified by a restrictive relative clause while serving as the predicate of an equational sentence, something like

Table 12–2 Subsystem of Finite Verbal Forms

	Present (*Habitual*)	*Past* (*Perfective*)
Pronominal Form:	Verbal adjective + personal pronoun *vaaṟanaan* *paTikkaṟanaan*	Verbal adjective + personal pronoun *vantanaan* *paTiccanaan*
Negative	Action verbal noun or verbal adjective + *illai* *vaaṟeellai, vaaṟatillai* *paTikkiṟeelai, paTikkirēatillai*	Action verbal noun+ *illai* *vantatillai* *paTiccatillai*

"(I am) an I (who did such and such)." The predicate could thus serve to assign an attribute (or more strictly, membership in a class) to the pronominal subject, parallel to "I am one who does such and such," rather than an identification ("I am he who"). From this, it would seem a short step to the current senses of these forms, and there is ample precedent elsewhere for the similar transitions from nominal to verbal forms.[9] It would also seem probable that the indefinite interpretation of the pronoun with which such a line of development commenced could occur most easily in the third person and spread to the others, but all of this must remain speculation until clear historical evidence is found.

For present purposes, it is enough to note that this subsystem as a whole contributes to giving the Jaffna Tamil verbal system a distinctive character, even though some of its individual features may be found in other dialects. If our presentation is of interest to students of Tamil dialectology and ultimately contributes to establishing the place of the Jaffna variety within the broad spectrum of Tamil dialects, we will have more than accomplished our purpose.

Addendum to the Reprinting

Sanford Steever (1988: 84–85), referring specifically to this paper, has claimed that the forms that we have designated as pronominal verb forms here (or as the PAST EMPHATIC VERB in Gair, Suseendirarajah, and Karunatilaka 1978: 291) does not have the derivation given here, claiming instead that they represent a survival of a "so-called past tense marker -(n)taṉ" which was "really a present perfect tense marker" ultimately from a auxiliary verb *man 'be' used in a serial verb construction (p. 84), parallel to a derivation he proposes for verbal forms in Pengo. Thus, for him, Classical Tamil va-ntaṉ-eṉ 'I have come' would implicitly represent the etymon of the Jaffna Tamil form vanta-naan (in the morphological division we have proposed here). Similarly, he analyzes the Jaffna Tamil form piTiccaniinkaL 'you have caught' as piṭic-can-īŋkaḷ 'catch-pres perf-2p', wheareas under our analysis it would derive from piTicca-niinkaL 'catch-past -REL+2pers. pron (setting aside the possibility of further decomposing the pronominal forms, as they indeed are in Suseendirarajah 1967). Without addressing the general thesis of Steever's account as it applies to other languages, it seems necessary to point out, at least briefly, some problems with his proposal as it applies specifically to Jaffna Tamil, since it directly contradicts the derivation that we have given here.

Steever states that the forms in question are "retentions of the [Classical Tamil] synthetic present perfect" and that the "only difference is in the allomorphy of the personal endings: while the personal endings in Classical Tamil have short vowels, those in Sri Lankan Tamil have long vowels." This, he further states, "can be explained as a side-effect of the historical changes that have progressively reduced the allomorphic variation among the personal endings in favor of those forms with long vowels." This is unfortunately, observationally incorrect. Even in the forms he cites, there is a qualitative as well as quantitive difference in the vowel of the first person singular affix: -(n)aa(n) versus -e(n). Note also that the latter form continues to exist in Jaffna Tamil. Even more importantly, if one goes beyond the first and second persons cited, the intermediate -*n*- (which I understand to be an integral part of Steever's derivation) disappears. Thus, we see, for example, the form *vantavar* (*vant-avar*) 'came-he' = 'came 3Sg Masc', which was, in fact, given in this paper. Note that the final part of this contrasts with the regular past ending *vant-aar*, but it is identical with the third singular masculine polite pronoun *avar*.

Similarly, we find *vant-avan* 'he came (pronominal, nonpolite) versus *vant-aan*; *vant-avaa* 'she came (pronominal) ' versus *vant-aa*; *vantavai* they came (polite, pronominal) versus *vant-inam*, and so on. If we assume the relative plus pronominal derivation, only one rule is needed: the sandhi that reduces -*a* +*a*- to single -*a*-; but this rule applies also across the board to the clear combinations of relativizing verb form with an *a*- initial pronominal head, as in *kaNT-avar* (<*kaNTa+avar*) 'the one I saw'. It even applied to the negative relativizing form *pookaatavai* '(*pookaata+avai*) 'those who didn't come' (Gair, Suseendirarajah, and Karunatilaka 1978: 306).[10]

In short, the pronominal past (or "past emphatic verb") forms exhibit three characteristics. First, they are homonymous throughout the paradigm with the pronominally headed relatives (Gair, Suseendirarajah, and Karuntilaka 1978: 291, 306), and out of context, the pronominal past forms are ambiguous with them, as stated earlier in this chapter. Second, they agree completely in form with the Jaffna independent pronouns, save for the one sandhi rule. Third, the pronominal past forms differ in their endings from other verb forms in either Jaffna Tamil or in other dialects that I know of in ways that a simple lengthening rule cannot easily account for (even if one were to invoke an additional nasal deletion rule applying to some forms).[11] Thus, by far the simplest, and hence null, hypothesis for their derivation would be the one advanced here.

Selections from the Review
of Southworth and Apte

This review appeared in Language *54(2), pp. 461–65. The section reprinted here addressed the three papers in that volume that were concerned with phonological aspects of the area as a whole, and it raised some questions of methodology that are still relevant to studies of this specific area and beyond.*

The papers by Emeneau, F. Kuiper, and Southworth, taken together, form a significant contribution to the study of South Asian prehistory. Kuiper's "The Genesis of a Linguistic Area" is by now a classic and scarcely requires comment. Subsequent research has shown him to be substantially correct in his view that "it will no longer be permissible to ignore the wider Pan-Indian perspective with regard to those innovations of Indo-Aryan that have striking parallels in the non-Aryan languages of India" (p. 146), and his paper remains a seminal contribution to that end. His hypothesis that such features as the gerunds, "must have emerged among the lower classes, and must have been used in colloquial speech, long before they found acceptance in the highly traditional religious poetry" (p. 151) has also been accepted and elaborated by others, such as Emeneau and Southworth. His paper and Emeneau's "The Indian Linguistic Area Revisited" are distinguished by the careful marshaling of detailed evidence through time; they are scholarly models that might well be emulated, whether or not one agrees with them in all details.

Emeneau's consideration of Sanskrit *api* and its descendants, as compared with Dravidian *-um*, demonstrates that the parallels go far beyond chance, and one important by-product consists of the etymologies provided for some problematic forms, notably Emeneau's derivation of particles with aspirate or *h* in several languages from an apparently unremarked Apabhraṃśa *vi/pi hu*. His other major example, the parallel use of social status terms, particularly paired masculine and feminine terms for caste and occupation, is by nature not as conclusive. Since such parallels are linked to social structure, the argument for linguistic convergence *per se*, rather than parallels born of similar social structure (though a product of diffusion) is not as strong as in the case of the grammatical functors, with their high degree of form–meaning arbitrariness. In conjunction with the larger picture, though, they are additional evidence for convergence.

Southworth's attempt to give a more specific geographical and sociolinguistic setting to early influences on Indo-Aryan (IA) in "Linguistic Stratigraphy of North India," despite some references to Ashokan inscriptions, draws evidence largely from the contemporary distribution of features—notably gender systems, classifiers, and the frequency of retroflex consonants. His argument for regional differences that resulted from early pidginization or creolization is based on two main points: First, there was a progressive weakening of IA features correlating with the southward and eastward spread of IA. By implication, this is also a function of time, with more contact time for "pidginization" in the outward areas. Second, there were different substrata in different areas: Dravidian languages in the west and south (strong retroflexion and a three-gender system) versus other languages in the east (no grammatical gender or dental–retroflex contrast).

This is a bold attempt to operate on a broad scale. Southworth's argument is plausible, and it agrees in general with Emeneau and others; but there are some problems regarding particular features, especially retroflexion. Southworth notes that "some of the Ashokan dialect differences noted by Bloch have either disappeared or become less prominent" (p. 211). However, his statement that "the absence of a distinction between *n* and *ṇ* (as also that between *l* and *ḷ*) precisely in the languages and dialects of the Ganges system still indicates, as it did in Ashoka's time, that the Gangetic area is distinct from the rest of IA" does imply a specific continuity. Though Bloch (1965: 60) noted that eastern Ashokan had only the dental nasal, at least graphically, the present-day *n/ṇ* and *l/ḷ* distinctions in the west are not direct continuations of Old Indo-Aryan (OIA) contrasts.

Except in Sinhala and Pali, OIA *n* and *ṇ* seem to have merged everywhere in Middle Indic, and the modern *n/ṇ* contrast is a later development, with *ṇ* derived from single intervocalic *n*. Not only does this fact create chronological problems for Southworth's argument, but the same development also appears to have occurred in the eastern language Oriya, and it may even have occurred in Assamese and Bengali with subsequent merger (cf. Pattanayak 1966, esp. 62–65). Modern *ḷ* is similarly a later development, and an *l/ḷ* contrast is doubtful for OIA in any case. Sinhala creates another problem, since it retained the *n/ṇ* and *l/ḷ* contrasts (but *ḷ* is also a later development, from *ḍ*) until about the ninth century. Though its geographical origin is disputed, the evidence favors the east, particularly since Karunatillake 1969 accounts for previously unexplainable umlaut phenomena on the assumption of an eastern type of nominal ending in -*e*, with subsequent *e > i* (a view bolstered by inscriptional evidence). This is a problem for the argument that retroflexion was weak or lacking in the east from earliest times.

Southworth's statistics are based on the text frequency of all retroflexes, so we cannot tell what effect the removal of *ṇ* and *ḷ* would have on them; but we can assume that his figures would not be affected for Hindi and Bengali, where those sounds do not occur, so that his lower frequency in the eastern regions would remain unchanged. To account for that, and to see what really happened, we must look at specific etyma, to see whether there was loss in some items toward the east or a gain in the west. It is true that the distinction was lost completely in Assamese, but this seems to have occurred after common changes linking Assamese with Bengali and Oriya, which also requires chronological explanation (Pattanayak 1966, esp. 62–65). Regarding gender, whatever the cause of its loss in the east, it is dubious to invoke Dravidian influence for its retention in the west since, as Southworth recognizes, if early Dravidian had a three-gender system, it was natural gender, not grammatical gender as in IA.

Regarding the much-disputed origin of the IA retroflex consonants, all three papers on prehistory accept the view of Dravidian origin, not only through loanwords, but also by the interpretation of (OIA) retracted allophones as retroflex by second-language speakers of OIA. On evidence of the kind advanced by Kuiper, this is an arguable proposition; but it still leaves us with a kind of chicken-and-egg problem for certain retroflexes, particularly intervocalic $ḍ$ and $ḍh$ from *$ẓd$ and *$ẓdh$. For the Dravidian hypothesis to hold here, the loss of $ẓ$ had to occur after the contrast in stops was introduced, since that loss would immediately have led to $d/ḍ$ and $dh/ḍh$ contrasts. Barring new evidence, this chronology is not likely to be definitively settled. Emeneau goes further, attributing the "spontaneous" retroflexes in items with IE dental etyma to mistakes in assignment by nonnative speakers of OIA. To judge from my experience with second-language learning, such mistakes are more likely to occur when speakers lack a distinction in the language being learned rather than the reverse; but Emeneau's argument is as good as any other to date, and at least it offers a nonmystical solution.

How Dravidianized
Was Sinhala Phonology?
Some Conclusions and Cautions

This paper was written for the Festscrift for Gordon H. Fairbanks, *edited by Veneeta Acson and Richard L. Leed (Oceanic Linguistics, University of Hawaii Press, 1985). That work was of special significance to me, since it was Gordon who was responsible for my interest in South Asian linguistics, and especially in Sinhala, not only in his classes in Sanskrit and historical linguistics and in numerous discussions, but especially by engaging me as research assistant in the project that resulted in the Fairbanks, Gair, and De Silva Sinhala text, an employment that altered the course of my academic career. I was particularly touched by his letter to me acknowledging the contribution of this paper, and especially delighted that he agreed with it. That was, unfortunately, one of the last letters that he wrote before his death. Because of this special regard for him, I have retained intact here the first, dedicatory paragraph of the paper as it appeared. It follows immediately as the remainder of this note.*

Those of us who were fortunate enough to have studied and worked with Gordon Fairbanks were exposed to a model of willingness to entertain new ideas combined with both a healthy skepticism and a respect for methodological rigor and the available data. He applied this attitude also to too-uncritical attempts to claim influences, such as substratum effects, as causes of language change where the identity of the substrate and the specific nature of the influence could not be established. Such attempts often violated his cherished principle that historical linguistics is a scientific endeavor and that a scientific statement is one that is capable of disproof. South Asia constitutes a linguistic area in which cross-language influence is generally accepted but in which its workings, or even existence, in particular cases are often matters of dispute. It thus affords a number of opportunities to make claims for such influence and to test them. This paper is an attempt to examine a set of claims that have been made concerning one language in a spirit that I hope is consistent with Gordon Fairbanks's principles and approach. It seems fitting that it deals with Sinhala, a language in which he had a special interest, especially since he was the one initially responsible for the author's own interest in and fascination with it. Needless to say, he cannot be held responsible for any lapses here from the standards he set.

A number of scholars, such as Bloch, Chatterji, and Grierson, had pointed out features that appeared to be common to the Indian or South Asian linguistic area and suggested cross-language influence as a possible cause, but it was Murray Emeneau's 1956 paper "India as a Linguistic Area" that focused the question and clearly introduced the *Sprachbund* notion into South Asian linguistics. Subsequently, areal studies formed a major theme in that field, resulting, among others, in such works as the Southworth and Apte's 1974 volume on contact and convergence, Masica's rich and stimulating 1976 work attempting both to define the area and place it within a larger perspective, and further works by Emeneau himself.

Much of this effort has invoked Dravidian influence on Indo-Aryan (IA) or, to a lesser extent, the reverse. In this connection, Sinhala, the Indo-Aryan majority language of Sri Lanka is of particular interest. Except for the closely related Divehi (Maldivian), it is the southernmost IA language, separated from its northern sisters by both the ocean and the southern Dravidian languages for over two millennia. During that time it has been in constant and often close contact with Dravidian languages particularly Tamil–Malayalam. As I have stated elsewhere (1976b: 259), Sinhala's very survival as a clearly Indo-Aryan language can be considered "a minor miracle of linguistic and cultural history."

The IA and hence Indo-European origin of Sinhala is now a matter of consensus among serious scholars, but the location of its ancestor on the subcontinent is not. Both eastern and western origins have been proposed by respected scholars, though there is fairly general agreement that whatever its primary origin, it ultimately incorporated some features of the other region (for a survey, and in my opinion a cogent argument for a generally eastern origin, see Karunatillake 1969 and 1977).

What we can be sure of is that the language was well established on the island by the third century B.C., thanks to the coming of Buddhism and the alphabet in that century, as well as the consequent presence of inscriptions slightly later than the Ashokan ones in India. Sinhala Buddhist tradition claims a date of arrival coincident with the *parinibbāna* of the Buddha—that is, in the sixth or early fifth century, depending on which proposed date we accept for that event. As a matter of fact, when we consider that important linguistic changes intervened between the split of Sinhala from mainland IA and the earliest inscriptions, an actual date around that time does not seem unreasonable.

In 1976, I remarked:

> No one who has worked on Sinhala, Tamil, and on Northern Indo-Aryan languages such as Hindi can fail to get some global feeling of similarities shared between the first two in contradistinction to the latter. There is a danger, however, in drawing too ready conclusions about massive Dravidianization of Sinhala, since it is easy to overlook similarities and differences in the opposite direction and ignore the less exciting question of the extent to which Sinhala has remained distinctly Indo-Aryan. What we need, of course, is not only a careful, point by point typological comparison of the present-day languages, but a study of apparent influences as they operated from period to period. Fortunately, the material for such a study is rich, thanks to the relatively continuous documentation of Sinhala since the earliest inscriptions, but that massive task remains to be done or even fairly commenced. (p. 260)

That assessment remains essentially true, though some small progress has been made (see for example, Ratanajoti 1975; Gair 1980). What I will do here is essentially elaborate on those remarks and the methodological principles implied, largely by examining some claims that have been made for Dravidian influence on Sinhala phonology and raising pertinent methodological and evidential issues along the way. At the end, I will touch lightly on possible syntactic influence (see also Gair 1976b).

Sinhala and the South Indian Dravidian languages are marked off as a subarea by at least two major features: the lack of a series of aspirated consonants in contrast with a nonaspirated series and their overwhelming left-branching syntactic character—in particular, the exclusive or overwhelmingly dominant use of preposed relativized clause structures.

We will return to the second of these features later. The first, interestingly enough, has been disturbed (if we include Telugu and Kannada) by the intrusion of aspirate consonants into the systems of some Dravidian languages largely through Sanskritic borrowings (see map). Sinhala has them only in its most formal varieties and they tend to be fugitive, in terms of pronunciation, even there. Somewhat ironically, the effect of (re)introduction in Sinhala seems even more marginal than in some forms of Telugu or Kannada, as the map in figure 14–1 suggests.

As a point of reference for the discussion of phonological influence, a summary of the systems involved will be useful. Diachronic and varietal considerations make it impossible to really present a single system for each of the languages involved,

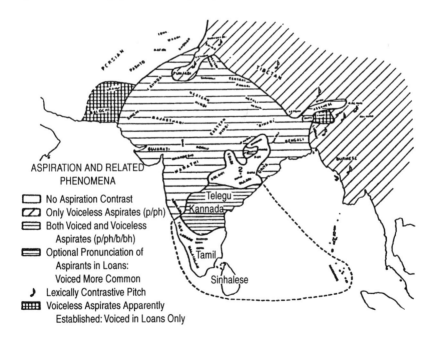

ASPIRATION AND RELATED
PHENOMENA

☐ No Aspiration Contrast
▨ Only Voiceless Aspirates (p/ph)
☰ Both Voiced and Voiceless
    Aspirates (p/ph/b/bh)
▭ Optional Pronunciation of
    Aspirants in Loans:
    Voiced More Common
♩ Lexically Contrastive Pitch
▦ Voiceless Aspirates Apparently
    Established: Voiced in Loans Only

Figure 14–1   Distribution of Aspirated Consonants in South Asia (from Ramanujan and Masica 1969) (Reprint permission from Mouton Publishers is gratefully acknowledged).

but the consonant systems given in table 14–1 will suffice. For Middle Indo-Aryan, I have used essentially the Old Sinhala system with the aspirates restored, and it can be taken to represent Pre-Old-Sinhala fairly accurately.[1]

For Tamil-Malayalam, I have used Jaffna Tamil, eliminating contrasts introduced by loanwords. I have, however, retained *L*, which has merged with *l* in Jaffna Tamil, since it was characteristic of Old Tamil. The result approximates quite well the older Tamil system as reflected in the orthography. (Note, however, that the alveolar stop *t* and its contrast with (trilled) *r* apparently represent a reconstitution of the system, not an inheritance, in Jaffna Tamil.)[2]

It is important to note that the system is phonetically richer than the inventory suggests. In particular, stops may have voiced and voiceless allophones, a point that will become important later.

The Sinhala system given is modern colloquial, but it agrees almost entirely with that reflected in thirteenth-century grammars and literary works. m̆b, n̆d, and n̆ḍ, n̆g represent prenasalized stops, the so-called "half-nasals"; the rest is relatively self-explanatory.

In light of the undoubted influence of Dravidian languages, specifically Tamil,[3] on Sinhala, it is not unreasonable to look for such influence in phonology as well as

Table 14–1   Consonant Systems

	Middle Indo-Aryan (Pre-OS)			
Lab.	*Den.*	*Ret.*	*Pal.*	*Vel.*
p	t	ṭ	c	k
ph	th	ṭh	ch	kh
b	d	ḍ	j	g
bh	dh	ḍh	jh	gh
m	n	ṇ	(ñ)	
v				
		y		
		r		
		l		
		s		h

Tamil (Jaffna)[a]							Sinhala (13th c. and modern)[b]				
Lab.	*Den.*	*Alv.*	*Ret.*	*Pal.*	*Vel.*		*Lab.*	*Den.*	*Ret.*	*Pal.*	*Vel.*
p	t	ṯ	t	c	k		p	t	ṭ	c	k
							b	d	ḍ	j	g
							m̆b	n̆d	n̆ḍ		n̆g
m	n		ṇ	ñ			m	n		ñ	ŋ
v		y					v		y		
			r						r		
			(L)						l		
		l	ḷ						s		h

[a]*r*, trilled retroflex; *L*, voiced frictionless lateral continuant; *c* represents s.
Notes on Sinhala:
[b]m̆b, etc., are prenasalized stops intervocalically.

in other areas of grammar. The broadest and strongest claims, partially recapitulating those made by others, seem to have been made by Elizarenkova (1972). She sees:

> paradigmatic influence of the Tamil phonological system towards the Sinhalese one . . . manifesting itself mainly in the loss of some opposition of distinctive features caused by the contact with Tamil . . . or in the change in volume of a certain opposition which has existed in Sinhalese previously. (p. 133)

In what follows, I address myself largely to Elizarenkova's paper, partly because it presents the fullest and most explicit set of suggested influences and partly because it exemplifies in a particularly clear fashion a method that might be called the inference from comparative inventory, one not uncommon in areal studies. As far as I know, it has not been spelled out explicitly, but in its essentials as reflected by its exemplars, it includes two major steps:

1. A number of common properties are surveyed across contiguous languages in some area, and/or subsystems are compared largely in terms of their inventories.
2. Historical inferences concerning cross-language influence are drawn, preferably in comparison with cognate languages outside the area of at least one of the language families being compared, so as to determine the limits and direction of influence.

These procedures may be amplified in various ways. For example, one can look at earlier stages with more or less thoroughness, and one may try to delineate the general area in terms of a number of features, in a manner similar to dialect geography, but the two steps above seem to be central.

Specifically, Elizarenkova proceeds by postulating a "New Indo-Aryan (NIA) model"[4] (p. 126) and then comparing Sinhala with both it and Tamil. All of her points of comparison and contrast cannot be considered here, but the most important ones seem to be (cf. Shapiro and Schiffman 1981: 138):

1. Sinhala has fewer phonemes (about 30) than is common in IA (though more than in Tamil).
2. In Sinhala, the "volume of opposition of cerebrality" (i.e., retroflexion) is less than in the rest of NIA.
3. The absence of diphthongs in Sinhala, unlike in Eastern IA.
4. The absence of nasalized vowel phonemes.
5. The partial neutralization of *s* and *h* in Sinhala, because of the change *s > h* "already at work in Sinhalese prakrit," with the result that *s* and *h* became "actually not opposed to each other" in the modern language (p. 129).
6. The opposition of long and short vowels, common in Dravidian, less so in IA. (This is particularly relevant for *e* and *o*, for which a length contrast is lacking in Sanskrit, much Middle Indic, and NIA; and for *æ*, which is lacking entirely in most IA).
7. The loss of aspiration in Sinhala commonly retained in IA.

The first point, the relative paucity of phonemes, actually follows from others, such as the loss of the aspirate series and the change $s > h$, with subsequent $h > \emptyset$. Similarly, the "decrease in cerebrality" (point 2) is, as far as I can follow it, a function of the loss of the aspirate series, so that there were fewer retroflex phonemes to oppose. These two points, then, require no special attention but stand or fall with the rest.

As for the absence of the diphthongs (point 3), I confess that I have not been able to make the argument precise enough to evaluate it. The extent to which Tamil has diphthongs would depend on dialect, register, and stage of the language. In Jaffna Tamil, for example, written (and presumably older) ay and $\bar{a}y$ are commonly represented by low front vowels relatively close to Sinhala α and $\bar{\alpha}$ (ay remains in monosyllables), so that, if anything, this could be taken to suggest interference in the opposite direction. Furthermore, the lack of diphthongs in Sinhala resulted largely from changes such as $ay(a) > e$ and $av(a) > o$ occurring prior to the earliest inscriptions and common also in mainland Middle Indic even where Tamil influence would be hard to posit convincingly. A later loss of diphthongs in final position somewhere before the eighth century (Karunatillake 1969: 96ff.) affected diphthongs that had arisen largely from the change of other intervocalic consonants into y and v. Hence, Sinhala eighth century $p\bar{a}$ 'foot' from OIA $*{}'p\bar{a}da$ ($> *p\bar{a}ya > *pay$), $r\bar{u}$ 'form' from OIA $*r\bar{u}pa$ ($> *r\bar{u}va > *ruv$) etc. Note that here we would have to account for the dipthongs that were lost having arisen in the first place in the face of the presumed Tamil influence. In any event, much requires explanation before we can accept Elizarenkova's assertion with confidence.

The absence of nasalized vowels (point 4), noted also by Ramanujan and Masica (1969) as a subareal feature, is difficult to treat briefly, since nasals constitute one of the most complex areas of Sinhala phonology, both synchronic and diachronic, but some considerations might be mentioned.

First, it is difficult to determine whether Sinhala did in fact develop nasalized vowels as a transitional stage following the loss of nasal consonants preceding voiceless consonants, probably before the fourth century (Karunatillake 1969: 60). For the development of nasal vowels under such circumstances, one can consider not only the northern IA languages such as Hindi but also languages such as French and, for development and subsequent loss, the pre–Old English change resulting in $g\bar{o}s$ from West Germanic $*gans$-.[5] The inscriptions give us no real evidence, since they fail to write nasals not only before voiceless consonants for the period in question but also before voiced consonants, where they must have been retained. Thus we see in inscriptions $saga$ monks (cf. Pali $sangha$). If nasal vowels were present, of course, we would be faced with another instance of the arising of an "un-Tamil" feature only for it to be eliminated later. (The possibility of different influence at different times suggests itself and will be considered subsequently.)

In any case, the loss of the nasal is itself a problem for the argument. The nasal was retained before voiced consonants but then shortened so as to produce a prenasalized consonant. This might be in accord with Tamil influence, providing the influencing dialect was one of those with nasal + voiced stop clusters. Present-day Tamil generally has a voiced stop here, earlier Tamil probably a voiceless one.[6] In no case, however, is there a voiced/voiceless contrast after nasal in Tamil, and it is significant that Sinhala clusters such as *nt* and *nd* did not merge as either *nd* or *nt*, the change that we might reasonably expect under Tamil influence. Rather, the result of the actual change was a most un-Tamil intervocalic single voiceless stop. (Elizarenkova herself notes the absence of a Tamil voicing contrast.) These considerations as a whole certainly militate against an easy assumption of Tamil influence in this case, too, unless one can provide some reasonable hypothesis as to how it might have operated in fact.

One way of saving the influence hypothesis might be to assume that the change VNC > ÑC (where C is a voiceless consonant)[7] occurred before Tamil influence, which was then responsible for the loss of the nasalization.[8] This would require a very early date for the VNC > ÑC change, especially if that Tamil influence were to occur as early as it has been postulated for other effects, such as the very early loss of aspirates (to be dealt with later), and we have noted that the loss of nasal itself involves un-Tamil consequences, so that the influence would presumably have had to come into play after that change. There were a number of changes affecting single consonants occurring in Sinhala between the second and fourth centuries A.D., such as the merging of voiced and voiceless nonlabial stops (see below) and subsequent changes affecting the results, such as *g* and *d* becoming *y*, *p* becoming *v*, and *ḍ* becoming *ḷ*. The single stops resulting from the loss of nasals in NC clusters did not undergo these changes, so that the latter change, and the possible subsequent loss of nasalization, would have to postdate the others, ruling out early Tamil influences here. It is clear that the timing of that influence so as to accord with all of these phenomena faces serious problems and contradictions, since at every stage there is some linked non-Tamil feature.

Point 5, regarding *s* and *h*, also touches on some complexities of Sinhala phonology, but with simplification, a general evaluation can be made. First of all, the assertion that Sinhala *s* and *h* do not contrast is simply wrong for any modern register. Compare Colloquial *hatə* 'seven' and *hiiyə* 'ploughing' with *satə* 'cents'; *siiyə* '100' and *visə* 'poisonous' with *ihələ* 'above'. In all of these, the *s* and *h* are stable, and examples could be multiplied with ease. Furthermore, *s* > *h* is not one change in the history of Sinhala, but it occurred twice. Ignoring a number of complications regarding positional variants and intersecting changes, the major developments are schematized in figure 14–2 (superscript numerals are for reference).

One result of these changes is modern alternations such as *miniha* 'man', *minissu* 'men'; *gaha* 'tree', *gas* 'trees'. There is also a great deal of variation within and across registers. Hence Literary *sata* 'seven', Colloquial *hatə*, but *hoodənəva ~ soodeneva* 'wash', *raha ~ rasə* 'tasty', both Colloquial, the last of each pair also Literary (with a different spelling). In the light of such alternations, reflected also in earlier documents as well as the successive changes above, it is not unlikely that there was never a time when Sinhala did not have both *s* and *h*, although they came from different sources at different times.

Even more important, it is hard to see how Tamil influence would lead to *s* > *h* so as to approximate some Tamil pattern while allowing a new s to arise at about the same time. Granting that both *c* > *s* and *s* > *h* have been suggested by Grierson to reflect possible Dravidian influence, but for different languages, it is hard to conceive of them operating at cross purposes in the same language at the same time (i.e.,

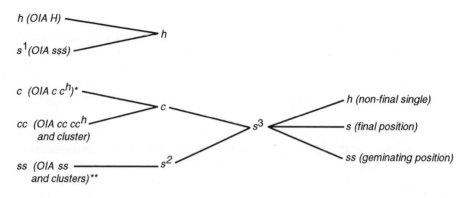

Note: Chronological order is left-right.
*Only initial *c* is retained and becomes s^3 Medial *c* had merged earlier with *j* and ultimately became *d*.

**The change of *ss*>*s* is part of a general, pre-8th century simplification of geminates. A new gemination of consonants, including s^3, ocurred after simplification to s^2, but obviously before s^3> h.

Figure 14–2   Contrast of *s* and *h*

so as to both eliminate and restore *s*). Worse yet, a plausible Tamil model is hard to conceive, since Tamil lacks an initial *h*. On the other hand, *c* may be represented by initial and/or medial *s* in some Tamil dialects (initial *c*, medial *s* in Jaffna) which lends some plausibility to *c* > *s*, though *cc* does not simplify and become *s* in any dialect that I know of. Note also that initial *c*, which may remain in Tamil, becomes *s* in Sinhala and that (original) intervocalic *c*, which is generally represented by *s* in Tamil, became *j* in Sinhala, a most un-Tamil effect. The resulting *j* later merged with *d*, and the result of that change, together with others affecting *c* and *cc*, was to completely eliminate the palatal series, another quite un-Tamil result.[9]

In sum, a point-by-point comparison of the entire relevant set of subsystems, taking some of the known history into account, makes the *s* > *h* change another unlikely candidate for Dravidian influence, though *c* > *s* (a change that Elizarenkova mentions but does not seem to take as Tamil influence) could conceivably reflect it.

Sinhala, like Tamil, has a short/long contrast for all vowels (except perhaps Sinhala *ə*), so that an influence hypothesis (point 6) is possible. However, somewhere before the eighth century, Sinhala long vowels merged with their short counterparts, so that vowel length was lost.[10] Pausing only to note that this is another most un-Tamil development and strongly suggests a lack of Tamil influence at that time, we may note that the later (and present-day) contrast in length arose from the general loss of *y*, *w*, and *h* between vowels or, finally, a development reflected from about the eighth century in inscriptions (Karunatillake 1969: 101ff.). To this day, there are variations, as in *bææ ~ bæhæ* 'can't' and *pohosat ~ poosat* 'rich'. While Tamil influence could conceivably have helped such a change along, it seems scarcely necessary to invoke it. The outcome may be more Tamil-like, but the mechanism of influence is hard to see. Note also that we cannot assume continuous influence, but we have to switch it on and off to accommodate the earlier un-Tamil loss of vowel length; we shall return to this point.

We now come to the last of the seven proposed points of Tamil influence, the loss of aspiration. Dravidian influence has been accepted here by a number of scholars including Geiger (1936: xviii), Wijeratne (1945: 590), and Ratanajoti (1975: 34), and Elizarenkova states flatly that "the loss of the opposition in Sinhalese is due to the contact with Tamil" (p. 132). Certainly, this is by far the strongest candidate among the set of proposed influences.

The fact that aspiration was lost in Sinhala somewhere before the third century is attested to by the inscriptional evidence, and particularly by fluctuations and backspellings, such as second century B.C. *jhaya* 'wife' (*cf.* Pali, OIA *jāyā*) or first century B.C. *rajha* 'king' (*cf.* Pali, OIA *rājā* (Karunatillake 1969: 12). To the best of my knowledge, no other IA language has undergone complete deaspiration,[11] although some IA languages have undergone deaspiration for particular series (as in Panjabi voiced aspirates), particular positions (final in Bengali), or sporadically (see Grierson 1931–33: 171ff). Considering this remarkable persistence of the feature in Indo-Aryan (which the map shows clearly), the thoroughgoing and apparently sudden change in Sinhala, apparently following upon its transplantation to the island, does raise a strong possibility of substratum effect. However, it may not be as obvious as it first appears that the substratum was Dravidian. To develop this point, I must first take a detour to consider another set of changes not mentioned so far.

Middle Indo-Aryan (MIA) (i.e., the Prakrits) reflects, with some dialectal differences, a general set of changes of the following sort:

1. the voicing of single intervocalic stops, presumably with lenition and, for some, subsequent loss and
2. the assimilation of consonant clusters, resulting in geminates, such as *sappa* 'snake' from OIA *sarpa*.

Since the lack of a voicing contrast in intervocalic consonants and the allophonic voicing of single intervocalic stops is a common feature of Dravidian, the first change has been attributed by some to Dravidian influence (as by Grierson 1931–33: 42–43, but with reservations). Furthermore, since Tamil lacks many of the medial clusters that were affected in MIA, but is rich in geminate voiceless obstruents, possible influence could be suggested for the second change as well.

The earliest Sinhala inscriptions reflect the assimilation of clusters,[12] but the voicing of intervocalic stops and the subsequent loss of some of them seems to have been a later development paralleling changes in the mainland (Karunatillake 1969: 41ff.). Clearly, it would be as reasonable to invoke Dravidian influence, and particularly substratum, in Sri Lanka as in the mainland; in fact, it would be more reasonable given the undoubted contact. However, a substratum effect, to be plausible, should involve approximation, preferably systematic, to the substrate language. In this instance, this is true only as long as we focus only on the (new) voiced stop and voiceless geminates, ignoring the system of contrasts within the subsystem of stops as a whole. When we look at the latter as represented in Table 14–1, the argument becomes less compelling.

Using the dental stop as an illustration, the Tamil basic allophonic pattern follows the pattern given in the first part of table 14–2. But the early Sinhala (and for that matter, wider MIA) pattern after those changes would follow the pattern in the second part of table 14–2. Clearly, the latter system lacked a voicing contrast only in the single intervocalic stops.[13] Most importantly, the contrast remained unaffected in initial position, where Tamil lacks it, but it was weakened intervocalically, where Tamil has it, at least as a redundant *phonetic* feature. Even there, the contrast was maintained in the geminates in Sinhala, quite unlike Tamil.

I would now like to invoke a methodological principle, or at least a heuristic one, that might be usefully employed in areal studies of this kind: looking at what did not, but might have, happened, as well as what did. In the example at issue, neither the initial stops nor the medial geminates lost their contrast in voicing. We might wonder why a substratum strong enough to effect one change would fail to effect the other but instead would lead only to a very restricted weakening in the superstrate of an opposition lacking in the substrate. As indirect but striking evidence bearing on the plausibility of our argument here, we might note that Tamil-speaking learners of Sinhala to this day have great difficulty with voiced initial stops and medial geminates, to the extent that it serves as the basis for some ethnic humor and has even been incorporated into some ritual interchanges depicting Sinhala–Tamil encounters.

Also, the lenition and voicing of intervocalic consonants is by no means an uncommon change. Grierson (1931–33), in fact, noted the parallel to Romance languages and thus restricted the role of Dravidian to encouraging an otherwise likely change. Taking all of the relevant arguments into account further suggests that Grierson's assertion was indeed the strongest that one could make with any degree of confidence.

Returning now to the loss of the aspirated series: As we noted earlier, the apparent suddenness and completeness of that change does make the assumption of substratum influence plausible, and Dravidian, with its lack of aspirates, is the obvious candidate. On the other hand, when we consider this change together with the others just discussed, the case for that identification becomes less compelling. The initial and geminate consonants would have had to pass through the same substratum filter that was strong enough to screen out the aspirates but remain unaffected. While this is not impossible, it certainly is puzzling, and it makes it far less obvious that the filter was Dravidian. One might rather consider the possibility of a substratum language that opposed voiced and voiceless consonants and preferably possessed a dental–retroflex opposition. While I do not have a specific candidate at present, the

Table 14–2   Allophonic Patterns of Tamil and Sinhala

	Tamil Pattern	
Word-initial	#[t]	
Medial single	-[VdV]- or -[VðV]	
Medial geminate	-[VttV]-	
	Sinhala Pattern	
Word-initial	#[t] -vs- #[d]	(i.e., in contrast)
Medial single	-[VdV]-	(or -[VðV]- ?)
Medial geminate	-[VttV]- vs -[VddV]-	(i.e., in contrast)

existence of a non-Dravidian population on the island seems clear, given the traditional history that mentions it and the actual existence of the Veddas (important in the Sinhala origin tradition as well).

The existence of lexical items in Sinhala which are neither IA nor Dravidian (see De Silva 1979: 16) is also interesting in this regard, and the problem deserves further research that has perhaps been diverted by the Dravidian assumption. A similar suggestion has recently been made in a paper by J. B. Disanayaka (1978).

In his 1966 article on Dravidian metaphony, Bright suggests vowel assimilation as a possible subareal feature extending to non-Dravidian languages. Elizarenkova notes the "synharmonism" of vowels in Sinhala, but she discounts it as Tamil influence, saying that "it can have no source in Tamil" since it is strongest in Tulu and Telugu, which are not contiguous to Sinhala. Bright himself notes (p. 322) that Sinhala vowel assimilation is different from that in both Dravidian and Indo-Aryan languages, since it involves adjustment in fronting, whereas in Dravidian (and Bengali), vowel height is affected. In particular, Tamil vowels are quite stable in backness. Sinhala vowel assimilation thus really sets it off as an isolate rather than placing it within an area.[14] Furthermore, the vowel *æ*, occuring both long and short, which arose from Sinhala "umlaut" (Geiger 1938: 18ff) is another quite un-Tamil phenomenon. It is also quite uncommon in Indo-Aryan[15] and is thus another specifically Sinhala feature.

Examples of the differential treatment of lexical items shared by Sinhala and Tamil (whatever the direction of borrowing) offer dramatic examples of the differences in phonological history, such as Tamil *katti* 'knife' and Sinhala *kætta* 'sickle' (following loss of gemination, fronting, and regemination, with loss of *y* < *i*), as well as Tamil *kanci* [kañji] 'rice gruel' and Sinhala *kæñdə*. By themselves, such examples should cast doubt on the notion of strong and constant Tamil influence.

Ramanujan and Masica (1969) note the absence of retroflex nasals and laterals as a feature setting off Sinhala from Dravidian, which possesses them. As a matter of fact, however, Sinhala appears to have retained the OIA distinction between retroflex and nonretroflex nasals longer than any other IA language. The distinction was retained in Pali: *aṇu* 'particle' verus *anu* 'prefix' and *ciṇṇa* 'practiced' versus *dinna* 'given', but they are merged in one direction or the other in later Prakrits except for Old Sinhala.[16] This by itself, of course, points to the relatively early transfer of Sinhala to the island, in time to miss the general merger on the mainland. The distinction was retained in Sinhala until about the eighth century, until after gemination took place, since the retroflexes did not geminate (Karunatillake 1969: 105–12), and then it was lost. The retention up to that point could, of course, be attributed to Tamil influence, but then we are faced with the subsequent loss, and once more, at the very least, we have to turn the influence on and off.

Roughly the same reasoning applies to the retroflex lateral, which merges with the dental at about the same time as the nasals merged, but its origin was within Sinhala from intervocalic -*ḍ*- before the eighth century (Geiger 1938: 55; Karunatillake 1969). Note that we might be tempted to invoke Tamil influence in that development since Tamil has a retroflex lateral, but whatever Tamil dialect would have been involved would most likely have had an intervocalic *ḍ* as well, at least as an allophone of /t/. It is thus hard to see what would have triggered the change, and that argument, too, loses much of its force.

We may now note briefly a few clearly un-Tamil developments in Sinhala phonology.

At some point, all final nasals merged to [ŋ]. This change is paralleled in Pali, but it is difficult to date in Sinhala. What is certain is that it occurred by the thirteenth century, when we have graphic evidence of it (Karunatillake 1969: 129ff.).[17] This is a most un-Tamil change, since Tamil retains the distinction in final nasals. Some mainland dialects (but not Jaffna Tamil) develop nasalized vowels there, but even then vowel quality gives a clue to the position of the earlier nasal.

Quite early, by the fourth century, all of the final vowels, -i, -e, -u, and -a in Sinhala, merged as /a/ (except in #CVC-# structures where -e > -a but the other vowels remained unaffected (Karunatillake 1969: 48ff.). Since Tamil distinguishes these vowels, this is another most un-Tamil development. Furthermore, the Tamil unmarked final vowel (occurring when some other vowel does not) is -u, not -a, a feature shared with some other Dravidian languages (Bright 1972).

Later, at some time before the eighth century, Sinhala lost final vowels under most conditions (Karunatillake 1969: 92ff.). This left obstruents in final position (subsequently the voiced and voiceless ones merged, much as in Germanic or Slavic). Clearly this change, too, was a most counter-Tamil one, since Tamil does not allow final obstruents.

One might point to the redevelopment of geminates, somewhere after the eighth century, as a development in a Tamil-like direction, but this followed upon their non-Tamil-like loss earlier, which reinstituted a contrast between voiced and voiceless single consonants, and it was the result of a quite common internal process of sound change, bearing resemblances to West Germanic gemination. Furthermore, retroflex consonants did not geminate, as mentioned earlier, though there is no such constraint in Tamil, where geminate retroflexes abound. In addition, Sinhala gemination reintroduced the most un-Tamil contrast between voiced and voiceless geminate stops, again in contradistinction to the Tamil pattern.

Looking back now at the phonological changes in the history of Sinhala that has been discussed, it is apparent that the great majority of them, when looked at closely, do not really result in more Dravidian-like patterns and that those that do often include un-Tamil consequences as well.

Earlier, I noted that proponents of strong Tamil influence would at the very least have to allow for that influence being turned on and off. We should accordingly look at how the changes arranged themselves in real time, since it is perfectly possible that there were periods of strong influence alternating with periods of weak or no influence. Ideally, one should also do this in relation to the social and political history, but I have not been able to carry out this task properly as yet. The history of Sinhala–Tamil relations is not yet all that clear, despite quite full documentation for the political and religious history, so that more research of a purely historical kind would be required to make such linkage possible. However, a simple plotting of most of the changes we have discussed with regard to their occurrence in time as shown by inscriptional evidence and their necessary sequencing, as given in table 14–3, shows that even the argument for differential influence at different periods faces serious problems. Most changes are counter-Dravidian (marked -D), but even those few that could be considered to be in a Dravidian direction (+D)

Table 14–3   Summary of Changes (in Rough Chronological Order)

Pre-OS	Loss of aspiration	+D
	Assimilation in clusters	+D(?)
Before Eighth Century		
	Simplification of geminates	−D
	Metaphony/vowel fronting	−D
	Word-final vowels merge as /a/	−D
	s > h	−D(?)
	c > s	+D(?
About Eighth Century		
	Loss of vowel length	−D
	Loss of final vowel with	
	resultant final obstruents	−D
	Loss of final *y, v*	±D (+v, -y)
	Reinstitution of vowel length	+D
After Eighth Century		
	Final nasals merge as [ŋ] (date uncertain)	−D
	Reintroduction of geminates	+Dᵃ
	(but) nongeminating retroflexes	
	ṇ, ḷ merge with *n, l*	−D

ᵃResembles Tamil only in terms of the surface outputs that resulted from changes under specifically Sinhala conditions that did not replicate Tamil.
Note: ±D means ± resemblance to Dravidian.

are interspersed, with plus or minus changes occurring with at least approximate simultaneity.

We can now attempt to summarize and to put the entire question of Dravidian influence in perspective with relation to possible influence on other parts of the grammar. Before doing so, it is worthwhile to gather together some of the methodological points that have surfaced along the way and make them explicit.

Assessing cross-language influence within a linguistic area is fraught with pitfalls, since the very nature of the problem makes it necessary to proceed on the basis of inferences most of which are ultimately probabilistic, since the changes involved are commonly such that they could have occurred independently. There are, of course, clear cases, such as lexical borrowings, idiomatic calques, and the borrowing of new sounds in lexical items, but these are not problems since they can be dealt with within well-developed methodology, nor are they usually the most interesting phenomena for area-historical studies. There is, of course, one general principle for assessing likelihood: The more marked (or in general terms, unexpected) a feature shared by languages in contact is, the more likely it is to represent borrowing. Complexity, in terms of the association of a number of not necessarily associated features, is, of course one important aspect of markedness in this general sense. (As I have indicated elsewhere, however, differential complexity in two languages does not necessarily indicate the direction of borrowing (see Gair 1980: 39). In attributing influence, as in other inferential endeavors, one must proceed with a healthy skepticism, and our examination of the Sinhala case has suggested some useful principles, largely cautionary in nature, to wit:

1. Do not consider only surface inventories with regard to single features, but look at whole systems or relevant subsystems.
2. Consider the likelihood that a change would have occurred independently, especially if it occurred in cognate languages outside the area. While this does not rule out influence, it may limit its function to that of a catalyst. In particular, consider whether the change was part of a wider change or set of changes, the remainder of which are not likely to be a result of influence.[18]
3. If a change appears to be toward the pattern of another language, look to see whether there are side effects or associated changes that run counter to that pattern.
4. Provide, if possible, a plausible mechanism for a change for which influence is suggested by indicating how that influence would have operated.
5. Look at what did *not* happen but might have under the proposed conditions of influence.

As a final methodological note: There will be instances in which we will of necessity be confined to making inferences on the basis of the synchronic distribution of features, since other evidence is not available. In that case, one is forced *faute de mieux* to employ and limit oneself to the inference from comparative inventory method. In this case, a large number of shared features can lend credibility to assertions of influence, but the cautions above can still largely be observed. Where historical evidence of other sorts is available, however, it should be used.

Examined in the light of these principles, the case for massive, or even strong, Tamil influence on the phonology of Sinhala has proved to be surprisingly weak. The most robust claim can be made for the loss of aspiration, but even there the character of the presumed substratum is in doubt. When we look at the Sinhala consonantal system in table 14–1 in that light, we are struck, in fact, with the surprising integrity of the system over time, not its vulnerability. Allowing for the very early lack of aspiration, the system largely retains its Indo-Aryan character despite a number of intervening allophonic and distributional changes. The largest single difference, aside from aspiration, is the series of prenasalized stops, a uniquely Sinhala feature in Indo-Aryan and also a non-Dravidian one arising from internal changes (Karunatillake 1969: 108ff.). It is also worth noting, as Elizarenkova does, that "Tamil influence . . . has never introduced any new phonemes into the phonological system of Sinhalese. Not a single phoneme or its variants specific to Tamil has ever been adopted by Sinhalese" (1972: 134).

We have not considered the vowel system as a whole, but enough has been said to indicate that Sinhala has undergone a number of changes setting it off from the other Indo-Aryan languages and that most of these have been most un-Tamil as well. The final result of some of these was to bring Sinhala into closer resemblance with Tamil in some respects, specifically the length contrast for *e* and *o*, but the existence of phonemic /æ/ and /ə/ and the metaphony that the first reflects (i.e., umlaut) differentiate it from both groups. In sum, though Sinhala is part of a southern subarea in terms of one or two features (notably thoroughgoing vowel length and lack of contrastive aspiration), it is in relation to phonology largely an isolate, with a unique character differentiating it from both Dravidian and northern Indo-Aryan.

If we turn to other areas of the grammar, the situation is quite different. Although, as I have claimed elsewhere, the influence in morphology and on at least some aspects of main clause structure have been limited, the effects on subordinate structures have been pervasive (Gair 1976: passim), and some of these effects have been noted by Ratanajoti (1975, especially chapter 5) and others, including Elizarenkova (1972: 135). The overall effect has been to convert Sinhala to a thoroughgoing left-branching language, much on the model of Tamil (or for that matter, Japanese, usually cited as the "consistent" language of that type). There has also been a borrowing of at least one important and complex main clause structure, a nominalizing cleft or focused construction, illustrated here with Sinhala in example (1) and Jaffna Tamil in example (2):

(1) *mame yanne   kolə̃mbəṭə.*
    I   go-Pres-Emph Colombo-DAT
    'It is to Colombo that I am going.'

(2) *naan pooratu   yaaLpaanattukku.*
    I   go-past/Nom   Jaffna-DAT
    'It is to Jaffna that I am going.'

I have dealt with this construction and its history elsewhere (1980, 1986b), but it is particularly important here since it does not seem to be a feature among the "consistent" set for left-branching SOV languages. It is thus a particularly convincing example of syntactic borrowing, since it is both complex and not likely to arise from a "drift toward consistency."

In his (1938) grammar of Sinhala, Geiger remarked:

> Sinhalese was probably influenced in its development by the neighbouring Dravidian languages. I do not refer to the vocabulary, which indeed contains a good number of Tamil loanwords, for loanwords do not touch the character of a language. . . . We must rather try to trace the Dravidian influence in grammar and style, and I should myself be very glad if a competent student of Dravidian would undertake this important task. (p. vi)

Though some progress has been made in the meantime, much if not most of that task remains to be done, and it is not without theoretical interest for area-historical studies. In any event, it is clear that Geiger knew where to look.

Selections from "The Verb in Sinhala, with Some Preliminary Remarks on Dravidianization"

This paper appeared in the International Journal of Dravidian Linguistics 5(2): *259–272. Some parts of that paper, particularly the survey of inflected verb forms, have been omitted here since they are redundant with other chapters in this volume. The sections reprinted here, with some minor revisions for clarity, are those concerned with the use of the forms and with cross-language parallels and influence, since one fundamental purpose of the paper was to establish a general context for the study of Sinhala in an areal context in reference to one set of phenomena. It thus sets the stage for studies such as chapter 11, "Sinhala Focused Sentences: Naturalization of a Calque."*

As probably the longest separated and most isolated of the South Asian Indo-Aryan languages,[1] Sinhala is of particular interest for the study of the South Asian linguistic area. The earliest Sinhala inscriptions of the late third century B.C. already show clear differences from the mainland Indo-Aryan languages, making it clear that the language had existed on the island for some time before that. Very little is known concerning contact with any non–Indo-Aryan and non-Dravidian languages that might have existed on the island earlier, but there has been steady contact with Dravidian languages, particularly Tamil–Malayalam, since before the beginning of the Christian era. The editors of the PTS Pali dictionary, in fact, argue that the influence of Dravidian on Sinhala was sufficiently strong and early to lead to some apparently Dravidian features finding their way indirectly into Pali through Sinhala in texts of the fifth and sixth centuries A.D. (Rhys-Davids and Stede, 1921–25: vi). Furthermore, Sinhala kingdoms were in constant contact with South Indian kingdoms, whether in wars, alliances, or marriage relationships from pre-Christian times to the last line of Kandyan kings, which itself originated in South India.

Although much of the history of the texture of Sinhala and Tamil (or perhaps more precisely Tamil–Malayalam) cultural relationships remains to be written, what we know of the circumstances would make it astounding if there were not heavy Dravidian influence on Sinhala, and in fact, the survival of Sinhala as a clearly Indo-

Aryan language might be looked on as a minor miracle of linguistic and cultural history. No one who has worked on Sinhala, Tamil, and some Northern Indo-Aryan language such as Hindi can fail to get some global feeling of similarities shared between the first two in contradistinction to the latter. There is a danger, however, in drawing too-ready conclusions about massive Dravidianization of Sinhala, since it is easy to overlook similarities and differences in the opposite direction and ignore the less exciting question of the extent to which Sinhala has remained distinctively Indo-Aryan. What we need, of course, is not only a careful, point-by-point typological comparison of the present-day languages but also a study of apparent influences as they operated from period to period. Fortunately, the material for such a study is rich, thanks to the relatively continuous documentation of Sinhala since the earliest inscriptions, but that massive task remains to be done or even fairly commenced.

This chapter is not an attempt to make a significant start on that major task or even to draw firm conclusions about particular points of similarity and their possible origins. Rather, it will be largely restricted to Sinhala itself and specifically to the verb within that language. Its primary goal is modest: to present a brief descriptive summary of major inflectional and syntactic characteristics of the Sinhala verb, followed by a few preliminary observations on some gross similarities to Tamil, together with some methodological observations. It is hoped that such a summary, by gathering those characteristics in brief compass, may be of some use to those interested in larger questions of language typology and the South Asian linguistic area.

As is well known, Sinhala presents an almost classic case of diglossia with sharply distinct written and spoken varieties (De Silva 1967, Gair 1968, Gair and Karunatilaka 1974, and chapter 18 here among others).[2] In any detailed study of Sinhala–Tamil relations, this varietal distinction, along with the parallel distinction operating within Tamil, would have to be taken into account, since influence would have operated on both levels, and probably with varying intensity at different periods. This paper is limited to Colloquial Sinhala, since the differences between the varieties are great enough to warrant separate treatment. It will also ignore dialectal variants, attempting to largely represent the speech of the educated around Colombo. Although a detailed dialect survey has not been done, material available so far indicates that despite the clear existence of regional differences, taking dialectal variants into account would affect the points made here only in trivial ways, and that the grammatical categories and constructions dealt with would remain essentially the same, despite some differences in the forms of morphemes and in lexical items.[3]

We may now briefly survey the syntactic uses of the inflected forms of the Sinhala verb. For this task, it is convenient to divide the forms into INDEPENDENT forms, which characteristically occur as the main verb in independent clauses, and DEPENDENT forms, which occur in dependent (i.e., embedded) clauses and whose inflectional affixes thus mark subordinate status. One form, the perfect participle, occurs freely in both types of clauses.[4] From an areal and typological point of view, the embedded forms are of special interest, and we will thus include in the discussion some periphrastic forms showing functional similarities with some of the dependent inflected forms.

Independent Forms

The basic forms, (i.e., those tensed forms ending in *-nəwa* or *-a(a)*, such as *kərənəwa* and *keruwa)* appear to be, semantically at least, the most neutral or unmarked forms; that is, they serve essentially as nonpast and past indicative forms:

(1) *mamə peṭṭiyak   hadənəwa /hæduwa.*
    I   box-INDEF   make   /made
    'I make (am making, will make)/made a box.'

The emphatic (-EMPH) forms (i.e., those tensed forms ending in *-nne* or *-e(e)*), are particularly interesting, since they appear to be a peculiarly Sinhala phenomenon among languages of the area.[5] They have two main functions. As main verbs they indicate that the focus is elsewhere than on the verb or verb phrase,[6] and they are likely to be accompanied by a shift from the unmarked (SOV) word order to a focus-last order. The most common English translation equivalent is a cleft or pseudocleft sentence. The following may be compared with their nonemphatic counterpart given earlier:

(2) *mamə hadanne   /hæduwe   peṭṭiyak.*
    I   make-EMPH   /made-EMPH   box-INDEF
    'It is/was a box that I made.'

    peṭṭiyak   hadanne   /hæduwe   mamə.
    box-INDEF   make-EMPH   /made-EMPH   I
    'It is/was I who made a box.'

The other main use of the emphatic form is before the negative auxiliary *nææ*:[7]

(3) *mamə peṭṭiyak   hadanne   /hæduwe   nææ.*
    I   box-INDEF   make-EMPH   /made-EMPH   nææ
    'I am not making/did not make a box.'

The hortative (*-mu*, as in *kərəmu* 'let us do', *yamu* 'let us go', etc.) and the imperative forms occur with the senses one would expect. The imperative marks singular and plural and shows several grades depending on status of speaker and addressee. There are numerous forms, of which a partial subset is given in table 15–1 (from De Silva 1960: 106, with transcription adapted). The infinitive (nonpast stem +

Table 15–1 Imperative Forms

		hadənəwa 'make'	*adinəwa* 'pull'	*wæṭenəwa* 'fall'
Ordinary	sg.	*hadəpan*	*ædəpan*	*wæṭiyan*
	pl.	*hadəpalla*	*ædəpallə*	*wæṭiyalla*
Nonhonorific	sg.	*hadəpiyə*	*ædəpiyə*	*?wæṭiyə*
	pl.	*hadəpiyaw*	*ædəpidaiyaw*	*wæṭiyaw*

nnə—with *nḍ/nṭə* as dialectal variants—as in *kərannə* 'to do') is also used as a polite imperative without distinction of number. No special attention need be given those forms here.

The volitive and involitive optative (respectively nonpast stem + *-nnan,* as in *kərannan* 'will do' and nonpast stem with lengthened vowel +*wi*—with *-(y)i* as dialectal variant—as in *kəraawi/kərayi* 'might do') have future reference and are in complementary or near complementary distribution in their occurrence with first and nonfirst person subjects. The volitive optative is restricted to occurrence with first person, singular or plural, whereas the involitive optative rarely occurs with the first person.[8] They could thus be considered first and nonfirst person future forms, but they have very strong modal senses. The volitive optative implies volition or determination:[9]

(4) *mamə pahaṭa   ennan.*
     I   five-DAT come-VOL-OPT
     I'll come at five.'

The involitive optative signifies the possibility of something's occurring—'might' or 'it could happen that':[10]

(5) *eyaa pahaṭə   witərə   eewi.*
     he   five-DAT about   come-INVOL-OPT
     He might come at about five.'

The perfect participle (participial stem ±*la,* as in *kərəla* 'has done/did'), in addition to its very common subordinate function (which will be dealt with later), also very commonly occurs as a main verb in Sinhala:

(6) *miniha meekə   hadəla.*
     man   this-one make-PERF-PART
     'He has made this.'

The sense is completed action, commonly with an implication of less direct observation of the action itself on the part of the speaker than is the case with the past basic form.[11] The perfect participle also occurs before *tiyenəwa* 'be/exist (inanimate)'[12] to form a perfect:

(7) *mamə ee   pættəṭə   gihilla   tiyenəwa.*
     I   that area-DAT go-PERF-PART be-PAST
     'I have gone to that area.'

The sense may be completed action with third person subjects, but it is usually, in all persons, that one has had the experience of doing something, for example: "I have been to Sri Lanka."

The perfective form (participial stem +*pi,* as in *kərəpi* 'has done') also signifies completed action, commonly with an implication that the action was undesired by the speaker. (The name "ohellative" that I once coined for the form, if somewhat jocular, conveys this implication somewhat better.) Thus:

(8) *miniha eekə   kapapi!*
     he   that-one cut-PERF
     'He's gone and cut it!'

The permissive (past stem +*aawe,* as in *keruwaawe* 'let X do') is also confined to third person and may convey exasperation or unconcern:[13]

(9) *miniha kaepuwaawe!*
     man   cut-PERMISS
     'Let him cut it (I don't care)!'

Dependent Forms

Sinhala embedded verbal structures are of particular interest from an areal standpoint. Here we will deal briefly first with adjectival clauses and then with the adverbial ones. We should first note that there are no clause-initial (or interclause) conjunctions in Sinhala, although there are clause-initial discourse-linking adverbs such as *namut* 'but'. All grammatical subordination is clause-final, either by verbal affix or some lexical item such as a complementizer.

Adjectival (Relative) Clauses

Sinhala has no relative clause in the strict sense involving a relative pronoun, nor has it correlative constructions like the Hindi *jo . . . vo.* Rather, the equivalent of relativization is accomplished by a preposed adjectival clause employing verbal adjectival forms: nonpast (nonpast stem +*nə* as in *kərənə* 'doing'), past (past stem +*ə* as in *keruwə* 'did/has done'), or participial (participial stem +*pu* as in *kərəpu* 'did/has done'). The latter two appear to be semantic equivalents:

(10) a. *miniha hadənə*   *peṭṭiyə*
        man   make-NONPAST-VERBADJ box
        'the box the man is making'

     b. *peṭṭiyə hadənə*   *miniha*
        box   make-NONPAST-VERBADJ man
        'the man who is making the box'

     c. *miniha hæduwə*   /*hadapu*   *peṭṭiyə*
        man   make-PAST-VERBADJ /make-PARTICIPADJ box
        'the box that the man made'

     d. *peṭṭiyə hæduwə*   /*hadəpu*   *miniha*
        box   make-PAST-VERBADJ /make-PARTICIPADJ man
        'the man who made the box'

     e. *lameya iskooleṭə   yanə*   *bas-ekə*
        child   school-DAT go-NONPAST-VERBADJ bus
        'the bus on which the child goes to school'

f. *mamə giyə*   *tænə*
   I   go-PAST-VERBADJ place
   'the place that I went'

The range of nominal forms that may be modified by such clauses approximates the range of those that can be modified by relative clauses in English.[14] That is, there are no restrictions concerning the modified noun in terms of its subject or object status in the embedded clause (or perhaps more accurately that of its deleted equi-NP), such as those that apply to Hindi participial modifiers of the *jaataa huaa* or *gayaa huaa* type, and that are linked to the transitivity and inflection of the verbal form.

Adverbial Clauses

There is one conjunction, *nan* 'if', that may follow a clause in independent form:

(11) *mamə yanəwa nan taatta hambəwenəwa.*
    I   go   if   father   meet
    'If I go, I will meet father.'

Otherwise, adverbial embedding is accomplished by using either of two kinds of forms.

The first method is to use one of the dependent forms of the verb, such as the conditional, concessive, contemporaneous, prior temporal, or reduplicated forms. These may be called CONJUNCT FORMS. As mentioned earlier, the perfect participle is thus both a conjunct and an independent form. The following examples illustrate the use of the conjunct forms and will roughly convey the senses involved:

(12) CONDITIONAL: *mamə peṭṭiyak   hæduwot   salli   hambəwenəwa.*
                 I   box-INDEF make-PAST-COND money receive
                 'If I make a box, I will get money.'

      CONCESSIVE: *mamə peṭṭiyak   hæduwat   salli*
                 I   box-INDEF make-PAST-CONCESS, money
                 hambəwenne næœ.
                 receive   not
                 'Even if I make a box I will not get money.'

CONTEMPORANEOUS: *mamə peṭṭiyak   hadaddi,   miniha kataakeruwa.*
                 I   box-INDEF make-CONTEMP man   talk-PAST
                 'The fellow talked while I made a box.'

   PRIOR TEMPORAL: *mamə peṭṭiyak   hæduwaamə   gedərə giyaa.*
                 I   box-INDEF make-PRIOR-TEMP home go-PAST
                 'I went home after I made a box.'

      REDUPLICATED: *mamə peṭṭiyə hadə hadə   kataa keruwa.*
                 I   box   make (redup) talk-PAST
                 'I made the box and talked (simultaneously).'

PERFECT PARTICIPLE: *mamə peṭṭiyak   hadəla   gedərə giyaa.*
                    I   box-INDEF make-PAST home   go-PART.
                    'I made a box and went home.'

As example (12) shows, Sinhala has the conjunctive participle construction on which so much stress as an areal feature has been placed by Emeneau and others dealing with the Indian linguistic area (see Masica 1971: 128ff. for a survey).

The second method is to use one of a number of forms (usually of nominal or verbal origin) following one of the adjectival forms of the verb or an infinitive.

Sinhala has a number of lexical items that may follow a verb in an adjectival form to create an adverbial clause. Like the conjunct affixes, they have special senses in addition to their function as markers of subordination, and there are limitations on which verbal adjectival forms some of these lexical items may follow. Some of them, with their meanings (and the verbal adjectival forms with which they occur indicated in parentheses) are: *nisaa* or *hinda* 'because' (all forms), *koṭə* 'when' (nonpast), *kan* 'until' (nonpast), *hæṭiye* 'as soon as' (past or participial), and *hamə* 'prior action' (past or participial). The following examples should suffice to illustrate the manner in which these forms occur:

(13) a. *taatta aawa   nisaa   mamə giyee   næœ.*
        father come-PAST-VERBADJ because I   go-PAST-EMPH not
        'Because father came, I did not go.'

     b. *mamə enə   kan gedərə   mə innə.*
        I   come-NONPAST-VERBADJ until home EMPH stay-INFIN
        'Stay at home until I come.'

     c. *mamə peṭṭiyak   hæduwə hamə   gedərə giyaa*
        I   box-INDEF make-PAST-VERBADJ home   go-PAST
        'After I made a box, I went home.'

The form *hamə* is particularly interesting because not only is it an equivalent of the prior temporal form in *-aamə*, but also it is clearly its etymological source as well. It thus furnishes a neat example of the way a periphrastic structure has become an inflectional form. All of the other conjunct forms appear to have similar histories, although not as obviously as this one.

There are also forms that follow the infinitive, with similar effects, such as *issella* 'before':

(14) *taatta yanə   issella mamə peṭṭiyak   hadannan.*
     father go-INF before I   box-INDEF make-VOL OPT
     'I will make a box before father goes.'

Verbal nominals deserve a brief mention. There are forms in *-iimə* and *-illə* (formed by adding the affix to a stem with "umlaut" and no thematic vowel: *keriimə/ kerillə* 'doing') that form gerundive nominals with the subject of the underlying clause appearing in the genitive (quite parallel to English "his doing that"):

(15) *minihage   pot   liviimə/livillə hoǹdə næc̄ə.*
     man-GEN books   write-NOM good   not
     'His writing books is not good.'

There is another, and colloquially more common, type of nominalization in which the verbal adjective is followed by *ekə*, etymologically the inanimate numeral "one." This nominalizes an entire clause, with no other change in form:[15]

(16) *minihə pot   liyənə   ekə hoǹda næc̄ə.*
     man   books   write-NONPAST-VERBADJ ekə good not
     'That he writes books is not good.'

As stated at the outset, this chapter does not attempt any detailed Sinhala–Tamil comparisons or their historical explanation. However, a few general observations, coupled with some cautionary remarks, are in order.

Despite the manifest influence of Dravidian languages, particularly Tamil, on Sinhala, further specification of that influence poses some very knotty historical problems, and a considerable amount of caution is called for. Noting resemblances is important, but insufficient; each observation must ultimately be accompanied by a plausible historical explanation if we wish to conclusively demonstrate cross-language influence of any direct kind.

The form of the causative affords one example of the difficulties involved in drawing conclusions from resemblances alone. Masica indicates that Sinhala employs not only -*wə* (his -WA-) as the distinctive sign of the causative but also "consonant strengthening" (i.e., gemination), and he mentions in passing that the latter is "a Dravidian device" (Masica 1971: 77).[16] This interesting observation could suggest direct influence, but the history of Sinhala offers an alternative explanation that makes such an inference unnecessary and in fact implausible. The Sinhala causative -*wə* (or orthographically -*va*) is the direct reflex of Sanskrit -(*ā*)*paya* (Geiger 1938: 154). Historically, the geminated causatives have the same source, through the changes CV *wə* > Cwə > CC (i.e., *kapəwə*- > *kapwə*- > *kappə*-), and alternate forms with Cw and CC are attested, particularly in Literary Sinhala: *nawatwə*- or *nawattə*- 'cause to stop'. These changes, dating from about the eighth to tenth centuries, are part of a set attributable to regular sound change, which involved *y* as well as *w*, that reintroduced geminate consonants into Sinhala. These by no means affect the causative alone; they also affect other aspects of verb morphology, as well as noun morphology, where no question of Dravidian influence of this kind would arise (Karunatillake 1969: 105ff.). Thus, any Dravidian influence would have had to operate through those regular sound changes rather than on the morphophonemics of the verb, and there seems no reason to invoke it. Since Sinhala historical phonology has been relatively well treated, we are on firm ground in dealing with such examples, but we have no equally comprehensive treatment of historical morphology and syntax. Thus any historical inferences from similarities in those areas, though well worth making, should be considered provisional at best.

A special problem with Sinhala lies in determining the period at which particular influences could have operated. Presumably, its pre–Sri Lanka ancestor was subject to prior influence on the mainland, leading to membership in the general South Asian linguistic area, but it is no simple task to separate the results of such influence from subsequent effects of influences operating independently but in a parallel fashion on Sinhala and its cognate languages.[17] For this we need further detailed studies of the area as a whole, such as Masica's, along with period-by-period analyses of both Sinhala and Tamil.

One impressive set of similarities does emerge from the summary above, however. Although Sinhala verbs in independent clauses do not seem to resemble in any obvious way those of Tamil any more than they do those of northern Indo-Aryan languages, subordinate verbal structures as a whole are of a strikingly Tamil and Dravidian character. The exclusive use of preposed adjectival clauses as the equivalent of relativization stands out here, as do the conjunct affixes such as the conditional and concessive (i.e., Sinhala *giyot*, Tamil *poonaal* 'if one goes'; Sinhala *giyat*, Tamil *poonaalum* 'even if one goes'),[18] as well as the use of particles or other forms following verbal adjectives so as to form adverbial clauses (Sinhala *yana koṭa*, Tamil *pookira poḷutu* or colloquial *poora appa* 'when one goes'). Whatever the problems in accounting for specific similarities, the cumulative effect is nothing short of overwhelming, particularly considering the lack in Sinhala of the alternate structures found in northern Indo-Aryan, such as correlatives and clause-initial conjunctions.

On the other hand, Indo-Aryan is not without parallels and possible sources, such as participial modifiers and such constructions as Hindi *aate samay* 'when one is coming' and or *aane ke baad* 'after coming'. One might venture the hypothesis that what occurred in Sinhala was a shifting toward Dravidian patterns of embedding by the re-formation of those Indo-Aryan structures most closely resembling those of Dravidian with similar functions so as to approximate the latter and that this was accompanied by the (gradual?) disuse of alternatives not bearing those resemblances. Fortunately, the relatively extensive documentation of Sinhala throughout its history should make it possible to treat this as an empirical question by observing changes through successive periods, but this task remains to be done. Why the effect seems to have been so much more marked in dependent than in independent verbal structures (i.e., operating in an "outer to inner" fashion) is also an extremely interesting question whose answer could cast some further light upon the way such influences operate—not only in this instance but elsewhere.

Addendum: The Quotative

Since this chapter is primarily concerned with verb forms and only secondarily concerned with the nature of embedding, no mention has been made of the quotative complementizer *kiyəla*. However, that form is itself a verbal derivative, it illustrates in its use the thoroughgoing left-branching complementation that has been referred to, and it has clear Dravidian parallels, so it deserves brief mention here.

Sinhala sentential complements of verbs of speaking, thinking, and so on occur, as we would expect, to the left of those verbs in the unmarked case, as do complements and objects generally, though they are often dislocated, as is common with heavier constituents. The complementizer for such sentences is, in Colloquial Sinhala, *kiyəla*, clearly the participial form of *kiyənəwa* 'say'. It is not limited to contexts of speaking, however, but occurs also with verbs of thinking and knowing as well as others, the full semantic range of which has not been described, to my knowledge.[19] Thus:

(17) [*gunəpaalə iiye gamə giyaa   kiyəla*]   *amma   kiwwa.*
     Gunapala   yesterday village went COMP   mother   said
     'Mother said that Gunapala went home yesterday.'

     mamə [*kææwa kiyəla*] *dannəwa.*
     I   ate COMP   know
     'I know that (someone) ate (it).'

Note that the last example, with a different bracketing, could also be interpreted as '(Someone) knows that I ate(it).'

This use of a "say" verb has clear Dravidian parallels, as for example Tamil *enru* (spoken *ennu*) and Malayalam *ennə*, which are also derived from a verb of speaking. In this context, we can also mention Dakkhini *bol ke* from *bolnaa* 'say', for which Dravidian, specifically Telugu, influence has been claimed (see Arora 1986), as well as Marathi *mhaṇūn* from *mhaṇṇe* 'to say' (Kachru 1979). Though Dravidian influence certainly appears likely here, one can also maintain some reservations in that the development of such complementizers is not unknown elsewhere (Hock 1991: 500; Kachru 1979: 75). One might also point to *bole* in Bengali, which is not in the southern South Asia area with Sinhala and the others, though Dravidian influence has been claimed there as well (Klaiman 1977). Current Literary Sinhala, as well as older Sinhala, has a quotative (*ya/yæ*) *yi*, not based on *kiyənəwa*, which appears to be at least in part a descendant of Old Indo-Aryan *iti* (Geiger 1941: 142), and certainly its replacement by a 'say' verb does suggest Dravidian influence, parallel to the forms in Dakkhini and Marathi. Interestingly, Dhivehi (Maldivian) retains the older form exclusively (Bruce Cain, personal communication). Although areal influence clearly appears to be at work here, the manner of its working is open to, and invites, detailed research, as do many other phenomena that have only been touched on here.

V

DIGLOSSIA

Sinhalese Diglossia

This paper appeared in Anthropological Linguistics *10(8): 1–15, in 1968, and it was, as far as I am aware, the first generally available description of the diglossia situation in Sinhala and the first attempt to characterize its varieties in precise structurally based terms. Although it has since been elaborated and given a historical account and a more specific theoretical and empirical base, as in the following two chapters, it still appears to me to be a clear and concise description and summary that has held up over time and to be fundamentally correct, despite some disagreement that it has engendered (for which see Chapter 18 on AGR and diglossia and the references therein.)*

Sinhalese, as used in Ceylon, exhibits the kind of distinction between major functional varieties for which Ferguson's term DIGLOSSIA has been generally accepted. This chapter is an attempt to characterize those varieties on a broad scale and to point out those characteristics that seem to be most central to them. In his by now classic paper, Ferguson (1959) defines diglossia as:

> a relatively stable language situation in which, in addition to the primary dialects of the language (which may include a standard or regional standards) there is a very divergent, highly codified (often grammatically more complex) superposed variety, the vehicle of a large and respected body of written literature, either of an earlier period or in another speech community, which is learned largely by formal education and is used for most written and formal spoken purposes, but is not used by any sector of the community for ordinary conversation. (p. 435)

This statement fits the Sinhalese situation in almost all particulars. For Sinhalese, however, as Ferguson himself suggested for other languages, the implied two-variety scheme requires some modification when the full range of current materials is taken into account. In this case, such modification becomes necessary when we attempt to go beyond everyday conversation on the one hand and formal writing on the other and to account for the language of much relatively formal speaking and informal writing.

Even a cursory survey of contemporary written and spoken materials at once reveals the existence of at least two sharply distinct varieties. First, there is the language used by everyone, at all social levels, educated and uneducated alike, for all normal face-to-face conversation. While there are recognizable subvarieties, they all share a large core of basic structural features so that they together constitute one major variety: COLLOQUIAL SINHALESE.

Distinct from Colloquial Sinhalese is the language of virtually all written materials, ranging from newspapers and magazines through official documents and learned journals to imaginative literature. Despite subvarieties showing a wide range of surface divergence, there is a shared set of structural features that serve to characterize another major variety. This may be called LITERARY SINHALESE, providing that term is not taken to imply a necessary connection with literature *per se*. Literary Sinhalese may also be heard in some public speaking and some radio programming on Radio Ceylon, including news broadcasting and station breaks, but it is fundamentally a written variety that is likely, even when spoken, to have been composed beforehand. There are people capable of impromptu speaking in it without violating its conventions, but they would use it only on formal occasions. It is no one's first language, but it is generally acquired within some formal learning situation. A significant amount of energy is expended within the education system in imparting and acquiring some productive and receptive control of it, whether in formal instruction directed specifically to that end or in dealing with materials using it. Accompanying this is a widespread attitude that it is the "real" or "good" variety of the language, and when someone in Ceylon speaks of learning Sinhalese, or of not knowing the language they are likely to be referring to the Literary variety, unless they are residents of one of those areas with a large proportion of Tamil monolinguals.

Colloquial Sinhalese, on the other hand, finds its life in speaking, and it is acquired simply by growing up where it is spoken. Many in Ceylon, whether from the Sinhalese or some other community, who would disown knowing Sinhalese, do in fact possess a more or less fluent control of the Colloquial variety.

Grammar—Inflection

Differences between Literary and Colloquial Sinhalese exist at all levels of structure of interest to the linguist. In grammar proper—that is, in both morphology and syntax—there are important differences between Literary and Colloquial Sinhalese, beginning with the inflection of nouns. In both varieties, nouns inflect for number (singular and plural), definiteness (definite and indefinite), and case. The partial paradigms in table 16–1 give forms in both varieties for three nouns that occur in both: the animate nouns *minihā* (Literary *minisā*) 'the man'[1] and *dena* 'the cow', and the inanimate noun *pota* 'the book'. (Variant forms are given in parentheses; those for Literary are somewhat less and those for Colloquial are somewhat more so).

In both varieties, there are further case forms, but those given will suffice for our purpose. Both varieties show a formal contrast between animate and inanimate gender, which is reflected in the forms of case affixes. In Literary, however, there is a further division into masculine and feminine within animate (seen clearly in the indefinite forms) leading to a three-gender system. In Colloquial, this is true only for those who use the -*ak* alternate for the feminine indefinite, which seems to reflect relatively careful speech. For those who do not use the -*ak* form, Colloquial has only

Table 16–1 Comparison of Colloquial and Literary Forms

| Case | Singular | | Plural |
	Definite	Indefinite	
Direct			
Coll	minihā 'the man'	minihek	minissu
Lit	minisā	minisek	minissu
Accusative			
Coll	minihava	minihekva	minissunva
Lit	minisā	minisaku(-eku)	minisun
Dative			
Coll	minihāṭa	minihekuṭa	minissunṭa
Lit	minisāṭa	minisakuṭa	minisunṭa
Genitive			
Coll	minihāge	minihekuge	minissunge
Lit	minisāgē	minisakugē (-ekugē)	minisungē
Direct			
Coll	dena 'the cow'	denek (-ak)	dennu
Lit	dena	denak	dennu
Accusative			
Coll	denava	denekva (-akva)	dennunva
Lit	dena	denaka (-aku)	denun
Dative			
Coll	denaṭa	denekuṭa (-akuṭa)	dennunṭa
Lit	denaṭa	denakaṭa -akuṭa)	denunṭa
Genitive			
Coll	denage	denekuge (- akuge)	dennunge
Lit	denagē	denakagē (-akugē)	denungē
Direct[a]			
Coll and Lit	pota 'the book'	potak	pot
Dative			
Coll and Lit	potaṭa	potakaṭa	potvalaṭa
Genitive			
Coll	potē	potaka	potvala
Lit	potehi (-ē)		

[a]Nouns of this type have no separate accusative in either variety; the direct is used instead.[2]

a two-gender system in noun inflection. More important, there are differences in the way the case forms are built that can lead to different analyses of the grammatical categories involved.

The Literary accusative has two functions: It occurs as an independent case form in certain syntactic positions and it serves as a stem on which the other nondirect cases are built. Thus Geiger's (1938) term "oblique" rather than "accusative" is quite apt for that variety.[3] In Colloquial, on the other hand, all nondirect case forms, including the accusative, are formed on an oblique stem (which in some instances is identical with the direct), but that stem is only a conditioned alternant whose occurrence is completely determined by occurrence with case affixes and not an independently occurring case form. Correspondingly, the Colloquial accusative is in its formation a case form on a par with the others and not the stem on which they are built.

The functional status of the Colloquial accusative also requires mention. Not only does the frequency of its use vary from speaker to speaker, but it is always optionally replaceable by the direct case form wherever it may occur. This is not true of the Literary accusative, which is obligatory in certain positions to be stated later.

There are also differences in pronoun inflection, as well as in pronoun inventory, between the two varieties. On the whole, the dimensions of difference are like those for the nouns and do not require special notice here, but there is an interesting difference in the gender system of pronouns, which is distinct from that of the nouns. In both varieties, there are numerous pronouns reflecting a number of categories such as animal versus human and degrees of proximity, respect, and status. Cross cutting these is a distinction between animate and inanimate, as there is for nouns. For Literary, there is again a masculine–feminine distinction within animate: *hetema* 'he' (human), *ōtomō* 'she' (human). For Colloquial, however, the distinction within animate is rather between GENERAL, encompassing both masculine and feminine reference, and FEMININE, used where specifically feminine reference is required *eyā* 'he, she' (human), *ǣ* 'she' (human).[4]

For verbs, differences in inflection between varieties are even more marked than those for nouns. Verbal inflection is more complex than nominal and is not easily summarized, but the most important difference is in the marking of person and number. In the present tense, Literary Sinhalese marks both, as the partial paradigm for *balanavā* 'look' (table 16–2) shows. On the other hand, the Colloquial present (probably better called "nonpast") marks neither person nor number, and one form, *balənəvā*, is used throughout.[5]

The past tense not only shows person and number in Literary Sinhalese—for example *bæluvemi* 'I looked', *baeluvemu* 'we looked', *bæluvēya* 'he looked'—but it also marks masculine versus feminine gender in the third singular: *bæluvāya* 'she looked'. Again, Colloquial Sinhalese uses one form throughout: *bæluvā*.[6]

Grammar—Syntax

In syntax, there are numerous differences between the varieties. Most importantly, Literary verbs agree with their subjects, as the verb forms above suggest, while Colloquial verbs do not.[7] Accompanying this are differences in the uses of cases, notably the direct and accusative. In Literary Sinhalese, the verb forms that show agree-

Table 16–2   Tense Marking in Literary Sinhala

	Singular	*Plural*
First Person	*balami*	*balamu*
Third Person	*balayi*	*balati*

ment occur primarily in independent clauses, and noun and pronoun subjects appear in the direct case only when they occur with such agreeing verb forms. Otherwise, they are in the accusative, which is also the case characteristically occurring as object of a postposition. The sum effect of all this might be called the ACCUSATIVE RULE and stated thus:

> When a noun or pronoun is not the subject of an agreeing verb and is not in a construction requiring some other oblique case form (as, for example, in a possessive construction with the genitive), it will be in the accusative case.

In Colloquial Sinhalese, however, the accusative occurs only as object of a transitive verb or in a few special sentence types. This difference in case syntax is an important one in distinguishing varieties. (Note that this distinction is relevant only for animate nouns, since inanimate ones lack a distinct accusative in either variety.) Colloquial Sinhalese has nonverbal sentences, such as:

(1) a. *mē   pota alut*
        This   book new
        'This book is new'

     b. *mēka potak*
        This book-INDEF
        'This is a book.'

There is no special mark of predication unless the nonverbal predicator is a vowel-final adjective, in which case the ASSERTION MARKER, of shape *-i* or *-yi*, occurs:

(2) *mēka rasayi*
     This tasty-yi
     'This one is tasty.'

In Literary Sinhalese, a different principle, which might be called FULL PREDICATOR MARKING, applies, and the assertion marker, of shape *yi, ya,* or *-i* occurs obligatorily in these and some other types of sentences, as in *meya alut ya, meya potaki, meya rasa ya.* Person-number affixes, like those of verbs, are sometimes used rather than the assertion marker, as in

(3) *mama goviyek   mi*
     I   a-farmer   1Sg
     'I am a farmer.'[8]

There are other differences in syntax, including constructions found in one variety and not in the other. As only one example, we may note a passive with the verb *lœbenava* or *labanava* that appears in Literary Sinhalese but not Colloquial:

(4) *mā   visin meya karanu lœbē*
     me(acc.) by   this   done   gets
     'This gets done by me.'

Lexicon

In distinguishing varieties of a language, vocabulary differences are likely to rank high in user awareness and to be an area in which one is conscious of the possibility of choice, even though they are in a real sense less central than grammatical or phonological differences. In Sinhalese, as elsewhere, lexical differences play a large part in contributing to the relative formality of an utterance, but there is one very important difference between the Sinhalese situation and that in many other languages, including the more familiar European ones, in that differences in lexical items extend to the functors to a quite thoroughgoing extent.[9] Forms like *visin* 'by', *siyallama* 'all', *pinisa* 'for', *siṭa* 'from', *pilibaňda* 'concerning, about', *saha* 'with', *samaga* 'with, accompanying', *kerehi* 'in relation to', *hetema* 'he', and *ōtomō* 'she' are restricted entirely or nearly so to Literary Sinhalese; forms like *atin* 'by', *okkoma* 'or', *sērama* 'all', *iňdala* or *hiṭaŋ* 'from', *gæna* 'concerning, about', *-t ekka* 'with, accompanying', and *eyā* 'he, she' pertain to Colloquial.

Sometimes such forms pair off relatively neatly as Colloquial and Literary variants, having the same function within their respective varieties, but other forms are substitutable only through part of their ranges or have no real equivalent in the other variety. (This does not mean, of course, that the same thing cannot be said in some other way, such as with a case affix or a different construction.) Thus *pilibaňda* and *gæna* seem to be essentially stylistic equivalents, while *kerehi, pinisa,* and *saha* seem to find no obvious Colloquial counterparts. For some sets of functional equivalents, the division is not bipartite, but there is a "ladder" of forms such that those at the ends are restricted to a single variety, but some in the middle are usable in either depending on the degree of formality desired. Such seems to be the case, for example, with sets of terms (going from Literary to Colloquial) for 'near': *asala, laňga, gāva,* for 'because': *bævin, nisā, hindā, handā,* and for 'when': *kalhi, viṭa, koṭa.*

With regard to the remainder of the vocabulary, we still require careful studies of the uses of different forms in different varieties, but a few broad generalizations can be made. The sources of the Sinhalese vocabulary are many, including, along with words inherited throughout its development, forms borrowed from Sanskrit and Pali as well as from Dravidian, particularly Tamil, and from European languages, specifically Portuguese, Dutch, and English, together with a scattering of others.

Sanskrit borrowings have taken place at various stages in the history of Sinhalese and with varying degrees of adaptation to the Sinhala speech habits of the time. Such borrowings are found at all levels of the vocabulary, but modern Literary Sinhalese, particularly in its technical or learned varieties, tends to make heavy use of forms or coinages based on Sanskrit, with only sufficient change in form to make them usable with the Sinhala inflectional pattern.[10] Examples are legion, such as *niyōjita mantrī mandalaya* 'House of Representatives', *aṃśya* 'division, department', *vārimārgaya* 'irrigation canal', *vibhāgaya* 'examination'. Sometimes, as in the last example, there is a semantic shift (Sanskrit *vibhāga* 'division, part').

The most interesting aspect of Pali loans is their comparative rarity in current Sinhalese contrary to expectations sometimes expressed. There are Pali borrowings, such as *tanhāva* 'thirst, desire' and *ñāya* 'wisdom', but they are insignificant compared to the vast number of Sanskrit forms, which are likely to be used even in discussing Buddhist concepts. For example, *dhamma* and *kamma* are heard usually only when Pali texts are being directly cited; otherwise, the forms *dharmaya* and *karmaya* are used instead, or, colloquially, the more adapted *darume* and *karume* are used. The doublets *vijjāva* 'magic' (Pali *vijjā-* 'knowledge, lore') and *vidyāva* 'knowledge' (Sanskrit *vidyā* 'knowledge') are interesting in that the Pali borrowing has been specialized in one of its meanings and is in common use in Colloquial.

Literary Sinhalese may also reach back to an older stage and the classical, or Eḷu, language for a stock of inherited terms no longer in common use. In contradistinction to commonly used inherited forms, these are likely to have an even more elevated ring than direct Sanskrit borrowings. Thus *riya* 'vehicle' and *viduhala* 'school' (< *vidyā śālā*) may seem more formal than *rathaya* and *vidyālaya*. There has been an active movement to revive such forms and bring about wide use of an Eḷu (or Hela) style, but it has met so far with only sporadic success in affecting the body of written material produced today as a whole.

Tamil words have been borrowed at all stages and are found at all levels of the language. Thus we see *urumaya* 'heritage', *palama* 'bridge', *akkā* 'older sister', *appā* 'father', *ilakkama* 'number', and many others.

Colloquial Sinhalese has been receptive, over the past few centuries, to borrowings from Portuguese, Dutch, and English, particularly when they labeled new items or concepts, as we might expect. Thus, from Portuguese we have such forms as *kamise* 'shirt', *kēju* 'cheese', *pādiri* or *pādili* 'priest', and *būruvā* 'donkey'. From Dutch were borrowed *artāpal* 'potatoes', *kokis* 'cakes', *notāris* 'notary', *baṃkalot* 'bankrupt', and *komasāris* 'commissioner'. English introduced such terms as *saykalē* 'bicycle', *mīṭima* 'meeting' , *saybōṭṭuva* 'sideboard', and *bas eka* 'bus'. Current Literary Sinhalese tends to eschew such forms when they are recognizable, replacing them as far as possible with Sanskrit, Eḷu, or combinations of both.[11] Hence *riyædurā* (Eḷu) 'driver' for *ḍrayvar*, *dūrakathanaya* (Sanskrit) for *ṭælifōn* or *tælipōn*, *dumriya sthānaya* (Eḷu plus Sanskrit) for *isṭēsama*, and *polis sthānadhipati tumā* (English plus Sanskrit plus Eḷu) for *inspækṭa*, or *inspæṭṭa mahattea*. In practice, these replacements seem to have the greatest effect on the English portion of the vocabulary, since it has the highest current visibility.

Phonology

Differences in phonology between Colloquial and Literary are not easily discussed as such, since one is essentially a spoken and the other a written variety. However, there are conventional ways of rendering Literary Sinhalese aloud, and the fit between spelling and pronunciation is such that given a set of general symbol-to-sound rules (plus a few rules that are specific to particular lexical items), the conversion is quite regular. The actual pronunciation habits used are, not surprisingly, fundamentally those of the spoken variety, in that the same basic phonemic inventory is employed, but there may be some additions, depending in part on the educational background of the speaker. Indo-Aryan aspirate consonants were lost centuries ago in Sinhalese, so that they are found written only in loanwords from Sanskrit and Pali. Some educated speakers have learned to pronounce the aspirate consonants as single units when reading Literary Sinhalese but others do not distinguish them in pronunciation from their unaspirated counterparts [k], [g], [t], [b], and so on, or they insert a vowel, commonly [a], thus rendering them as [Cah].

Even when no new sounds are required, items existing in both varieties may find different pronunciations in each because of artificial conventions in reading. Thus *gonāṭa* 'bull' (dative) and *māmāṭa* 'maternal uncle' (dative) have different vowels before the [ṭ] in Colloquial [gonāṭə] but [māmaṭə], but carefully read Literary may have [gonāṭə], [māmāṭə] in accordance with the spelling.

The simplicity of spelling-to-sound conversion does not hold in the opposite direction. While a given symbol is generally rendered in a single way in a given environment, some sound elements are represented in more than one way. Thus three sibilants: ශ් <ś> , ෂ් <ṣ>, and ස් <s> are written, but the last is pronounced as an alveolar sibilant [s] and the first two both as palatal [š]. Similarly, ල් <l> and ළ් <ḷ> are both [l], and ණ (ṇ) and න (n), both [n].[12] Also ම (m), න (n), and ං (ṃ), are all produced as [ŋ] in statable environments, most importantly in final position.[13] Though these double values cause no serious difficulty in reading, they do introduce an additional complication in the other direction, since a word one knows with [ŋ] might be written, with ම (m), න (n) or ං (ṃ). All of this leads to some problems in spelling, since [malə], for example, might be either මල (mala) 'flower' or මළ [maḷa] 'dead' and [gaŋ] can be ගං [gaṃ] 'rivers' or ගම් [gam] 'villages'. If the aspirate consonants are not distinguished in pronunciation from their unaspirated counterparts, they constitute additional instances.

These problems, however trivial when compared to English, nevertheless constitute a very important difference between the varieties from the point of view of Sinhalese-speaking children learning the written variety, and they loom large in their (and their teachers') consciousness as a fertile source of mistakes and uncertainties.

General

If we now turn to look again at current Sinhalese as a whole, attempting to classify it exhaustively according to the two varieties and their characteristics as given so far, there will be a sizable remainder that does not fall cleanly into either variety. First of all, and least important, occasionally Colloquial habits will refuse to remain suppressed in an otherwise Literary passage. Setting aside such sporadic backsliding from the artificial conventions of the Literary variety, there remains a significant body of material blending the characteristics of both varieties in a less haphazard fashion. In much of it, a consistent pattern can be discerned. Main verbs are in their Colloquial form, and the marking of other predicators generally accords with Colloquial usage rather than with the principle of full predicator marking. However, one and usually more of the structural features of Literary Sinhalese will be observed with full or relative consistency so that there may be Literary case forms, the observance of the accusative rule, specific literary constructions such as the *læbenəwa* passive, and the use of Literary verb forms in some or all subordinate constructions. Literary functors are also an important and very common characteristic. Considerable use may also be made of formal vocabulary, but this may be considered of less importance than the structural features in classifying varieties, however important for stylistic variation within varieties. Sinhalese of this kind finds a number of present-day uses, not only in childrens' books and readers intended to be transitional between the varieties but also in public speaking, radio talks and lectures, and sermonizing. Thus, from a children's book:[14]

vāsanā ǣta enu duṭu goviyan prītiyen kǣ gasanna paṭan gattā.

'The farmers, who saw Vasana coming from a distance, began to shout for joy.'

Here *enu dutu* 'saw coming' is Literary in form, but the main verb *paṭan gatta* 'began', as well as the infinitive *kǣ gasanna* 'to shout', which is dependent on it, are in Colloquial form. The accusative rule is followed with *goviyan* (direct *goviyo*) 'the farmers' in the accusative case since the Colloquial main verb cannot agree with it. This sentence illustrates an interesting consequence of the intersection of the accusative rule with Colloquial verbs, which is found here and in other examples of this style. Since there can be no verb agreement, there will never be an occasion for a noun or pronoun having distinct direct and accusative forms to appear in the direct case, so that the contrast between those cases is effectively wiped out in verbal sentences. Another example, from the speech of a Buddhist priest at the ceremonies for a restored dagoba (stupa):[15]

udaya giri purāna rajamahā viharasthānaya daenaṭa avurudu ekdas aṭasiyēkaṭa pamaṇa ihatadī udaya maharajatumā visin ārambhakaraṇa laddā vū ati pǣraṇi vihārasthānayak.

'The Udayagiri Rajamaha Viharasthanaya is a very ancient temple which was established about one thousand and eight hundred years ago by King Udaya.'

This sentence is an equational one with no main verb, but the nominal predicator *vihārasthānayak* lacks the assertion marker called for under full predicator marking, and main verbs throughout the remainder of the talk are in Colloquial form. However, the functors *pamaṇa* 'about', *ihatadī* 'previous, ago', and *visin* 'by' are all Literary, as is the passive attributive construction *ārambhakaraṇa laddā vū* 'was (or had been) established.' Also, the aspirates were pronounced as such. A sentence from a recent letter also exemplifies this kind of Sinhalese:[16]

obagen liyumak lǣbī apamana satutata patva īta piliturak . . . evvā.

'Having received a letter from you, I was very happy and sent a reply.'

Here the verb *evvā* 'sent' is Colloquial, but the participles *lǣbī* 'received' and *patva* 'got (to a state)' are Literary in form. Sinhalese of this kind certainly constitutes a recognizable current variety or subvariety, and it will be found to have a number of subvarieties of its own depending on the particular structural features employed. The constant feature that distinguishes it, however, is the use of Colloquial main verbs, generally accompanied by the lack of full predicator marking, coupled with clearly Literary Sinhalese features. It seems to be filling a real need by providing a variety to be used when more formality than that provided by Colloquial is called for, impromptu delivery is involved, and/or there is a desire to avoid some of the artificiality of Literary.

Sinhalese speakers often point to the verb agreement of Literary as their greatest source of difficulty in producing it. This accords with our selection of that feature as a crucial defining characteristic of varieties. It also helps to account for the wide use of the intermediate variety in relatively formal but impromptu situations, since one can avoid constantly encountering vexing problems with agreement and the accusative rule by using Colloquial main verb forms while employing the relatively easily learned nonagreeing Literary forms used in subordinate constructions along with lexical substitution.

This variety clearly fits Ferguson's characterization of intermediate or middle varieties blending the characteristics of the other varieties in diglossia situations. However, it also finds wider employment than he suggests for such varieties on the basis of the languages he describes. It occurs with relative frequency in at least two situations for which he indicates that the superposed variant (his H, for "high") is required—sermons and political and parliamentary speeches—and it is also employed in at least some academic lectures and radio talks.[17] The actual regularity with which it is employed for these and other uses, however, remains to be carefully determined on the basis of a much fuller sample of current practice. Since it does find much of its life in speaking, and it shares verb forms and a lack of agreement and predicator marking with the Colloquial variety, it is fundamentally closer to Colloquial than to Literary. Thus I would class it and Colloquial together as subvarieties of one broad variety of SPOKEN SINHALESE.

Conclusion

In summary, then, the following overall classification is proposed for contemporary Sinhalese:

1. Literary Sinhalese is Sinhalese showing Literary main verb forms and the attendant subject–verb agreement. This will normally imply the presence of the other features of Literary outlined earlier.
2. Spoken Sinhalese is Sinhalese that does not show Literary main verb forms and agreement. (This term should not, of course, be taken to exclude occurrence in written materials). Spoken Sinhalese has two main subvarieties. One, FORMAL SPOKEN, is characterized by the employment of one or (usually) more structural features of the Literary variety with relative consistency. Spoken Sinhalese that does not show such features is (SPOKEN) COLLOQUIAL.

The varieties outlined above are not, of course, internally homogeneous. Literary has numerous subvarieties—a matter of interest as much for the literary critic as for the linguist—though the latter is likely to throw a wider, if less refined, net. Spoken Formal also has numerous varieties consonant with its varied uses, as implied earlier. About the varieties of Colloquial, we have as yet very little systematically collected data and objective analysis, at least judging from what has appeared so far. This lack of data is a matter of some urgency, since social change—particularly with increased education and literacy, mass communications, and social and geographic mobility—is breaking down the old patterns. There are quite clearly regional varieties, but their defining features and the precise extent of each of them remain to be systematically ascertained and described. There are also other dimensions crossing this one, such as a rural–urban, or perhaps more precisely, a sophisticated dimension, and not unconnected with this, formal and informal Colloquial variants within a given locality.[18]

One very interesting point does emerge from the limited observations made so far. All regional dialects of Colloquial Sinhalese seem to involve the same basic phonemic system, with differences in the number of phonemic contrasts relating instead to the sophisticated–unsophisticated dimension and the pronunciation of loan words. For example, some speakers without regard to region have [š] in Sanskrit or English loans where called for, in contrast with inherited [s], while some have only the latter.[19] Regional differences are found rather in the different phonemic composition of specific items, in the use of different items entirely, or in different grammatical forms. For example, there are regional differences both in the inflectional forms of verbs and in the system of interrogatives, as well as in kinship terms[20] and the use of pronouns. As yet, however, we have very little systematic information of this sort for the island as a whole, so that it is too early to draw firm conclusions about significant speech regions and their boundaries.

17

Sinhala Diglossia Revisited,
or Diglossia Dies Hard

This paper appeared in Bh. Krishnamurti et al., eds. South Asian Languages: Structure, Convergence and Diglossia *(1986: 322–36) and was a revised and expanded version of one by the same title given at the First International Conference on South Asian Languages and Linguistics, Urbana, July 1978.[1] Unlike the other diglossia papers here, its primary concern was not with the linguistic characterization of the varieties and their relationship but with the sociolinguistic setting of Sinhala diglossia, particularly the aspects of that situation that led (and continue to lead) to its apparent stability despite other rapid social and cultural changes in the relevant time span. It also proposed a general schema for the classification of diglossic situations in terms of factors that would affect the possibilities for both stability and kinds of change. The observations made here appear to continue to hold, and in that regard the attention of the reader interested in more detail may be directed to the later extended study by John Paolillo (1992), which describes essentially the same situation in greater detail, especially in chapter 3.[2]*

In 1959, Charles A. Ferguson published an important paper called "Diglossia," in which he defined diglossia as:

> a relatively stable language situation in which, in addition to the primary dialects of a language (which may include a standard or regional standards) there is a very divergent, highly codified, (often grammatically more complex) superposed variety, the vehicle of a large and respected body of written literature, either of another period or in another speech community, which is learned largely by formal education and is used for most written and formal spoken purposes, but is not used by any sector of the community for ordinary conversation. (p. 336)

Subsequently, I carried out some investigations of diglossia as it obtained in Sinhala (Sinhalese), the majority and official language of Sri Lanka (formerly Ceylon) during fieldwork in 1964–65 (Gair 1968), and I was able, some twelve years after my first observations, to observe some of the changes that had taken place in the interim. Though relatively short, that time span seemed long enough, under current conditions of rapid change, to allow some tendencies to emerge. This paper was first

---

17

Sinhala Diglossia Revisited, or Diglossia Dies Hard

This paper appeared in Bh. Krishnamurti et al., eds. South Asian Languages: Structure, Convergence and Diglossia *(1986: 322–36) and was a revised and expanded version of one by the same title given at the First International Conference on South Asian Languages and Linguistics, Urbana, July 1978.[1] Unlike the other diglossia papers here, its primary concern was not with the linguistic characterization of the varieties and their relationship but with the sociolinguistic setting of Sinhala diglossia, particularly the aspects of that situation that led (and continue to lead) to its apparent stability despite other rapid social and cultural changes in the relevant time span. It also proposed a general schema for the classification of diglossic situations in terms of factors that would affect the possibilities for both stability and kinds of change. The observations made here appear to continue to hold, and in that regard the attention of the reader interested in more detail may be directed to the later extended study by John Paolillo (1992), which describes essentially the same situation in greater detail, especially in chapter 3.[2]*

In 1959, Charles A. Ferguson published an important paper called "Diglossia," in which he defined diglossia as:

> a relatively stable language situation in which, in addition to the primary dialects of a language (which may include a standard or regional standards) there is a very divergent, highly codified, (often grammatically more complex) superposed variety, the vehicle of a large and respected body of written literature, either of another period or in another speech community, which is learned largely by formal education and is used for most written and formal spoken purposes, but is not used by any sector of the community for ordinary conversation. (p. 336)

Subsequently, I carried out some investigations of diglossia as it obtained in Sinhala (Sinhalese), the majority and official language of Sri Lanka (formerly Ceylon) during fieldwork in 1964–65 (Gair 1968), and I was able, some twelve years after my first observations, to observe some of the changes that had taken place in the interim. Though relatively short, that time span seemed long enough, under current conditions of rapid change, to allow some tendencies to emerge. This paper was first

224

presented after that visit, but a later extended visit for fieldwork extended the time of observation to almost twenty years and served to further confirm the tendencies noted in it. In rereading Ferguson's work, I was struck with how many important insights there were, often couched in a few sentences, that I had overlooked and noticed only after that later work; in particular I was struck by his comments on the stability of diglossia in view of the apparent persistence of it in Sinhala. What I propose here is to outline some factors that seem to operate—whether positively or negatively—to maintain it. Along the way I shall discuss some of the changes that have taken place in some varieties of Sinhala. My remarks can best be regarded mainly as an interim report and in part as a program for further research.

In commenting on the stability of diglossia, Ferguson noted some trends that could possibly lead to its demise:

> Diglossia seems to be accepted and not regarded as a "problem" by the community in which it is in force, until certain trends appear in the community. These include trends toward (1) more widespread literacy (whether for economic, ideological, or other reasons), (2) broader communication among different regional and social segments of the community (e.g., for economic, administrative, military or ideological reasons), (3) desire for a full-fledged standard national language as an attribute of autonomy or sovereignty. (p. 338)

All of these trends apply strongly in Sri Lanka. There is an impressive mother-tongue literacy rate (approximately 80 percent overall and over 90 percent in some districts). Moreover, as table 17–1 shows, unusually high literacy for a third world country is a relatively long-standing phenomenon, so that this factor has had some time to operate.

Table 17–1   Mother Tongue Literacy in Sri Lanka

Year	All	Male	Female
1881–1963 (Population over 5 years)			
1881	17.4	28.9	3.1
1891	21.7	36.1	5.3
1901	26.7	42.0	8.5
1921	39.9	56.4	21.2
1946	57.8	70.1	43.8
1953	65.4	75.9	53.6
1963	71.9	79.4	63.8
1971 (Population over 10 years)			
Overall	78.1	85.2	70.7
Rural	75.9	83.8	67.6
Urban	85.6	87.5	81.5

Source: 1953 Census and 1970 *Statistical Pocketbook* for 1881–1963. The 1971 data are from the Population of Ceylon (*Census monograph*) 1971.

The twentieth-century history of Sri Lanka is largely one of increased social mobility and democratization, which have accelerated since independence. In particular, individual participation in government and direct communication between the individual and agencies or officials has increased tremendously. In sum, I would consider it to be, in relation to the region, a remarkably open society. The state-operated Sinhala radio service is active, the largest-circulation newspapers and magazines are in Sinhala and find a large and receptive audience, and book publishing in Sinhala is impressive (though somewhat curtailed by paper shortages).[3]

Sri Lanka has instituted a national language policy, particularly since the official Language Act of 1956, calling for the use of Sinhala as an official language largely at the expense of the colonial language, English, and to some extent of minority languages (some official provision has subsequently been made for the reasonable use of Tamil, the major minority language, but I shall not be concerned with that, and the complex issues involved, in this paper.) This policy has been energetically implemented. Though there is still a great deal of what has been called the "unostentatious" use of English in government and commerce (Fernando 1977, following De Souza 1969), government servants are required to be able to carry out their work in Sinhala, and they must deal with correspondence in it. Furthermore, education from the primary level through the tertiary is officially (and overwhelmingly in actuality) in the mother tongue, with some few exceptions, such as medicine, where English is commonly used.[4]

Nevertheless, despite the strong presence of all three trends, Sinhala diglossia shows few, if any, signs of weakening. Before dealing with this question, it will be useful to briefly review my earlier (1968) statement of varieties as background. The varieties in Sinhala diglossia were given as:

I. *Literary Sinhala.* The chief defining characteristic is Literary main verb forms, particularly the subject–verb agreement lacking in other varieties. Generally, these verb endings will entail the other grammatical and lexical features of Literary. It should be noted that this is the variety characteristic of virtually all written Sinhala, not just of literature *per se.*

II. *Spoken Sinhala.* It lacks Literary verb agreement, but has two main varieties:
   A. *Formal Spoken*, which makes use of one of (usually) more grammatical features of Literary Sinhala (other than verb agreement) with relative consistency. It characteristically makes considerable use of a formal lexicon shared with Literary, and
   B. *Colloquial Sinhala*, the language of ordinary conversation.

Perhaps needless to say, there are further varietal distinctions within these varieties, such as the geographic ones within Colloquial. For present purposes, we can view this as a three-variety schema, with Literary Sinhala corresponding to Ferguson's *H* (or high) form, Colloquial to his *L* (or low), form and Formal Spoken Sinhala to the intermediate variety for which he makes provision. I had taken the agreeing verb endings as the primary defining mark of Literary, and further observation and discussions with native speakers have confirmed their salience in that respect. Certainly their use entails other Literary characteristics, while the reverse is not the case.[5] The partial summary in table 17–2 illustrates the differences in verbal affixes and agreement between the varieties.

In examining some of the causes of diglossic persistence in Sinhala and some of the changes that have occurred within varieties, it will be convenient to proceed under the three rough categories of prestige and acceptance, varietal functions, and effects of literacy. I will also attempt to relate the persistence of diglossia in Sinhala to some more general considerations and propose a partial typology of diglossia for that purpose.

Prestige and Acceptance

Literary Sinhala is the vehicle of an impressive body of literature going back to the tenth century (and beyond, but the earlier literature has been lost save for inscriptions and some graffiti of literary quality). It is essentially the language of that earlier literature as revived in the eighteenth century after a break in the tradition, partly in reaction to colonial learning. It was thus an important symbol of the Sinhala heritage to those educated in the vernacular, notably the Sinhala teachers, the Buddhist clergy, and Ayurvedic physicians, the three props of the *Swabhasha* movement culminating in the Language Act of 1956. (See De Silva 1974 and 1967 for a more detailed account.) De Silva (1976) feels that "the polemics on the 'purity' of Sinhala

Table 17–2 Verb and Pronoun Forms and Agreement

	Colloquial			*Literary*	
Pers–No.	*Subject*	*Verb*	*Pers–No.*	*Subject*	*Verb*
Present Tenses ('I go, you go', etc.)					
1s.	*mamə*		1s.	*mama*	*yami*
2s.	*ohee, oyaa, uṁbə*		2s.	*to, oba*	*yahi*
3s. (M,F)	*eyaa*		3s. (M)	*he, hetema*	*yayi*
(F only)	*ææ*		(F)	*ōtomō, ō*	
(Inan)	*eekə*		(Inan)	*eya*	
1pl.	*api*	*yanəwa*	1pl.	*api*	*yamu*
2pl.	*oheela, oyaala, uṁbəla*		2pl.	*topi, obala*	*yahu*
3pl. (Hum, An)	*eyaala*		3pl. (Hum, An)	*owuhu*	*yati*
(Inan)	*eewa*		(Inan)	*ēwā*	*yayi* (=3s)
Past Tense (Third person Human only)					
3s. (M,F)	*eyaa*		3s. (M)	*hē*	*giyēya*
3s. (F only)	*ææ*	*giyaa*	3s. (F)	*ōtomō*	*giyēya*
3pl. (M,F)	*eyaala*		3pl. (M,F)	*owuhu*	*giyōya*

Note: In Colloquial Sinhala, doubled vowels indicate length. Literary forms are transliterated.

have ensured that the Literary variety is not widely recognized as a symbol of the Sinhalese heritage" (p. 53) and states that "people, when questioned individually, have shown comparatively little enthusiasm for the continuation of diglossia in the Sinhalese community" (p. 101). Yet, as he himself notes, there is no organized movement against it (p. 101). There have been authors and scholars, some very well known, who have employed the Colloquial variety for purposes for which Literary is customarily used, but such attempts have not been widely emulated, and efforts at forming movements for the purpose have not met with much success. Nor is it a simple matter of prestige or enthusiasm. The written style has significant overtones to which a wide spectrum of the public appears to be sensitive, and they are expected in the appropriate contexts. (An example confirming this is the way a dramatist, like Simon Nawagatthegama, in his recent widely popular ironic historical drama *Subha saha Yasa,* can make extremely effective use of the resonances resulting from an interplay of styles.) Also, even if Literary Sinhala per se is not a symbol of the Sinhala heritage, the Sinhala language itself is, and most people simply accept Literary Sinhala as the "real" variety of it. In fact, my (unquantified) observations suggest that diglossia is simply accepted as a given, and in a culture with a traditionally high regard for learning, the written variety is one sign of it.

There may be, however, a great deal of uncertainty as to what constitutes proper Literary Sinhala. As De Silva (1980) showed by giving a number of teachers a text to correct, there is wide, if not wild, variation in what is considered correct or incorrect. Nevertheless, this uncertainty, whatever its ultimate effects on the language itself, does not seem to translate into any doubt that *some* form of Literary Sinhala should be used for any serious written purpose.

Similarly, in relation to language standardization, there are disputes, often acrimonious, between advocates of different types of Sinhala. Since these involve educational policy and textbooks, they often gain considerable public attention, but they are essentially about the proper nature of Literary Sinhala and not its elimination. Thus, for example, they may include disputes as to the proper form of grammatical endings but not about the propriety of their existence.[6]

Particularly important is a factor that is lacking: Literary Sinhala is not clearly identified with any social group or cultural feature regarded negatively by a large portion of the population (compare, for example, Brahmin Sanskritized Tamil). Though it may have been advanced by a nativizing elite of sorts, which in any event seems to have been widely respected and not resented, it is not the property of any caste, class, or group, save (of course) those educated in the vernacular. Furthermore, widespread education in Sinhala is generalizing, not narrowing, that group. Put otherwise, a command of Literary Sinhala is a result of effort and ability, not opportunity or privilege.[7]

Varietal Functions

One striking aspect of Sinhala diglossia is the sharp limitation in the functions of Literary Sinhala, and this restriction is more marked than in the cases described by Ferguson, as a glance at table 17–3 will show. In fact, it is even more marked than Ferguson allowed for in his definition, since Formal Spoken, not Literary, Sinhala is

Table 17–3 Functions of *H* and *L*—Sinhala and Others

	Ferguson's Chart		Sinhala	
	H	L	H	L
Sermon in church or mosque	X			F
Instructions to servants, waiters, workers, clerks		X		C
Personal letter	X		(X)	F-C
Speech in parliament, political speech	X		(X)	F
University lecture	X			F
Conversation with family, friends, colleagues	X			C
News broadcast	X		X	
Radio "soap opera"		X		C
Newspaper editorial, news story, caption on picture	X		X	
Caption on political cartoon	X			C
Poetry	X		X	
Folk literature		X		?
Government documents, forms			X	
Novels				
Nonconversational parts	(Not given in		X	
Conversational parts	Ferguson)			C
Airline announcements			X	

For Sinhala, *L* has been further specified as: F = Formal Spoken, C = Colloquial.
? = Probably, but insufficient observation as yet.
() = Sometimes, often under special circumstances.

the language of "most . . . formal spoken purposes." Though the overall distribution of functions among varieties seems not to have changed significantly, there has been much elaboration and expansion of functions in Sinhala as a whole, particularly since the Official Language Act. Fernando has summed this up nicely in discussing the place of English:

> The most striking feature marking the use of English and Sinhala in present-day Sri Lanka is the invasion by Sinhala of almost all the areas held by English alone. (1977: 348)

She further remarks, concerning the effects on Sinhala:

> In sum, what is more striking about present-day Sinhala is, firstly, the enormous and impressive functional elaboration it has undergone, and secondly, the very substantial influence of English upon Sinhala. These two phenomena are, of course, related. (p. 358)

Setting aside the nature and extent of English influence, which operates differently in different varieties, that functional elaboration represents largely the extension of Sinhala into official and technical domains, where "technical" should be taken to include not only technology proper, commerce, and aspects of agriculture but also education, including the social sciences and the more Westernized of the liberal arts (as opposed to traditional Oriental learning, where Sinhala already held sway), and Western medicine (as opposed again, to the traditional, indigenous variety). As a whole, these might be conveniently referred to as "imported" functions. One result is a great expansion in occasions on which such matters require public presentation or discussion in an impromptu or seemingly impromptu manner: such as university lectures, conferences, and radio presentations such as panel discussions or interviews on matters such as agriculture, medicine and health education, and economic policy.

There are two features that make full-blown Literary Sinhala unsuitable for such purposes. First, it is difficult for most people, even the educated, to produce it in a spontaneous, extended fashion with correctness, though there are virtuosi who can do it. The verbal endings, involving agreement not found in Colloquial Sinhala, seem to cause particular difficulties on this score, along with some other special rules of Literary Sinhala. Second, Literary Sinhala is fundamentally a written variety, and the use of full Literary forms seem to militate against a sense of spontaneity and re-sult in distancing or an air of impersonality. This seems also to render it unsuitable for occasions on which the audience, even though passive, is to be engaged in some sense. Thus, Literary may be suitable for news broadcasts and even airline or train announcements but not for political speeches or exhortations (note that I am talking here only of oral presentation).

The simplest strategy, then, is to use the proper lexicon both for technical pur-poses and for giving the necessary formality for public presentation, then to also employ some Literary grammatical features within a basically spoken grammar.[8] What this process will result in, in terms of the schema given earlier, is essentially Formal Spoken Sinhala. Furthermore, whatever English influence there may be, this usage is also an extension of a tradition by which Formal Spoken Sinhala, or its ancestor, was used for public debates and Buddhist sermons at least as far back as the nine-teenth century. (It is also noteworthy that English lexicon is rare in such uses, though there may be Sanskritized calques on English aplenty, whereas in informal discus-sions among colleagues, carried out in Colloquial Sinhala, English loans abound.) It is also interesting that lyrics of popular songs, including the omnipresent rock, show formal characteristics, as do political songs, however scurrilous (at least to the oppo-sition). In short, public presentation tends to bring forth formal characteristics. Some formal oral presentations, ritualized in a general sense, such as acknowledgements and introductions of events or speakers, call for Literary Sinhala, even if impromptu. Here the function of the Literary style seems to be to call attention to the occasion rather than the message.[9]

On the other hand, as soon as one puts pen to paper, one is likely to produce Literary Sinhala, or the best approximation one can muster. Exceptions would be where Literary endings would have too great a distancing effect, as in letters to ac-quaintances, sometimes resulting in such phenomena as a letter essentially in Spo-ken Sinhala, bracketed by Literary. Official or formal correspondence and reports, however, require Literary Sinhala.

In sum, a large share of the increase in communication resulting from social mobility and what can loosely be termed modernization is being handled by other varieties than Literary, and particularly by Formal Spoken Sinhala, which, with some adaptation, is quite adequate to the purpose. Thus, strong pressure to replace H by some form of L for those functions is lacking, at least until such a time as greater demands are made upon a wider segment of the population as writers. Even there, widespread free mother-tongue education mitigates the problem by increasing the number with a competence reasonably adequate to those demands. What effects an increase in the volume and number of producers of Literary Sinhala is having on that variety remain to be seen. (What is needed, of course, is an investigation along the general lines of Fries's now much neglected *American English Grammar*.)

This specialization also means that there is no direct competition between H and L across any significant range of functions, as might be the case where H and L have overlapping functions with the choice between them in that range determined by other, largely social, factors. Such seems to be the case, for example, in Haitian Creole versus French. The closest Sri Lankan analogue is not Literary versus Spoken, but English versus Sinhala for a sector of the population.

Effects of Literacy

De Silva (1970, 1974) has pointed out that the added grammatical complexities of Literary Sinhala can be regarded as redundancies from the point of view of Collo-quial Sinhala, and it is true that once a native speaker knows the script, the major bar to understanding is lexical, a point substantiated by De Silva's tests showing that those with a limited command of Literary Sinhala have little difficulty in comprehension once lexical adjustments are made. An implication of this is that we can expect little reaction against diglossia from the literate population in their role as receivers. As noted earlier, though, change could occur as a result of increased demands on that wider population for written correspondence and in education.

It would seem that weakening could take place in two ways. The written variety could approach the spoken and merge with it. De Silva (1974) has pointed to a num-ber of "hybridisms" in Literary Sinhala, most of which are mistakes from a puristic standpoint. If they become cumulative and systematically recurrent, they could weaken the sharp line between varieties. At present, however, they seem to lack that systematic, general character, though they are often explicable in terms of the intru-sion of Colloquial habits. Also, the verb agreement system would have to go, by losing its saliency in some fashion.

One possibility here may be found in what can be called a "nominalizing strat-egy." Sinhala has both nominal and adjectival sentences that lack an overt verb and in which the copula may properly be a nonagreeing form. It also has a rich system of nominalizing devices. It is possible to combine these features so that something that might be stated in a sentence with an agreeing verb is in fact said in one with a nominalized sentence subject and a nominal or adjective as predicator. The copula may then be a nonagreeing form or a third person singular form to agree with the nominalized subject. In either case, the complexities of verb agreement are then avoided. Newspapers, for example, though written in a kind of Literary Sinhala, seem to show a lower incidence of agreeing endings than one might expect a priori, and this seems explicable as the result of that strategy. One result is that there are whole stretches of sentences that differ little if at all from possible sentences in Formal Spoken Sinhala. This, together with an increased exposure to the Formal Spoken used for formal purposes, might have the required weakening effect, particularly as that variety continues to develop for a variety of uses.

The second possibility for the weakening to take place would be for the Spoken variety simply to replace the Literary, perhaps as the result of a movement engendered by the increased demands on the population as writers, through bureaucratic exigencies and otherwise. This would be more effective if it could be given a democratizing rationale, but at present there are few, if any, signs of it.

On the contrary, it seems that in the short run at least, literacy and education are strengthening Sinhala diglossia. One factor involved was mentioned earlier, in that H becomes even less the property of an elite. Also, the variety sees greater use, and exposure to it is vastly increased. Where H is restricted to a largely classical literature, it may become *de facto* a kind of museum piece, impinging little upon the consciousness of the population apart from a small group of custodians of the cultural heritage. Where, however, it is not only the medium of official writing in an increasingly democratized and bureaucratized state but also the medium of the printed mass media widely and eagerly read by a large literate population (as in the case), as well as of a popular prose literature (such as the popular novels that account for a large and apparently profitable share of Sinhala book publishing), the situation is quite different. There is, indeed, a large and active Sinhala reading public (see, for example, the Marga Institute's 1974 study) so that the Literary variety is becoming more familiar and diglossia even more of an established fact.

Indeed, the Sinhala case suggests that a high literacy rate may not pose a serious immediate threat to diglossia if it is achieved steadily over a period of time—that is, if there is at no time a sudden dramatic upsurge in the number of people who have to struggle, with limited success, to master H, as could be the case where there was a sudden drive for literacy as the result of the exigencies of modernization. A massive literacy drive, on the other hand, could produce not only widespread dissatisfaction but also strong practical imperatives for displacing H in the interests of immediate needs for wider communication. In the Sinhala case, however, a large section of the population has been gradually habituated to the acceptance of H, and, as we have seen, they have been called on more in their capacities as receivers than as producers.

Diglossia Dies Hard

Before concluding, I would like to relate the Sinhala situation to some general observations concerning the stability of diglossia in relation to fundamentally different kinds of diglossic situations, and in doing so, I would like to propose a partial typology of diglossia in terms of the population using L as their everyday language vis-à-vis that using or acknowledging H.

In particular, I would suggest that we distinguish between two general types of diglossic situations, building on a distinction that was in fact implicit in Ferguson's paper and in his examples. In what I propose calling Type I, or "congruent" diglossia, H and L are varieties of the same language, and the speech communities for H and L are essentially coterminous (I will avoid the problem of defining "same language" here except to say that the varieties are recognized as such, which suffices for this proposal). H is not used by some other speech community, as their standard or otherwise, and while all speakers of L may not have a full command of H, they do recognize it as the H—or "proper" or "real"—variety of their language. Type I diglossia is represented graphically in figure 17–1. There may be subvarieties, both regional and functional, of L, and these may include a standard or standards. These possibilities are represented by dotted lines in Figure 17–1.

Examples of Type I diglossia are Sinhala, Tamil, and Arabic (In increasing order of regional varietal distinctions in L). In Type I, H is likely to be essentially an older written or at least literary form of the language, and that is the case with all examples I am aware of. (This does not, of course exclude changes within H or require that contemporary H be precisely like some earlier actually employed variety.)

In Type II, or "included" diglossia, represented in figure 17–2, only a portion (Community A) of the speech community using or recognizing H is diglossic. H is also employed by some other speech community (Community B) and in fact is characteristically the standard language of that community, for whom it is likely to be a part of continuum of functional varieties and for whom there may be regional varieties as well (both possibilities again indicated in the figure by dotted lines).[10]

Examples of Type II diglossia include Swiss German, where H is Standard German, Haitian Creole, where H is French, and Havyaka Kannada (Ullrich-Baylis 1974) where it is Standard (Brahmin) Kannada, among many others. The fact that H as used by Community A may actually differ to a greater or lesser degree from the standard of Community B does not concern us here. For example, Jamaican Standard English

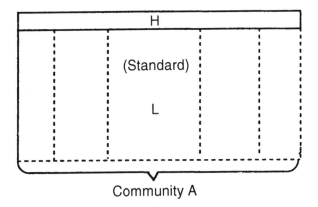

Figure 17–1   Type 1 (congruent diglossia).

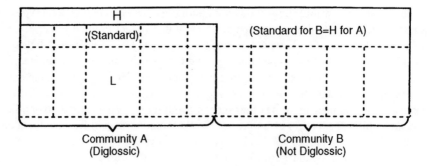

Figure 17-2   Type II ((included) diglossia).

differs from British English, but it is felt to be the same; that is, British English is the professed model (De Camp 1971).

In both Type I and Type II diglossia, H and L are varieties of the same language. There are similar situations where they are different languages. This is commonly the case in colonial and postcolonial situations, for example. Such situations of functional bilingualism have been called diglossia, but there is good reason to employ some other term, such as "diglossic bilingualism," for them, since the dynamics of change are potentially quite different from either Type I or Type II true diglossic situations.[11] I shall not pursue this issue further here save to remark that not only do factors of language allegiance bearing on stability operate differently but also the hybridization affecting L and/or H in diglossia is different in important ways from the convergence that may affect L in diglossic bilingualism.

Now, returning to diglossia proper, a number of factors affecting the stability of diglossia operate very differently in Type I and Type II situations, such as those relating to language allegiance, solidarity, and sense of identity. In Type II diglossia, stability is affected by the sense of identity of Community A (the L-using group) versus Community B. The Swiss Germans, for example, have a high degree of pride in their language and a strong sense of identity. As Moulton (1962) points out, this is a factor in the stability of Swiss German diglossia. In such situations, L is unlikely to be displaced by a merger with H. On the other hand, if a sense of pride and identity become associated with a cultural assertivist and antioutsider movement, diglossia could be threatened by the displacement of H by some variety of L for Community A, but this seems unlikely where H has high functional value as the language of wider communication, as is commonly the case. What we might get instead is a more complex situation with a literary form of L operating side-by-side with (old) H for Community A. To some extent, this appears to have happened in Switzerland.

In Type I diglossia, the situation is quite different, and the continuation of diglossia may depend on the extent to which the community feels H to be a repository and symbol of their cultural heritage. Such is the case in Arabic, where H is felt to be not only prestigious but also divine, as well as the only "real" form of the language and a symbol of Arabic cultural unity. As we have seen, Sinhala falls into this category as well, though less strongly. In such cases, anti-H movements cannot be tied to irredentist sentiments and movements. Rather, the relevant factor is the relation of the H-commanding community to the remainder of the society. Where that group represents an elite or powerful political faction definable in other terms as well, a revolutionary or democratizing movement can be in part an anti-H movement.

Something of that sort appears to have happened in Greece, with a newer democratic government moving to eliminate the official status of *Katharevusa* (though Greek diglossia seems to have been precarious in any case). An interesting example of another possibility is Tamil, in which an antielite movement had as its aim not the elimination of diglossia but a change in the nature of H, particularly by substituting "pure" Dravidian Tamil forms for Sanskritic forms with their Brahminic overtones. In Sinhala, as we have seen, anti-H movements have not been able to attach themselves to any other widespread social movement, and they have lacked strength thereby. Also, the controversy over the proper nature of Literary Sinhala has not taken on any strong caste or regional character, though it has not been entirely free of such overtones. Thus anti-H movements have had to base themselves on more nebulous aspects of educational democratization or on efficiency, causes not very capable of arousing strong sentiments in the general public for the elimination of H.

Ferguson pointed out that H "may succeed in establishing itself as a standard only if it is already serving as a standard in some other community and this diglossic community, for reasons linguistic and non-linguistic tends to merge with that other community" (p. 437). Or, in our terms, this could occur only in Type II situations.[12] Connected with this is the narrowness of functional specialization of H, likely to be much greater in Type I than in Type II situations. In Type I diglossia, H, existing only within the L-using community, can be limited to a narrow subset of functions, as is the case in Sinhala. In Type II, however, H by virtue of its use elsewhere as a standard for a wider range of functions, is likely to possess a ready-made set of associated functional varieties for wider use. These can easily seep over into the L-using community and lead to an overlap between H and L in some functions, as when H is used in day-to-day contact with outsiders. This seems to be a common mechanism by which H becomes the spoken standard of the L-using community. It is also only in Type II that we find the postcreole continuum, with the complexities and uncertainties that it entails.

In Type I diglossia, it appears that the demise of diglossia can take place in one of two ways, which we have already discussed in relation to Sinhala. That is, it can be overthrown or go out of use in favor of L, perhaps displaced by some literary form of L, as was the case with Latin in Romance-speaking Europe or Sanskrit in India (though the process may take a long time and include successive revivals). This is the possibility envisioned by Ferguson "by which H may fade away and become a learned or liturgical language studied only by scholars and specialists and not used actively in the community" (p. 437). As we have seen, this appears unlikely to occur with Sinhala in the near future, and a long-term but widespread increase in literacy may deter the process.

The second manner of demise is the blurring and gradual disappearance of the lines between H and L. In this case, H can be absorbed into L, being restructured so as to become the higher variety in a continuum. As we have seen, hybridization and the nominalizing strategy are possible mechanisms by which this could occur in Sinhala.

At present, Sinhala diglossia, as an example of Type I in which none of the diglossia-threatening factors operate very strongly, appears stable. At the same time, L seems to be becoming richer in terms of functional varieties, though some regional differences may be weakening. A standard spoken variety seems clearly to be developing, based largely on the regional varieties of the southwest, but not exclusively on that of the capital (and largest) city, Colombo. As we noted earlier, Formal Spoken Sinhala is developing an increased range and flexibility as it fulfills a wider range of functions. The drama is flourishing to an amazing degree, with dialogue in L in most styles, but both imaginative and technical prose continues to be overwhelmingly in Literary Sinhala, save for the conversational stretches in fiction—which are, however, set in a Literary frame. Certainly Sinhala gives no support to Wexler's semiserious suggestion that the term *diglossia* "should be retained to describe a speech community with a high percentage of illiterates" (1971: 337).

In any event, in the Sinhala case as in many others, diglossia, as Ferguson implied, dies hard.

Syntactic Theory, AGR,
and Sinhala Diglossia

Present-day Sinhala is a diglossic language with sharply distinct spoken and written varieties that exhibit the complementarity of function and other features that characterized diglossia in Ferguson's classic definition of diglossia as

> a relatively stable language situation in which, in addition to the primary dialects of a language (which may include a standard or regional standards) there is a very divergent, highly codified (often grammatically more complex) superposed variety, the vehicle of a large and respected written literature, either of another period or in another speech community, which is learned largely by formal education and is used for most written and formal spoken purposes, but is not used by any sector of the community for ordinary conversation. (1959: 336)

In a 1968 paper that was, as far as I know, the first published general description of the Sinhala situation as diglossia, I claimed that there was an initial binary division—corresponding to Ferguson's H(igh) and L(ow) varieties—between the variety used for most written purposes, called Literary Sinhala, and the other varieties as a group, referred to collectively as Spoken Sinhala. The crucial defining distinction was taken to be the presence of grammatical agreement in the Literary variety. The classification proposed there and reiterated in Gair (1986a) is given below. Note that the description not only allows, but asserts, the existence of subvarieties; it specifies two of them for the Spoken hypervariety (elaborated somewhat in Gair 1986a):

Literary Sinhala. The Chief defining characteristic is Literary main verb forms, particularly the subject–verb agreement lacking in other varieties. Generally, these verb endings will entail the other grammatical and lexical features of Literary Sinhala. It should be noted that this is the variety characteristic of virtually all written Sinhala, not just of literature per se.

Spoken Sinhala lacking Literary verb agreement, but with two main varieties: (a) *Formal Spoken,* making use of one, and usually more, grammatical features of Literary Sinhala (other than verb agreement) with relative consistency. It characteristically makes use of a formal lexicon shared with Literary. (b.) *Colloquial.* The language of ordinary conversation.

This view was challenged, notably by M. W. S. De Silva, who asserted that there was a continuum rather than a sharp binary division, since lexical items from the Literary variety could be substituted at any point in a Colloquial sentence (De Silva 1974, but see also the reply in Gair 1978).[1] However, these positions did not really meet head-on. De Silva's view was on the basis of lexicon, whereas the original distinction was on structural grounds, so that both could be true simultaneously, depending on which features one considered primary.

In a later paper (Gair 1992a), I argued that the original claim, which took the single structural feature agreement as the crucial distinguishing characteristic between the varieties, was in fact well-founded and that it found an explanation in terms of interim developments in grammatical theory. Specifically, it was possible to view Literary Sinhala agreement as representative of an abstract element AGR(eement), which was included within the Government and Binding (GB) version of what has come to be called the Standard Theory (Chomsky 1981, 1982, 1986b). The nature of that element was such that its presence, absence, or nature in specific languages could be linked in a parametric way to a constellation of features that indeed were exhibited in Literary Sinhala in contradistinction to the spoken varieties.[2]

Recently, John Paolillo has presented the results of a detailed study of Sinhala diglossia on the basis of a number of actual texts carefully selected to represent actual varieties in use (Paolillo 1991, 1992), thus making available a much wider and more systematic database. In the course of this work, he has challenged my theory-based conclusions on several grounds. His was essentially a form of the continuum argument, but his argument was based primarily on structural features and their distribution across varieties (Paolillo 1991, 1992, esp. ch. 2).[3] Essentially, his claim was that the constellation of features that I had attributed to AGR was instead a set of independent features distributed within a continuum ranging from Colloquial through Formal Spoken to Literary. Thus he held, in relation to two of three central features that I had cited, that "AGR has no explanatory role in describing the distribution of agreement and accusative case in Sinhala Diglossia" (Paolillo 1991: 57). Rather, the distribution of such features was held to be governed by their functional communicative values related to "social and contextual factors."

In this paper I will reiterate, expand, and justify with some further observations my earlier expressed view that current linguistic theory, specifically with reference to concepts developed in GB theory, can indeed have relevance to the study of diglossic situations. I will first provide as background a general description of a number of relevant grammatical features of the Sinhala situation, especially case assignment, agreement, and operations such as the passive that are commonly viewed as case-related within that theory. I will also invoke some data and observations not included in that earlier paper, some of which I owe to Paolillo's critiques. I will also attempt to clear up some apparent unclarities and apparent misunderstandings revealed by those critiques. The aim here is not polemic, but at the end, I will address the major points in the critiques referred to and demonstrate that the "functional articulation" view embodied there and the view that invokes grammatical theory are not necessarily in direct conflict, but that the latter may place some constraints on the former.

Some Fundamental Characteristics of Sinhala Diglossia: Morphological Prerequisites

The varieties encompassed in Sinhala diglossia differ at all levels of structure. A general account was given in Gair 1968, and a more detailed and elaborate one, in general agreement with the first but based on a wider range of data, is included in Paolillo 1992 (see also the papers by De Silva cited in the references). This chapter will be primarily concerned with some crucial syntactic features representing dimensions along which the varieties differ, but a general account of some morphological features is necessary as a prerequisite.

Noun Forms

Literary Sinhala nominals inflect for six cases: nominative, accusative, dative, genitive (=locative), instrumental (=ablative), and vocative, as well as for two numbers, (singular and plural) and definiteness (definite and indefinite). This is shown in the partial paradigm in table 18–1 for *minisā* 'man'. Vocative is omitted, since it involves a number of complications that are irrelevant here. Note that here and throughout, Literary forms are cited in transliteration and Colloquial in an essentially phonemic representation. This has the effect that the same lexical item may be presented differently in the two representations, as in, for example, Literary *venavā*, 'be, become' but Colloquial *wenəwaa*.[4] For an explanation, see Gair 1968 and Paolillo 1992.

Note in table 18–1 that there is no nominative–accusative distinction in the definite. As the paradigm shows, the accusative case form serves as the base upon which the oblique case forms are built morphophonemically. This is a familiar pattern, with variations, in Indic languages, and the case called "accusative" here could equally well be referred to as "oblique." In fact, as I shall point out later, some mis-

Table 18–1   Nominal Inflections in Literary Sinhala

	Sg Def.	*Sg. Indef.*	*Plural*
Nom.	*minisā*	*minisek*	*minissu*
Acc.	*minisā*	*minisaku*	*minisun*
Dat.	*minisāṭa*	*minisakuṭa*	*minisunṭa*
Gen-Loc.	*minisāgē*	*minisakugē*	*minisungē*
Inst-Abl.	*minisāgen*	*minisakugen*	*minisungen*

understandings concerning my account of case assignment might have been avoided had I used the latter term.

Colloquial Sinhala Case marking on nominals is exemplified in table 18–2 with the animate noun *miniha* 'man', which is equivalent to the Literary form *minisā*, which was given in table 18–1. As can be seen by comparing these tables, Colloquial Sinhala differs in a number of ways from Literary in form. These differences extend to other nouns and pronouns as well, such as the lack of degemination in the nonnominative plural in Colloquial nouns and the length of the genitive affix, which is always long in Literary but not in Colloquial Sinhala. These details need not concern us here.

One aspect that will be of importance, though, is the form and status of the accusative. In Colloquial—as in Literary— Sinhala, distinctive accusative case marking is limited to animate nouns, with the Colloquial being marked by the invariant affix -*wə*. Note that the Literary plural -*n*- is reduced in Colloquial Sinhala to a morphophonemic variant serving as a base for the nonnominative forms, and it does not occur as an independent case form. Thus, Colloquial Sinhala has no independently occurring "oblique" form. This fact, when related to differences in distribution of the forms, will be of crucial importance to my account.[5]

Verb Forms and Agreement in Literary Sinhala

Sinhala verb forms differ across varieties such that there are relatively few that are shared in the same phonological shape at the two extremes by the Colloquial and the Literary varieties. Characteristically, forms in one variety have functional counterparts in the other, but there are also forms specific to one variety without counterparts in the other.[6] The feature that will concern us the most, however, is the strong presence of verbal agreement in the Literary variety and its complete absence in the spoken varieties. In unmarked, independent tensed sentences, Literary Sinhala verbs show agreement for person, number, and gender, as shown in example (1):

(1)   a. *mama gamaṭa   yami.*
        I   village-DAT   go-PRES-1 Sg
        'I go to the village.'

      b. *hē gamaṭa   yayi.*
        he village-DAT   go-PRES-3 Sg
        'He goes to the village.'

Table 18–2 Nominal Inflections in Colloquial Sinhala

	Sg Def.	Sg. Indef.	Plural
Nom.	miniha	minihek	minissu
Acc.	minihawə	minihekwə	minissunwə
Dat.	minihaṭə	minihekuṭə	minissunṭə
Gen-Loc.	minihage	minihekuge	minissunge
Inst-Abl.	minihageŋ	minihekugeŋ	minissungeŋ

c. *ovuhu gamaṭa   yati.*
they   village-DAT go-PRES-3 Pl
'They go to the village.'

d. *otomō gamaṭa   giyāya.*
she   village-DAT go PAST-Fem-3 Sg[7]
'She went to the village.'

Special mention must be made of inanimate nouns in relation to agreement. As mentioned earlier, neither Literary nor Colloquial inanimate nominals show a nominative–accusative distinction in any category, and when Literary inanimate forms occur as subjects, their verbs occur invariably in the third person singular, as in (2):[8]

(2)   *mē pustakālayehi puskola pot/pota tibē.*
this library-GEN ola-leaf books/the book be-PRES-3 Sg
'There is/ are ola leaf books/the ola leaf book in this library.'

Colloquial Verb Forms and Nonagreement

In contradistinction to the Literary variety, spoken Sinhala exhibits no verbal agreement. A single verb form within any given tense–mode combination serves for all numbers, genders, and persons, as illustrated in (3). (Unless otherwise required, Colloquial Sinhala will generally be used for exemplification of spoken forms):

(3)   a. *mamə /oyaa /eyaa /api /oyaala /eyaala pansələṭə   yanəwa.*
I   /you /(s)he /we /you-Pl /they   temple-DAT go-PRES
'I/ you/ (s)he/ we/you-all/ they go to the temple.'

b. *mamə /oyaa /eyaa /api /oyaala /eyaala pansələṭə   giyaa.*
I   /you /(s)he /we /you-Pl /they   temple-DAT go-PAST
'I/ you/ (s)he/ we/you-all/ they went to the temple.'

Agreement in Nonverbal Sentences

As with verbs, The Literary and spoken varieties also show a sharp difference in the marking of nonverbal predicates.[9] In spoken Sinhala, they lack both an obligatory copula and agreement of any sort, as in (4):

(4)   a. *mamə   goviyek.*
I-NOM farmer-INDEF
'I am a farmer.'

b. *ee   mahattəya   guruwərəyek.*
that gentleman-NOM teacher-NOM-INDEF
'That gentleman is a teacher.'

The situation is quite different in Literary Sinhala, in which all such sentences require predicate marking of some sort. In the third person, this is an agreement form *ya,* which may in some cases can also take the form *(y)i* and does not show number agreement, as in (5):

(5) a. *ovuhu goviyō ya.*
      they   farmers-NOM-3
      'They are farmers.'

   b. *hetema   goviyek ya / goviyeki.*
      he-NOM farmer-NOM -3
      'He is a farmer.'

In other persons, they take essentially the same agreement affixes as verbs, as exemplified in (6), for the first person:

(6) *mama   goviyekmi.*
    I-NOM farmer-NOM-1 Sg
    'I am a farmer.'

In any person, they may alternatively occur with a copula verb *venavā* 'be, become', with the usual agreement affixes, as in (7):

(7) a. *mama   goviyek vemi.*
      I-NOM farmer   NOM be-PRES 1Sg
      'I am a farmer.'

   b. *hetema   goviyek veyi.*
      he-NOM farmer   be-PRES 3Sg
      'He is a farmer.'

In Gair 1992a (and 1986a), I referred to the *ya/(y)i* marker as a copula, though I did state later that it represented or included AGR. However, as was pointed out by John Paolillo (personal communication), it seems clear that it is best considered an agreement affix or clitic, especially in view of its participating in a paradigm with the undoubted agreement affixes in the other persons, as in (6). Once this is recognized, the identification with agreement in verbal sentences (which of course include those with an overt copula) becomes even more direct, and no special provision is made for *ya/(y)i.* The crucial point to note here is that the obligatory occurrence of agreement on nonverbal independent finite sentences and its absence in Colloquial Sinhala parallels the situation with verbal sentences.

Case Marking in Verbal Sentences

Case Marking in Colloquial Verbal Sentences

Colloquial Sinhala exhibits lexically realized subjects in an unusually wide variety of cases. This will be demonstrated later. For now, what should be noted is that the case of the subject and other nominal arguments remains constant throughout the full range of constructions for any given verb.[10] Thus the nominative and dative subjects occurring respectively in (8a) and (8b) are seen also in the focused (or cleft) sentences in (9) and the relative clause structures in (10):[11]

(8) a. *mamə ee potə kiyewwa.*
I-NOM that book read-PAST-FIN
'I read that book.'

b. *maṭə ee missunwə penuna.*
I-DAT those men-ACC see-PAST-FIN
'I saw those men.'

(9) a. *mamə kiyewwe ee potə.*
I-NOM read-PAST-FOC that book
'It was that book that I read.'

b. *maṭə penune ee minissunwə.*
I-DAT see-PAST-FOC those men-ACC
'It was those men that I saw.'

(10) a. *Siri mamə kiyewwə potə kiyewwe næœ.*
Siri I-NOM read-PAST-REL book read-PAST not
'Siri did not read the book that I read.'

b. *Siri maṭə penunə minissunwə dannəwa.*
Siri I-DAT see-PAST-REL people-ACC know-PRES-FIN
'Siri knows the people that I saw.'

Case Marking in Literary Verbal Sentences

The situation is very different in Literary Sinhala. There, the equivalents of (8) through (10) are as in (11) through (13):

(11) a. *mama ema pota kiyevuvemi.*
I-NOM that book read-PAST-1Sg
'I read that book.'

b. *maṭə ema minissu penunōya.*
I-DAT those men-NOM see-PAST-3Sg
'I saw those men.'

(12) a. *mā kiyevuvē ema potə ya.*
I-ACC read-PAST-FOC that book 3Pers
'It was that book that I read.'

b. *maṭə penunē ema minissu /minissun ya.*
I-DAT see-PAST-FOC those men-NOM /men-ACC 3Pers
'It was those men that I saw.'

(13) a. *Siri mā kiyevuva potə nokiyevuvēya.*
Siri I-ACC read-PAST-REL book not read-PAST 3Sg
'Siri did not read the book that I read.'

b. *Siri maṭə penuna minisun danī.*
Siri I-DAT see-PAST-REL people-ACC know-PRES-3Sg
'Siri knows the people that I saw.'

The subject of the agreeing verb in (11a) is in the nominative, parallel to that in the Colloquial sentence. However, the equivalents of the Colloquial nominative subjects in the focused and relativized sentences (12a) and (13a), where their verbs do not show agreement, are in the morphologically marked accusative. Note also that the nondative NP in (11b) is in the nominative and agrees with the verb, but in (8b) it is in the accusative, and agreement is not relevant. The variation in (12b) will occupy us later.

Some Generalizations on Literary Case and Agreement

There is clearly an intimate relation between case and agreement (AGR) in Literary Sinhala, which I initially formulated as the "accusative rule":

> A nominal that is in a construction with an agreeing finite verb form will be in the nominative case. Otherwise, it will be in the accusative, unless it is in some other case required by the construction. (Gair 1968, 1992a)

Actually, there are two generalizations concerning Literary Sinhala embodied here, which for reasons to be made clear shortly, I would reformulate as separate nominative and accusative rules:

> The nominative rule: Only a nominal that is coindexed with (finite) agreement will be in the nominative case.[12]
>
> The accusative rule (proper): A nominal not coindexed with (finite) agreement will appear in the accusative unless it is in some case required by the construction.

In retrospect, it probably would have been better to use the term "oblique" for what has been referred to as the Literary "accusative" form, since, as the foregoing will have made obvious, it is by no means limited to syntactic accusative contexts. However, the latter term has by now been established in the works of others as well. In what follows, therefore, I will generally continue to use the term "accusative" to refer to the relevant form, but I will use "oblique" where the context demands.

Case Marking in Nonverbal Sentences

In Colloquial Sinhala, as noted earlier, no agreement or other marker of finiteness appears in nominal equational sentences, and their subjects and predicate nominals are both in the nominative, as illustrated in (4) above, repeated as (14):

(14) a. *mama   goviyek.*
         I-NOM   farmer-INDEF
         'I am a farmer.'

      b. *ee   mahattəya   guruwərəyek.*
         that man-DEF-NOM   teacher-INDEF-NOM
         'That man is a teacher.'

In Literary Sinhala also, when agreement is present, both nominals are in the nominative, as illustrated in (5) and (6), repeated here as (15a) and (15b):

(15) a. *mama   goviyekmi*
        I-NOM   farmer-NOM-1Sg
        'I am a farmer.'

     b. *hetema   goviyek ya/ goviyeki.*
        he-NOM   farmer-NOM-3
        'He is a farmer.'

However, the kinds of agreement-related differences in case marking that were observed between Colloquial and Literary Sinhala in verbal clauses emerge again when we look at relativization. Neither Colloquial nor Literary Sinhala can form relative clauses directly from nominal equational sentences without an overt copula. In Colloquial Sinhala it is in fact difficult to form relative clauses that are equivalents of "the man who is a teacher" at all because of the lack of a copula to bear the relativizing affix (Gair and Paolillo 1988). Thus, one must resort to some circumlocution, such as using two sentences. Though it is possible to use the relativizing form of the verb *wenəwa* 'become', the "change of state" sense shown in the corresponding independent sentence (16) is generally preserved, so that the relative is not a true equivalent for the copuleless independent sentence.[13] Nevertheless, as in the corresponding independent sentence (16), both the subject and the predicate nominal are in the nominative, as shown in (17):

(16) *ee   mahattəya   guruwərəyek   wenəwa.*
     that man-DEF-NOM   teacher-INDEF-NOM become-PRES-FIN
     'That man is (becoming) a teacher.'

(17) a. *guruwərəyek   wenə   mahattəya huñgak dannəwa.*
        teacher-INDEF-NOM become-PRES-REL man-DEF I much know-PRES-FIN
        'The man who is becoming a teacher knows a lot.'

     b. *mamə guruwərəyek wenə   bawə eyaa danne   næœ.*
        I   teacher-INDEF become-PRES-REL fact he   know-PRES-AFF not.
        'He doesn't know that I am becoming a teacher.'

In Literary Sinhala, however, independent equational sentences can appear either with the agreement marker alone or with the verb *venavā* as noted earlier and illustrated in (18). No change of state is necessarily involved, which makes it possible to form equational relative clauses using the verbal variant to bear the relativizing affix, as in (19):[14]

(18) *mama   guruvarayek   (ve)mi.*
     I-NOM   teacher-INDEF-NOM (copula)-1Sg
     'I am a teacher.'

(19) a. *guruvarayaku   vana   mahatmayek bohō deval danī.*
        teacher-INDEF-ACC COP-PRES-REL man   much things know-PRES-3Sg
        'A man who is a teacher knows many things.'

b. *mā   guruvarayeku   vana   bava hē no-danī.*
   I-ACC teacher-INDEF-ACC COP-PRES-REL fact he NEG-know-PRES-3Sg
   'He doesn't know that I am a teacher.'

The subject of a Literary relative clause, if present, is in the accusative as expected, since the relativizing affix does not show agreement. However, the Literary predicate nominal in such constructions is also marked accusative, as in both examples in (19). This casts light on the nature of case assignment in Literary copular sentences. The obvious conclusion is that the agreement in nonverbal predicate sentences, with or without a copular verb, assigns case to the subject, and the case of the predicate nominal is assigned through case coindexing with that subject. As (19a) shows, this remains true if the subject of the relative clause is the relativized element and hence an empty category. Thus, the case of both nominals is dependent on the occurrence of AGR, so that we have another exemplar from Colloquial Sinhala of the difference that relates to the linkage of case with agreement.

The Relevance of Grammatical Theory to Sinhala Diglossia

Initially I claimed (Gair 1968) that the presence or absence of agreement made for a sufficiently sharp and important distinction between the main varieties of Sinhala so as to constitute their defining feature; this claim was based on observations of use rather than on theory. One especially suggestive observation was the difficulty that Sinhala speakers encountered in coping with the Literary variety, especially in producing it, unless they had practiced sufficiently to become virtuosi. Along with this came the observation that the major part of this difficulty appeared to center on agreement.[15] However, it was not obvious why this one feature should have a critical defining role. More recently, I suggested (Gair 1992a) that recent work in grammatical theory, stemming from Chomsky 1981, provided a principled explanation when taken together with the observations concerning case and agreement made above.

Within Government and Binding Theory in particular (as represented in Chomsky 1981, 1982, and 1986b), verb agreement in finite clauses has been identified with an AGR element within INFL(ection), governing and assigning case to the subject with which it is coindexed. This feature in turn has been linked to a number of other features, so that AGR has been assigned crucial roles in the grammar that go well beyond its traditional subject-identifying function. There has been further treatment and elaboration in the literature since, but the crucial insight here is the connection between at least one kind of agreement (symbolized as AGR)[16] and case assignment. This connection has been put forward clearly by Chomsky:

> The agreement element [AGR-JWG] of INFL is associated (we have assumed, coindexed) with the subject, which it governs, since they share all maximal projections, and assigns it nominative case. (1986a: 188)[17]

In what follows, I shall argue, as in my earlier (1992a) paper, that verbal agreement in finite clauses in Sinhala is a surface exemplar of AGR and that its presence in Literary Sinhala and absence in the spoken varieties has, as the theory just characterized would lead us to expect, wide-ranging effects in the grammars of those two major Sinhala varieties that result in their being sharply distinct typologically. I shall thus claim once more that the recognition of the presence or absence of AGR, surfacing as agreement,[18] has explanatory power in distinguishing them in a nontrivial way by unifying a number of apparently separate defining characteristics. In the process, I will also address what appear to me to be the major points in the critiques of my earlier paper, and I will make some corrections and clarifications of that earlier presentation that have been suggested in those critiques. In addition, I will present some further AGR-linked features that distinguish the varieties.

Relating AGR to the Varietal Differences

Literary Case Assignment and the Case Filter

In my earlier (1992a) paper , I claimed:

> What we have shown so far is that at least three features distinguishing Literary from Spoken Sinhala: agreement, case marking, (specifically the Literary accusative rule) and the occurrence of the copula, can be related in a unified fashion to the presence of AGR, as represented by overt agreement, in Literary Sinhala . . . and its absence in Spoken. (p. 187)

Though I still believe this claim to be true in essence, it requires some further clarification and justification, inspired in large measure by Paolillo's critiques. It has by now been amply demonstrated that nominative case marking of Literary Sinhala subjects is dependent on agreement (now taken as representative of AGR) and its alternation with accusative/oblique in the absence of that agreement. The copula referred to in my earlier claim was the apparently invariant *ya/(y)i*, which I have now identified with agreement, hence AGR, so that it can be conflated with the other person–number endings. It is also clear that independent finite sentences in Literary Sinhala, whether verbal or nonverbal, require the presence of agreement/AGR, in sharp contradistinction to Colloquial Sinhala. Thus, no further justification is needed on these points.

However, the situation with regard to the accusative rule, and the assignment of accusative case in general, is more complex than that earlier statement assumed. On reflection, it is clear that the accusative/oblique rule does not follow ineluctably from any observations made so far, since it is easy to imagine alternative case marking scenarios for the nominals affected, while retaining the nominative linkage with AGR. That is, the nominative rule could hold without the accusative rule holding. To address this problem, some further observations on case in general are necessary.

In the general theory we are working in, a clear distinction is made between structural case and inherent case,[19] as well as between case assignment (referring essentially to abstract case) and case realization (which may be expressed in morphological case). The former distinction, as expressed by Chomsky, is:

We distinguish the "structural Cases" objective and nominative, assigned in terms of S-structure position, from the "inherent Cases" assigned at D-structure. . . . Inherent Case is associated with θ-marking while structural Case is not. . . . Thus we assume that inherent Case is assigned by [a form] α to NP if and only if it θ-marks NP, while structural Case is assigned independently of θ-marking. (1986b: 193)

Chomsky uses "Case" to signify abstract case. Here, "θ-marking" refers to the assignment of a θ ("thematic") role to a nominal, where "thematic role" refers to "the semantic properties assigned by heads" (Chomsky 1986b: 93). What is of relevance here is that structural case is assigned by categories such as V or INFL/AGR without association with any specific thematic role. The thematic role assigned along with Case by an inherent case assigner, however, is a lexical property of that head and, hence, specific.

Structural case is abstract and does not require any one-to-one surface morphological realization. Rather, its crucial effects are more indirect—specifically, the licensing of NPs and motivating NP movement under certain circumstances. Thus it is perfectly conceivable that accusative marking of Literary Sinhala nominals is by a default, or "otherwise," rule and applies to nonnominative NPs not assigned some lexical case. In fact, that is implied in the accusative rule as stated either in its original form or in the combination of nominative rule and accusative rule. Under that assumption, structural nominative would surface, but structural accusative would not, so that the accusative case on direct objects would represent the default case both there and in the other positions in which it occurs. However, it would obviously be preferable if we could unify all instances of accusative by relating them to some general principle.

As a first step, let us note two characteristics of Literary accusative (oblique) marking. First, titles of books and similar "freestanding" nominals are generally in the nominative. Thus the disjunction of the nominative and oblique rules applies only to nominals "in construction"—in some relation to a head—as complement or specifer. Second, despite the general way the accusative rule has been expressed, in actuality there appear to be only three environments in which it applies, as has been pointed out by Paolillo (1991: 54). These are nonagreeing subjects, (direct) objects, and postpositional objects.[20]

For adpositions and verbs to assign a single case to their complements would not, of course, engender any surprise. Such is the situation, for example, with the objective case in English. The question we must then address is how accusative case is assigned to subjects of nonagreeing verbs. That question, though not adequately addressed in my earlier paper, is far from trivial, since failure to account for it runs afoul of a fundamental principle of GB theory, the necessity for licensing of nominal expressions. One proposal for guaranteeing such licensing was the Case Filter:

*[NP a] if a has no case and contains a phonetic matrix or is a variable. (Chomsky 1981: 175)[21]

Paolillo quite properly raised this issue, albeit somewhat indirectly, pointing out that:

In Government–Binding theory, if a governing case assigner is absent, Case is not assigned and the NP will not be licensed. However, the nonagreeing subjects of Literary Sinhala appear in the accusative, and subjects of nonagreeing verbs in

Colloquial Sinhala appear in the nominative. Therefore absence of AGR entails that Case is assigned by some other means. According to Gair's hypothesis, when AGR is present in the variety [i.e., Literary Sinhala-JWG], but is lacking in the immediate clause, an alternative case assigner appearing in INFL must be invoked to assign accusative case, and no agreement morphology surfaces. This constitutes the "accusative rule." . . . When AGR is absent in the variety altogether, as in Colloquial Sinhala, no agreement morphology surfaces, and the subject is assigned nominative case directly by the verb. (1991: 48–49)

I shall address the question of Colloquial Sinhala case assignment later but only briefly, since I have addressed it elsewhere (Gair 1991b). Actually, I did not suggest that some case assigner in Literary INFL assigned accusative in the absence of AGR, as Paolillo implies, but clearly, when the Case Filter is taken into account, I should have done so, or else proposed some other case assigner or licensing element.

TENSE as a Case Assigner

Paolillo (1991, 1992) explicitly rejected the possibility that the case assigner could be TENSE. Before dealing with his reasons for that rejection, I will first suggest the approach that a solution involving TENSE and the verb as the required case assigner might take within the general theoretical framework here.

A Technical Interlude: TENSE as a Functional Head

It has frequently been proposed that subjects as well as other arguments originate within the VP (as in Koopman and Sportiche 1986). I have proposed this elsewhere (Gair 1991b) for Colloquial Sinhala, arguing in addition that all relevant case assignment takes place there, thus accounting for the wide range of Colloquial Sinhala subject cases. For Literary Sinhala too, I will also assume that all arguments originate within VP, but I will also claim that the presence of AGR carries with it the assignment of a structural case that surfaces as nominative. This is a familiar, essentially orthodox, analysis that has been proposed for many other, more familiar, languages.

This, then, constitutes the basic distinction between Literary and Spoken Sinhala. So far, I have invoked only a unitary INFL, which could include AGR, but some work, particularly stemming from Pollock (1989) and represented in Chomsky (1989), has decomposed INFL into several functional heads, commonly including T(ense), AGR, and NEG(ation), with each defining a projection of its own. For Literary Sinhala, I would assume that the canonical configuration (omitting NEG) is as in (20).[22]

(20)

The verb, by head movement, moves from within VP to adjoin to T(ense) in tensed clauses. The subject NP, originating within VP (probably in spec VP), will move accordingly to spec T.

From this point on, there are at least two general lines of analysis that we could follow. Under one of them, we make the not unreasonable assumption that T and AGR will only project maximal projections if they are instantiated. Thus if there is AGR, the V+T will move there to form a V+T+AGR complex. The subject NP will now move to spec AGR in the usual fashion and receive nominative case there by spec–head agreement.

If there is no AGR, no AGRP is projected, and the subject NP does not go beyond spec T, where it receives case from V+T. I assume V+T assigns case and licenses the NP, also by spec–head agreement. Under either scenario, proper case assignment will be assured by case checking at S structure.[23] If there is a direct object, accusative is, of course, assigned to it in the usual way.

However, in the cases in which AGR is present, and the verb raises all the way to it, we must resolve the apparent problem of case conflict. When the verb raises, its trace must still be able to assign case to the direct object. Then, in the structure in which it raises to AGR and the subject NP raises to spec AGR, how do we prevent its intermediate trace in T_0 from assigning the accusative to the trace in spec T, as the V+T does in the case where raising is only to that position? We might claim that this does not happen because there is no nominal in that position when case is checked, but this scarcely seems satisfactory by itself. What one could claim is that the nominative case assigned by AGR is in some way "stronger" than that assigned by TENSE (or V+TENSE) alone. That does not seem unreasonable, given the unique form and the narrower distribution of the nominative, which is clearly tied to agreement. Thus, TENSE by itself would be sufficient to license the occurrence of an NP, but only AGR, as represented by agreement, could assign the nominative.

There is an alternate scenario by which there is an AGRP even if AGR is not instantiated. Under that assumption, as well, we would have to say that nominative is somehow "stronger" than oblique. One way of accomplishing this is to say that in the tensed accusative subject sentences, V+TENSE raises to AGR_0 as before, but that AGR there is featureless, and that only AGR with nominal-type features (i.e., some selection of person, number, and gender) can assign nominative. Case is then assigned by TENSE (or V+TENSE), as before. This avoids the case conflict in the NP chain and has the virtue that AGRP is always projected in Literary Sinhala, which is consistent with the claim that I am making here about its typological properties. Thus, I prefer this account to the previous one, but on theory-internal grounds, since I know of no empirical evidence to support it. If, for example, we were to find independent reasons that both nominative and accusative subjects had to be in spec AGRP, there would of course be such empirical evidence, but at present I am not aware of any.

Counterexamples to TENSE as a Licensing Element

Paolillo's (1992) rejection of TENSE as an accusative case assigner was based on empirical, not theoretical, grounds:

I have explored this possibility [that the case assigner for accusative subjects is TENSE] in earlier research on Sinhala diglossia (Paolillo 1987); briefly, in this research I concluded (reluctantly) that it is not possible to identify accusative case assignment with TENSE, since certain tensed clauses appear in obligatorily controlled positions and hence cannot have lexical subjects. (p. 88)

Note that the implied counterexamples thus have to do with the nonoccurrence of overt NPs in some tensed structures rather than on the occurrence of overt subjects in tenseless ones, which is the immediate problem here. However, the proposed counterexamples should be taken into account.[24] Although no exemplification accompanied Paolillo's just quoted statement, a similar statement in Paolillo 1992 makes reference to an earlier paper (Paolillo 1987) in which the relevant forms are treated.

One set of exceptions consists of adverbial clauses formed with the present tense relativizing form and the forms *sē, lesa, paridi,* and *men.* The form *ayuru* could also be added here. Though their distributions and semantics differ, all have a "manner" or "kind" sense of some sort. With the apparent exception of *men,* they all may appear with overt subjects as adverbial clauses. Since these have tensed verbs but no agreement, and since the subjects are in the accusative, as in (21) (from Gair and Karunatilaka 1974: 224), they present no problem.

(21) *apa*   *dakvana*   *ayuru meya kiyaviya yutu ya.*
      we-ACC show-PRES-REL way   this   read   must 3Sg Neut
      'This is to be read as we indicate.'

However, sentences with these forms also occur as complements of verbs with null subjects coindexed with some NP in the matrix clause. Depending on the specific forms involved, the controlling NP may be a subject or a dative case NP, which we may assume to be an indirect object, as in (22a) and (22b). (Examples are again from Gair and Karunatilaka 1974):

(22) a. *sī-sāna*   *men goviyō*   *kuṁburaṭa*   *yati.*
        plow-PRES-REL as   farmer-PL-NOM paddy-field-PL-DAT go-PRES-3Pl
        'The farmers go to the fields to plow.'

      b. *ō*   *sora-sæmiyāṭa* *sangavena paridi sælæsuvāya.*
        she-NOM paramour-DAT hide-REL   so-as   arrange-PAST-3 Sg-Fem
        'She made arrangements for her paramour to hide.'

What such examples demonstrate is that null subjects of some tensed clauses can occur in control domains, a phenomenon that has been noted in other languages. A precise definition of CONTROL DOMAIN for such instances has been the subject of considerable attention in the literature, and I will not attempt one here, but I will simply note that the Literary Sinhala environments here are classical instances of such domains.[25] The possibility of null controlled elements occurring in specific environmental contexts in the same sentential structures in which overt NPs occur in other contexts (hence requiring a case assigner) is thus well attested and does not tell us anything in general about the identity of that assigner.

The other proposed counterexample appears to concern the verb form referred to as the progressive participle. This form not only is tensed but also has agreement morphology. However, it also appears to have obligatorily controlled null subjects. Examples are given in (23) (from Gair and Karunatilaka 1974):

(23) a. *hē   vanaṭa   yannē*   *muwaku duṭuvēya.*
    he-NOM   forest-DAT   go-PROGPRT-PRES-3 Sg   deer   see-PAST-3 Sg Masc
    'Going to the forest, he saw a deer.'

  b. *Kuvēṇi   Vijaya   duṭuvā*   *biya   vuvāya.*
    Kuveni-NOM   Vijaya-ACC   see-PROGPRT-PAST-3 Sg Fem   afraid become-
    PAST-3Sg Fem
    'Kuveni, seeing Vijaya, was afraid.'

If these sentences do indeed have null subjects, the same general considerations apply as for the forms with *men, paridi*, and so on, except that the null element would apparently have nominative case (as would be true of controlled *pro* in other languages, and hence presents no problem in itself).

However, the analysis of these structures is as yet not clear. The agreement affix is not precisely the same as that in finite clauses, lacking the final *-ya*—compare the final finite forms in the same sentences in (34), as well as with (22b). Thus it is not clear that it would have the same case-assigning properties. Also, some type of coordination may in fact be involved, so that it is not clear which sentence the overt NP is the subject of (L. Sumangala, personal communication). Even pending such an analysis, however, they do not appear to constitute a serious obstacle to TENSE as a licensing case assigner.[26] Though these examples suggest interesting questions about control structures and the licensing of null elements in Literary Sinhala (and in general), they do not constitute material for arguments for rejecting an explanation for the otherwise overwhelming and pervasive pattern in Literary Sinhala by which tense is a necessary condition for the occurrence of phonologically realized subjects. (Since AGR always accompanies tense, nominative subjects do not constitute exceptions.)

The Accusative Rule Restated

The Literary Sinhala accusative rule was earlier broken into two parts, which are repeated here for convenience:

> The nominative rule: Only a nominal which is coindexed with (finite) agreement will be in the nominative case.

> The accusative rule (proper): A nominal not coindexed with (finite) agreement will appear in the accusative unless it is in some case required by the construction.

Both of these rules refer to surface case marking, but they are actually somewhat different in the kinds of case assignment they pertain to, as reflected in the essentially positive condition in the nominative rule and negative condition: the accusative rule. That is, nominative rule assigns a specific structural case and associates a specific case inflection with it. The accusative rule, on the other hand, specifies a particular inflection that must appear when a nominal that is not assigned some inherent (i.e., lexically assigned) case does not fit the nominative rule.

In view of the foregoing discussion, we can now restate these rules more precisely and in the process achieve the unification of accusative case marking that was stated earlier as a desideratum. Note that the distinction between case assignment and case marking is crucial here and is reflected in the different terms case (marking) versus Case (structural):

> Nominative Case is assigned only by AGR, represented by verbal agreement. It surfaces as nominative case inflection.

> Accusative (oblique) case inflection occurs on nominals that are licensed in a syntactic construction but are not assigned Nominative Case (or some lexically assigned case).

The licensing referred to in the new Accusative rule does not necessitate any specific case; it only requires the assignment of some Case as required to escape the case filter. In some work, the emphasis has been placed on licensing of NPs by spec–head or head–complement relations, rather than by Case (see, for example, Toribio and Gair 1991). For present purposes, this is not important. Licensing of NPs in general is a separate issue, and though the new Accusative rule crucially refers to licensing, both it and the new Nominative rule, as stated, are essentially neutral with regard to the necessary involvement of Case in it.[27] One point that should be made clear, however, is that accusative case, as assigned to the complements of verbs, does not have any specific marking in Literary Sinhala, but those nominals are part of the general set in the Accusative rule that receive accusative case inflection. Again, had the accusative/oblique distinction been made at the beginning (Gair 1968) in terms of case assignment versus case marking, much potential confusion would have been avoided, but that was scarcely possible in terms of the theoretical situation at the time.

Typologically, we could view Literary Sinhala in case-marking terms as an essentially "well-behaved" language of the nominative/accusative type, with the interesting exception of the accusative subjects of nonagreeing forms. However, in view of the preceding discussion, "nominative/oblique" might be a more accurate label, given the lack of an accusative form restricted to object position and the wide distribution of the form that has been designated accusative. Interestingly, a similar characterization also holds for much Colloquial English, as reflected in the case marking of pronouns. There, too, overt NPs are not barred from nonfinite structures under all conditions, nominative occurs only in connection with agreement,[28] and a case that has been referred to as objective appears in nonagreement patterns, as exemplified in "Him doing that was pretty disgusting."

Colloquial Sinhala Case Revisited

Colloquial Sinhala has subjects in a wide variety of cases—in fact, in all cases but the genitive,[29] as exemplified in (24) with both transitive and intransitive sentences:[30]

(24) a. NOMINATIVE: *miniha   duwənəwa.*
man-NOM run-PRES
'The man runs.' (intransitive)

siri   adə   apəṭə   ballekwə   dunna.
Siri-NOM today us-DAT dog-INDEF-ACC give-PAST
'Siri Gave us a dog today.' (transitive)

b. DATIVE: *minihaṭə   diwenəwa.*
man-DAT run-INVOL-PRES
'The man runs (involuntarily).' (intransitive)

məṭə   dæŋ aliyawə   peenəwa.
I-DAT now elephant-ACC see-PRES
'I see the elephant now.' (transitive)

c. ACCUSATIVE (INTRANSITIVE ONLY):
minihawə gaṅgəṭə   wæteewi.
man-ACC river-DAT fall-OPT
'The man might fall into the river.'

d. INSTRUMENTAL: *ehee poliisiyeŋ   innəwa.*
there police-INSTR be (exist)-PRES
'The police are there.' (intransitive)

aanḍuweŋ   eekəṭə   aadaarə denəwa.
government-INSTR that-DAT support give-PRES
'The government gives support for that.' (transitive)

I have treated subjecthood and case assignment in Colloquial Sinhala in detail elsewhere (Gair 1991b) and will not repeat it here. In brief, the argument held that the assignment of argument case, including subjects, is carried out within VP, and that case is assigned by the verb within the θ-grid. Movement of the subject nominal was motivated not by the necessity to receive structural case but by a requirement that spec INFL be filled. There was thus no AGR to enforce nominative case assignment, and the wide variety of subject cases was thus made possible by the absence of AGR.[31]

In the present context, the important point is that the Colloquial pattern is obviously quite different from that we have seen in Literary Sinhala, which displays a much more restricted array of subject cases, one more reminiscent of that in the familiar European languages, especially those with "quirky case" (dative subjects will be dealt with later). Colloquial and Literary Sinhala are thus typologically quite distinct, and that difference is linked to a difference in a functional category—specifically AGR—and the specifics of case assignment.

Some Further Structural Reflections of Case Assignment and Agreement

There are other characteristics that are consonant, in terms of later theoretical work, with the differences in AGR agreement between the two varieties. These include focused (cleft) sentences, dative experiencer sentences, the passive, and the occurrence of null subjects with arbitrary reference.[32]

Focused Sentences and Agreement

Focused sentences, also referred to as emphatic or cleft sentences, are much more common in both Literary and spoken Sinhala than their usual English translations as clefts would suggest (Gair 1983b, 1986b; Gair and Paolillo 1988; Paolillo 1992). They are formed in both Literary and spoken Sinhala by adding an affix *-e/ee* (always *-ee* in Literary Sinhala but metrically determined in Colloquial) to the tensed stem of the verb of the presupposition. The affix is invariant and does not show agreement in Literary Sinhala. Examples were given for Colloquial focused sentences in (9) and for Literary focused sentences in (12); they are repeated here for convenience. As noted earlier, subjects in such Literary sentences (i.e., of the presupposition) are in the accusative:

(9) a. *mamə   kiyewwe   ee   potə.*
      I-NOM read-PAST-FOC that book
      'It was that book that I read.'

    b. *matə   penune   ee   minissunwə.*
      I-DAT see-PAST-FOC those men-ACC
      'It was those men that I saw.'

(12) a. *mā   kiyevuvē   ema potə ya.*
      I-ACC read-PAST-FOC that book 3 Pers
      'It was that book that I read.'

    b. *matə   penunē   ema minissu   /minissun ya.*
      I-DAT see-PAST-FOC those men-NOM /men-ACC 3 Pers
      'It was those men that I saw.'

Historically, the *-e/ee* affix was a third person nominalizing form, but that is no longer the case in Sinhala (see Gair 1986b, Paolillo 1990, Sumangala 1992). The important point to note here is that in Colloquial Sinhala, no further marking is necessary, but in Literary, the focused element must occur with the third person agreement affix *-ya/(y)i*, or with the lexical copula in the third person, as in (25):

(25) *mā   kiyavannee   ema potə veyi.*
    I-ACC read-PRES-FOC that book be-3 Pers
    'It was that book that I read.'

The situation with focused sentences is thus parallel to the nominal predicate sentences that they resemble, since in Literary, but not Colloquial, some form of agreement is necessary. The agreeing affix in Literary is coindexed with the entire presupposition and not with its subject. Thus that nominal is in the accusative. Focused sentences thus exhibit a set of AGR-linked properties.

Dative Experiencer Sentences

Like other South Asian languages, Sinhala has dative subject sentences (see Verma and Mohanan 1991 for a general survey and relevant analyses). The type that I will illustrate here is an experiencer type, expressing sensations or emotion, corresponding roughly to psych verbs in some languages. Such sentences exhibit very different characteristics in Literary and Colloquial Sinhala in a way that is clearly related to AGR and case assignment and thus in accord with my hypothesis. An example for Colloquial was given as (8b):

(8)   b. *maṭə   ee   missunwə penuna.*
      I-DAT those men-ACC see-PAST-FIN
      'I saw those men.'

As the example shows, Colloquial Sinhala allows the nondative nominal (which I will refer to for convenience as NP2, to avoid complications concerning their object or nonobject status in both varieties) in sentences of this kind to appear in the accusative.[33]

Literary Sinhala, however, does not seem to allow this (*modulo* the difference in case form) even with the equivalent verbs. Dative subject sentences of this type are not common in Literary texts, but the Sinhala speakers adept in that variety whom I have consulted require NP2 to be in the nominative, and the verb agrees with it, as in (26).[34] This also accords with Paolillo's (1992) findings:

(26)   *ema kumārayāṭa sundara kumārikāva   penunāya.*
      that prince-DAT beautiful princess-NOM see-PAST- Fem/3Sg
      'That prince saw the beautiful princess.'

Thus, Literary Sinhala, but not Colloquial, belongs to the class of languages, which includes at least Hindi and Marathi among South Asian languages, that requires NP2 in such sentences to be in the nominative. This also a feature of "quirky case" languages that has initiated a considerable amount of discussion, but there is general agreement that the nominative case assignment is linked to INFL/AGR, whatever the precise mechanism might be (for an account and relevant references, see Harbert and Toribio 1991).

However, cross linguistic comparison demands that some caution be exercised here. While one may associate the nominative case NP2 with INFL/AGR, as in the recent literature on other languages, one cannot simply go on to say that allowing accusative/oblique is a function of the absence of AGR if AGR is assumed to always be represented as overt finite verb agreement. Tamil and Malayalam both allow accusative/oblique NP2s, but while the latter lacks agreement, like Colloquial Sinhala, the former has strong verbal agreement. It is suggestive that the Tamil forms involved are "neuter verbs," but further work is needed here. What we can say conservatively regarding Sinhala is that the requirement for nominative NP2 in the Literary variety does coincide with the presence of AGR in that variety.

The intersection of dative subject sentences with focusing does provide some further suggestive data bearing on the analysis of both. We may naturally assume that the presupposition contains an empty category that is in some way coindexed with the focused element. In Colloquial Sinhala, the focused element is always in the case that would be proper to that empty category.[35] In Literary Sinhala, this is true of lexically assigned cases like the dative in (25):

(27) *mā   giyē   gamaṭa   ya.*
I-ACC go-past-FOC village-DAT 3Sg
'It is to the village that I went.'

However, when presented with a situation in which the object of a dative subject sentence is to be focused in Literary Sinhala, as in (24b), even informants who unhesitatingly supply the nominative in the simple sentence commonly hesitate, vacillating between the nominative and the accusative, but generally show preference for the accusative, as in (12b).

(12) b. *maṭə   penunee   ema   minissu   /minissun   ya.*
I-DAT see-PAST-FOC those men-NOM /men-ACC 3Pers
'It was those men that I saw.'

This is not surprising, in terms of the AGR hypothesis by which we assume that the nominative is somehow assigned by agreement AGR. The focused sentence resembles a nominal equational sentence in which the predicate would be nominative, and the case of the relevant nominal would be nominative in the corresponding nonfocused sentence in which it is in an agreement relation with the verb. Thus there is some inclination toward that case. However, under the AGR hypothesis, nominative would be a structural, not a lexical case. In the Literary focused sentence, coindexing of the *ya/(y)i* agreement affix would be with the presupposition, not the empty category within it (accounting for the invariant third person neuter nature of that agreement). Thus the condition for nominative assignment to the focused element is not fulfilled, and the accusative is called for. As far as I have been able to ascertain, no prescriptive rule applying to this particular situation is ever taught, so that the informants are thrown back on the competence that they have acquired in that variety and behave accordingly.

Passive versus Null Arbitrary Subjects

The Passive

Literary Sinhala has a passive, which uses the verb *læbenavā* 'obtain, receive', as illustrated in (28):[36]

(28) a. *apa   visin mema væḍə karanu   læbē.*
us-ACC by   this work do-PART obtain-PRES-3Sg
'This work is done by us."

b. *lāŋkikayō   koṭas kihipayakaṭa   bedanu   læbeti.*
lankans-NOM groups several-INDEF-DAT divide-PART- obtain-PRES-3Pl
'Sri Lankans are divided into several groups.'

As comparison of (28a) with (28b) shows, the passive does show the kind of agreement that we expect from what we have seen of case assignment.

Colloquial Sinhala, on the other hand, lacks a true passive, making use of other devices, such as active verbs with empty subjects and arbitrary reference (see Gair

1970; Gair and Wali 1988; also see Gunasinghe 1985, which includes extensive discussion and exemplification). While passive is still a subject of discussion and debate in recent work, there is quite general agreement that it involves movement of the underlying object to a position assigned case by INFL (generally following Chomsky 1981, 1982). The existence of passive in Literary Sinhala and its absence in Colloquial are thus perfectly consistent with the differences in case assigning mechanisms associated with ±AGR in INFL that have been described here. The crucial observation here is that the passive is characteristic of Literary Sinhala but not Colloquial, and this appears to be no coincidence given their other properties.

Not only does Colloquial Sinhala lack a passive, but in fact it appears entirely to lack any "moving to subject" (or argument externalization) operations that do not retain the original case of the moved element (see chapter 6 this volume). While consistent with the lack of nominative-assigning AGR, this does not constitute in itself a varietal difference, since such operations aside from the passive seem to be equally lacking in Literary Sinhala. While the lack of AGR might well militate against such processes, there is, of course, no reason that its presence would necessarily induce them.

Empty Arbitrary Subjects

Sinhala is a language of what could be called the SUPER-PRO-DROP type: not only subjects but also objects and other arguments may be null. Most interestingly, it has finite transitive sentences without overt subjects but with "arbitrary agent" readings. These, as illustrated by (29a) and (29b) are true transitives in that the verbs are never used intransitively (unlike, say English 'grow' and 'close'). They are the discourse-functional equivalent of passives or English "arbitrary they" sentences, but Sinhala has no lexical equivalent of "they" in this function. Note that they contrast with otherwise identical sentences that have referential NPs or phonologically null pronouns (*pro* in current terms), as in (29c)and (29d):

(29) a. *mee pætte huňgak wii wawənəwa.*
       this area much   rice grow (transitive)-PRES
       'A lot of rice is grown in this area.'
          =They grow a lot of rice in this area.

   b. *kantooruwə wahanne   hatərəṭə.*
       office   close-PRES-FOC   four-DAT
       'It's at four that they close the office.'
          = It's at four that the office closes.

   c. *api/ Ø mee pætte huňgak wii wawənəwa.*
       we/ Ø this area much   rice grow (transitive)-PRES
       'We/*pro* grow(s) a lot of rice in this area.'

   d. *lipikaruwo/ Ø kantooruwə wahanne   hatərəṭə.*
       clerks/   Ø office   close-PRES-EMPH   four-DAT
       'The clerks/*pro* close(s) the office at four.'

Sentences like (29a) and (29b) thus appear to afford clear instances of phono-logically null pronouns with arbitrary reference (pro_{arb}), since the empty categories involved occur in a position in which lexical NPs and referential null pronominals (*pro*) may also occur, namely as subject of finite tensed sentences.[37] Taken in con-junction with the other properties that we have considered, a natural explanation for these suggests itself: The lack of AGR within INFL (or at the least of a strong AGR with specific features to be discharged through coindexing) allows the occurrence of "featureless" governed null arguments, namely, pro_{arb}.[38] In my observations so far, this type of sentence is uncharacteristic of Literary Sinhala, which employs the passive instead. However, this particular linkage with the AGR/non-AGR character-istics of the varieties must be proposed with some uncertainty, since it is possible to conceive of an empty pronoun that is linked to agreement, possibly third person plu-ral, i.e., a phonetically realized equivalent of English arbitrary "they." This is almost the case, for example, in Hindi, in expressions like Ø *kahte hāī ki* '(they) say that', though there one might say that the empty subject is a function of pro-drop of a form like *log* 'people'. Nevertheless, it is interesting that the difference between the vari-eties does exist and particularly that the Colloquial Sinhala null subject appears to have only the feature "human."

Coherence and Specialization of the Features Across Varieties

I believe that I have now made, or remade, the case that three crucial features of Literary Sinhala—verbal agreement, the *ya/(y)i* marking (or other agreement affixes) of nonverbal sentences, and nominative subject case in alternation with accusative—can be directly attributed to AGR as reflected in surface agreement. In addition, the plausible linkage to AGR of several other properties of Literary, in contradistinction to Colloquial, has been shown. Thus the typological character of the Colloquial and Literary varieties, as at least polar types in Sinhala diglossia, has been shown to be plausibly linked to the existence or content of AGR in those varieties. However, the question as to whether Sinhala diglossia represents a fundamentally binary division or some sort of continuum remains to be dealt with.

The crucial question in this regard is of course whether the constellation of fea-tures that we have observed in Literary Sinhala and related to AGR are indeed ex-clusive to that variety in some significant way. The counter case has been put clearly in one of the critiques of that view by Paolillo:

> Clearly Gair's account of the grammatical differences between Colloquial and Liter-ary Sinhala is not correct, since the AGR hypothesis wrongly predicts that agreement, the accusative case, copula marking, and the accusative rule are categorically linked. These features must be grammatically independent, since their distribution in differ-ent varieties is independent. Some grammatical linkage, of course, must be recog-nized; the accusative rule could not exist without the accusative case. (1991: 56)

Subsequently, on the basis of more detailed analysis of extended data, that con-tention has been considerably softened, resulting in the following observations:

It now appears that the grammatical features predicate marking [i.e.,*ya/(y)i* -JWG] and agreement can be assigned identical communicative attitude values—the range of contexts they occur in is entirely co-extensive. Second, we could now *explain* the close occurrence of agreement and predicate marking by identifying the two as exponents of the same grammatical category; in other words, predicate marking is a special sub-case of agreement. . . . In this case, examination of textual evidence provides support for the view expressed in Gair (1968, 1991) that agreement and predicate marking represent the same grammatical category. (1992: 198)

We have observed implicational relations between features such as agreement and accusative case, such that there are no varieties with agreement that do not also have accusative case. (1992: 304)

Thus, his final conclusion is that, "on the whole, the basic observations of Gair's AGR hypothesis remain intact" (p. 310).

Though this might appear to close the case, at least with regard to AGR and case marking, one might still ask whether the properties that I have seen as AGR related are so distributed across the spectrum of Sinhala varieties and subvarieties as to be consistent with the binary view of Sinhala diglossia. It has been claimed (Paolillo 1991, 1992) that this is not the case, but that their distribution demonstrated a functionally determined continuum of varieties. The possibility of intermediate varieties in diglossia has been recognized since Ferguson's original (1959) study, and at least one such variety in the form of Formal Spoken (see my original classification at the beginning of this chapter) has been recognized in Sinhala diglossia studies from Gair 1968 on. The fundamental question here is that of the status of intermediate varieties, including Formal Spoken with regard to an essentially binary view of the Sinhala situation. The main proposed counterexamples to the binary view (Paolillo 1991, 1992) consisted in the use of the accusative rule and the occurrence or nonoccurrence of *ya/(y)i* marking in two special varieties (some children's readers and one kind of puristic Formal Spoken), and in the occurrence of Literary accusative/oblique NPs in some Formal Spoken texts. I will take them up in turn.

The Language of Elementary Readers: Children's Literary Sinhala

In my earlier (1992a) paper on AGR and diglossia, I noted that the centrality of agreement and its attendant difficulties are at least tacitly recognized in Sinhala teaching in the schools. In the textbooks for the earliest grades, Colloquial Sinhala is generally employed. However, in the next step up, we find in at least some textbooks a unique variety of the language, which appears to be designed as a bridge between the varieties (how explicitly, I do not know, since I know of no stated rationale for it). I had thus referred to it as a facilitating variety. In this variety, the verb forms are Colloquial and thus lack agreement, but the accusative rule is followed. If this is carried out consistently, the result is that *all* nominals, with an exception to be noted, appear in the accusative, since there is no AGR to license the nominative.[39] Thus the subject in (30a) and the direct object in (30b) are both in the Literary accusative form, though only the latter would be eligible to appear in the Colloquial *-wə* accusative form (for examples in other positions, see Gair 1992a). The italicized nominals are the crucial ones and are in the Literary accusative form:

(30) a. *issara   kālē   andarē nam   **kavaṭayaku**   siTiyā.*
    previous time-LOC Andare named jester-INDEF-ACC be(Animate)-PAST
    'Once there was a jester named Andare.'

   b. *(mē raja) vēdanāven peḷena   **nayaku**   dækkā.*
    (this king) pain-INST writhe-PRES-ADJ cobra-INDEF-ACC see-PAST
    '(This king) saw a cobra writhing in pain.' (Gair 1992, from Amararatna 1981)

What we see in the children's Literary variety is the accusative rule as expressed in both its original and reworked versions imported into an essentially spoken variety lacking agreement. Given that lack, however, conditions for the application of the nominative rule in its first and second versions cannot occur. Thus, all nominals, regardless of grammatical function, must occur in the accusative. Though this simple characterization holds true for verbal sentences, nominal predicate sentences pose some complications. In the text from which I drew my examples, the *ya/(y)i* marker appeared, as in Literary Sinhala, on nominal predicates of equational sentences, as in (31a), and on the focused constituent of focused sentences, as in (31b):

(31) a. *gam   væsiyangen   bohō denek   goviyōya.*
    village dwellers-INSTR many people-INDEF-NOM farmer-Pl-NOM COP
    'Most of the village dwellers are farmers.' (p. 5)

   b. *mā   siṭinnee   piṭisara gamekaya.*
    I-ACC be-PRES-FOC rural   village-INDEF-LOC-COP
    'I live in a rural village.' (p. 5)

The subject and object in (31a) are in the nominative, and they thus constitute an exception to the generalization that the underlying system should force all nouns to be in the accusative. Therefore, I proposed that the *ya* marker, which I had regarded as a nonagreeing copula, could serve, like agreement, to license the nominative. Paolillo (1991) pointed out, however, that his investigations included children's readers in which the-*ya* did not appear on equational sentences, but their subjects were in the nominative, even though they lacked agreement and followed the accusative rule elsewhere. He took this as evidence that the features I had claimed to be linked with AGR were in fact independent and thus provided a strong counterexample to the AGR hypothesis (1991a: 50–54).

However, the status of the *ya* in sentences such as (31) is not really clear. It could be seen as a representative of agreement, as in Literary Sinhala. What may be then the case in these textbooks as a group, as Paolillo subsequently concluded, is that they represent mixed agreement systems, with some introducing the Literary system in nonverbal sentences and others maintaining the Colloquial one for case assignment in equational sentences, even though all of the readers enforced the accusative rule. This seems to me to be quite possible and quite consistent with the view of case assignment expressed here. If so, to the extent that the readers embody different agreement and/or case assignment systems in different types of sentences, they do indeed fail to fit neatly into the binary classification. Another possible explanation is that in examples like (31a), the case is assigned as in Colloquial Sinhala without agreement, presumably by case coindexing with the predicate nominal, and what is being introduced is simply a predicate marker, not an exemplar of AGR. This analysis would have some precedent in Colloquial Sinhala also, since a marker of that type does occur on adjective predicate sentences in Colloquial, and can occur on nominal and focused sentences as an emphatic clitic (See Gair 1970 and 1983b for a description; see Gair 1986b for a historical account).

However, it does not seem productive to attempt to further outguess the producers of the children's texts, and in the present context it does not much matter which analysis is in fact the case. In any event, we are dealing with an artificial variety designed to facilitate the transition from one actual variety to the other as essentially a second language (L2). In more advanced readers, the full Literary conventions are introduced, and the real change there is the introduction of agreement as a representative AGR and the application of the nominative rule. The real question, of course, is how the features cohere in the real varieties. That, as we have seen, is clear, so that these readers form at most an interesting, but not very important, exception to a strict binary view.[40]

Hela Havula Formal Spoken Sinhala

A group of puristic writers and scholars known as *Hela Havula*,[41] follows in the tradition of the brilliant, influential Sinhala grammarian Munidasa Kumaratunga. *Hela Havula* espouses and uses a variety of Sinhala that has as a prominent feature the nativistic purging of Sanskritic and other loanwords in favor of forms occurring in classical Sinhala of roughly the thirteenth and fourteenth centuries or forms coined on their model (De Silva 1967, 1976). The Formal Spoken Sinhala of the adherents of this school is likely to exhibit, like the children's readers, the application of the accusative rule in the absence of agreement, and in fact some of the characteristics of those readers have been attributed to the influence of that group in education (Paolillo 1991, citing Karunatillake, personal communication). Thus, the same considerations apply here, and no further treatment is necessary. However, despite the special features of *Hela Havula* Formal Spoken Sinhala and the implementation of some distinct grammatical rules and lexicon in both their spoken and written productions, their Literary Sinhala still has the fundamental characteristics that obtain in that variety in general.

The Literary Accusative/Oblique in Formal Spoken Sinhala

The use of the Literary accusative/oblique form in Formal Spoken Sinhala, which lacks agreement, is illustrated in (32). The first example, (32a), in which the accusative is the object of a postposition, is from a student speech on a formal occasion (Karunatillake 1990, cited in Paolillo 1992). The second example, (30b), in which the accusative appears on the object of a (nonagreeing) verb, is from a speech by the president of Sri Lanka (from Paolillo 1992):

(32) a. *śiśayan   waśayen api-t   mee aayatanaṭa   enne   loku*
      student-Pl-ACC as   we-NOM-also this institution-DAT come-FOC big
      balaaporottu ætuwa.
      expectations having
      'As students, it is with great expectations we also come to this institution.'

    b. *gewalwəla   innə   pudgaliyan api aarakša kərənəwa.*
      house-Pl-LOC individual-PL-ACC we-NOM protection   do-PRES
      'We (will) protect the individuals who are in those houses.'

Note that in these examples, the subjects are in the nominative case. Thus the nominative rule has not applied, as we would expect given the nonagreeing verbs. What appears to be the case in this kind of Formal Spoken Sinhala is that the Literary accusative form is used on objects of both verbs and postpositions in order to strengthen the formality by more closely approaching Literary Sinhala. These environments share a feature: Both involve complements, so that case is assigned under sisterhood and thus strict head government. It is also not surprising that objects of verbs and adpositions might appear in the same case: Standard English provides one example.

In examples like those just cited, there is a systematic employment of the Literary accusative, and that use seems to be common to much Formal Spoken Sinhala. However, given the formal and literary associations of the Literary accusative, it would not be surprising to find it used in formal circumstances, even where it is not grammatically justified. It does indeed appear to be subject to hyperurbanism, and this may well be the reason that Paolillo found it used sporadically and in fluctuation in his texts. While this hyperurbanism is often found in Spoken Sinhala, it may also occur in some writers' attempts at Literary, leading to the accusative overuse that he refers to as "substitution" in which accusative forms, commonly pronominal, are substituted for nominative in all contexts. An example, in which the accusative *mā* 'me' is used for the correct *mama* with an agreeing verb, is given in (33) from a personal letter cited by Paolillo (1992: 213):

(33) *mā   suvemi.*
    I-ACC healthy-1Sg
    'I am well.'

As he quite correctly points out, such texts "do not exhibit a genuine accusative marking pattern; they use an accusative form as an alternant of the nominative case" (1992: 213).

To return to the more systematic instances of the accusative in Formal Spoken contexts, as in (32a) and (32b), such usage appears to reflect the grafting of a local rule assigning the Literary accusative form under head–complement relations onto the spoken Colloquial pattern. One thing that facilitates its use is the local and limited nature of the assignment. Thus, Formal Spoken Sinhala is not difficult to master enough to use in oral presentation on one's feet, as compared with agreement, which involves more complexity. With the postpositional objects, it may also be facilitated by the fact that Formal Spoken Sinhala commonly uses postpositions used in Literary, so that the accusative can also be reinforced as a lexical property and learned along with those postpositions. In any event, though the use of these forms increases the resemblance of this variety to Literary Sinhala, a quite different system is actually at play. The combined nominative and accusative rules have not been applied, since AGR is not involved; rather, the subjects of the nonagreeing verbs remain in the nominative, presumably under the kind of case assignment applicable there.

On Grammatical versus Functional Approaches

I have now dealt with those basic grammatical aspects of Sinhala diglossia that I take to be linked with AGR differences across varieties, and hopefully I have remade and strengthened the original case. However, since a functional approach has sometimes been presented as opposed to and exclusive of the grammatical theory-driven approach represented here, something should be said about the relation of those features to communicative function.

One reason for undertaking this investigation in the first place, as represented in Gair 1992a, was to develop a kind of initial rapprochement between current grammatical theory and the study of language varieties, as in studies of diglossia (and their practitioners), by affording an illustration of the way the former could illuminate our understanding of at least one instance of the latter. An approach that attempts to characterize more precisely and in explanatory terms a major difference between varieties where that difference appears to be most clearly expressed in terms of some constructs of current theory would also seem to be of obvious potential value to the typology of diglossia. It seems clear that many cases do not exhibit possibly parametrically linked differences between varieties such as those proposed here for Sinhala. (Bengali appears to be one such, judging from the accounts that have been given of it.)

I had by no means claimed that a contribution in the other direction—from varietal studies to theory—was not possible. In fact, the problem raised by the different case-assigning properties in the two main varieties of Sinhala, and especially the problem raised for the case theory by the oblique subjects in Literary, provide a small example of such a contribution.

However, one can neither demand of each kind of investigation what is not relevant to it nor deny to each its own sphere of enlightenment. As one example, Paolillo, in pointing to the fact that some varieties of Formal Spoken observe the accusative rule and others do not, states:

> Thus, there is socially conditioned variation in the employment of the accusative rule in Formal Spoken Sinhala. Gair's AGR cannot accommodate this variability, and thus does not account for the distribution of accusative case found in Formal Spoken Sinhala. (1991: 55–56)

It is, of course, true that the AGR hypothesis cannot account for the functional distribution of that rule, nor is there any reason it should do so, any more than it can be called on to explain the distribution, say, of Sanskritic, classicized Sinhala, and ordinary colloquial lexical items. On the other hand, relating grammatical features, or constellations of them, in different varieties to general principles of grammar in no way constitutes a denial that those features may indeed have communicative–functional values. There may also be a further bonus in that we may come to understand better the nature of those varieties. Thus in the case of at least some Formal Spoken Sinhala, it appears that there is not just a different distribution of properties exhibited but also the application of a different rule. This only became clear, however, when we compared that distribution in a systematic way with the distribution predicted by the AGR hypothesis. It also appears fair to claim that the discovery that the presence of agreement implied accusative case marking as stated by Paolillo (1992: 148) came as a result of testing that hypothesis.

There is at least one way, however, in which the application of syntactic theory might indeed make a more direct contribution to our understanding of why certain grammatical features have the communicative–functional values that they do. Ferguson's definition, as quoted at the very beginning of this chapter, includes in parentheses the phrase "often grammatically more complex" in relation to the H variety. In the present case, it is not immediately clear, in the absence of a workable evaluation metric couched in some unified theory, that Literary Sinhala is indeed more complex. It is true that the verbal paradigms of Literary Sinhala are enriched by agreement in comparison with Colloquial and that the nominal paradigm might be considered at least marginally more elaborate. However, Colloquial Sinhala has complexities of its own, such as the complex system by which the wide range of subject cases is licensed and assigned. Also, to the extent that a set of features falls out of universal principles, they might be counted as one and, hence, as less complex.

We might, however, look at the situation in a somewhat different way, beginning with two observations, one grammatical, one functional (or at least situational):

1. Under the AGR hypothesis, Literary Sinhala is typologically distinct from the Spoken varieties in a fundamental way.
2. Literary Sinhala is nobody's native language, but is acquired, like H varieties in other languages, in a formal setting.

In this light, there is a marked resemblance between the acquisition of Literary Sinhala and the acquisition of a second language, despite the undoubted shared features, grammatical as well as lexical, across the varieties. Given those shared features, it is also not unreasonable to expect that the most difficult things to acquire to the point of fluency are precisely those features that represent major structural differences—in this case, AGR and its consequences. If we now progress through the varieties and subvarieties from Colloquial through Formal Spoken to Literary, we can ask whether a case can be made that there is an increasing degree of complexity from the point of view of the learner in terms of ease of acquisition. Colloquial Sinhala is, of course, the L1 analogue. We have seen that the children's literature is relevant to the extent that it involves a conscious stepwise introduction of features, of which the full agreement and case pattern is the last (of those dealt with either here or in Paolillo's work—rhetorical features and lexicon are another matter). As I have shown, the use of the accusative case in Formal Spoken Sinhala, in so far as it is systematic, is a matter of local case assignment, with clearly realized surface correlates. It thus should not be a great problem to acquire, particularly in the case of postpositions, where the lexical items, which are drawn from Literary Sinhala, also commonly differ from Colloquial. It is AGR cum agreement, with its complex surface effects in case assignment, that clearly appears to present the most difficulty, and indeed observations of actual practice appear to bear this out.

What I would suggest in this connection is that the typological uniqueness of Literary Sinhala, in addition to setting it off from the rest as the most prestigious—in fact, required—variety for use in written contexts is at least a contributing factor to one important and well-noted aspect of Sinhala diglossia: the strength of the complementarity between H and L in comparison to some other diglossias. This has, in fact, led Krishnamurti to wonder whether Sinhala diglossia is in fact true diglossia in Ferguson's terms, since the Literary variety is not used for "most . . . formal spoken purposes" as incorporated in the definition (1986: lxix, xxi).[42] Literary Sinhala, even in its oral manifestations, is almost invariably written first. It follows from what has been said here that Literary Sinhala is the most difficult variety to learn to use spontaneously. My observations of actual speakers tend to bear this out, as do De Silva's (1970, 1976) investigations. This, then, would seem to be a likely factor in its restriction to primarily written or written-initial contexts. In fact, Paolillo (1992) has proposed the felicitous term "edited" to characterize the primary defining functional feature of the Literary variety.

In recent years, Formal Spoken Sinhala has been elaborated and has met with an increasingly wide range of uses; this development has been attributed to the need for a variety to be used in a number of new or expanded functions that result from social change and language policy (Fernando 1977; Gair 1983b, 1986a). I can now add that it is its essential typological unity with more informal varieties, and the consequent relative ease of acquiring its defining features, that makes it a suitable candidate for such use, where both formality and at least apparent spontaneity are called for, as in political speeches, debates, sermons, and formal television and radio interviews.

There is also a possible link with the very active research now being conducted that investigates language acquisition in relation to current linguistic theory. Of most relevance here is the significant amount of suggestive research into L2 acquisition that has begun to appear based on the principles and parameters approach within GB theory (Several chapters in Flynn and O'Neil 1988 and references therein; White 1989 and the works cited there; Martohardjono and Gair 1991; and Gair, Flynn, and Brown 1993).[43] Under the view I have taken here, the connection with L2 research becomes relevant, and a new and quite possible promising line of research is opened up into the acquisition of H varieties and the resulting degrees of competence in them in relation to the defining differences between varieties.

The observed relative difficulty in producing the Literary variety as opposed to Formal Spoken raises an interesting point in this connection. If the differences between Literary and Spoken are as a set reducible to a parameterized difference in AGR, as I have suggested, the acquisition of the relevant features of Literary Sinhala should be relatable to parameter resetting, as discussed and debated in much of the L2 literature referred to above and amenable to investigation in that framework. As an initial hypothesis for the Sinhala situation, I would tentatively suggest that to stay essentially within the Spoken variety and add (or replace) lexicon and graft on specific rules is simpler than to acquire a variety that is typologically difficult, even though it is parametrically related. On the other hand, one might predict that once the AGR functional category is acquired, we will find coherence among those other features. This suggests an empirical program of research, as well as possible cross-linguistic investigation of different types of diglossia situations in that vein.

All of these are matters to be investigated. If they prove fruitless, so be it, but the one thing that we must not do is shut off legitimate investigation, whatever theoretical perspective it may come from. Unfortunately, if we begin from the premise that any theory can prima facie have nothing to contribute to varietal studies, we can have just that unfortunate result, as we would if we begin from the assumption that if a particular presentation is flawed, the entire enterprise must be without possible value.

VI

THE DEVELOPMENT
OF SYNTAX

Acquisition of Null Subjects and Control in Some Sinhala Adverbial Clauses

WITH BARBARA LUST, LELWALA SUMANGALA, AND MILAN RODRIGO

An earlier version of this paper was given at the Stanford Conference on Child language Development in 1989 and appeared in the Proceedings *(29: 97–196). The syntactic analysis of the Sinhala structures dealt with has not been changed, except for some additional bracketings for clarity, and we have not changed the associated trees to fit later developments in phrase structure such as the fragmentation of INFL, since that would not affect the essential arguments. The sections presenting the acquisition data and their analysis have, however, been revised and expanded, and some figures have been added. The fundamental purpose of the paper—to illustrate the two-way interaction of acquisition research with linguistic theory and the analysis of specific language analyses—remains the same.*

This chapter reports selected results from a large project concerned with the acquisition of empty categories in Sinhala, an SOV language of the Indo-Aryan family that is spoken in Sri Lanka. It concerns itself specifically with empty categories that occur in a subset of adverbial clause types that differ with regard to the kinds of null subjects they permit. Some of these are CONTROL STRUCTURES, which are obligatorily coindexed.

There have been a number of studies of the first language acquisition of control structures in English (e.g., Cohen Sherman 1983; Cohen Sherman and Lust, 1993; Hsu, Cairns, and Fiengo, 1985). To date, however, there has been little or no study of the acquisition of such structures in other languages, such as Sinhala. (See, however, Lust, Wakayama, Snyder, Mazuka, and Oshima (1985) for a related study of Japanese acquisition; also see Lust, Gair, Goss, and Rodrigo 1986 for an earlier study of the acquisition of Sinhala empty categories).

Typological Background

Sinhala is verb-final and strongly—in fact almost exclusively—left branching and right headed. Both complements and modifiers appear to the left of their heads, as shown in (1):

(1) NP: *laŋkaawe   tee*
          Sri Lanka-GEN tea
          'Sri Lankan tea' / 'tea of Sri Lanka'

          gunəpaalə gænə kataawə
          Gunapala about story-DEF
          'The story about Gunapala'

     VP: *tee biwwa*
          tea drank
          'drank tea'

          ikmənəTə diwwa
          quickly   run-PAST
          'ran quickly'

     AP: *huñgak rasə*
          much   tasty
          'very tasty'

     PP: *laŋkaawə ætule*
          Sri Lanka within
          'in(side) Sri Lanka'

Recursive sentence embedding shares this left-branching character. As exemplified in (2a), relative clauses always appear to the left of their heads. As (2b) illustrates, finite adverbial subordinate clauses appear to the left of the main clause in the unmarked order:

(2) a. [[*mamə gunəpaalətə   dunnə*]   *potə*] [[[*apee iskoole   ugannənə*]
         I   Gunapala-DAT gave-REL book   our school-loc teach-REL
         guruwərəyek   liwwə]   ekak].
         teacher-INDEF wrote-REL one

         'The book that I gave Gunapala was one written by a teacher who teaches in our school'

     b. [[*iiye   gedərə iñdəla ţawmətə   yanəkoţə] mamə loku nayek dækka*].
         yesterday house from town-DAT go-when I   big cobra see-PAST
         'I saw a big cobra when I was going from home to town yesterday.'

Variant orders are, however, possible, generally with discourse-pragmatic effect. Thus, in a simple sentence, in addition to the unmarked SOV order, all possible orders of major constituents are acceptable with the proper intonation. This freedom extends also to subordinate clauses, including the -*aamə* and -*la* clauses that we will be chiefly concerned with in this paper.

Three further characteristics of Sinhala are extremely important here. First, finite verbs, even if tensed, fail to show agreement of any kind in the spoken varieties of the language,[1] as shown in (3):

(3) *mamə /oyaa /eyaa /api /oyaala /eyaala pansələţə   yanəwa /giyaa.*
    I   /you /(s)he /we /you-PL /they   temple-DAT go-PRES /go-PAST
    'I/ you/ (s)he/ we/you-all/ they go/went to the temple.'

Second, Sinhala is a language of the kind that might be called SUPER PRO-DROP, which allows empty categories in all argument positions, governed or ungoverned, except for object of postposition (cf. Sumangala 1988a). Example (4a) illustrates this phenomenon for simple sentences, (4b) illustrates it for complex ones. Thus, empty categories in Sinhala are widely determined by pragmatic context or discourse context for resolving ambiguity.

Third, although lexical pronouns (e.g., *eyaa* '(s)he') and lexical anaphors/reflexives (e.g., *tamaŋ/tamuŋ* 'self') do exist in Sinhala, their appearance is far less common than that of null pronouns and is used to show contrast, give emphasis, or resolve ambiguity (cf. Gair 1970). Comparison with English translations in (4) will illustrate this. As (4b) especially illustrates, the freedom of occurrence of null pronouns can lead to multiple ambiguity:

(4) a. TICKET AGENT: *mennə noonage   ţikət-ekə.*
                      here   lady-GEN   ticket-DEF
                      'Here is your ticket (madam).'

    CUSTOMER: *Ø Ø Ø denna.*
                 Ø Ø Ø give-INF
                 'Give (me) (the ticket).'

   b. *Ø maTə enəkoţə   Ø   okkomə   kaala iwəray.*
      Ø I-DAT come-when Ø (=they) all (everything) eaten finished
      'By the time Ø (=it) came to me, all (=food) was eaten and finished.'[2]
      or 'By the time Ø (=it/they) came to me, all(everybody) had finished eating.'
      or 'By the time Ø (=it/they) came to me, all(everybody) had finished eating
      Ø (=it).'

As current linguistic theory would predict, however, while Sinhala empty categories are prolific and often pragmatically (nongrammatically) determined, their *distribution* in Sinhala is grammatically constrained, and their *interpretation* is grammatically differentiated. For example, an empty pronoun may not c-command its antecedent, as illustrated in example (5), and coreference with a c-commanding antecedent in a local domain is not possible with a coreferential interpretation, as in example (6). This constraint is, of course, quite parallel to the constraints on lexical pronouns in English, as the glosses show:

(5) $Ø_{*i/j}$ *gunəpaaləge$_i$ ammaţə   kæmətiy.*
    Ø   gunapala-GEN mother-DAT like
    'He$_{*i/j}$ likes Gunapala's$_i$ mother.'

(6) *gunəpaalə$_i$ $Ø_{*i/j}$ kannaaḍiye dækka.*
    Gunapala   Ø   mirror-LOC saw
    'Gunapala$_i$ saw him$_j$ / *himself$_i$ in the mirror.'

One effect of the combination of lack of agreement, relatively free word order, and the wide distribution of empty categories is the severe attenuation of surface signals accompanying different empty categories in Sinhala. This lack of constraint might be expected to heighten the problem of first language acquisition to the degree that this acquisition depends on such signals. As we shall see, this problem is even further compounded in the case of one set of adverbial clause structures.

The Adverbial Clause Structures at Issue

The -*la* Conjunctive Participle

Sinhala shares with many other languages of South Asia a type of embedded clause structure sometimes referred to as the CONJUNCTIVE PARTICIPLE.[3] This is commonly cited as an important areal feature (Emeneau 1956 and much subsequent work; see particularly Masica 1976). The form fulfilling this function in Sinhala is the -*la* participle, which is illustrated in example (7). The sense is commonly, though not necessarily, temporal, with the action of the embedded clause preceding that of the main clause and commonly linked to it in some fashion:[4]

(7) *mamə gedərə gihilla kææmə kææwa.*
     I   home go-*la* food   eat-PAST
     'I went home and ate.'

The embedded -*la* clause in (7) is in its unmarked position preceding the remainder of V″ (VP), and it is clearly within the minimal dominating S (I′). This relation is shown by a number of characteristics, such as inclusion in the scope of negation of the main verb. We will not pursue this feature here, but it is perhaps illustrated most dramatically by the possibility of sentences like (8a). In such sentences, the subject appears in the nominative case, as required by the main verb *diwwa* 'ran', although the verb of the embedded -*la* participle *æhila* (*æhenəwa* 'hear') would require the dative, as shown in (8b):[5]

(8) a. *mamə   saddəyak   æhila   diwwa.*
        I-NOM   sound-INDEF hear-*la* run-PAST
        'I heard a sound and ran.'

     b. *matə   saddəyak   æhuna.*
        I-DAT   sound-INDEF hear-PAST
        'I heard a sound.'

A crucial characteristic of conjunctive -*la* clauses in this type of sentence is obligatory coreferentiality between main and -*la* clause subjects, as in (9a): they are control structures. Their control properties include the fact that they do not allow an overt NP, as in (9b):

(9) a. [$_S$*mamə*$_i$ [$_{VP}$[$_S$ Ø$_{i,*j}$ *gedərə gihilla*] *kææmə kææwa* $_{VP}$]$_S$].
        I   home   go-*la*   food   eat-PAST
        'I went home and ate.'

b. * [$_s$*mamə* [$_{VP}$ [$_s$ *Kalyaani gedərə gihilla* $_s$] *kææmə kææwa* $_{VP}$]$_s$].
  I   Kalyani home go-*la*   food   eat-PAST
'Kalyani went home and I ate.'

We thus hypothesize that the basic structure for (7) and (9a) is as in (10), with the -*la* clause as an adjunct to VP.[6] Here, the empty category subject in the -*la* clause occurs within a nonfinite clause; it is c-commanded in a basic control configuration (cf. Huang, 1989).

(10) Conjunctive -*la*

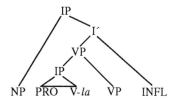

  In some languages of South Asia, this coreference is a necessary characteristic of the form appearing in the embedded clause. This is the case, for example, with Hindi V-*kar* (Davison 1986b). In current Sinhala, however, the -*la* participle is not so restricted, though that is its favored use in subordinate structures, and it appears in noncoreferential contexts as well. These will be described later, after we present the second type of adverbial structures. One important aspect of this chapter will be the use of acquisition data in distinguishing these structures in a principled way.

The -*aamə* Adverbials

The empty category in the conjunctive -*la* structure can be contrasted with the one that occurs in a finite tensed adjunct subordinate clause, such as the -*aamə* 'when/after' clauses illustrated in (11). The -*aamə* form is made by adding that affix to the past tense adjectival form of the verb, and its chief use is to form relative clauses as exemplified in (2). The adjectival form with -*aamə* is always past tense. Hence from *dunnə* 'gave (relativizing)' is formed *dunnaamə*.[7] The sense is "prior temporal when," with differences from the similar use of -*la* that need not concern us here.

  The -*aamə* construction easily involves the lexical expression of two separate subjects, as shown by (11a). Coreference is not required of a null subject, as in (11b). A lexical pronoun may replace an empty category in an -*aamə* construction, as in (11c), although a lexical pronoun in this case, as in many cases in Sinhala, tends to favor a noncoreferential reading:

(11) a. *mahattəya aawaamə   mamə wædə kərannaŋ.*
      gentleman come-*aamə* I   work do-OPT
      'I will work when (after) the gentleman comes.'

  b. *gunəpaaləi gamətə   giyaamə* $Ø_{i,j}$ *gañgee   nææwa.*
      Gunapala village-DAT go-aamə Ø   river-LOC bathe-PAST
      'When (after) Gunapala$_i$ went to the village (he$_{i,j}$ bathed in the river).'

c. *gunəpaaləi gaməṭə   giyaamə eyaa ᵢ.ⱼ gañgee   nææwa.*
   Gunapala   village-DAT go(when) he/she river-LOC bathe-PAST
   When (after) Gunapalaᵢ went to the village hₑᵢ,ⱼ bathed in the river).'

Given these characteristics of -*aamə* clauses, especially their noncontrol properties,
we assume that they are adjuncts outside the minimal S (=IP), and that their subjects
are not c-commanded in a control domain by the main clause subject, as in (12).

(12)   -*aamə* Clauses

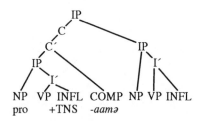

NP VP INFL COMP NP VP INFL
pro   +TNS   -*aamə*

We may now ask whether the child acquiring Sinhala knows the subtle differences between the empty categories in -*la* and -*aamə* constructions, and if so, what
is the nature of the development of this knowledge? We have already noted the paucity of surface cues such as agreement, fixed constituent order, and narrowly restricted
distribution of empty categories. One obvious possibility would invoke the subordinate morphology itself, namely, the cooccurrence of different empty categories with
those affixes. However, this possibility is confounded by the lack of one-to-one
cooccurrence between -*la* and subject empty category type that was mentioned earlier. This is a function of the fact that Sinhala -*la* has other, nonconjunctive, uses,
which we will briefly describe.

Absolutive and Finite -*la*

A structure with -*la* may occur productively as a finite sentence, as in (13), and such
sentences are by no means uncommon. (Note that (13c) shows both conjunctive and
finite -*la*.) The use of the conjunctive participle form in an independent sentence is,
as far as we have been able to ascertain, a characteristic unique to Sinhala among the
languages of South Asia:

(13) a. *mahattəya   kantooruwəṭə gihilla.*
        gentleman-NOM office-DAT   go-*la*
        'He (hon.) has gone to the office.'

     b. *gunəpaalə   mee wæḍə okkomə iwərəkərəla.*
        Gunapala-NOM this work all   finish-*la*
        'Gunapala has finished all this work.'

     c. *kalageḍiyə   meeseŋ   wæṭila kæḍila.*
        water jug-NOM table-ABL fall-*la* break-*la*
        'The water jug has fallen off the table and broken.'

Furthermore, *-la* also occurs in an ABSOLUTIVE construction.[8] This is a subordinate structure, but it allows a lexical subject and shows none of the syntactic reflexes of a control structure. Noncoreference between subjects is not only allowed but also common, as in example (14):

(14) a. *amma gamǝțǝ   gihilla, mamǝ   seerǝmǝ gedǝrǝ wǽḍǝ kǝrannǝ oonǝ.*
     mother village-DAT go-*la* I-NOM all   house   work   do   necessary
     'With Mother gone to the village, I have to do all the housework.'

   b. *loku mahattayațǝ asǝniipǝ welaa,   mehee kaurut   wǽḍǝ kǝranne nǽǽ.*
      big boss-DAT   sick   get-made-*la* here   everybody work do   NEG
      'With the big boss sick, no one here is working.'

On theory-internal grounds, we assume that the *-la* clause in (14) reflects an underlying adjunct structure like the *-aamǝ* clause in (12), and not one like the control *-la* structure in (10). Thus, in (14a) and (14b), the *-la* clauses are outside the minimal S containing the main verb, and their subjects are not c-commanded by the main verb subject.

The relevant properties of the three *-la* constructions are compared with each other and with *-aamǝ* in table 19–1. As the table shows, *-aamǝ* patterns with the absolutive and finite *-la* in relation to the type of subjects it permits, though it is never used as the main verb in independent sentences. Thus, the problem of the noncongruence of morphology with nominal type is rendered even more complex. The learner must deal with four structures, of which three involve the same verbal morphology. The control structure involving *-la* is not morphologically distinct from the other two *la* structures, which pattern with *-aamǝ* in terms of the kind of subjects allowed (and for the absolutive one, in control properties).

The Acquisition Problem

Given the lack of straightforward surface cues in Sinhala, we can hypothesize that only abstract syntactic structure, presumably configurational differences, can account for this differentiation of empty categories in adverbial structures. Critically, Sinhala does not allow the child to depend solely on surface cues of morphology, as the foregoing has made clear. For children acquiring Sinhala, then, only a sensitivity to such

Table 19–1   Subject Properties of *-la* and *-aamǝ*

	-la			
	Control *(Conjunctive)*	*Noncontrol* *(Absolutive)*	*Independent* *(Finite)*	*-aamǝ*
Obligatory Subject Coreference	+	–	–	–
No Possible Overt Subject	+	–	–	–
C-commanded by Main Subject	+	–	n.a	–

structural differences could account for their differentiation of empty categories in this set of adverbial types. Critically, if the child acquiring Sinhala is found to differentiate not only the empty categories in the control -*la* and the -*aamə* constructions but also the different types of -*la* where no morphology is available, then we have a powerful argument for such sensitivity.

In the remainder of this chapter we will adduce both experimental and natural speech evidence for this STRUCTURE DEPENDENCE in early acquisition, specifically in Sinhala. A strong theory of Universal Grammar would predict that the child is equipped with such principles of structure dependence (Chomsky 1986b), and recent work has argued that children evidence such principles continuously in early stages of first language acquisition in other domains of anaphora (Lust 1986, 1987).

The Acquisition Evidence

We will draw on a study of Sinhala acquistion that is one of a series of ongoing cross-linguistic experimental studies of acquisition carried out at Cornell under the direction of Barbara Lust and involving a number of languages that differ in their fundamental structural characteristics.[9] The Sinhala research, like that for several other languages, included three types of data: natural speech, elicited imitation, and act-out (coreference judgments). In this chapter, we will focus on the first and third types of data and touch only lightly on the results of the elicited imitation task.

Natural Speech

We have begun to study the natural speech of 74 children acquiring Sinhala as a first language, from the ages of 2 years and zero months (2;0) to 4;0, with a mean age of 3;01, divided into four six-month age groups. Each speech sample had a mean of 133 utterances and was collected by a native speaker in village homes or schools in the Kadawatha area of Sri Lanka. These analyses revealed a total of 438 utterances with various -*la* constructions; they ranged from a mean of 3.5 per child in the youngest age group to 10.5 in the oldest age group. In contrast, only 47 utterances with -*aamə* were found; they remained at a low mean rate of use over development ranging from .07 in the youngest group to .84 in the oldest. However, from the earliest age group, all three types of -*la* construction were evidenced, as table 19–2 exemplifies. The control type "conjunctive" -*la* is productive at all age levels.

Experimental Data

Although the observed productivity in natural speech does suggest both an early knowledge of the Sinhala control structure and a differentiation of closely related adverbial structures, the natural speech data alone do not unambiguously identify the factors that children are consulting in differentiating these structures and their empty categories. To test the nature of children's knowledge more precisely, we have conducted a series of experiments to evaluate the specific factors that may be involved in the child's representation of these structures.

The Comprehension Test

SUBJECTS AND DESIGN   In one of these studies, our subjects were 169 Sri Lankan children from 2 to 6 years of age (mean 4;8) who were acquiring Sinhala. We tested them on a set of sixteen experimental sentences in a standardized "act-out" test of comprehension. Half of these involved a *-la* construction' and half involved an *-aamə* construction, as exemplified in table 19–3. All the sentences involved an empty category in subject position of one clause. Each of these sentences was

Table 19–2   Examples from Children's Natural Speech: Different Uses of *-la*

	(S#; AGE; Utt#)
Group 1	

(1) conjunctive: mee, gaumak æñdəla innəwa.
    look, frock   wear-la be(animate)-PRES
    'Look, she is wearing a dress.'
	105; 2.00;149)

(2) absolutive: nangi-t   kaar-ekee nægəla yanəwa   nangi-t   ekkə
    little sister car-LOC   enter-la go-PRES little sister-also with
    'Little sister is going in the car with the little sister.'
	(105;2.00;67)

(3) finite: oon,   amma genælla, nee?
    there,   mother bring-la, TAG
    'There, mother has brought it, hasn't she?'
	(109;2.04;101)

Group 2	

(4) conjunctive: budiyənəkotə maduruwo   æwilla   kanəwa.
    sleep-when   mosquitoes come-la bite-PRES
    'When I sleep, mosquitoes come and bite me.'
	(212;2.11;115)

(5) absolutive: bakti-giitə   gihilla aawa   andə-beree.
    'bhakti'-song-Pl go-la   come-PAST (andə)-drums
    'Bhakti songs passed and the (andə) drums appeared.'
	(209;2.07;102)

(6) finite: belt ekə kædila.
    belt-one break-la
    'The belt is broken.'
	(211;2.11;5)

Group 3	

(7) conjunctive: api mee paak ekətə   gihilla meekə   eləwanəwa nee?
    we this park-DEF-DAT go-la   this one   drive-PRES TAG
    'We will go to that park and drive it, won't we?'
	(317;3.01;57)

(8) absolutive: ekkan-ævilla, amma innəwa   gedərə.
    bring-la   mother be(animate)-PRES home
    'Having been brought, mother is at home.'
	(306;3.04;62)

(9) finite: arəka-t   peralila.
    that one-also overturn-la
    'That one, too, has been overturned.'
	(308;3.01;9)

Group 4	

(10) conjunctive: akki   æwilla   aait   yanəwa.
    big-sister come-la again go-PRES
    'Big sister came and is going back.'
	(401;3.08;88)

(12) absolutive: pettiyəkə   daala tibbe   meekə.
    box-INDEF-LOC put-la be-PAST-FOC this-one
    '(Someone) having put (it) in a box, this (=it) remained.'
	(413; 4.00;25)

(13) finite: ewunge   amma   ævilla.
    they-GEN   mother come-la
    'Their mother has come.'
	(405;3.08;99)

Table 19–3 Experimental Sentences: Act Out Task

-la

Forward Left

1. wañdura keselgediyə ahulala   Ø ate   wanənəwa
monkey banana   (having) picked -up Ø hand waves
'When the monkey picked up the banana, Ø waves the (his) hand.'

2. koṭiya bas-ekə perələla`   Ø rawumak duwənəwa
tiger   bus-the   (having) knocked-down Ø circle   runs
'When the tiger knocked down the bus, Ø runs in a circle.'

Forward Right

3. wañdura naṭənəwa Ø keselgediyə wiisikərəla
monkey dances   Ø banana   (having) thrown
'The monkey dances when Ø threw the banana.'

4. gemba pinumak gahanəwa Ø ṭopiyə pahurugaala
frog   somersaults   Ø toffee   (having) pawed
'The frog somersaults when Ø pawed the toffee.'

Backward Left

5. Ø boole pahurugaala   puusa kakulə dikkərənəwa
Ø ball   (having) pawed cat   leg   stretches
'When Ø pawed the ball, the cat stretches the(his) leg.'

6. Ø keselgediyə bimədaala   gemba pinungahanəwa
Ø banana   (having) dropped frog   somersaults
'When Ø dropped the banana, the frog somersaults.'

Backward Right

7. Ø rawumak duwənəwa puusa bas-ekə ataærəla
Ø circle   run   cat   bus-the   (having) dropped
'Ø runs in a circle when the cat dropped the bus.'

8. Ø kakulə ussənəwa balla ṭopiyə wiisikərəla
Ø leg   raises   dog   toffee   (having) thrown
'Ø raises the(his) leg when the dog threw the toffee.'

-aamə

Forward Left

9. wañdura boole ahulapuwaamə Ø appudigahanəwa
monkey ball   pick-up(when) Ø hand-claps
'When the monkey picked up the ball, Ø claps the(his) hands.'

10. gemba bas-ekə ædepuwaamə Ø muuṇə atullənəwa
frog   bus-the   pull(when)   Ø face   rubs
'When the frog pulled the bus, Ø rubs the(his) face.'

Forward Right

11. wañdura nondigahanəva Ø bas-ekə allapuwaamə
monkey limps   Ø bus-the touch(when)
'The monkey limps when Ø touched the bus.'

12. balla oluwə hollənəwa Ø galə paagəpuwaamə
dog head   shakes   Ø stone step-on(when)
'The dog shakes the(his) head when Ø steps on the stone.'

Backward Left

13. Ø bas-ekə ahuləpuwaamə puusa udə paninəwa
Ø bus-the pick-up(when) cat   up   jumps
'When Ø picked up the bus, the cat jumps up.'

14. Ø boole roolkərapuwaamə koṭiya pinungahanəwa
Ø ball   roll(when)   tiger   somersaults
'When Ø rolled the ball, the tiger somersaults.'

Backward Right

15. Ø nondigahanəwa aliya   galə   wiisikərəpuwaanə
Ø limps   elephant stone throw(when)
'Ø limps when the elephant threw the stone.'

16. Ø udə paninəwa balla galə tallukərəpuwaanə
Ø up   jumps   dog   sonte push(when)
'Ø jumps up when the dog pushed the stone.'

varied in design according to two syntactic factors, as the table suggests: BRANCH-ING DIRECTION and PROFORM DIRECTION. In left-branching (LB) sentences, the adverbial clause was preposed, and in right-branching (RB) sentences it was postposed. In forward proform-direction sentences, the empty category followed the subject name, and in the backward ones, it preceded the subject name. Finally, seventy of these children received the experimental sentences with an initial PRAGMATIC LEAD to the name in the sentence. For example, sentence 1 in Table 19–3 was preceded by a sentence similar to "Now I am going to tell you a little story about the monkey."

One point should be noted concerning the placement of the nulls in these sentences. In the forward left -*la* sentences (1 and 2), the nulls appear as they would if they were the subject of the main clause. This makes these structures quite parallel to the corresponding -*aamə* sentences (9 and 10), and they were designed with that in mind. However, though that placement is perfectly possible and grammatical in an absolutive structure with a lexically realized subject, it is clearly inconsistent with the structure that we have proposed for the conjunctive participle sentences in examples (9a) and (10). In the event, this led to a particularly interesting and revealing—though unanticipated—result that we will deal with later.

This design allowed us to test the following hypotheses regarding children's knowledge of -*la* and -*aamə* strucures:

Hypothesis 1: If children do distinguish -*la* structures as "control" structures in distinction from the -*aamə* adjunct structures, then they should assign significantly more coreference in their interpretation of the -*la* structures, which involve obligatory coreference, than in their interpretation of the -*aamə* structures. They should assign significantly more disjoint reference responses to the -*aamə* structures, which involve a free empty category, than to the -*la* structures. They should also allow the pragmatic lead to influence their interpretation of the empty category in the case of the free empty category in the -*aamə* clause significantly more than in the controlled empty category in the -*la* clause.

Hypothesis 2: In particular, if children distinguish -*la* and -*aamə* sentence types in terms of their abstract representation, as in 10 and 12, then children should differentiate the -*la* sentences according to the factors we varied experimentally.

RESULTS   For the first hypothesis, we initially consider the main effects, computed by ANOVA, on the amount of children's judgments of coreference (CRJ) between the empty category in the sentence and the name, taking the pragmatic lead (+PL and –PL) conditions together: $F(1,161) = 8.26$, $p = .005$.

As predicted, the children made significantly more coreference judgments when responding to a sentence with -*la* than to a sentence with -*aamə* when the -*la* and -*aamə* sentences were analyzed as a total set: $F(1,95) = 7.98$ ($p = .006$). Overall, children computed a mean number of 1.23 coreference judgments (CRJ) with -*la*; 1.13 with -*aamə* type sentences. (score range = 0–2). A higher amount of CRJ on -*la* was consistent over development. They made significantly more disjoint reference judgments (DRJ) when responding to a sentence with -*aamə* than with -*la* : -*aamə* .08; -*la* .02; $F(1,61) = 10.75$ ($p = .001$).

The factor of PRAGMATIC LEAD significantly affected CRJ on both -*la* and -*aamə* overall. However, analyses of interactions among the factors we varied showed that in the case of -*la*, the effects of PL were more limited, as we shall see below.

For hypothesis 2, children did differentiate the -*la* structures according to the experimental factors manipulated. For example, the -*la* sentences 1 and 2 had the highest amount of CRJ (1.53, about 75% of the data), overall for either -*la* or -*aamə*. The corresponding sentences with -*aamə*, 9 and 10 on table 19–3, had less CRJ (1.24).

The amount of CRJ with and without PL are shown in figure 19–1. There was no significant effect of PL on the paradigm control -*la* sentences 1 and 2 (1.56 vs. 1.51 with and without PL, respectively). However, there was a significant effect on -*la* structures overall—$F(1,161) = 8.90$ ($p = .003$)—as there was for -*aamə* overall—$F(1,161) = 12.98$ ($p = .0004$). For rightward -*aamə* with forward anaphora, the effect was particularly striking, raising the amount of coreference judgment to equal that of leftward -*la* with backward anaphora (1.56) to yield an interestingly symmetrical patten for these two.

What appears to be at work here is the tendency of the null *pro* subject in -*aamə* structures, and especially in preposed ones, to be particularly sensitive to discourse reference. This leads to low CRJ in the backward left condition without pragmatic lead, but pragmatic lead to the overt NP increased the CRJ by providing a referential link to the overt nominal that is consonant with the null in the -*aamə* clause. In the postposed cases with null subject -*aamə*, the pragmatic lead to the overt nominal in the main clause also identifies that with the discourse topic, thus strengthening coreference. In both preposed and postposed conditions, then, pragmatic lead significantly increases coreference for the null subject of -*aamə* clauses, though forward coreference remains higher than backward in all conditions, as figure 19–1 shows. Also, the children sometimes use themselves as the referent for the null form. This is more common in preposed backward (i.e., null subject) subordinate structures, particularly with -*aamə*. These count in the scoring as noncoreference cases and do suggest a sensitivity to sentence-external reference. They also undersore the difference between -*la* and *aamə* in terms of the higher possibility for disjoint reference for the latter, while at the same time demonstrating the possibility of absolutive reading for the preposed -*la* cases with a null, (i.e., *pro*) subject. In any event, there are some interesting aspects of the interaction of null pronouns with discourse to be followed up here, illustrating the possibility for acquisition research both to cast light on old problems and to suggest new ones.

Earlier, we mentioned the possibility of alternative interpretations (control vs. absolutive) for the forward left sentences (1 and 2 on table 19–3). These sentences with -*la* produced high CRJ values (1.56 with PL, 1.51 without PL), and the overall figure is the highest for any structure. This corroborates our basic hypothesis in a serendipitous way that was not entirely anticipated under the original design. As we indicated earlier, these sentences were designed under the assumption that they could and would reflect empty categories as shown on the table—that is, that the overt NP subject would form part of a -*la* clause, outside of the main clause, analogous to the -*aamə* sentences. In other words, they were expected to be interpreted as in (15a) and (15b), with a tree structure parallel to the -*aamə* clause in (12).

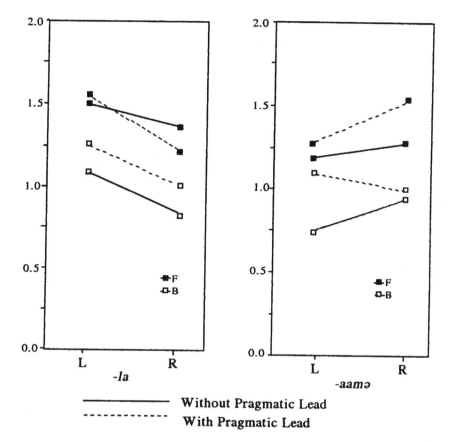

Figure 19–1   Children's coreference judgments (CRJ) on *-la* and *-aamə*.

(15) a. [*waňdurai keselgedi ahuləla*] $\varnothing_{i/j}$ *atə*   *wanənəwa*
        [monkey$_i$ banana   pickup-*la*] $\varnothing_{i/j}$ hand waves

    b. [*koṭiya$_i$ bas-ekə perələla*] $\varnothing_{i/j}$ *rawumak duwənəwa*
        [tiger   bus   knockdown-la] $\varnothing_{i/j}$ circle   runs

However, these sentences 1 and 2 in table 19–3 are also susceptible to interpretation
as in (16a) and (16b)—as the canonical control structure of the tree representation in
(10), and they map onto it in a straightforward fashion:

(16) a. *waňdura$_i$* [$\varnothing_i$ *keselgedi ahuləla*]   *atə*   *wanənəwa*
        monkey$_i$ [$\varnothing_i$ banana   pickup-*la*] hand waves

    b. *koṭiya$_i$* [$\varnothing_i$ *bas-ekə perələla*]   *rawumak duwənəwa*
        tiger$_i$ [$\varnothing_i$ bus   knockdown-*la*] circle   runs

Note that the surface linear order of constituents here is the one that occurs commonly in the children's natural speech for conjunctive structures where there is an overt main subject, namely the relevant natural speech examples in Table 19–2. In both natural speech and experimentally, the children appear to have strongly favored that control mapping, accounting for the fact that this category of sentences shows the highest CRJ and resistance to the effects of pragmatic context. Contrast this with the backward right sentences 7 and 8 in table 19–3. In these, not only is the -*la* clause extraposed out of the canonical control domain, but the presence of an overt nominal in the postposed -*la* clause blocks the control -*la* interpretation and forces the absolutive one. These show the lowest CRJ (.82) of any of the types tested. The corresponding -*aamə* sentences, 15 and 16, showed higher CRJ (1.01) than 7 and 8, signifying once again the child's distinction between -*la* and -*aamə* clauses.

The Imitation Task

The results of the imitation task are not dealt with here, and they require separate extensive presentation.[10] However, we do show in figure 19–2 the number of correct responses on the left-branching structures for a set of sentences parallel to those in table 19–3. Note that the children do significantly better on the canonical control -*la* structures (left forward) than on the left-backward ones, which are most straightforwardly interpreted as left-dislocated control structures under the syntactic analysis proposed here. For the -*aamə* sentences however, there is no difference in success of imitation that correlates with the direction of the null in relation to the overt nominal. This demonstrates once again, with a quite different task, the ability of the children to differentiate between the two kinds of structures in a structure-dependent

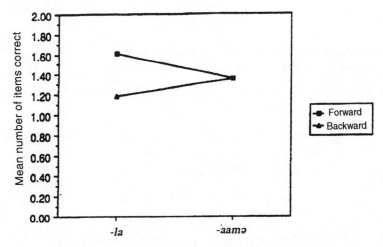

Figure 19–2   Amount of children's correct imitation task responses on Sinhalese left-branching structures.

way. It is also clearly consistent with the analysis of those structures that we have proposed and is thus another exemplar of the value of acquisition research in elucidating syntactic structures.

Conclusions

These experimental results suggest a continuous stucture dependence in children's early hypotheses about the prolific empty categories in Sinhala, including those involved in control structures. As we have shown, Sinhala empty categories are not differentiated by surface cues such as verb morphology or surface agreement. Thus, the fact that children did distinguish the interpretation of empty categories in the full set of adverbial forms we tested appears to reflect sensitivity to the abstract structure of these forms. Critically, in *-la* sentences 1 and 2, which were susceptible to the canonical control structure, children opted for a control interpretation. They clearly did not assimilate these to the adjunct *-aamə* sentences.

In terms of linguistic theory, the full set of results appears consistent with a generalized control theory such as that proposed by Huang (1989), wherein empty categories are significantly differentiated by the configuration in which they appear, although this remains a direction for future research. In terms of first language acquisition, these results cohere with results attained on English acquisition of control by Cohen Sherman (1983) and Cohen Sherman and Lust (1986, 1993), which provide evidence for continuous structure dependence in the child acquiring English control structures. They also cohere with results attained from experimental study of Japanese acquisition of adverbial structures (Lust, Wakayama, Snyder, Mazuka, and Oshima, 1985). The results raise the crucial question: If it is abstract structure that is consulted critically by children in the differentiation of empty categories, how is this knowledge determined—how is it mapped correctly to various surface structures? What principles does the child use to determine what constitutes a paradigm control stucture as opposed to an adjunct structure? The experimental results reported here for Sinhala begin to identify the type of structural factors that were consulted in this mapping and point the direction for future research in these areas.

A Parameter Setting Paradox: Children's Acquisition of Hindi Anaphora in *jab* Clauses

WITH BARBARA LUST, TEJ BHATIA, VASHINI SHARMA, AND JYOTI KHARE

The Relevance of Acquisition Research

There has been a considerable amount of research linking investigation of language acquisition to linguistic theory, especially syntactic theory as represented in a Universal Grammar (UG) approach (Chomsky 1981 and subsequent work by him and others). The bulk of this theory-driven acquisition research has been devoted to children's acquisition of their first language (e.g., Lust, Hermon, and Kornfilt (eds.) 1994). However, there have also been an increasing number of extensions to second language acquisition, much of it using, adapting, and sometimes extending the methodology of the first language work (for examples and a survey, see Flynn and O'Neill 1988; White 1989).

Theory-driven research into language acquisition also feeds back into the theory on which it is based by providing a testing ground for that theory and providing new hypotheses to be tested. This is even more true when it is extended to cross-language research. In addition, such research, whether in first or second language acquisition, can furnish important new insights into the structures of the languages under investigation by forcing explicit and testable accounts of the structures at issue, as well as by providing empirical tests of those structures. Also, there have been some promising attempts to explore the possible implications of that aquisition research for language pedagogy (see Gair 1995 and the works by Flynn, White, and others cited therein).

This chapter deals with the acquisition of a South Asian language, Hindi, and represents an instantiation of the first link in the chain of research just outlined. As that link, it presents a general hypothesis about language acquisition, proposes specific structural characteristics of the language concerned, and formulates and implements an empirical test of those hypotheses. For those teachers and researchers concerned with principled approaches to language pedagogy, the nature of the languages taught and the manner in which they are acquired cannot fail to be of interest. Thus this chapter, though it does not deal directly with pedagogical extensions, is presented as an example of the research paradigm described above as applied to a South Asian language. We hope that such efforts, especially when extended to second language research, will ultimately lead to such pedagogical extensions.

The Fundamental Premise

Linguistic theory describes a module of Universal Grammar (UG) that proposes both to formulate essential properties of all natural languages and to characterize the initial state of human competence for language. In this chapter, we assume that empirical studies of the initial state, specifically of CONSTRAINTS on first language acquisition, are necessary to the test of specific proposals regarding the content of UG. In particular, we investigate constraints by parameter-setting on the first language acquisition of certain forms of anaphora in Hindi.

Our fundamental hypothesis is that UG-determined principles and parameters, by constraining the course of first language acquisition, contribute to the explanation of how first language acquisition is not only possible but also effectively achieved during the first few years of life, regardless of the input language. Here, we engage in a test of that hypothesis, concentrating on the role of one particular phrase structure directionality parameter that we will define.[1]

Constraint on Anaphora in First Language Acquisition

One of the most fundamental domains of language knowledge concerns the interaction of structure and linear order. Current research is concerned both with possible cross-linguistic variation in this area and its proper theoretical representation in Universal Grammar. This interaction of structure and linear order is critical in the study of first language acquisition, particularly in the area of anaphora.

In English, it has been observed that early periods of first language acquisition are characterized by an apparent constraint on anaphora:

> The Forward Directionality Constraint: In early acquisition of anaphora, the proform (null or pronoun) should follow, not precede, the antecedent.

Here, we use the term "anaphora" in a general sense to refer to relations between PROFORMS and their antecedents, where proforms may be lexical—like the English pronoun *he* or Hindi *vo*, for example—or phonologically unrealized (null) (cf. Lust et al. 1995).

In accord with the forward directionality constraint, experimental and naturalistic studies have shown that children acquiring English as their first language resist backward anaphora (where a proform precedes an antecedent) in both production and comprehension. The constraint in English has been found to involve lexical pronouns and to generalize to certain forms of null proforms (e.g., Lust, Solan, Flynn, Cross, and Schuetz 1986). Subsequent research has attempted to define the nature and source of this constraint. (See Lust 1986a for review; see Lust 1987 and Lust and Mazuka 1989 for discussion.) One might hypothesize, for example, that children have a universal "processing" principle that determines that only prior terms may be anaphorically referred to. Such a principle might be predicted, for example, if children's early competence for language were determined by principles of discourse or computational complexity more strongly than by principles of Universal Grammar. Alternatively, we might ask if this forward directionality in the acquisition of anaphora in English is explained in some way by UG itself (cf. Lust 1986). That is, do the principles and parameters of UG provide some form of constraint that underlies the forward directionality constraint, or is there some functional or processing effect at work?

Parameter-Setting

The work reported here is part of a larger cross-language project conducted by Barbara Lust at Cornell, in which it is hypothesized that the forward directionality constraint that was observed in English acquisition may be at least partially based on children's sensitivity to configurational factors involved in parameter-setting for the English language. Thus it was further hypothesized that the forward directionality constraint reflects the presence of a basic property of UG, STRUCTURE DEPENDENCE. In other words, the child (or an adult learner) does not operate on unstructured linear strings but on the structures that underlie the surface language data (see Chomsky 1981, 1982).

Several parameters that determine English configuration and differentiate it from other languages have been proposed. For example, Lust proposed that the principal branching direction parameter may provide a testable formulation of a critical dimension for language organization that is consulted by the young child acquiring a first language. While this parameter formulation is related to a head-direction parameter that has been proposed (e.g., Chomsky 1982), it is not identical to it. (See Lust, in preparation, for discussion, and Lust and Mangione 1983.)

> Principal Branching Direction Parameter: The branching direction that holds consistently in unmarked form over major recursive structures of a language, where "major recursive structures" are defined to include embeddings of sentences under either NP or S heads. Specifically, relative clauses in complex NP and adverbial subordinate clauses are critical to the definition of this parameter.

Although this definition will suffice for the purposes of this chapter, it also allows a formulation in terms of the X-bar theory of phrase structure, as below. See Lust, in preparation, and Lust 1994 for articulation of the relations between these formulations.

Corollary: The PBD parameter is defined over the head direction of the
Complementizer Phrase (CP) and the adjunction direction it correlates with. This
can be exemplified by the schemata below, where C-zero is either a *left* or *right*
head in CP, and adjunction is either right branching or left branching, respectively:

[C-zero [IP]]   (left-headed, right branching)
[[IP] C-zero]   (right-headed, left branching)

In Lust 1986, 1994 it was proposed that it is because English is principally
RIGHT BRANCHING on this parameter and because the child's acquisition is constrained
by the principle of structure dependence that the forward directionality constraint
holds for English acquisition. Because English is right-branching, the directional
constraint will have as one consequence that a forward proform will generally not
command[2] its antecedent, thus respecting a basic principle of UG whereby proforms
may not command their antecedents (cf. Principle C in Chomsky's binding theory,
e.g., Chomsky 1986b; Reinhart 1976; Lust, Eisele, and Mazuka 1992). It was hypothesized (e.g., Lust 1986) that children were sensitive to the right-branching
direction of English and deductively established linearity relations between antecedent and proform to accord with it in their general theory of the grammar for the
language they were acquiring. This constraint on anaphora in acquisition would
thus guarantee a critical component of UG that has been referred to as structure
dependence:

Constraint on Anaphora in Acquisition: In early child language, the direction of
grammatical anaphora is constrained to accord with the principal branching direction (PBD) of the specific language being acquired. If the PBD of the language they
are acquiring is rightward, children establish anaphora in a mainly *forward* direction. If the PBD is leftward, they establish a backward direction of anaphora as
unmarked.

"Grammatical anaphora" here refers to the interpretation of proforms that is
represented at some level in sentence grammar and that involves construal as well
as coreference relation between terms. Grammatical structure is a necessary condition for either the existence of, or the blocking of, such anaphora.

A wide number of experiments have tested various types of anaphora acquisition for their susceptibility to this proposal.

Initial confirmation for the hypothesis that the right-branching nature of English
was the source of the forward directionality acquisition constraint was found when
Arabic, another right-branching language, showed a forward directionality constraint
in first language acquisition of similar forms of anaphora, while three left-branching
languages (Japanese, Sinhala, and Chinese) showed no such forward directionality
constraint in first language acquisition. Rather, in these left-branching languages,
children found backward anaphora as accessible as (or in some cases more accessible than) forward anaphora in systematically matched experimental designs that
tested similar anaphora types. (See Lust, in preparation, for review.) The anaphora

type involved in this first set of experiments involved free pronominal anaphora in adjunct adverbial subordinate clauses, as in "When *he* came home, *John* cooked dinner." This was the type of anaphora that had motivated the forward directionality constraint in studies of English acquisition.

Hindi

Given these empirical results and the proposed forward directionality constraint, Hindi becomes a critical language for testing the proposed phrase-structure parameter, and for testing that constraint and evaluating its nature. Although Hindi may be described in terms of surface typology as basically SOV, like Japanese or Sinhala, it differs from them in regard to its embedded and adjunction structures. Those other languages are thoroughly left-branching. Their relative clauses precede (i.e., occur to the left of) the head, as illustrated by the Sinhala example in (1a) (with heads in boldface). Complementizers entirely, or nearly so, follow their clauses (i.e., their complements occur to the left of them), as in (1b):

(1)   a. [*mamə gunəpālətə   dunnə*]   ***potə*** [[*apē iskole   ugannənə*]
           I   Gunapala-DAT gave-REL book our   school-LOC teach-REL
           guruwərəyek   liyəpu*]   ***ekə.
           teacher-INDEF wrote-REL one
           'The book that I gave Gunapala is the one that a teacher in our school wrote.'

      b. *īye   gedərə iṅdəla ṭawməṭə   yanə- koṭə mamə loku nayek dækka.*
           yesterday home   from   town-DAT go-REL when I   big cobra saw
           'Yesterday when I was going from home to town, I saw a big cobra.'

Hindi, on the other hand, is not fully left-branching in that way. Rather, on the PBD parameter (as well as on several other versions of a phrase structure parameter), Hindi appears to be mixed. That is, both values of the parameter setting appear to be unmarked. As examples (1) and (2) show, Hindi relative clauses may appear to the right of their heads as in (2), or to the left as in (3). (Examples here are from Srivastav, personal communication.) The exact analysis of these structures is still a matter of some dispute. For one account and a summary of research, see Srivastav 1991:

(2)   a. *vo dhobī*   [*jo mere sāth āyā*] *ḍākṭar kā bhāī   hai.*
           that washerman who me   with came doctor's   brother is
           'The washerman who came with me is the doctor's brother.'

      b. *vo dhobī   ḍākṭar kā bhāī   hai* [*jo mere sāth āyā*]
           that washerman doctor's   brother is   who me   with came
           'The washerman who came with me is the doctor's brother.'

(3)   a. [*jo   dhobī   mere sāth āyā*] *vo ḍākṭar kā bhāī   hai.*
           which washerman me   with came he doctor's   brother is
           'The washerman who came with me is the doctor's brother.'

b. [*jis   ghar   mẽ māĩ   rahtā thā*]   *vo   usne kharidā hai.*
   which house   in I   live   used to that he   bought has
   'He has bought the house I used to live in.'

Participial modifiers, however, occur left of their heads, as example (4) shows, and cannot follow them:

(4)   *usne* [[*kamre mẽ baiṭhe   hue*] *logõ*] *ko cāy pilāī.*
     he   room   in   seated   people   to tea drink-caused
     'He offered tea to the people who were sitting in the room.' (Kachru 1980: 35)

As (5) shows, adverbial subordinate clauses (e.g., *jab* (when) clauses) may also occur either before (left) or after (right) main sentences. Traditional Hindi grammars represent the *jab* clause as sentence-initial, or left-branching (for example, McGregor 1972: 83 ff.). However, in apparent accord with mixed PBD, both right and left adjunctions and embeddings may appear in colloquial Hindi, as in (3a) and (3b). Thus Kachru (1980: 141) claims that "relatives, complements and other subordinate clauses are relatively free with regard to their order with respect to main clauses." Kachru (1980: 139) gives the example in (5a). Our informants also allow (5b).

(5)   a. *jab   māĩ kalkatte mẽ thā tab   har   garmī   mẽ dārjīling   jātā thaā.*
       when I   Calcutta in   was then every summer in Darjeeling go   used-to
       'I used to go to Darjeeling every summer when I was in Calcutta.'

     b. *har   garmī   mẽ dārjīling   jātā thā   jab   maĩ kalkatte mẽ thā.*
       every summer in Darjeeling go   used to when I   Calcutta in   was
       'I used to go to Darjeeling every summer when I was in Calcutta.'

In addition, in striking contradistinction to the strongly left-branching languages mentioned earlier, Hindi finite complements of verbs always occur to the right (see Davison in preparation). Compare the Hindi example in (6a) with the Sinhala example in (6b):

(6)   a. *rām ne   kahā* [*ki   shyām kal   āyā*].
       Ram ERG   said   COMP Shyam yesterday came
       'Ram said that Shyam came yesterday.'

     b. *gunapālə* [*Siri īye   āwa kiyəla*] *kiwwa.*
       Gunapala Siri   yesterday came COMP said
       'Gunapala said that Siri came yesterday.'

It has even been argued (Singh 1975) that the position of COMP as right or left of the clause, may be "mixed" in Hindi. (For further study of Hindi relative clause formation, see Verma 1966; Masica 1972; Bhatia 1974; Donaldson 1971; Kachru 1978; Subbarao 1984; Davison in preparation; Srivastav 1991). We may then—given the hypothesized constraint on anaphora in acquisition and the facts in (1) through (3)—question whether the first language acquisition of anaphora in Hindi will be constrained and if so, how?

Research Design and Method

Design

In the research reported here, we tested children in India. We were looking for their production and comprehension of complex Hindi sentences with proforms and possible NP antecedents (potential pronominal anaphora) that varied factorially in both the linear and the configurational relations between proform and antecedent. We report only production results here.

The experimental sentences involved adverbial *jab* clauses, as shown in table 20–1. Half of these sentences were right-branching—they had the *jab* clause on the right of the main clause as in sentences 1, 2, 5, and 6 in table 20–1. Half were left-branching—they had the *jab* clause on the left of the main clause, as in sentences 3, 4, 7, and 8. All of the sentences involved one proform in subject position, either in *jab* clause subject position or in main clause subject position. The proform was either an empty category (null) as in sentences 1 through 4 or a lexical pronoun, *vo*, as in sentences 5 through 8, both of which are allowed by Hindi. We will refer to these two types of proforms as PROFORM TYPES. Half the sentences involved what we will call FORWARD directionality of proform: the null site or the pronoun *followed* a lexical NP subject, as in sentences 1, 3, 5, and 7. Half the sentences involved BACKWARD directionality of the proform: the null site or pronoun *preceded* a lexical NP subject, as in sentences 2, 4, 6, and 8. All sentences were tensed (present imperfective) in both main and subordinate clauses. They had equal syllable length (14 syllables) and near equal word length (8 or 9 words).

Method

Production was elicited through use of a standardized ELICITED IMITATION TASK, in which subjects were asked to repeat a sentence after the experimenter. Through standardized scoring procedures, the differential success rates and the nature of children's errors (i.e., their changes of the stimulus sentences) were assessed in terms of the factors involved in the design of the stimulus sentences. Imitation results alone do not display the subjects' anaphora (coreference) judgments directly. However, previous research has shown the elicited imitation task to be sensitive to these judgments, which appear to underlie the child's mental representation of the stimulus sentence it is imitating. The task also provides results that generally converge with those from comprehension tasks. (See Lust, Chien, and Flynn 1987 for a study of the elicited imitation methodology.) The elicited imitation task directly reveals the child's hypotheses about the *distribution* of proforms.

Analyses

As the sentences illustrate, this study performed analyses of variance on correctness of children's productions of such complex sentences according to an experimental factorial design with repeated measures. The factors exemplified in the experimental sentences included BRANCHING DIRECTION (2) (Right Branching or Left Branching) × PROFORM TYPE (2) (null or lexical (*vo*) pronoun) × PROFORM DIRECTION (2) (forward or backward.)

Table 20-1 Hindi Study Imitation Sentences

	Forward	Backward
	Null	

Right Branching

1. samīr reḍiyo suntā hai jab Ø sarbat pītā hai.
Sameer radio listens when Ø punch drinks.
'Sameer listens to the radio when (he) drinks punch.'
2. rām khilaune se kheltā hai jab Ø gānā gātā hai.
Ram toy with plays when Ø song sings.
'Ram plays with a toy when (he) sings a song.'

5. Ø khiṛkī band kartā hai jab rām sīṭī bajātā hai.
Ø window closes when Ram whistle blows
'(He) closes the window when Ram blows the whistle.'
6. Ø samosā khātā hai jab ramesh pānī pītā hai.
Ø samosa eats when Ramesh water drinks
'(He) eats the samosa when Ramesh drinks water.'

Left Branching

3. jab shyām gānā gātā hai Ø katorā letā hai.
when Shyam song sings Ø bowl takes
'When Shyam sings a song, (he) takes the bowl.'
4. jab mohan ballā rakhtā hai Ø cārpāī khīctā hai.
when Mohan bat puts down Ø cot pulls-out
'When Mohan puts the bat down, (he) pulls out the cot.'

7. jab mithāī lātā hai kishor jūtā utārtā hai.
When Ø sweet brings Kishor shoe takes off
'When (he) brings the sweets Kishor takes off shoes.'
8. jab Ø bādām khātā hai shyām palang haṭātā hai.
When Ø almond eats Shyam bed moves
'When (he) eats the almond, Shyam moves the bed.'

Lexical Pronoun

Right Branching

9. munnā cāklet khātā hai jab vo dūdh pītā hai.
Munna chocolate eats when he milk drinks
'Munna eats the chocolate when he drinks milk.'
10. mohan ālū letā hai jab vo kāpī girātā hai.
Mohan potato takes when he notebook drops
'Mohan takes the potato when he drops the notebook.'

13. vo darvāzā kholtā hai jab rohit cāy pītā hai.
he door opens when Rohit tea drinks
'He opens the door when Rohit drinks some tea.'
14. ho cāval khātā hai jab rām reḍiyo suntā hai.
he rice eats when Ram radio listens
'He eats rice when Ram listens to the radio.'

Left Branching

11. jab manu kitāb paṛhtā hai vo pānī pītā hai.
when Manu book reads he water drinks
'When Manu reads the book he drinks water.'
12. jab amit pensil pakartā hai vo paisā phēktā hai.
when Amit pencil holds he penny throws
'When Amit holds the pencil, he throws the penny.'

15. jab vo pān khātā hai mohan kitāb detā hai.
when he leaf eats Mohan book gives.
'When he eats a betel-nut leaf Mohan gives a book.'
16. jab vo sarak par caltā hai rām patthar phēktā hai.
when he road on walks Ram stone throws
'When he walks on the road Ram throws a stone.'

In addition, by design, a factor of presence or absence of pragmatic lead (±PL) was also tested on the imitation of these sentences. While half the subjects were asked to imitate the sentences in isolation, the other half were asked to imitate each sentence only after it had been introduced by a pragmatic lead to the NP subject named in the sentence. For example, in the +PL condition, a sentence such as 2 or 5 in Table 20–1 would be preceded by a lead like "Now this one is going to be a little story about Rām." The addition of the pragmatic lead factor to the design was motivated by the question, To what degree are children's early hypotheses regarding anaphora dependent upon pragmatics versus grammar? In particular, to what degree are the early hypotheses about directionality dependent on pragmatic context?

Standardized scoring criteria were applied. There were two replication items for each condition, giving a score range of 0 to 2.

This study tests whether the children acquiring Hindi are sensitive to the experimental variables we manipulate. It also examines their initial hypotheses regarding unmarked linear and configurational domains for the two forms of pronominal anaphora, namely, null and the lexical pronoun, *vo*.

Adult Judgments

According to our informants (as well as the native-speaker coauthors), adult native speakers do not easily allow coreference (anaphora) between the proform and NP subject in the sentences with backward null proforms (Ø) in table 20–1, as in 5, 6, 7, and 8. For the rejection of the right-branching structures of 5 and 6 as anaphoric, a ready explanation presents itself in accord with Principle C of the binding theory (see the text associated with the principal branching direction corollary above). That is, although the structure of these right-branching sentences is not totally clear, there is a plausible analysis under which the proform would command the antecedent, as it does in English. However, Principle C would not explain the rejection of 7 and 8 (left-branching). Adult informants allow possible coreference (anaphora) on the sentences with forward proforms, e.g., sentences 1 through 4 and 9 through 12. However, a noncoreference judgment is preferred for lexical pronouns (*vo*) in general in these structures (9–12). Adults, then, prefer coreference only with forward nulls like 1 and 2 in these sentence types.

Subjects

All of the children in this study were residents of India (mainly Agra and Hyderabad areas), where they were tested by a trained experimenter whose mother tongue was Hindi. All children were monolingual Hindi speakers, with no overt language handicap.

There were 145 subjects in all (mean age 4;10). Of these, seventy-five subjects from 3;0 to 6;11 (mean age 4;9) were tested without the pragmatic lead. Another seventy subjects from 3;1 to 6;11 were tested with a pragmatic lead. The children in each group were divided into four subgroups, each of which had a one-year range. All children were administered all sentence types in random order.

Summary of Results

We will summarize our results here. The interested reader is referred to the appendix for a more detailed report of the empirical results:

1. First language acquisition of Hindi is not characterized by a general preference for one branching direction over another in complex sentence formation (with temporal adverbial subordinate (*jab*) clauses), as it is in other languages.
2. First language acquisition of Hindi is not characterized by a general forward directionality (precedence) constraint on proforms, as it is in English (and as it may be in adult Hindi).
3. First language acquisition of Hindi is not characterized by a general preference for a phonetically realized lexical pronoun. On the contrary, it is characterized by a preference for a null.
4. Lexical (*vo*) pronouns and null pronouns pattern similarly in Hindi, in spite of the overall advantage of the null. That is, the factors Branching Direction and Proform Direction that were tested affect them both similarly. First language acquisition of Hindi is thus characterized by the child's generalization over both types of proform (whether phonetically realized or not).
5. Proform Direction and Branching Direction are precisely linked in Hindi first language acquisition (for both nulls and pronouns). Directionality of proform correlates with direction of branching (i.e., subordinate clause embedding) in the following manner: Forward direction is associated with right-branching structures and backward direction is associated with left-branching. See figures 20–1 and 20–2 in the appendix.
6. Pragmatic lead did not uniformly *improve* imitation success, nor did it *reverse* the Proform Direction results. That is, presence of pragmatic lead did not induce a significant preference for forward direction in left-branching structures; nor did it neutralize the significant interaction between Branching Direction and Proform Direction in the data. Thus, the data suggest that the grammatical factors tested are to a degree independent of this pragmatic factor in Hindi acquisition. Precedence effects, when they exist, are linked to structure and are not totally explained by pragmatic context.

Conclusions

Cross-linguistic Comparisons

In terms of cross-linguistic patterns, Hindi acquisition resembles English acquisition in certain ways. The primary resemblance is that in right-branching structures, forward directionality of proforms is strongly preferred.

However, Hindi differs from English and resembles left-branching languages like Japanese and Sinhala in that backward proforms are preferred in left-branching structures. In fact in Hindi, this preference for backward proforms in left-branching structures (e.g., Figure 20–1b) may even be even stronger than it is in these left-branching languages. Hindi acquisition also differs from English acquisition and resembles Japanese and Sinhala in that it shows an overall preference for null proforms in the adverbial subordinate clause contexts tested here. Hindi thus shows a mixed acquisition pattern, as its mixed value of the PBD parameter would predict.

Theoretical Consequences: The Adult Model and UG

Several aspects of these results clearly were not necessary given the "primary language data" (adult Hindi) to which the child is exposed.

First, as we noted above, traditional Hindi grammars represent the *jab* clause as sentence-initial, or left-branching. However, it does not appear, according to our acquisition data, that either left- or right-branching *jab* clauses are more "marked" in the initial state. Thus, if children's early imitations resembled the adult grammarian's analysis, a left-branching preference could have been found in these data. It was not.

Second, linguists have proposed that forward pronominalization may be required in Hindi. Kachru and Bhatia (1975: 45) proposed that reflexivization, for example, occurs only in a forward direction. As in English, lexical pronouns like *vo* occur productively forward in Hindi. In addition, Bhatia (1974) has argued that a similar forward directionality constraint may hold for certain pronouns in Hindi. In relative clauses, as in (7) for example, forward pronominals (whether relative clauses or demonstratives) are allowed in (7a) through (7c), but backward ones are questionable or disallowed for at least some Hindi speakers, as in (7d) through (7f).

(7) a.   *vo laṛkā merā bhāī   hai [jo   New York   mẽ rahtā hai]*
          that boy   my   brother is   REL. New York in   lives
          'The boy who lives in New York is my brother.'
     b.   *[jo laṛkā New York mẽ rahtā hai] vo merā bhāī hai*
     c.   *vo laṛkā [jo New York mẽ rahtā hai] merā bhāī hai*
     d. ? *vo merā bhāī hai [jo laṛkā New York mẽ rahtā hai]*
     e. ? *[jo New York mẽ rahtā hai] vo laṛkā merā bhāī hai*
     f. * *vo [jo laṛkā New York mẽ rahtā hai] merā bhāī hai*

As we saw earlier, adult judgments on our sentences with nulls showed preference for forward direction. Given the adult model, then, the child acquiring Hindi may well have been expected to show a preference for, even a constraint to, forward directionality of proforms, just as the child acquiring English did. However, these children preferred forward direction of proforms only in right-branching structures, and in fact they reversed this preference to a preference for backward direction of proforms in left-branching structures. They did so for both nulls and pronouns similarly. The child acquiring Hindi thus has clearly not established linearity relations between proform and antecedent on the basis of induction from surface linearity alone.

Third, it is also the case for many adult speakers that lexical pronouns (*vo*) in adverbial subordinate clause contexts are not judged to be more marked than null pronouns in these positions. In fact, for some adults, lexical pronouns appear to be more unmarked than nulls in these domains. For the child, however, nulls were consistently preferred to pronouns in these positions, although the child applied general principles similarly over both.[3]

These nonnecessary acquisition results clearly suggest that the child acquiring

Hindi is not forming generalizations relative to the potential organization of proform and antecedents on the basis of induction from the surface facts (i.e., adult "model" language) *alone*. Critically, the child appears to be organizing surface linear relations between proforms and possible NP antecedents with reference to the configuration in which these terms appear. The child acquiring Hindi thus is forming generalizations that are paradigmatically "structure-dependent." In accord with other cross-language comparisons, we reason that the child is consulting this configuration differently from children acquiring other languages, depending on a parameter of phrase structure organization, which has been proposed to be the principal branching direction (cf. Lust, in preparation).[4]

The findings with regard to pragmatic lead, wherein this factor was found to be independent of the grammatical factors to a degree, confirm that the Branching Direction and Proform Direction effects observed in Hindi acquisition must, in part, relate to the grammar of Hindi that the children are acquiring and not only to general pragmatic or discourse factors. Because the pragmatic lead did not cause children acquiring Hindi to reverse their preference for backward Proform Direction in left-branching structures, it is clear that Proform Direction is not simply pragmatically determined. The depression that children show on left-branching structures, when a pragmatic lead exists, suggests that this left-branching structure (preposed *jab* clause) with *any* form of anaphora, is somehow inconsistent with a pragmatic lead. Apparently, some aspect of Hindi discourse structure is at work here, but we have no specific proposal at present for what that might be.

Disambiguating Previous Results

Finally, these results have several consequences for disambiguating previous results in English. Both English and Hindi provide high-frequency modeling of forward proforms, particularly forward pronouns. The fact that Hindi acquisition (where Hindi is mixed in PBD), does not show the overall general forward directionality constraint in acquisition, which English acquisition does, suggests that it is the principally right-branching direction of English that is responsible for the strong forward constraint in English acquisition. It clearly confirms that a universal forward processing constraint or discourse does not determine this aspect of first language acquisition (cf. Lust and Mazuka 1989). In turn, it suggests that in both languages, "constraint" on anaphora direction in first language acquisition is at least in part a reflex of more fundamental structural principles.

In English acquisition, as we mentioned earlier, children showed a preference for the lexical pronoun (and finite clause structure) in adverbial subordinate clause structures. The opposite results that we found in Hindi also suggest that a preference for a phonetically realized proform does not necessarily characterize first language acquisition but is a function of the grammar of the language being acquired.

The Hindi acquisition data appear to be in remarkable accord with the theoretical proposal that the PBD provides a dimension for grammatical organization that "constrains" first language acquisition. Because Hindi is mixed on this parameter, its acquisition shares properties with both the right-branching and left-branching language acquisition patterns and is not totally consistent with either.

The parameter formulation at issue—namely, principal branching direction—seems strongly supported by these data. First, this parameter predicts, in general, that the Hindi acquisition pattern should differ from that of either clearly principally right-branching or clearly principally left-branching languages. Second, in Hindi, the branching direction differences across stimulus sentences (in whether they are right-branching or left-branching examples) correlated with different Proform Direction preferences—that is, with whether the proforms were backward or forward—just as it did across languages whose grammars were either principally right or left branching.

In addition, the Hindi first language acquisition data reveal a paradigm example of "structure-dependence": Children modulate antecedent–proform direction so that it is forward in right-branching Hindi structures and backward in left-branching Hindi structures. Configuration thus clearly determines linearity just as it is predicted to in strong theories of UG. Neither pragmatic factors nor the adult model will predict these results.

The Hindi pattern of association of right-branching with forward proforms and left-branching with backward proforms, which was observed in our results, appears to even more precisely correlate with the constraint formulated in the Principal Branching Direction corollary, which hypothesizes that anaphora direction is linked to branching direction.

A Paradox

The paradox these data raise, is however, the following: If the children in first language acquisition are as structurally sensitive as they are shown to be in these Hindi results, why is a parameter necessary at all? Clearly the parameter is evidenced empirically in the cross-language acquisition differences. Children acquiring Hindi, Japanese or Sinhala (left-branching), or English or Arabic (right-branching) show three distinct patterns of anaphora acquisition. They thus would appear to reflect the parameter value differences of these languages. In general, the child acquiring Hindi appears to show much more modulation of Proform Direction with modulation of the grammatical structure involved in the stimulus sentence than either of the other two groups of children acquiring languages with a uniform, regular PBD.[5] One might say then that the parameter setting determines the particular form that structure-dependence may take in language acquisition and that the child acquiring Hindi is grammatically more flexible because of its mixed parameter setting.

In the principles and parameters theory of UG, however, parameter setting is theorized to aid first language acquisition, because setting to a particular value would provide a wide set of deductive consequences that differentiate languages. One would have imagined then that a mixed parameter setting would have been detrimental, rather than advantageous, as the facts suggest. In general, after all, how is it even possible for a parameter to be set in two directions at once?

We do not attempt to resolve this paradox or these questions here. However, the Hindi acquisition data suggest that in the absence of a consistent parameter setting for the language they are acquiring, children fall back on a more exaggerated structure-dependence, for which they are competent. After all, the parameter, itself, in UG must make both directions—*both* values of the parameter—available to be set.

Further research on the structure of Hindi relative clauses (e.g., Srivastav 1991) will be crucial to the resolution of this paradox. Gambhir (1981), and Srivastav (1991), for example, have discovered that right- and left-embedded Hindi relative clauses are not equivalent in several of their crucial syntactic and semantic properties. If this is the case, Hindi may not be in fact "mixed" in branching direction parametrically. Srivastav suggests, in fact, on the basis of her analysis, that Hindi may be principally right-branching with regard to relative clauses. If that is indeed the case, however, the apparently exceptional facility with left-branching backward proforms in Hindi acquistion would remain to be explained. In any case, Hindi has important contributions to make to acquisition research and, through it, to general theory.

APPENDIX

Here we report a summary of the experimental results based on statistical analyses by analysis of variance (ANOVA). Factorial analyses of children's elicited imitation success on these sentence types provided the following results. We report first the neutral condition without pragmatic lead.

Branching Direction (BD)

There was no significant difference due to Branching Direction of the stimulus sentences overall. In general, subjects imitated right-branching (1, 2, 5, 6, 9, 10, 13, 4) in table 20–1 (.58) and left-branching sentences (3, 4, 7, 8, 11, 12, 15, 16) in table 20–1 (.57) with equivalent ease: F (1,71) = 0.02 (p = .89). This contrasts with results from English, where right-branching structures are significantly more accessible than left-branching, and also with results from Japanese and Sinhala, where left-branching structures are significantly more accessible than right-branching in imitation.

Proform Direction

There was also no significant effect overall due to Proform Direction in these Hindi acquisition data. That is, in general it was not significantly easier for children acquiring Hindi to imitate proforms in a *forward* direction over those in a *backward* direction. Conflating over proform type and Branching Direction in which the proform appears, the effect is not significant $F(1,71) = .57$ (p = .45); forward = .56, backward = .59. This result differentiates Hindi from English acquisition, as well as from Arabic, where forward proforms are generally superior to backward. It more closely resembles Japanese or Sinhala, where there is no general forward directionality constraint (although in Japanese and Sinhala a preference for backward proforms is found in certain structures).

Proform Type

There was a significant effect of proform type. Children acquiring Hindi imitated the sentences with nulls (1–8 in table 20–1) significantly better than those with lexical *vo* pronouns (9–16 in the table).

A large number of the errors on sentences with the lexical pronoun *vo* involved a change of the *vo* to a null (33% of items, 60% of errors). These imitation changes occurred on both forward (36% of items, 63% of errors) and backward (31% of items, 56% of errors) forms of the pronoun sentences. (Only 4% of items and 15% of errors on sentences with null subjects involved conversion to *vo*.)

This result differentiates Hindi from English acquisition. In sentences with adverbial subordinate ("when") clauses, young children acquiring English prefer the pronoun to the null form in a similar domain, productively converting a nonfinite sentence like "John saw Tom when Ø walking down the street" to a finite adjunct with lexical pronoun such as "John saw Tom when he was walking down the street." They do so systematically in a forward direction (Lust, Solan, Flynn, Cross, and Schuetz 1986).

This Hindi result resembles results in Sinhala or Japanese, where the null proform is the preferred form in first language acquisition, as in the adult grammar. It also resembles results in acquisition of Arabic, which is a pro-drop language.

Interaction of Proform Direction and Branching Direction

Critically, there was a significant interaction between Proform Direction and Branching Direction, which modulated the effects we have just reported. As shown in figure 20–1, in right-branching Hindi structures, (figure 20–1a) forward proforms were significantly easier for the children to imitate than backward proforms (whether null or *vo* pronoun). However, in left-branching structures (figure 20–1b), just the opposite is true. In Hindi left-branching structures, children find it significantly easier to produce backward proforms (whether null or pronoun) than forward. (There is no significant interaction between Branching Direction and proform type or between these and Proform Direction.) In both Branching Directions, the difference between Proform Directions is significant. In right branching sentences, forward proforms (.70) are superior to backward (.46), $F(1,71) = 33.13$ ($p = .00$). In left-branching sentences, backward proforms (.72) are superior to forward (.43), $F(1,71) = 29.93$ ($p = .00$). Thus there are significant Proform Direction effects in the Hindi data. They apply to both nulls and pronouns, but they are critically linked to the Branching Direction of the sentence.

Overall, when imitation "errors" (i.e., changes of the stimulus sentences) were analyzed, "anaphora errors" (i.e., imitations that changed some aspect of the relation between name antecedent and proform in the sentence) occurred to a similar degree in both left-branching and right-branching sentences, and in both forward and backward proform directions. However, in right-branching structures there were more anaphora errors on backward proforms (36 percent of items) than on forward (27 percent); on left-branching structures there were more errors on forward (32 percent) than on backward (27 percent) proforms. The interaction of Branching Direction × Proform Direction was significant in analyses of these anaphora errors: $F(1,71) = 9.04$ ($p = .004$).

Effects of Pragmatic Lead

Figure 20–2 shows the results when a pragmatic lead was added. When a pragmatic lead to the antecedent preceded the stimulus sentences (and anticipated the subject named in the sentence), there was still no overall Branching Direction effect. Again, the children still significantly prefer null to pronoun. The Hindi data do, however, show a forward directionality effect. That is, with pragmatic lead, forward proforms are now significantly favored over backward: $F = .51, B = .34; F(1,66) = 16.31$ ($p = .0001$). However, these data with pragmatic lead also show a significant interaction between Branching Direction and Proform Direction—

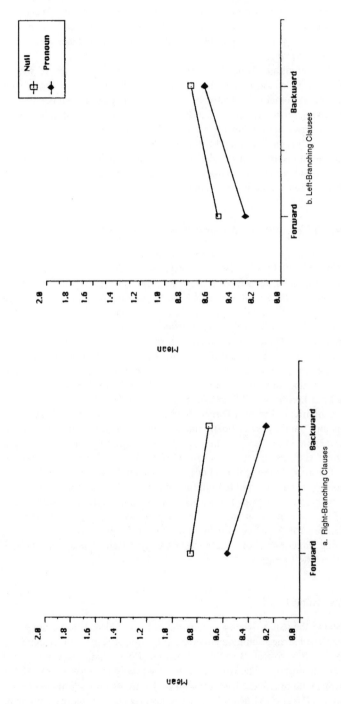

Figure 20–1 Amount correct imitation by children on Hindi sentences with *jab* clauses (in condition without pragmatic lead).

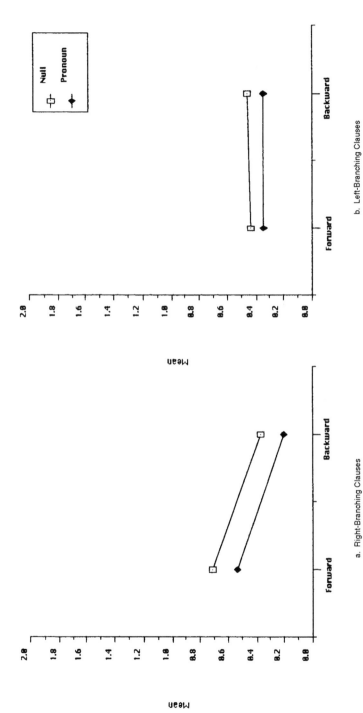

Figure 20–2 Amount correct imitation by children on Hindi sentences with *jab* clauses (in condition with pragmatic lead).

a. Right-Branching Clauses

b. Left-Branching Clauses

303

$F(1,66) = 13.72$ ($p = .0004$)—as figure 20–2 shows. Even with pragmatic lead, Branching Direction and Proform Direction are linked by the child acquiring Hindi. Figure 20–2a shows that right-branching structures again show a significant preference for forward direction of both types of proforms when there is a pragmatic lead. The effect of pragmatic lead is minimal on pronouns in right-branching structures, appearing to cohere with it fully, and pragmatic lead only intensifies the forward directionality preference for nulls in these (right-branching) structures. The critical effects of pragmatic lead are on the left-branching structures. As figure 20–2b shows, when there is a pragmatic lead, these left-branching structures no longer show a preference for backward direction of proforms. Rather, as figure 20–2b shows, there is no longer any directionality effect in the left-branching structures when a pragmatic lead to the antecedent is administered before the sentences. The pragmatic lead depresses both backward pronouns and backward nulls in left-branching structures similarly.

In summary, a comparison *across* the two (+/– PL) shows that there is a significant interaction between pragmatic lead and proform direction in the data as a whole: $F(1,137) = 13.31$ ($p = .0004$). Pragmatic lead depresses imitation success in general—$F(1,137) = 5.57$ ($p = .0197$), –PL = .43)—but depresses backward proforms particularly: $F(1,137) = 11.20$ ($p = .001$), -PL = .59, +PL = .34. Also, as figures 20–1 and 20–2 show, a significant interaction of Branching Direction and Proform Direction characterizes the data as a whole: $F(1,137) = 56.79$ ($p = .000$). Forward direction of proforms is significantly preferred to backward in right-branching structures, and backward is preferred to forward in left-branching structures overall. The latter can be modulated by pragmatic lead so that no directionality effect characterizes the left-branching structures.

NOTES

Introduction

1. A still later treatment in the Government and Binding framework appeared in the 1991 paper "What to Focus in Sinhala" with L. Sumangala, not included here. Further modifications were suggested by the coauthor in Sumangala 1992.

Chapter 1

This paper appeared in the *South Asian Review*, 6: 51–64, which was edited by P. J. Mistry, who had also chaired the original panel. I would like to thank him and Professors H. P. Kulkarni and Satya S. Pachori, who had initiated and arranged for the panel, and the participants who offered useful comments and suggestions.

1. It must be noted here that Sinhala, like some other South Asian languages, including Tamil, is a language exhibiting diglossia; that is, it has sharply different varieties used for written and spoken purposes. The variety used in virtually all serious written materials is referred to as LITERARY SINHALA. Other varieties, including the Colloquial variety (or varieties) used in most face-to-face communication, are referred to as SPOKEN SINHALA (see Gair 1968 and De Silva 1979, especially 39ff. and references therein). The phenomena discussed in this paper hold generally for both main varieties, except where otherwise noted.

2. This development is also shared by Divehi (Maldivian), and it is thus more accurately referred to as a Sinhala–Divehi development. It is one feature that links the two languages into a single subgroup. The change from clusters of nasal + voiced stop to prenasalized stop in Sinhala appears to have occurred between the second and fourth centuries A.D. (Karunatillake 1969: 60), and therefore it is of special interest in determining the date of separation of these two languages.

3. In pronouncing loan words from Sanskrit and Pali, particularly learned borrowings on formal occasions, some speakers do attempt to render the aspirated consonants, with more or less success and consistency. This, of course, does not count for present purposes.

4. This is quite different from the use of he/his/him as a "genderless" pronoun in English, since the Sinhala general form is widely used even when the one referred to is clearly feminine, and not just in abstract situations (i.e., for unspecified gender).

5. Sinhala appears to have lost the correlative construction very early. A correlative construction with an indefinite sense—whoever does that, (he) is my enemy—is encountered in formal Sinhala, but it is restricted to that use and may be a reborrowing from Sanskrit and/ or Pali. Interestingly, the South Dravidian languages have also borrowed the Indo-Aryan correlative to different extents.

6. This final sentence was added in this reprinting, and it holds true for research right up to the present (1996), including the relevant papers in this volume.

Chapter 2

Parts of this paper were included in a paper read at the Linguistic Society of the University of Ceylon on July 8, 1965. At the time of writing, the only other attempt at setting forth a systematic overview of Colloquial Sinhala inflection and parts of speech known to me was that in De Abrew 1963. That aspect of the part-of-speech system dealing with the classification of nouns and noun modifiers in nominal phrases had also been treated in D. D. De Saram, "Nominal Phrases in Colloquial Sinhalese," Cornell University master's thesis, 1964. The major part of the research reported herein was carried out while working with G. H. Fairbanks and M. W. S. De Silva on a textbook for Colloquial Sinhala under an Office of Education grant at Cornell University, 1961–62, and during a stay in Ceylon under an Office of Education–Fulbright–Hayes research grant, 1964–65.

1. See chapters 16, 17, and 18.

2. In Gair 1963, the accusative was treated as the syntactic occurrence of a particle, and this treatment was continued in Gair 1965 in disagreement with De Abrew's (1963) treatment of it as a case. The present treatment (like Gair 1970) agrees with De Abrew.

3. The criteria for phrasal inflection are those of Hockett 1958: 212.

4. My previous analyses (1963, 1965, 1970) differ from the present one in distinguishing a set of "stem-based forms" distinct from both tense and participial forms. These are the forms given here as "nonpast only" tense forms. Nonpast tense was implicitly taken as unmarked, and these forms were considered not to have tense, since they neither were marked for past nor had past tense counterparts. However, they now appear quite clearly to be formed from the nonpast theme, and there seems no reason to treat them differently in principle from "past only" forms made from the past theme but lacking nonpast counterparts. Accordingly, they are now included under forms built on tense stems. A quite different analysis of verbal inflection is given in De Silva 1960 and another in De Abrew, 1963: passim.

Later note: The participial adjectival form was so called simply on the basis of form: it was based on the participial theme. In meaning, however, it appears to be identical with the past tense adjectival form. This has caused some misunderstanding on the part of Sinhala speakers, including some linguists, who think of it as a past form, which functionally it is. For at least some speakers, it appears, in fact, to be displacing the past tense adjectival form throughout its range (including the distribution in the following note), at least in casual speech. Also, all of these forms could, with perfect justification, be called "relativizing" forms, since their primary (but not exclusive) function is to form relative clauses, always prenominal in Sinhala.

5. Later note: There are also verbal nominals formed with any of the adjectival forms of the verb+ekə (the inanimate numeral 'one'): kərənə-ekə, adinə-ekə, teerenə-ekə, kerua-ekə kərapu-ekə, and so on. These can nominalize an entire sentence without any internal changes: miniha eekə kərənə-ekə/kərəpu-ekə (hoňdə nææ). 'The man that do-Pres-Adj-ekə/do-Participial adjective-ekə (good not)' = 'His doing/having-done that (is not good)'. These were not mentioned in the original paper because they were periphrastic, but they are more common in Colloquial speech than the gerunds, which do require genitive subjects: minihage (Gen eekə keriimə 'His (the man's) doing that.'

6. There are some cooccurrence restrictions between verb form and subject. Not unexpectedly, some imperative forms are second person only. Also the volitive and involitive optative forms are restricted to first person and nonfirst person subjects, respectively, in independent clauses. Even if this is considered agreement, however, it is minimal. Actually, the restriction of the involitive optative to nonfirst person is not absolute, and there are limited circumstances in which it may occur. See Gair, Karunatillake, and Paolillo 1987: 91.

7. Later note: Boris Volkhonskii has pointed out to me that there are other verbs of this type, including *aṅduranəwa/aṅdunənəwa* 'be acquainted with, recognize'.

8. Hockett 1958: 221.

9. The type of environment in which the *-y* is obligatory is more precisely specified in Gair 1963 and 1970, passim.

10. The term "deictic particle " is taken from De Abrew 1963.

11. Partial classifications of second person pronouns by grade, or differential status, may be found in De Silva 1960: 106 n and De Abrew 1963.

Chapter 3

Part of the work reported here was conducted under an NDEA–Fulbright–Hays grant in Ceylon in 1964–65. The help of the United States Educational Foundation in Ceylon for facilitating fieldwork there is also gratefully acknowledged. In particular, I would like especially to single out, belatedly by name, Dr. Richard Arndt, Cultural Affairs Officer, the late S. Perinpayagam, then director of USEF, and Ms. Lylee Perera, all of whom went out of their way to facilitate research for me and other scholars. I have profited by discussions with several colleagues, but particular thanks are due to Mr. W. S. Karunatillake, not only for furnishing and checking many of the examples but also for stimulating discussion and comment. Any errors of fact and interpretation, however, are mine.

1. "Participant," as used here, should be taken most simply as roughly equivalent to the subject of an English nonpassive or the object of "by" in a passive sentence. In Sinhala, this involves a number of grammatical functions, depending upon the type of sentence, as will become apparent. Note that "speaker" and "participant" are separate notions and are the same only for the first person.

2. Later note: The terms A, P, and C were introduced in Gair 1963 and 1970 to refer to verb types. While these terms were clearly derived from the "Active," "Passive," and "Causative" designations used in some earlier works, they were intended simply to designate the presence or absence of the relevant morphemes. Despite the obvious interactions that will form part of the discussion here, they were not intended to equate with the syntactic distribution of the forms, especially in view of some of the mismatches that will also be referred to subsequently. Limiting them in that way was, in fact, the intention in using only the single capital letters. Unfortunately, that appears to have contributed to some misunderstandings, particularly when P was taken literally to indicate "passive." See also note 4.

3. Later note: The original paper had *kiuna* [=*kiyuna*], but *kiyəwuna* appears, on the basis of later work, to be the actually occurring form here. The difference is, in any case, only morphophonemic relating to the P forms of A verbs ending in -yə.

4. Later note: The use of "passive" to characterize this type was carried over from Gair 1963 and 1970 and has occasioned some criticism in subsequent work by others who have argued that Colloquial Sinhala lacked a syntactic passive (see particularly Gunasinghe 1978, 1985). In those earlier works and the one here, I had used "passive" simply as a label for an identifiable clause type, for lack of a better one, and had not intended to identify that type directly with the English passive. The description in Gair 1963 and 1970, in fact made it quite clear that it had a special character, and it was, as here, clearly considered an "impersonal"

type. Thus the apparent dispute is, to a great extent, simply terminological, and in hindsight, it might have been better to have used some other term for the type and to have clearly labeled the *atin* constituent as "involitive or accidental agent" rather than "agentive constituent." Although that would have been awkward at best, it would have been descriptively apt, as the paper here attempts to show. Note also that the chapter on AGR and diglossia clearly agrees with Gunasinghe's statement (1985: 115): "that Colloquial Sinhala has no derived passive structure is well supported."

5. Later note: The verb *lissənəwa* is in apparently free variation with *lissenəwa* in this construction, but it is an A verb in form. This furnishes an example of one kind illustrating the lack of a full match between the morphological (A, P, or C) composition of verbs and their syntactic behavior.

6. As noted earlier, some speakers may not use the accusative here, but the type is still distinct even though not as clearly marked.

7. The motivations for analyzing such sentences with inanimate nominals as inactive are discussed under the latter heading in Gair 1970.

8. It is possible, and perhaps simplest from a synchronic grammatical point of view, to analyze *gæhenəwa* 'shiver, start' as a separate P verb without corresponding A or C verbs. However, this does not affect the argument here, since by either analysis we have isolated *gæhenəwa* 'shiver' sentences as semantically distinct.

9. Some minor types, some of which may have other kinds of forms as predicators, are left out of consideration here. For them, see Gair 1963 and 1970.

10. It must be stressed that *innəwa* as 'stay, remain' must be distinguished here from *innəwa* as 'be', which pairs off with *tiyenəwa*, since in the former function it is clearly active and purposive. Similarly, *tiyenəwa* as a main verb 'be' must be distinguished from *tiyenəwa* as an auxiliary in the perfect (*gihilla tiyenəwa* 'has gone', etc.), since the restriction to animate nominals does not apply in the latter function.

11. Their special semantic characteristics actually reinforce their grammatical distinctiveness from other adjectives, most noticeably the freedom with which they enter into transformations resulting in allocative sentences with infinitives and their behavior with relation to the assertion marker -Y. See Gair 1970.

12. This is in keeping also with the terms "volitive" and "involitive optative" to designate these forms, which we have used elsewhere, as in Gair 1963, 1967 and 1970.

Chapter 4

1. The {P} used to designate the involitive morpheme, while it was used to maintain some continuity with earlier work such as De Silva 1960 in which it was referred to as "passive," was intended essentially as an arbitrary tag. However, it occasioned some mild misunderstanding by others later, and in retrospect, it might have been better to have used the symbol *I* for "involitive."

2. Thus, according to Chomsky 1958 (which, however, only became available in 1962, when CSCS was essentially complete): "The structure is not given by the phrase structure rules, because the sentence is a transform. The question is difficult. There are some possible answers, but it seems to me that all answers I have seen so far are ad hoc, and eventually end up by producing some very un-English sentences sooner or later. I think there is some important insight that is still lacking" (p. 158). The problem was naturally compounded in Sinhala, given the characteristics mentioned, and it was solved in an essentially ad hoc way by specifying the structures of the output as well as the input of transformations. In later versions of generative theory, of course, the problem disappeared, or was at least in part shifted to other grounds, by eliminating transformations of the earlier kind, leaving only "Move α with at-

tendant changes in the treatment of phrase structure, and by invoking constraints on both movement and phrase structure.

3. Interestingly, the idea that at least some languages exhibited a flat structure, for reasons that were at least in part those outlined here, emerged later in discussions of X* or XP* languages (Hale 1978, 1981, and 1983) and in treatments of other languages of a type similar to Sinhala, such as Malayalam in Mohanan 1992. It was also, at least in principle, allowed by a configuration parameter and by the linked α/β representation proposal in Chomsky 1981 subsequently employed in Chapter 5, "Nonconfigurationality, Movement, and Sinhala Focus." In fact, the issue has not died; thus Inman (1993) argued for a flat structure for Sinhala contra Sumangala 1992. In any event, it is certain that the proposals that have been advanced so as to allow a hierarchical X-bar analysis to be extended to languages exhibiting the characteristics at issue as for the more rigidly "configurational' ones like English have been an important component in the development of current syntactic theory and have contributed significantly to its enrichment.

4. Later work by others on some of the phenomena treated in CSCS includes, among others, Fernando 1973, Gunasinghe 1978 and 1985, Sumangala 1992, and Inman 1993, all of which contain further references and some critiques of the treatment in CSCS.

Chapter 5

I must thank W. S. Karunatillake and Milan Rodrigo for data, judgments, and discussion; Barbara Lust, Wayne Harbert, and John Bowers for comments and discussion; and those present at the LAGB meeting for comments and questions, particularly Liliane Haegeman and Neil Smith. Errors and misunderstandings, as usual, are my own.

1. This problem holds in both nonconfigurational languages and in configurational languages (e.g., Chinese) where "moved" elements appear in situ (Huang 1982).

2. I am dealing with focus here only as a specifically syntactic phenomenon, not with its semantic aspects. In this respect, the treatment of Sinhala focus represented here fits into a research paradigm such as represented by Horvath (1981 [1985]) and Kiss (1981) for Hungarian and Ortiz de Urbina (1983) for Basque.

3. Not unexpectedly, some emphasis-like differences characterize example (1) and the sentences in (2). There are also restrictions on possible orders (not yet sufficiently studied) for Sinhala (as there are for Warlpiri, Hale 1979, 1981). It seems clear, however, that Sinhala is, in terms of possible orders, less configurational than Japanese (which is taken by Hale to be a typical X-bar language) or than Malayalam, as described by Mohanan (1981, 1983), although it may be more configurational than Warlpiri.

4. In examples (8) and (9), the single superscript "f" here indicates that there is no focus external to the verb. All root sentences do have a focus, as will be apparent later from the possibility of focus-marking forms occurring in both neutral and focused sentences. The domain of focus in neutral sentences like 8 may be any constituent stretch including the verb, up to S.

5. This contrasts with languages such as Tamil, in which constituents can be questioned without triggering the focused form of the verb, as in

cuntaramaa neettu   cennekki   poonaaru
Sundaram-Q yesterday Madras-DAT   go-PAST-3sg(Hon)
'Was it Sundaram who went to Madras yesterday?' (Asher 1982: 98).

6. Though examples (21) through (25) may involve subtle differences in something like emphasis, they all have the same focus-presupposition structure. In all, the focus will receive highest pitch.

7. In this respect it differs from Malayalam clefting (as described by Mohanan 1983), which bears a close surface resemblance to it. Thus the analysis offered by Mohanan for Malayalam sentences like (ii) paralleling Sinhala (i), according to which (ii) is not a cleft, but an existential sentence with relative expression as subject, is not possible in Sinhala.

(i) *amma   horəkankerua   kiyəla   lamea   kiwwe^f   mee* potə^f.
    mother   stole   that-COMP   child   said-E   this book
    'It is this book that the child said the mother stole.'

(ii) *amma   moosticcu   ennə kutti   paran–n–ata ii   pustakam aanə.*
     mother   stole   that child   said-it   this book   is
     'This is the book that the child said the mother stole.'

8. Example (38) is actually ambiguous. *Siripaaləṭə* could be the indirect object of *kiwwe* with the Ø giving arbitrary reference and with the reading, "Karu told Siripala that Gunapala hit someone," but this reading is irrelevant here.

There is also a possible analysis of these sentences that does not involve double focusing. The entire lower S may be focused, and it may also be focused within itself. The lower focus has then been rightward placed, following from free order possibilities of Sinhala. Other orders, including one with the focus in its original position within the lower clause are possible, as shown by (i), with bracketing in (ii):

(i) *Gunəpaalə gæhue siripaaləṭə tamay/də kiyəla Karu kiwwe.*

(ii) [$_{S1}$ [$_{S2}$ *gunəpaalə   gæhue^f   siripaaləṭə^f   tamay/də*]$^F_{S2}$ *kiyəla   karu*
                         Gunapala   hit-PAST-E   Siripala-DAT   EMPH/Q   Karu   say-
     kiwwe^F]$_{S1}$
     PAST-E

This is the analysis that I presented in an earlier conference paper on focus extraction, based on the meaning suggested by the English translation but also dictated by the fact that the model I was contemplating could not allow *both* focusing of a lower element within its own and a higher clause—i.e., double focusing—and focusing directly into a higher clause from a lower since there was only one node through which movement can take place, and movement was cyclic. The present analysis, however, can accommodate both, and in fact both meanings do appear to be possible, though the meaning difference is understandably subtle.

9. Interestingly, quantifier WH-forms do not have this semiobligatory focusing but behave like other (non-WH) constituents:

pot   kiiyak   gatta   də?
books how-many-INDEF buy-PAST Q
'How many books did you buy'
versus
pot   kiiyak   də gatte
books how-many-INDEF Q buy-PAST-E
'How many books was it that you bought?'

The lack of WH movement stated here was intended to relate to syntactic movement. I was in fact assuming LF movement of WH, including WH forms that were in situ, whether blocked by subjacency or not, under the assumption that LF movement was not subject to subjacency as in Huang 1982. That was in fact the motivation for taking focus movement to be syntactic and not LF movement, since those blocked forms would indeed have to move at LF—see the discussion of examples (37) through (40). For a full discussion of this problem, see Sumangala (1992), who argues for essentially that position and assumes an LF focus movement as well, but one distinct from syntactic focus movement, though he disagrees with some of the conclusions here, and his analysis differs in detail, being couched in a later theoretical framework.

10. We could try the approach of reducing subjacency to the Empty Category Principle (ECP) along the lines of Kayne 1981, but this runs into serious problems. See, for example, Huang 1982. This would also require, as will become obvious later, establishing levels within LF so that subjacency cum ECP applied in one level and FOCUS or WH raising in a second level.

11. β structure is sometimes referred to in Chomsky 1992 as "lexical structure" (LS). It is not clear whether he means the identification between β structure and lexical structure to be complete. He does refer to his examples 11–13 on page 131, however, as representing β structure (p. 132), which he has earlier described as "lexical structure" representations. Mohanan 1982, also following Chomsky, has used LS for essentially the same type of representation as β representation. Hale, in his subsequent 1983 paper, uses LS in a way closer to Bresnan's "functional structure." Since it is not clear that all of the characteristics required of β structure in this paper—e.g., COMP and FOCUS nodes, as well as other nodes not strictly subcategorized—can be projected in a straightforward manner from the lexicon, I will use the β structure designation here in a manner somewhat autonomous from lexicon.

12. Rather than as the "one's" and "two's" of Relational Grammar or the "subject" and "object" of Lexical–Functional Grammar.

13. For example, in the application of the case filter, Chomsky writes (1981: 130), "By assumption, NP cannot be assigned a case within VP since *rare* absorbs case."

14. Note that this assumption conflicts with Chomsky's statement that "the configurations that determine GF's are not represented in the syntax in the X-bar system in D or S structures in Japanese" and, by extension, in nonconfigurational languages generally. I maintain this view only for α structure.

I set aside here the question of whether β structure involves only dominance or also linearity, such as that involved in head direction. It seems not unlikely that such linearity may be specified in one or both α and β structures in nonconfigurational languages. Thus a language like Japanese, which appears very strongly "right-headed" on the surface, may specify head direction in α structure, with a schema such as the W*X suggested by Chomsky or X-bar*X suggested by Hale. Latin, with much freer surface word order, may specify this type of linearity in β structure. For reasons too complex to go into here, Sinhala may be in between Japanese and Latin, with linearity specified in β structure but reflected in a structure in a category-specific way. Alternatively, even the strong right-headedness of Japanese may be represented in β structure, with constraints on the (α, β) mapping.

15. For Hungarian, Horvath (1981[1985]) has proposed a focus position under V-bar, preceding V and governed by it. Ortiz de Urbina (1983) has suggested a similar position for Basque, an SOV language resembling Sinhala in important respects. For Sinhala, however, this does not appear to be the case. The position right of the verb under V-bar in Sinhala seems clearly to be the proper location for the negative *næə* and perhaps for some other AUX-like forms. This *næə* not only cooccurs with focus, but it also takes the -E affix, in the form *nætte*, as in:

mamə kəranne nætte ee   wædə.
I   do-E   not-E   that   work
'It's that work that I don't do.'

(The -E affix on the verb 'do' here is determined by the following *næə*, and it appears whether or not focusing takes place. For details, see De Abrew 1980).

16. Reinhart (1981) adopts a similar configuration for her two COMP structures in Hebrew for the same reason. The two differ primarily in that her "escape hatch" COMP is

"inside" and ours "outside" the other node dominated directly by S-bar. This order difference is largely a reflection of the different surface orders of complementizers and WH or focused forms in the two languages.

17. We leave open the question of whether a form moved into FOC position is left-adjoined to a base-generated focus marker or whether FOC has a branching character. In any event, the entire contents of the FOC position must be moved on subsequent moves to higher Ss. Also, the proper treatment of "neutral" sentences, which may have focus-marking forms following the verb or other predicator (but naturally, no -E affix) is not dealt with here. Neutral sentences might be accommodated by allowing an entire S, or perhaps VP, to move into FOC, requiring no special rule. It appears that entire focused (embedded) Ss, at least, like any other focused constituent, may move upwards, suggesting that such a possibility is necessary. The lack of -E marking on verbs of neutral Ss followed by focus markers like *də* 'question' or *yi* or *tamay* 'emphatic' would follow without further specification, since the verb would be internal to FOC, so that the "external focus" condition on that affix would not be met. The scope of focus in LF in such Ss would also follow in straightforward fashion.

18. It will also be necessary to block movement to COMP of the highest (root) S, but that would of course be necessary for other constituents, as well. What is required, of course, is some sort of requirement that COMP may only be occupied by forms so designated in the lexicon or by traces.

19. One reason for this assumption is that it is the possibility, referred to earlier, of focusing some constituents within NPs, notably genitive attributes. This would not be possible if S rather than S-bar was the bounding node, given our assumption that FOC is dominated by S-bar. Even if the tree in Figure 5–3 were changed to have FOC dominated by S rather than S-bar, so that movement from NP to FOC would not cross S, unbounded focusing of such constituents would be blocked, but this does not appear to be the case.

20. Note that this is also consistent with Chomsky's statement, quoted earlier, that α and β are identical in languages like English, since the latter is a direct projection of the former.

Chapter 6

1. Interestingly, this represents approximately the same range of singular NPs that take plural agreement in British (but not American) English; cf. "*The government are considering. . . .*"

2. For many speakers, in fact, either nominative or instrumental variants are acceptable in sentences like (1d), though instrumental may be preferred.

3. The qualification "animate" is repeated for pronouns here to avoid misunderstanding by those familiar with other South Asian languages. It is not the case in Sinhala that the accusative marker appears normally on animate nouns and all pronouns, animate or inanimate, in direct object position, as is the case, for example with Hindi *ko* (setting aside the conditions of specificity that apply to the latter).

4. Although the boundaries are not yet clear, these *wə*-less varieties appear to include Southern dialects ranging at least from Ambalangoda to Matara. People from those areas commonly acquire the form when migrating to the western (Colombo) region, as, for example, when they enter universities there.

5. For details see Gair 1968, 1985, and De Silva 1979 and references therein.

6. There is an interesting problem here, however. The P-morpheme processes that we discuss next can apply in a straightforward way to causatives of intransitives, as if they were base transitives, and even to "true" causatives, (with expressed causees) from transitive bases. If we consider those processes to be lexical not syntactic, as we must for reasons given below,

it is difficult to see how causativization could be a syntactic process, as claimed, for example, in Baker 1988, since clearly lexical processes would operate on its output.

7. One might attempt to link *teerenəwa* 'understand' to *toorənəwa* 'explain', but synchronically the link is tenuous at best.

8. In addition, there are verbs for which the A and P forms are simple alternants, such as *lissənəwa* 'slip', which has the same range of occurrence and case frame as the P verb *lissenəwa*. Both take accusative subjects: *maawə lisseewi/lissaawi* 'IACC might slip.'

9. Most of these do, however, have causatives, which act as transitive or ditransitive verbs, but that is not relevant here. For details, see Gair 1970.

10. In particular, embedding sentences with volitional subjects in *atiŋ* sentences is difficult, apparently for pragmatic reasons having to do with clash in volitionality. On the other hand, attempting to embed any *atiŋ* sentence faces other obvious difficulties. If the presumed *atiŋ* phrase is a controlled empty category, one cannot be sure that the embedded S is not in fact one of another involitive type with a differently marked NP, since the remainder of the sentence would be identical. Some interesting work is being carried out in this regard by Michael Inman (Inman 1988, 1993), and the results so far seem to indicate that the *atiŋ* phrases are less subject-like than the dative ones with regard to such properties as control of empty categories.

11. See Gair 1970 for *atiŋ* examples; the instrumental "passive" type involves similar problems. Although it seems to require a potential matching sentence with a volitive agent, there may not be a straightforward A–P morphological relation in the verbs. For many speakers, for example, the natural sentence equivalent for (13a) would use the P verb *idenəwa*, which has also the general sense 'ripen, mature', instead of *hædenəwa*. However, there is no counterpart A verb **udənəwa* or **idənəwa* in either sense, and the usual counterpart would be *uyənəwa* 'cook'. One could, somewhat artificially, use a "cooked up" P-verb *iyəwenəwa*, but that would not, of course, solve the problem of the derivation of *idenəwa*.

12. These sentences involve a number of interesting questions concerning the content and possible combinatory possibilities of θ-roles that cannot be dealt with here. For example, the content of the θ-role of the "accidental agent" expressed by *atiŋ* phrases does not accord neatly with any of the proposals for such content that I am aware of. The closest may be instrument, but such sentences do not completely exclude a true instrument, as in *maŋ atiŋ lanuwə pihiyeŋ kapuna* 'I-*atiŋ* string knife-INSTR cut-P = 'I accidentally cut the string with the knife' (while using the knife volitively, perhaps for something else).' A complete theta theory would, of course, somehow have to account satisfactorily for the variations in volitionality and potential control of action exhibited in the range of forms in (14). See also Gair 1971 for further examples and considerations.

Note: In the version that appeared earlier, I neglected to point out that although the data reported in (14) is authentic, and certainly possible for some speakers (L. Sumangala, personal communication), it might be possible that others find (14b) strange, using *atiŋ* only where there is an affected, generally physical, object (as in 'The glass got broken'). Although *atiŋ* is etymologically the instrumental of *atə* 'hand', it is now clearly a distinct form with a distinct function, as pointed out in Gair 1970, since in many if not most contexts, no hand is involved. However, there may be a change still in progress here, such that an observed difference between those who have the "physical context" restriction and those who do not may reflect a further widening of the semantics of the form for the latter, whereas the former retain some of the physicalness that the "hand" etymology would clearly imply. In any event, the argument here is not affected.

13. In this context, it should be noted that even setting aside questions of suppletion, etc., one cannot attribute to the the P-morpheme the characteristics that have been claimed for it in recent work, whether "absorption" of case/θ-role or itself being assigned a θ-role.

See Baker 1988 for discussion and further references. Given the range of sentence types in which the P-morpheme functions and the degree of irregularity involved, this is clearly not an option, unless one argues for homonymity of that morpheme, and it is difficult to see how that could be accomplished without vicious circularity.

14. See Gair 1971 for an attempt to accomplish essentially this task, though couched within a quite different syntactic framework.

15. This would, of course, be the case if Sinhala was in fact ergative, as Gunasinghe suggests.

16. Cf. Williams's rule (1981: 87): "If there is an Actor, it must be external for V."

17. A dative subject with *dannəwa* also characterizes the Sinhala of some native speakers of Tamil, who apparently model it on Tamil *teriyum,* but it is also found in the speech of some monolingual speakers of Sinhala.

18. This is not true of Literary Sinhala, in which the unmarked case is the accusative. See Gair 1968 and 1992 and Gair and Wali 1988. See also chapter 18, "Syntactic Theory, AGR, and Sinhala Diglossia," this volume.

19. This is not true of nonverbal sentences (see below).

20. In responding to a question by Peggy Speas, I apparently failed to grasp its implications, and hence my response was not entirely clear. The problem that she raised was that if only accusative can be assigned under adjacency, then it can reasonably be argued to be a structural case. However, not only can dative also be assigned there in both transitive and intransitive structures, but also nominative can in fact so occur, in active intransitive structures. If the tree structures and lexical arrays here are retained, then, the restriction is that nominative cannot be assigned under adjacency if another argument is present, and the association of nominative with external argument, which I did invoke, would by itself account for this restriction. The interesting implication of this proposal is that the Sinhala cases are assigned lexically, but they are subject to structural conditions on their positions of occurrence. In addition, those positions for accusative and nominative resemble, in the unmarked case, those relating to structural case assignment in straightforward nominative–accusative languages. In Sinhala, however, those positions also allow a range of other cases, which is, of course, the fundamental problem that this paper attempted to address.

21. Possibly, some special provision must be made for "weather verbs" (see Gair 1970) if they do not in fact have pleonastic subjects.

22. For an argument that this does not account for similar phenomena in Hindi, however, see Davison (1988).

23. Examples for first person with -*wi* are simple to find, as for example *maawə wæṭeewi'* I might fall.' Examples for -*nnaŋ* are rare, but some are provided by Reynolds (1980: 111). What appears to be involved here is the general avoidance in Sinhala of attributing volition to others, which extends well beyond this case but explains, for example, why many speakers will judge *mahatteaṭə yannə oonə* 'The gentleman wants to go' as bad but *mahatteaṭə yannə oonə lu.* 'It seems (or 'is said') that the gentleman wants to go' as perfectly acceptable.

24. Including the phonologically unrealized AGR that has been claimed elsewhere for Hindi (Gair and Wali 1989).

25. We can also add Italian to this list if we can assume that *piacere* psych-verb sentences are the essential equivalent of "quirky case" (Belletti and Rizzi 1988). The situation is complicated in Icelandic by the fact that while dative-subject sentences preclude anything but nominative objects, and such objects occur only with dative subjects (Andrews 1982: 472), there are apparently double accusative sentences, judging from the range of examples given (Andrews 1982: 461).

26. Or, interestingly, in the nearby Dravidian language Tamil—see Gair, Suseendirarajah, and Karunatillake 1978 and Asher 1982. Though its range of subject cases is less than Sinhala's,

Tamil does allow accusative objects with dative-subject verbs. It also, however, has far from minimal verbal agreement in person, number, and gender. Thus the element responsible for nominative assignment, either exclusively to subject or to other positions, cannot be associated with the simple presence of "strong" phonologically realized agreement. Similarly, the closely related (to Tamil) Malayalam does not appear to differ in the relevant object case-marking features but does lack agreement. This is consistent with our dissociation of such phonological agreement from abstract AGR, as in the papers cited, and requires further investigation in languages such as Tamil and Malayalam.

27. It has also been suggested (Gair and Wali 1988) that the existence in Sinhala of null subjects of finite sentences with arbitrary reference as in *e mee pætte huñgak wii wawənəwa pro* this area much rice grow (TRANS)-PRES' = 'A lot of rice is grown in this area'/ 'They grow a lot of rice in this area' follows from the lack of AGR. This is consistent with the "weak INFL" analysis here, since INFL does not have either nominative case or person–number features to discharge.

28. These constructions must be distinguished from *puluwaŋ* 'can' sentences with dative experiencers, such as *maʈə yannə puluwaŋ* I go-INF can = 'I can go.' The difference is established by control properties, as well as case marking and the semantics of the constructions, but it is not necessary to pursue that here.

29. Such a structural case cannot, however, be assigned by INFL if there is an S-structure or PF adjacency requirement for such cases (Baker 1988; Chomsky 1986), since in the unmarked SOV order, all other arguments intervene. This would preclude structural nominative's being assigned in INFL in any SOV verb and INFL-final language, which is obviously too strong, so that we assume that no such adjacency requirement holds here, consistent with the "strong case" character of Sinhala.

30. This approach was suggested to me by Wayne Harbert. See the introductory note to this chapter.

31. See Fukui 1986, which argues against SSC effects in a similar structure in Japanese, for relevant arguments.

32. This is a slight simplification, since P morphemes may also occur with morphologically complex and even compound stems (see note 6), but that is not of importance here.

33. The impossibility of purpose clauses in such sentences as an indication of the lack of an implicit agent was pointed out to me by L. Sumangala.

34. This is assuming that we understand Williams's rule correctly, which may not be the case. Although the statement of it appears clear enough, it is difficult to follow some of the examples. In dealing with the French middle, he states it as an internalization rule—i.e. *vend* (A, Th) > *vend* (A, Th). However, it is not simple to follow what happens to the argument represented by Th, especially since he says in a note (p. 113 n 2), that "in the middle there is only one thematic position, the object position," which suggests that an argument has been lost somewhere. In any event, the Sinhala case does appear to afford a clear example of the suppression of an argument.

35. I am indebted here, as I so often am, to W. S. Karunatillake for pointing out these facts.

Chapter 7

This paper is a revised and expanded version of one given at SALA (South Asia Languages Analysis) at Champaign–Urbana in May 1986, and it appeared in the *Cornell Working Papers in Linguistics 8,* Fall 1988 (Special issue on South Asian Linguistics), pp. 39–77. We wish to thank many people for discussion, examples, and grammaticality judgments, particularly Wayne Harbert, W. S. Karunatillake, Barbara Lust, Milan Rodrigo, Lelwala Sumangala, and

Veneeta Srivastav. We also thank those who offered comments at the initial presentation, especially Hans Hock and Sanford Steever. We are also grateful for the constructive comments made by the reviewer for the *Cornell Working Papers*.

1. What is said in this paper is intended to apply only to Spoken Sinhala and cannot be projected directly onto the Literary variety, which is used for virtually all written materials. Sinhala is a diglossic language, and the Literary variety differs sharply in very fundamental respects from that variety generally used in face-to-face communication, at whatever level of formality. For further particulars, see Gair 1968, 1986a, and De Silva 1979, which includes an extensive bibliography.

2. Here we deal only with predicates headed by members of the major categories, although adverbial predicates are dealt with glancingly. There are also sentences with numeral phrases (Gair 1970: 101ff.), which pose special problems and are not considered here.

3. This usage is fundamentally consistent with the use of that term in Gair 1970, although there a flat structure was assumed for S in Sinhala, an assumption not carried into this chapter.

4. For the free word order and nonconfigurational properties of Sinhala, see especially De Abrew 1981 and Gair 1983b.

5. Some optative and imperative forms may appear to constitute minor exceptions by showing a kind of agreement, but this is not "standard" subject–verb agreement and appears to be explainable on semantic and pragmatic grounds. See Gair 1970, 1976, Paolillo 1986.

6. Focused (sometimes called emphatic) sentences are dealt with in some detail in Gair 1970, Fernando 1973, and Gair 1983b, 1986a (the second of which also gives a historical account).

7. It is not yet clear whether the affixes related to focus belong here, nor is it clear whether a rule such as this is called for, with *aux* represented by auxiliary verbs or other forms. For arguments that Colloquial Sinhala lacks AGR, see Gair and Wali 1988; also Gair 1992a and chapter 8.

8. As we will see, there is a change in the form of adjectives. Also, there is a class of forms called QUASIVERBS (Gair 1970) that do not have tense but do have distinct Basic and Emphatic forms. These include *æti* 'might(be)' and the negator *næ̃æ*.

Boris Volkhonskii has pointed out to me (1994) that in NP NP sentences, adverbs cannot apparently be clefted (i.e. *sinhəya vanee rajjuruwo* 'lion forest-LOC king' = 'The lion is king in the forest' but not **sinhəya rajjuruwo vanee tamay* 'lion king forest-emphatic', though the subject can, as in *vanee rajjuruwo sinhəya tamay* 'forest-LOC king lion-emphatic' = 'it is the lion who is king of the forest' and in the examples here. Actually, the data is not entirely clear here, since at least some speakers allow such sentences with an contrastive focus (i.e., "only") reading. However, if this does prove to reflect a general constraint, it constitutes a difference from verbal predicator types (and apparently adjectival ones as well).

One possibility that might be pursued here is that this relates to the content of INFL, under a more recent analysis, as in Gair and Sumangala 1991, by which the emphatic (focus) affix on verbs, and presumably the *-yi* on adjectives (or its absence) is in (a segment of) INFL, and the focused element is at some stage in a SPEC–head relationship with it. This would connect the limitations on focusing in NP NP sentences with the absence of any clefting (-EMPH) inflection on nominals. Thus, if this analysis proves plausible, it might constitute additional evidence against the "hidden verb" analysis for equational sentences rejected here, if it could be established that (other) phonologically unrealized verbs could take a form that could license a clefted focus. Such phonologically unrealized verbs might be a possible analysis for the examples in (21) through (25) here that have foci negated by *nemey* but no overt verbs. Such sentences appear to be restricted to having motion/goal or existential/location senses, and one might consider that they, and their noncleft counterparts, did indeed include phonologically unrealized (or ellipsed) forms of *innəwa/tiyenəwa* 'exist' or *yanəwa* 'go', which would always be recoverable from context. We did, in fact, consider an analysis along those lines for such sentences but did not include it in this chapter. At present, however, I can only offer these proposals for nominal and postpositional sentences as interesting hypotheses requiring further investigations (JWG).

9. Whether this -*yi* is to be identified with the homonymous focus-marking -*yi* will not be considered here, but they do have distinct ranges of functions.

10. See De Abrew (1981) for a detailed explanation of the various negation strategies available in Sinhala.

11. In fact, *næ̃æ* does not replace *tiyenəwa* or *innəwa* when they occur in the sense of 'remain' or 'reside, live, stay'; when they are used in these senses, *næ̃æ* occurs following them, as with other verbs. This is more common, understandably, with *innəwa* than it is with *tiyenəwa*.

12. See De Abrew 1981 for details on the separability of *næ̃æ* from the verb.

13. Whether there is movement to FOC in this case is a special problem for which there is yet no compelling solution and that we will consequently not discuss here. What is important here is that there is no difference between the sentences headed by different categories in this regard.

14. One class of sentences, NEGATIVE INDEFINITE SENTENCES, poses a special problem since these sentences are exceptional in terms of both case marking and negation. An example is *mee kæ̃æmə kisimə rasak næ̃æ* 'this food at-all taste-INDEF *næ̃æ* = 'This food isn't tasty at all.' These constitute a special case not dealt with here. For discussion, see Gair 1970, Perera 1976, De Abrew 1981. A still different analysis is suggested in Paolillo 1986.

15. The semantics of these sentences seem to us to lend support to this view, since they are compatible with either the partial or whole sentence focused reading mentioned for verbal and adjectival sentences with *nemey*. De Abrew (1980: 61), however, claims that these NP+NP *nemey* sentences are "neutral." The judgments here are understandably slippery, but syntactically the solution suggested here clearly appears to be consistent with all of the data.

16. Example (22b) is in fact possible, but not with the relevant structure. Rather, it represents a nonfocused sentence with scrambled or "front shifted" *næ̃æ*, a possibility that also exists for verbal sentences. The difference in structure also corresponds to a difference in interpretation, and the reading in which (25b) is ungrammatical is the one in which *meese uḍə* 'on the table' is outside the scope of the negation—i.e., in which there is a presupposition of the existence of something on the table, and the negation applies only to the suggested identity of that item. The reading in (24b) is possible for (25b), where the identity is presupposed, and its suggested location is negated. Either *næ̃æ* or the constituent *meese uḍə* in this reading has been scrambled, and neither the PP nor the NP subject are focused. See De Abrew 1981 for further details on the scrambling of *næ̃æ*.

17. There are other postpositional and adverbial sentences that do not take *næ̃æ* but always take *nemey*. These do not have existential readings and have all the characteristics of focused sentences. Their analysis would take us too far afield here, but a number of interesting problems are involved. See De Abrew 1981 for one promising analysis, carried forth by Paolillo 1986.

18. For verbless sentences, there are no distinct tense forms, as we would expect. However, all verbless sentences may have past, present, or future time reference when an appropriate time adverb is employed. Thus, verbless sentences are indeed tenseless, though this must be distinguished from time reference. See Paolillo 1986 for further details.

19. In Literary Sinhala, the equivalent relativized expression, with *wenawā* functioning as a 'be' copula, is fine. It also appears that some speakers can have that sense for sentences

like (31b), which appears to be an importation of the Literary form, and it will be interesting to watch whether this will become a more widespread variant in the Colloquial language.

20. Colloquial Sinhala also has accusative subject verbs, always intransitive, as in the example below:

> *maawə bimə wæṭeewi*
> I-ACC ground fall-OPTATIVE
> "I might fall down'.

These have led Gunasinghe (1985) to claim that Sinhala has ergative properties. While a number of interesting issues are involved here, we do not consider such verbs in the present context. Though they might give further evidence for case assignment, it is also possible that they are "unaccusative" or "ergative" verbs (Perlmutter 1978; Burzio 1986), in which event case assignment would still be involved, but initially within VP. (The accusative marker could also be considered an "inherent" case marker, as in Belletti 1988). Lexical properties would still be a factor, however, since not all intransitives behave in this way. [In this connection, see chapter 6.]

21. Although there is an obvious connection between participant role and θ-marking, the specific case is not predictable on that basis alone for verbs, nouns, or adjectives. Perception and "knowledge" verbs such as *teerenəwa* 'understand' and *peenəwa* 'see, be visible' take dative subjects, but *dannəwa* 'know' does not (although it does in some dialects, and there is no reason for thinking that the dialect distinction is a function of different semantics). Similarly, many adjectives such as *keenti* 'angry' take dative, but *santoosə*' pleased' does not. One could always construct a semantic difference for such examples on a case-by-case basis, but finding independent justification for it is difficult, to say the least. For the general connection among case, verb marking, and volitionality, see Gair 1976b, 1971, and 1991b.

22. These were described first in Gair, Karunatillake, and Paolillo 1987 as "activity-equational sentences" and treated under the same name in Paolillo 1986.

23. One might hold that the experiencer arguments originate within the predicative NP or AP and thus that they are not external arguments but bind a trace in an internal argument position (cf. Williams 1981: 92ff.). One could then attempt to extend this to the Agent ones in a mechanical manner, but this would not only be intuitively quite unconvincing, it would also overlook the fact that nouns do not subcategorize for direct case Agent nouns within NP, except, circularly, here if that tack were taken.

Later note: Actually, though dismissed here, a proposal of this kind becomes more appealing under an analysis, as in chapter 6, that generates all arguments within VP (extended to PredP for the sentences here) and has them move to SPEC IP. Extending such an analysis to nonverbal sentences would further unify the types and thus is an approach worth pursuing further. [JWG]

24. A general descriptive account of some facts relating to these characteristics may be found in Gair 1971.

Chapter 8

This paper appeared in a marginally different form in B. Lakshmi Bai and B. Ramakrishna Reddy, eds., *Studies in Dravidian and General Linguistics: A Festschrift for Bh. Krishnamurti*, Osmania University Publications in Linguistics 6, Hyderabad, 1991. In writing it, I profited particularly from discussions with W. S. Karunatillake, John Paolillo, and Barbara Lust. I also wish to thank Milan Rodrigo and Nandana Karunanayaka for checking and supplying data. Errors of fact and interpretation are, of course, my own.

1. In current Colloquial Sinhala, the forms *mææ* and *ææ*, have a derogatory tone, and the forms of the *meyaa* set are used instead, without gender distinction.

2. This distinction remains in Jaffna (Sri Lanka) Tamil, but it appears to have been lost in most, if not all, dialects of mainland Tamil, with the loss of the *u-* member. For details and examples, see the relevant sections of Gair, Susendiraraja, and Karunatillake 1978.

3. It is difficult to say from the descriptions given whether any of the four-term systems listed by Anderson and Keenan are in fact like Sinhala, since their sources did not necessarily look for the same things. Thus, the fourth member in languages like Sre (p. 287), described in terms of (non)-visibility, "remote, out of sight (either socially or temporally)" could well turn out, if looked at in that way, to resemble Sinhala *e-* forms. Certainly, the occurrence of such systems elsewhere should not be surprising, since there are other systems that integrate a category of "previous mention" (e.g., Hausa; see Anderson and Keenan 1985: 289).

4. Examples (1) and (2) are from Fairbanks, Gair, and De Silva 1981, part 1. It should be mentioned here that Sinhala is a diglossic language and that this chapter deals with Colloquial Sinhala only. Whether the same observations hold true in the Literary variety remains to be investigated.

5. Anderson and Keenan state that "in most systems . . . the intermediate term of the deictic series is often a general anaphoric element" (1985: 287). It is difficult to say how far this holds, however, since they give exceptions (i.e., Sre), and in Japanese, at any rate, the statement that such is the case seems certainly not to be so (see, for example, Kuno 1973; Hinds 1973; Kamio 1979; among others). Either way, this does not affect the analysis here.

6. There is one very limited exception to this statement. The form *ehaa*, 'that way (direction)', which pairs with *mehaa* 'this way (direction)', is used in an immediate spatial context, as in *ehaaʈə yannə* 'go that way (away)'. I have simply treated this set as exceptional and eliminated it from the discussion, since it is unique in this regard. Surprisingly, Fernando 1973: 78 n8 says that "in fact, the distinction between *arə* and *ee* is somewhat blurred in current use, and both may generally be used in the 'near neither you nor me' or 'aforementioned' sense." This is certainly not the case in the data available to me, nor does it reflect the judgments of numerous informants, (extensive classroom observation has also revealed native speakers correcting students on just this point). In part, at least, Fernando's observation difference may be a function of the degree to which observation is detailed and the complexity of usage of these forms, which we try to capture here. The *e-* (APH) forms can be used when the referent is still present, as in examples (1) through (3) here and subsequent ones. What needs to be noted is the sequence of occurrence. Also, *arə* (DIST) forms do have a discourse anaphoric use, as will be shown later, but it is restricted and different from *e-*. Thus, Fernando's statement is in the broadest sense true (though not representing a "blurring" of categories). It is, of course, possible that there are dialects in which a merger of functions is occurring (see also note 15 below), but in any case, the description and analysis here does hold for a considerable body of data and is based on much observation by me and others, so that it certainly represents a genuine and widespread variety.

7. In this chapter, I do not deal with the use of these forms in a temporal context, but it might be noted that the same observations hold in that case. Thus *ee dawaswələ* '(in) those days (GEN)' and *mee dawaswələ* '(in) these days (GEN)' are both possible and common. Also, *oyə dawaswələ* '(in) your days', seems highly possible, in the sense of either 'in your time' or 'in that time you are talking about'. However, **arə dawaswələ* seems highly unlikely, quite in accord with its essentially negative specification for discourse or nonspatial deixis.

8. This example and those in the remainder of this chapter are drawn from Gair, Karunatillake, and Paolillo 1987, unless otherwise noted.

9. Note also the exceptional status of *ehaa,* as stated in note 7.

10. Note that this statement refers only to cross-sentential anaphora. Intrasentential anaphora with *ee-* forms, though less common than cataphora, do occur. This is, in fact, a crucial difference in the use of such forms as "true" anaphors, as opposed to discourse anaphors; however, I do not deal with that here, but elsewhere (see note 19).

11. My "immediacy" is clearly the same as Kuno's (1973) characterization of the Japanese *ko-* deictic as "referring to something as if it were visible both to the speaker and hearer at the time of conversation . . . thus impart[ing] vividness to the conversation."

12. For those who are wondering how the story came out: Andare goes to the field, places an arecanut spathe on his shoulder as a carrying device, and asks the farmers to lift and place the rock there so he can fulfill his bargain and carry it away.

13. I am indebted to G. D. Wijayawardhana for bringing these facts to my attention.

14. Nandana Karunanayaka also informs me that he knows of dialects in which *arǝhemǝ* 'like that (DIST)' is used with discourse reference in the way that *ehemǝ* 'like that' (APH) is in the dialects dealt with here, in the sense 'Is that so?' This use requires further investigation to see how far it (and other uses of the DIST form in that variety) accords with the analysis made here.

15. I assume that temporal use can be subsumed under "conceptual."

16. This assertion that the APH forms are unmarked in this respect does not in fact conflict with the earlier assertion that those forms are marked. There it was the categories represented by the forms that were at issue, and the APH forms were the only ones possessing a plus value for *only* the discourse deixis feature and hence marked for it. In the present context, however, I am talking of the *use* and not the feature content of these forms. I am indebted to Linda Waugh (personal conversation) for making this distinction clear.

17. There is ample evidence that backward intersentential anaphora with lexical pronominal forms, as in (22c,) is grammatical in Sinhala. However, it is also clear that there is a strong preference for forward in general, where it is allowed by grammatically linked constraints.

18. Some observations on the intrasentential anaphoric properties of pronouns in Sinhala and their interactions with the relevant deictic categories have been made in Gair 1985a. Much of the material in this chapter was also included in the first half of the 1985 paper, but this chapter represents a substantial reanalysis and revision of that material, partly on the basis of subsequent data. (A more detailed analysis of intrasentenial anaphora is given in chapter 9, which was actually written subsequent to the present one though presented prior to its publication.)

Chapter 9

This paper was originally presented at SALA XII, at Berkeley, June 8, 1990. We would like to thank Lelwala Sumangala and Milan Rodrigo, who provided coreference and grammatical judgments as well as lively discussion, along with John Paolillo, Barbara Lust, Wayne Harbert, Jim Huang, John Bowers, and John Whitman. The usual disclaimers apply.

1. "R-expression" includes nonpronominal NPs (along with some types of empty categories), and "free" means not bound in the technical sense above.

2. A useful survey of versions of c-command up to its date may be found in Saito 1984.

3. A fuller account of Sinhala deictic and pronominal forms, and their function in discourse, is given in Gair 1991a.

4. The original had *mahattea* 'sir, the gentleman/master' as a term of reference rather than a title 'mister', but the latter sets the discourse better in this excerpt.

5. The verb *wahanǝwa* is transitive, and its subject here is not the office, but an arbi-

trary empty pronominal (i.e., pro_{ARB}). See Gair and Wali 1988, and Chapter 18 of this volume for a fuller account of such forms.

6. The clitic *mə*, which will be characterized further later, may also appear on argument or genitive t*aman/tamun* to add further emphasis; *eyaa, with -mə*, is also used as an emphatic adjunct. Interestingly, both of these as adjuncts appear to be limited to coindexing of some kind to the subject of the minimal S, so that *mamə nimalwə tamam(wə)mə dækka* 'I saw Nimal himself' is not possible.

7. In addition, *eyaa*+the emphatic clitic *mə*, to be considered shortly, is possible here in the genitive form *eyaagemə*—see example (8). The reading is then understandably biased toward the subject, whereas in example (6) as it stands, *eyaa* is less likely to be linked to the subject than *tamun*. The possibility of anaphoric linkage of simple *eyaa* with the subject is, however, clear to all informants that I have checked.

8. When the form is *taman*, the sense is roughly that 'Siri himself' or 'Nimal himself' must go. However, despite the English translation, this does not represent the emphatic use of *taman/tamun*, which would appear as *tamummə/tamammə*. In fact, *eyaa tamammə* or *tamun tamummə*, with the emphatic following the form in question, are possible (L. Sumangala, personal communication).

9. In examples (12), (13), and (15), the clauses in question have been moved leftward or rightward from the normal complement position, which is directly to the left of the verb as the SOV, left-branching structure of Sinhala dictates. This is usual in natural Sinhala speech, as it apparently is in Dravidian languages such as Tamil and Malayalam, presumably as a kind of "heavy constituent shift." If the clauses are left in their base position, awkwardness, and particularly the piling up of adjacent NPs, results, which can cloud judgments of acceptability. The right or left shifting might raise questions about whether the forms in question are actually bound in these examples under a strict definition requiring c-command. However, it is clear that these forms are commanded in the relevant sense since principle C applies. Thus, both *[Gunəpaalə giyaa kiyəla] eyaa kiwwa* 'Gunapala went COMP he said = He said that Gunapala went' and particularly *eyaa kiwwa [gunəpaalə giyaa kiyala]* 'He said Gunapala went COMP = 'He said that Gunapala went are generally unacceptable with coreference. (With the first of these, there is a complication in that the embedded clause may be topicalized so that the sentence becomes acceptable with the proper intonation.) The tree structures of these sentences with scrambling or right shifting are not completely clear, but the relevant type of command may be adjunction to IP (=S) together with M-command specifying maximal projections rather than first branching node (Chomsky 1986b). In any event, the full range of examples given clearly suffice to illustrate long-distance referential dependency.

10. For simplicity, I ignore the possibility of Gunapala as an antecedent here, since the concern is with demonstrating the command structure along with the possibilty of non-c-commanding antecedents.

11. Although in general, null possessives are not allowed, the relationship noun *pawulə* strongly implies coreference of an implied possessor with Gunapala in this example. I will set aside for now as irrelevant the interesting and as yet unsettled question of whether such nouns license a null possessive pronominal.

12. Of course, *eyaa* and *eyaamə* are possible here when the reference is external.

13. The problem is not limited to infinitives. Similar considerations obtain with other nonfinite, or at least participial, forms, which allow or disallow lexical subjects in relation to the environment in which they are embedded. An analysis, with supporting data from acquisition, may be found in Gair, Lust, Sumangala, and Rodrigo 1989. Similar phenomena also occur in Malayalam, as we discovered only after this paper was written. See Mohanan 1982 and Srikumar 1991.

14. It is not yet clear to what extent *pro* may share the property of possible genericity in situations such as those described here. There is clearly a *pro* with arbitrary reference in Sinhala, however, so that it would appear likely (see note 4).

15. Although it has not emerged fully from the discussion here, it is necessary to specify the higher predicate in addition to both the dominance structure and the verbal inflection of the embedded S, since there are higher predicates that allow both lexical (noncoindexed) and obligatorily empty (if coindexed) subjects in their complement infinitival clauses, where there is no reason to assume different tree structures. Thus, *siriṭəi [ei vibaage paas wennə]oonə* 'Siri (DAT) wants to pass the exam' as opposed to *ammaṭə [Siri vibaage paas wennə] oonə* 'Mother (DAT) wants Siri (NOM) to pass the exam.' It is clear that the subject of the embedded infinitival clause is assigned its case locally within that clause, because, among other reasons, it will appear in the case required by infinitive (cf. example (29b) above).

Chapter 10

This paper was given at the Parasession on Agreement at the 1988 Chicago Linguistic Circle Meeting, and appeared in D. Brentari, Greg Larson, and Lynn MacLeod, eds. *Papers from the Parasession on Agreement in Linguistic Theory* (*CLS 24*(2): 1988) pp. 87–104. The form in which it appears here is essentially unchanged, except for some alterations in format, minor corrections, and an added paragraph incorporating some later work.

1. Literary Sinhala examples are given in transliteration, but Colloquial Sinhala examples are given in phonological transcription. The situation is actually more complex than described here. Colloquial Sinhala is actually a subtype of Spoken Sinhala, and the agreement characteristics dealt with in this paper are characteristic of Spoken Sinhala in general (see the papers on diglossia in this volume). Since the system is shared by the varieties of Spoken Sinhala, however, colloquial examples suffice for this paper.

2. Claims of this general type, though differing in detail, have been made for Japanese, a language typologically similar to Sinhala, by Kuroda (1986), Fukui (1986, 1987), and Fukui and Speas (1986). However, although we are indebted to the latter authors in our argument here, we have not followed them by claiming the lack of an INFL node (and other functional nodes) for Sinhala, as they do for Japanese. Our assumption is, rather, that there is an INFL node defining the subject position, even though it lacks an AGR element. The status of INFL in Sinhala is a topic undergoing research and the outcome is not yet clear, but either way it does not affect our argument here, in which the claim extends only to AGR.

3. As stated earlier, the verbs in these sentences are not used intransitively. There are related intransitive verbs *wæwenəwa* 'grow' and *wæhenəwa* 'close', but these are involitive and exclude an agent, whereas the sentences under discussion not only imply an agent but *must* be used if agentivity is involved. Thus they do include, in terms of the theory employed here, a phonetically unrealized nominal, to which the agent θ-role is assigned.

4. Gender agreement is limited to cooccurrence with certain other categories, specifically past tense and certain nonfinite forms. For details, see the relevant passages of Gair and Karunatilaka 1974.

5. In earlier works, this was referred to as the "emphatic" form (EMPH).

6. In spoken Sinhala focused sentences, this rule does not hold, as we would expect, and all arguments appear in the same cases as in the nonfocused variant. Example (3b) provides an illustration.

7. Later note: The status of the form glossed as AGR in (6a) through (6c) is not entirely clear. In this paper as originally given, it was glossed as COP(ula) and had the form *yi*, but later work, such as that represented in Chapter 8, indicate not only that the *ya* variant is preferable in these sentences but also that it shows properties of agreement. For example, it var-

ies with person (but not number) in equational sentences: *mama goviyekmi* 'I farmer-INDEF-1 Pers = I am a farmer' versus *hē goviyek ya* 'he-farmer 3Pers = He is a farmer,' *ovuhu goviyō ya* they farmers 3Pers = They are farmers.' Note also that it occurs as the final element in both masculine and feminine past agreement in example (4). Thus it does appear to be at least in part an agreement form, and taking it as such actually strengthens the point of view here and in subsequent work concerning the relation of AGR to Sinhala diglossia. In any event, it, or some other agreement element, is necessary in any Literary Sinhala finite sentence, a rule that is absent in Spoken Sinhala. For discussion concerning the status of Literary *ya/yi*, I am indebted to John Paolillo and Lelwala Sumangala (Sunil Kariyakarawana) . For some discussion of these forms and their history, see Gair (1970, 1980, 1986b; Fernando 1973. Literary focused sentences are described in Gair and Karunatilaka 1974.

8. More precisely, the perfective affix -(*y*)*aa* does not show person but only gender and number. However, there are auxiliary forms that do show person, and they will be in the third person where they accompany the perfective form.

9. That these dative nominals are in fact subjects is shown by several properties, including antecedence of reflexives. See particularly Kachru et al. 1976; Davison 1985.

10. For c-command, we employ the "first branching node" definition of Reinhart 1976, but as far as we have been able to determine, our analysis would go through under any of the modified definitions that have been proposed.

11. See Gair and Wali 1987 for a more precise definition and justification.

12. Unlike Hindi, which has a two-gender system, Marathi has a three-gender system: masculine, feminine, and neuter.

13. For both Hindi and Marathi, this may also be identified with the agreement element on adjectives, which it resembles in form (for Marathi, see Kavadi and Southworth 1965: 200, Sec. 3.122), but this is not of importance here.

Chapter 11

I would like to thank Milan Rodrigo for her help in finding and discussing relevant Sinhala examples, particularly from earlier texts. I have also profited at various points from discussions with numerous colleagues, especially Leonard Babby, John Bowers, Kamal De Abrew, Wayne Harbert, Barbara Lust, Claudia Ross, and Margarita Suñer. None of them is, of course, responsible for any errors or misinterpretations. A shorter paper including many of the points dealt with here, but from a different perspective, was given at the sixth Berkeley Linguistic Society meeting, February 16–18, 1980.

1. Because I am examining focused sentences from several languages, I have added to the example numbers letters that indicate the source of the example. They are (in order of appearance): S = Sinhala; T = Tamil; M = Malayalam; K = Kannada; G = example from Gair, Suseendirarajah, and Karunatilaka 1979; SG = Sigiri graffiti; SA = Sinhala *Amāvatura.*

2. In Colloquial Sinhala, EMPH is represented by -*nne* in the present tense and -*e* or -*ee* (added to the past tense stem) in the past tense. Sinhala is a diglossic language, and in Literary Sinhala, the variety used for virtually all written purposes, EMPH is represented by -*nnē* or -*nuyē* and -*ē*. This does not affect the argument of this chapter, however, and except where otherwise noted, this chapter deals only with Colloquial Sinhala.

In other papers, this affix has been glossed as FOC(-using form), or -E, but that represents only a terminological change.

3. Tamil examples used herein are from Sri Lanka (Jaffna) Tamil, since that is the variety for which I have the fullest relevant data. The transcription is as in Gair, Suseendirarajah, and Karunatilaka 1979. Examples from other Dravidian languages are from the sources cited and in the transcriptions used therein.

4. There are in fact, sentences with V-EMPH that could be considered to represent another type, or at least a special subtype, of focused sentences. These are represented by such sentences as:

arə   enne   gunəpaalə.
There come-EMPH Gunapala
'The one coming is Gunapala' or 'There comes Gunapala now.'

As in this example, such sentences involve situational deixis and contain an appropriate deictic form. If other focused sentences are given a transformational derivation, these do not fit it neatly, and they are distinct in that way, as well; not considering them separately here will not affect the argument. It is interesting, however, that they can be considered to have sentences such as (SA4) as their forerunners, and they would require treatment in a full study of the history of Sinhala focused sentences.

5. I have not specified which constituents may be focused, but in general they include any phrasal constituent dominated by S or VP. Some details will be found in Gair 1970, but there are additional possibilities, such as some constituents of embedded Ss, for which details have not been worked out but are currently under investigation. (See Chapter 5, "Nonconfigurationality, Movement, and Sinhala Focus"; also see Gair and Sumangala 1991, Sumangala 1989b.)

6. This term is adapted from M. Suñer's "naked noun constraint" to characterize a somewhat similar phenomenon in Spanish.

7. The "simple" form of the verb is the tensed form usually occurring in finite nonfocused sentences. For a fuller description of verb forms, see Gair 1976b and the references therein.

8. There is also a focus-marking emphatic *may*, but this is an emphatic *mə+yi* and is thus a subcase of the latter. Sinhala has forms like *mə* 'emphasis' and *-(u)t* 'also', which mark "emphasis" of some sort but that do not require clefting (i.e., -EMPH) and thus are not focus-marking forms in the sense in which that term is used here. Note also that the definition of focus clearly leaves out other phenomena of a kind that have been called "emphasis," or "focus," including "focus" marked by intonational prominence. This distinction is important, as is the distinction between "focus" and "topic," and it is dealt with at greater length in Gair 1976a.

9. There is a third negative form, a prefix *no-* occurring in embedded Ss and on some verb forms in independent sentences, including verbs with EMPH. It is not necessary to deal with it in this chapter, however. For details, see Gair 1970: 156 and De Abrew 1980.

10. In such sentences, *næ̃æ* is not the focus as the result of any sort of focusing operation, transformational or otherwise, and no recent study has treated it as such to the best of my knowledge, despite the obvious desirability of unifying all the structures with the *(nn)e* form if possible, and consequent temptation to do so.

11. Although *næ̃æ* may be moved by low-level scrambling rules, that does not make any form preceding it the focus, and even then it leaves traces of its former location in the form of constraints on what may follow the verb and precede *næ̃æ*. For details see De Abrew 1980.

12. The association of WH-form and Q is so strong that dictionaries such as Carter 1924 and De Zoysa 1964 list them as single entries—*koheedə* 'where', *kohomədə* how', etc.—and do not list the WH-forms alone.

13. One should perhaps say with greater precision, "with two kinds of focus, involving both semantic and syntactic differences." This distinction requires more extended treatment than I can give it here. Note, however, that it is paralleled by Sinhala forms allowing *mə* (see note 7) versus those allowing forms like *tamay* or *-yi*. I use "focus" here only for the latter in Sinhala. See also note 8.

Later note: The similarity between Sinhala and Malayalam is actually closer than this may imply, since WH-forms in Malayalam are generally clefted like those in Sinhala. Also, although it is clear that clefting of questioned constituents requires *aaNū*, I do not have decisive data on whether constituent questions, with *-oo* but without *aaNū* and clefting, are possible. Lindholm's (1972) statement is not quite clear on this point. See also note 22.

14. In current Colloquial Sinhala, NP NP equational sentences lack an overt copula, but NP Adj sentences obligatorily take *-yi* if the adjective is vowel-final (as most are): *meekə hoňday* 'This-one good-*yi* = 'This one is good.'

15. Although *-yi* may cooccur with *də*, cooccurrence is restricted to special circumstances involving, in rough terms, another level of focus, as, for example, when asking for confirmation: *meekə hoňday də* 'Is this one really good?'

16. Thus, in an equational sentence: *atu meesa* (*y*) *aaNū* (George 1971: 10).

Later Note: Given the common cross-language association of clefts and pseudoclefts with equational sentences, the occurrence of the copula in both is not surprising. Thus the question to be asked is whether the copula was not a subsequent development in clefts in Malayalam but was there from the beginning, as it (or at least agreement) was in Sinhala as stated in the paragraphs that follow. See further note 20.

17. Forms of *venavā* as copula inflect for tense and number–gender to agree with the subject in Literary Sinhala. Thus: *mama goviyek vemi* 'farmer-INDEF be-PRES-1Sg.' = 'I am a farmer.' However, *yi* and its variants do not show agreement. Hence, *mama goviyek ya/ yi* (or *goviyeki*).

Later note: Subsequent work showed this to be inaccurate as it stands, since *mama goviyek mi* is not only possible, but preferable; see note 19 and the further reference there. It is also the case that some speakers, if not most, prefer *-ya* or *-i* in even third person nominal equational sentences and may in fact reject *-yi*.

18. Compare, for example, (SA1), given later, from a twelfth-century text.

19. Later note: Whether or not *-yi* and its *ya/i* variants is truly a copula is, on the basis of subsequent work, somewhat doubtful, and it might indeed be better considered a form of agreement (see note 17 and Chapter 8). However, the historical line of development outlined in this chapter is not seriously affected even if this change in identification is made, and it is found that an agreement rule rather than a copula rule (as stated here) is relaxed in the transition to current Spoken Sinhala. In fact, that revision brings the historical development more neatly in line with the view of Sinhala diglossia taken in part five, since it involves a loss of agreement. The multiple function of *ya/yi/i* and its somewhat uncertain status is not a recent phenomenon. Thus Piyaseeli Wijemanne, in her excellent (1984) study of the grammar of *Amāvatura*, which appeared after this paper was written, calls it "the assertion marker," (apparently following the use of that term for its modern Colloquial descendent in Fairbanks, Gair, and De Silva 1968, taken up in Gair 1970). She presents a number of functions for it, including its "functioning as a copula" (p. 171). In any case, it is unlikely that the final word has been spoken on these forms, and they present some interesting problems, both descriptive and historical.

20. Later note: The situation here is actually more complex and more interesting than was apparent at the time this chapter was written. As pointed out in note 16, there is a well-known connection between clefts/pseudoclefts and equational sentences, which makes the Sinhala–Malayalam parallel not too surprising, and as noted, the Sinhala copula (and/or agreement) was there from the beginning of the construction. However, it does raise questions about the history of the forms in Malayalam and Tamil and for South and South-Central Dravidian languages in general. One might reasonably surmise, in the absence of other than synchronic evidence, that the present Tamil situation evolved from one like Malayalam or Sinhala through the loss of a copula. However, the problem there is that as far as I can determine, there appears to be no evidence for a copula in earlier stages that preceded the Malayalam–Tamil split, and in general, the works on comparative Dravidian languages that

I have consulted assume the absence of a copula to be a general property of Dravidian languages. Thus, for example, Zvelibil (1990), in listing "a few very fundamental syntactic traits
valid for all Dravidian languages . . . [that are] so typical and so general . . . [that they] could
point towards a proto Dravidian syntax," says: "Equational sentences [in Dravidian] usually
do not have a verb expressed" (pp. 42–43). Similarly, Steever (1987), in discussing Dravidian
languages generally asserts: "No copula is required with predicate nominals," though he notes
that "some Dravidian languages possess a variation on the . . . pattern in which the predicate
nominal is inflected to agree with the subject," which is found also in Old Tamil (p. 8). This
pattern also parallels Sinhala, as described here, in an interesting way (see also note 19). I
have not been able so far to find any information regarding the same phenomenon on clefts in
early Tamil and South Dravidian.

All of this raises intriguing and important questions for comparative Dravidian syntax,
as well as interesting possibilities for the detailed nature of the influence on Sinhala and
the direction of that influence. For the present, at least, I still assume that the Sinhala–
Malayalam developments regarding focus marking with copular forms are parallel developments, explained at least in part by the universal connection—or at least basic tendency—
for clefts and nominal equational structures to be connected (see also Gair and Sumangala
1991 and Sumangala 1992 for Sinhala). This aspect of South Asian languages has been
addressed, in at least a preliminary fashion, in Gair 1994, but much remains to be done. It
is also interesting that *aaNū* in Malayalam is omissible in NP NP sentences (Andrewskutty
1971: 139) but apparently not in clefts (A. P. Andrewskutty, personal communication), which
resembles a probable earlier stage in Sinhala development. Also, Madhavan (1987), while
claiming that *aaNū* in Malayalam clefts is the finite verb, notes that it is also, in some sense
the "focus marker" and suggests that it is "cliticized" to the focus (p. 67).

There are a number of questions here, of theoretical as well as historical and areal interest, that have arisen in large part because of work, especially on Malayalam and Sinhala, done
since this chapter was written. However, the line of development presented in this chapter
still appears to me to be correct, though some of these issues suggest modifications of detail,
especially regarding the precise nature and direction of contact. Also, a 1994 paper by John
Paolillo deals with the internal developments in Sinhala in more detail than this chapter, is
generally in agreement with it, and offers an interesting explanation for their trajectory in
terms of grammaticalization and interaction with semantic shift.

21. Judging from the examples given by Schiffman (1979), the verificatory particle *-oo*
may also be subject to that rule (p. 132), though this point is not stated.

22. Later note: Actually, semiobligatory clefting of WH-forms does indeed occur in
Malayalam, as demonstrated and discussed in Madhavan 1987, Jayaseelan 1989, and Srikumar
1992, though this information was not available when this paper was written. However, given
the unlikelihood of contact influence, particularly in the time span involved, independent
development seems more than likely. It is, of course, interesting to speculate on the reasons
for the parallel, and that was indeed considered, if briefly, in Gair 1994. There also appears
to be a difference in what triggers the clefting syntactically in Malayalam and Sinhala. In
Sinhala, as noted, WH-forms cooccur with the Q particle, and clefting occurs when Q immediately follows WH. Thus, though the clefting–question connection may be pragmatically
motivated, it appears to be Q that triggers clefting syntactically (like some other forms), and
WH clefting can be considered a subcase of constituent question clefting. In Malayalam,
however, Q does not cooccur with WH, but *aaNū* does, so that the association appears to be
with focus, as marked by *aaNū* and clefting. Note also that the occurrence of *aaNū* is true for
focused non-WH constituent questions in Malayalam, as described earlier. Also, Malayalam
WH-forms, unlike Sinhala, may occur immediately preceding the verb without *aaNū* or clefting
(Jayaseelan 1989).

23. Thus, from *Amāvatura* (twelfth century):

mee   væni   siŋhanadayek   anekhata   vanne   no   veyi.
This   kind   lion-voice-INDEF   another-DAT   be-EMPH   not-be   3Sg
'This kind of a lion voice could not be (i.e., belong) to any other.'

24. The difficulties of reaching definite conclusions as to Dravidian influences under-lying the existence of two negatives of this sort have been set forth by B. Lakshmi Bai in her paper at the 1980 Hyderbad conference and included in Krishnamurti, Masica, and Sinha 1986. Also, given the existence of two "be" verbs and a negative prefix, the likelihood of indepen-dent development is quite strong.

25. Actually, *bææ* does not inflect with EMPH, but in focused sentences it appears as *bæri,* which also serves as an adjectival (or relative participle) form. Since it does have par-ticipial forms, however, it clearly belongs with the quasiverbs, and it is simplest to treat *bæri* in focused sentences as resulting from a spelling-out rule operating on *bææ*+EMPH or from an equivalent rule.

26. Later note: It appears that this is another respect in which Malayalam and Sinhala resemble each other. Thus Moag 1986 remarks: "This sentence type is really much more common in Malayalam than in English . . . because the grammatical equivalent in English is used mainly for emphasis which is much less common than is focus" (p. 204). Furthermore, and clearly related to this, is the "semiobligatory" requirement for clefting of WH in Malayalam (Jayaseelan 1987, Madhavan 1987, Srikumar 1992). Here again, I assume independent de-velopment, especially in the light of the documented history of Sinhala as outlined here, which clearly shows that the rule developed subsequent to any likely time of influence. If so, how-ever, it affords a most interesting example of universal tendencies (this term may appear to be an oxymoron, though I lack a better one to describe this type of phenomenon) at work in syntactic change, and it invites further investigation.

27. Later note: Whether the form glossed COP(ula) in this and subsequent examples is actually a copula or not in all cases can be questioned, but that does not seriously affect the argumentation and line of development presented here. See note 19.

28. Evidence from *Amāvatura* must be interpreted with caution, since the text is an archaizing one largely based on Pali originals (Reynolds 1970: 32–33). However, there is no apparent Pali model for focused sentences of the type we are considering. Also, there is no obvious Pali model for *də* and certainly none for its cooccurrence with WH. Pali influence would thus be looked for in the absence rather than the presence of *də* with WH, but parallel examples were also found in the Sigiri graffiti. Hence, our conclusions, though limited, seem relatively safe.

For the relationship of *Amāvatura* to the Pali originals, with numerous examples, see Wijemanne 1984, a study that also presents a great deal of other relevant information concern-ing that text. Had that admirable study been available when this chapter was written, not only would my work have been much easier but I would also have been able to be much more certain and specific. However, Wijemanne's careful and detailed work does bear out the conclusion here that the cleft sentence existed at the time of *Amāvatura* but had not acquired its present form and constraints. The work by Paolillo cited in note 20 also makes excellent use of Wijemanne's work in dealing with this subject in more detail than was possible in this chapter.

Chapter 12

We would like to thank those who served as informants for Jaffna Tamil, especially Ratnamalar Periyathamby, Parvaty Kanthasamy, and V. Subramaniam, as well as others too numerous to name individually. Part of the work presented here was carried out in Sri Lanka by James W.

Gair under a U.S. Office of Education research grant (1969–70) and a Fulbright lecturing grant (1976–77).

1. At the time that this chapter was first written, Professor Suseendirarajah was at Kelaniya University, but he has since gone to the University of Jaffna.

2. At the time of writing this chapter, the most recent published census of Sri Lanka (1971) did not give language statistics. However, rough estimates could be made from figures on community and ethnic origin. Thus the Ceylon Tamil population of Jaffna in 1971 was 665,857, and for the adjacent districts of Mannar and Vavuniya it was 39,977 and 58,431, respectively. Allowing for intervening population increase, our estimate for Jaffna Tamil thus seemed reasonable.

3. The transcription used here for Jaffna Tamil should be sufficiently self-explanatory, but a few points reflecting differences from other dialects require mention: *t*, *ṯ* and *T* are respectively dental, alveolar, and retroflex stops and are generally voiceless initially and when geminate and voiced when single intervocalically and (usually) after nasals. Initial *T* is an exception in being voiced. (Tamil scholars should note that while this three-way distinction is reminiscent of an earlier one in Tamil, it does not represent a straightforward survival of that earlier situation, with *ṯ* in particular having several etymological sources.) The *ṟ* is a voiced postalveolar retroflexed trill and *L* is a retroflex voiced lateral. In Jaffna Tamil, *L* represents a merger of earlier *ḷ* (ளி) and *zh* (ழ்). In the transcription used here, we do not distinguish *ñ* (ஞ) and *ŋ* (ங) from *ṉ* (ன), since that distinction has only graphemic relevance. For further details on Jaffna phonology, see Gair et al. 1978; Suseendirajah 1966, 1967, 1973a; M. Shanmugam Pillai 1962; and Thananjayarajasingham 1962, 1966.

4. In addition, *alla* is used with emphasized constituents and in clefts, as in *kaTaikku alla, viiTTukkupoonkoo* 'Don't go to the shop, go home.'

5. It may be noted that Kanapathi Pillai writes *vantani* (னி) rather than *vantanii* (னீ) as we have rendered it, indicating a shortening of the *nii* (நீ) pronoun in that position in the dialect represented. That shortening does not, of course, adversely affect our argument here, but it actually furnishes additional justification for treating these forms as inflected verbs originating in verb–pronoun sequences.

6. The instrumental case is also used as an ablative (source) in Jaffna Tamil. This appears to be another unusual feature of the dialect and one that it shares, interestingly, with Sinhala.

7. These action nouns contrast with identical sequences representing relative clause formations with a third person nonhuman pronoun as head, as in *vantatu* 'the one that came' or 'the coming', *paTiccatu* 'the one that was studied' or 'the studying'. For a justification of analyzing the action nouns and the relative formations as distinct but homonymous, see Lindholm 1972.

Note that the third person nonhuman past pronominal form of the verb will also be formed from the same sequence of verbal adjective and pronoun and thus will be homonymous with *both* the relative clause with a third person nonhuman pronoun as head *and* the action verbal noun, allowing a three-way ambiguity. Thus the sequence *inta pas yaaLppaaNattaalai vantatu* 'this bus Jaffna-INST came-ADJ PRONOUN (3Sg nonhuman)' can be, in the proper context, any of the following: (1) an equational sentence with pronoun-headed relative formation as predicate, 'this bus is the one that came from Jaffna'; (2) a sentence with a past pronominal verb, 'this bus came from Jaffna'; or (3) a deverbalized nominal clause, 'the coming (past) of this bus from Jaffna'.

8. Here and in the previous example, irrelevant internal bracketing within the VP has been omitted. We have not labeled *atu* in this second bracketing. Though it clearly serves a nominalizing function, whether or not it should be treated as a complementizer leads to a number of syntactic complexities that, however interesting, are not necessary to deal with here.

9. Professor Jay Jasanoff has pointed out to us the parallel with the Sanskrit periphrastic future, which is also based on a nominal form.

10. The earlier analysis of the forms at issue in Suseendirajah 1967 treats the endings somewhat differently by decomposing them morphemically, into intermediate morpheme plus ending. The analysis of those combinations, however, is quite parallel to his analysis of the pronouns, and treating them as such synchronically is quite consistent with the existence of those verb forms as independent finite forms in present-day Jaffna Tamil. Most importantly, he based the forms at issue on the relativizing form in the 1967 work as well, which is inconsistent with Steever's proposal, and he was one of the authors of both the later analysis in Gair, Suseendirarajah, and Karunatilaka 1978 and in this chapter.

11. Steever (1988) does in fact give a nasal degeminating rule, but that would clearly not account for the forms completely lacking the nasal. Also, judging from the derivations, it appears to apply together with vowel lengthening in Jaffna Tamil (p. 86) but not in Pengo (pp. 81-83). This would present a problem for an analysis that holds them to be the same rule in the different languages, but of course this ceases to be a problem under the pronominal derivation here.

Chapter 14

Throughout this chapter, my indebtedness to my colleague and former student W. S. Karunatillake will be evident from the numerous citations to his work at crucial points. What will not be so evident, but is of equal importance, is the number of stimulating discussions (and occasionally disputes) that I have had with him on these and related matters. His careful and precise application of structural criteria to the inscriptional and documentary evidence in his 1969 work built on the pioneering and indispensable contributions of such scholars as William Geiger and P. B. F. Wijeratne, and it enabled us to date a number of changes with more confidence than was earlier the case. Since he is also a member of the *guruparamparā* of Professor Fairbanks, the contribution of his work to this chapter is particularly fitting. I am also grateful to Jay Jasanoff for his insightful comments on an earlier version of this paper.

1. Note that the Pre-Old Sinhala system as given agrees quite well with Pali and other Middle Indic dialects, though it lacks the retroflex *l* found in Pali, for which Sinhala inscriptions give no evidence. Note also that the similarity to Modern Northern Indo-Aryan languages such as Hindi testifies to the remarkable persistence of the system over time, despite numerous changes in allophones and phonotactics.

Transcriptions and transliterations for these languages vary with regard to their use of *v* and *w*, but in no case is there any contrast involved, though different phonetic values may be implied. For the sake of consistency, I have used *v* exclusively here and throughout (thus differing from some of my own transcriptions for Sinhala presented elsewhere).

2. Briefly: The Jaffna Tamil aleovelar stop is a reflex of *r* (ʃ) intervocalically and initially, and of *rr* (ṭ ṭ) when geminate (sometimes arising from assimilation in clusters). Current *r* (trilled) is a reflex of *r* (ṭ) intervocalically.

3. Although Tamil is specifically invoked by Elizarenkova and others, including Hettiaratchi (1959: 42) and Ratanajoti (1975: 34ff.). "Tamil-Malayalam" might be more accurate for much of the time span involved. Not only was there interaction with both (present-day) Kerala and Tamilnadu, but much of the evidence suggested predated the split of Tamil and Malayam (ca. ninth through tenth centuries). In what follows, however, I will refer simply to "Tamil" for simplicity, but the caution just expressed should be kept in mind.

4. The model does not present entire subsystems, as in the consonant charts above, but rather the presence or absence of specific features such as aspirate consonants, dipthongs, vowel length, and nasal vowels.

5. As is well known, it is necessary to postulate an intermediate nasalized vowel to account for the different vowel quality in OE.

6. The voicing after nasal in Tamil has been the subject of some dispute, but it seems to have occurred quite early and, in any event, before the Tamil-Malayalam split (Krishnamurti 1968: 359) that took place around the tenth century. The Sinhala loss of nasal appears to have considerably predated that, so that we cannot be sure whether an influencing dialect would have had [nd] or [nt]. If [nt], the argument for influence is even weaker, since it was in such clusters that the Sinhala nasal was lost.

7. The assumption that lengthening accompanied the loss of nasals here is required by other subsequent changes; see Karunatillake 1969: 57ff.

8. This possibility was suggested to me by Jay Jasanoff.

9. There was a subsequent restoration of *c* and *j* through borrowings, including Dravidian borrowings for *cc*. Interestingly, the *Sidatsaṅgarā*, the classical thirteenth-century grammar, includes *j* but not *c* in its list of phonological–orthographical elements.

10. Vowel length is not written in inscriptions prior to the eighth century, except sporadically. However, its presence and origin in part from compensatory lengthening accompanying the later simplification of assimilated consonant sequences can be inferred from other changes requiring length as a conditioning factor (see Karunatillake 1969: 93ff for the relevant changes and their sequence). Like other MIA dialects, Old Sinhala had no length contrast for *e* and *o*.

11. Later note: The original paper neglected to note that Divehi (Maldivian) would have to be an exception here along with Sinhala. Given their clear relationship, this is no problem, but it does suggest, of course, that the split between them occurred after the presumably common loss of aspiration. Some other Sinhala changes given here were also shared with Divehi, and the extent to which these were common innovations is, of course, important in determining when the split occurred, but that is beyond our concerns here.

12. The inscriptions do not write geminates: thus *guta* for *gutta* < *gupta*, *puta* for *putta* < *putra*. However, other evidence makes it evident that a geminate stage was involved (Karunatillake 1969).

13. Intervocalic -*p*- did not follow the general pattern, not merging with its voiced counterpart -*b*-. It subsequently merged with -*v*- and remained distinct from -*b*- (largely from -*bh*-). Thus we see later *pav* 'sin' (Sanskrit *pāpa*), *laba* 'gain' (Sanskrit *lābha*). While this does not affect the general argument here, note that the retained contrast, in whatever form it took prior to the merger of -*p*- with -*v*-, is another un-Tamil development.

The subsequent history of the other intervocalic stops and consonants, alluded to later in connection with the loss of preconsonantal nasals, is also interesting in this regard. Between the second and fourth centuries A.D., -*d*- and -*g*- became -*y*- (possibly -*v*- in some contexts, judging from later variants such as *nuvara* city, *niyarī* 'urban'; *cf.* Sanskrit nagara): -*ḍ*- became -*ḷ*-, and -*j*- remained but later merged with *d* in all contexts, as mentioned earlier (*cf.* note 10). The geminates, both voiced and voiceless, simplified to single consonants, thus reintroducing a voicing contrast between single intervocalic stop, a most un-Dravidian result. For details of the changes and their dating, see Karunatillake 1969: 48–91.

I do not concern myself with consonant positions other than those given, such as postnasal stops, since they do not seriously affect the argument at this point; but note that there, too, Tamil lacks a voicing contrast, whereas Sinhala, prior to the loss of nasal, did not.(cf. note 6).

14. In fact, the Sinhala developments bear more resemblance to West Germanic, in particular Pre- and Early-Old-English, than they do to Dravidian, though no one would of course suggest areal influence there.

15. Though some dialects of Hindi have a low front vowel, it is not a result of umlaut but represents the dipthong *ay*. Bengali has *æ*, as does Konkani on the other side of India, but it results from a lowering of *e*. In none of these cases is the origin parallel to Sinhala *æ*.

16. Some of the IA languages, such as Marathi, reinstituted a contrast between retroflex and nonretroflex nasals and laterals later, but that is beside the point here. For remarks on a related topic, see Gair 1978: 463–464.

17. In fact, Karunatillake has found some evidence pointing to an even earlier date (personal communication). In the tenth-century *Dhampiyā aṭuvā gaeṭapadaya*, the alternation *nelum~nelun(ut)* is found. This is parallel to modern colloquial alternations with *m* intervocalically, *ŋ* finally, and *n* before clitics, as in *liyumə* 'letter', *liyuŋ* 'letters', *liyunut* 'and the letters', which requires an intermediate neutralized nasal [ŋ], which then appears as *-n-* when a clitic is added: i.e., $mV > \eta\# > nV$.

18. For a specific application of this caution, see my comments on Masica's interpretation of gemination in causatives to Dravidian influence in Gair 1976b: 271.

Chapter 15

1. Later Note: This overlooks Divehi (Maldivian), for which the same separation and isolation appears to hold. The relationship of these languages to each other and to the area are of great interest, and in 1995, research in that direction was under way with Bruce Cain and Kathy Cain at Cornell.

2. Later note: See also the other chapters on diglossia, and references therein.

3. The original paper included paradigms of verb forms. These can be found in the chapter "Colloquial Sinhalese Inflectional Categories and Parts of Speech." A few imperative forms have been incorporated in the text here, as have a few others as examples where such inclusions seemed necessary if the reader did not wish to turn to chapter 2 for details. Following the paradigms, there was a discussion of the A, P, and C verbs and a brief sketch of their uses, but since this is also covered in different ways in the chapters "Action Involvement Categories" and "Subjects, Case, and INFL," as well as in the selections from *Colloquial Sinhala Clause Structures*, it was not felt necessary to repeat them here as well.)

The examples of forms that have been added here are given in the form pertinent to regular Class 1 verbs (those with a present stem in *-ə-*). For the morphophonemic variants, see chapter 2 and De Silva 1960.

4. De Silva 1960: 104–5 thus calls the perfect participle (his "*-la* form") a "common form" as opposed to his finite and participial forms, which are essentially equivalent to our independent and dependent forms, respectively.

5. It is true that the "pronominalized verb" of Tamil and other South Dravidian languages shows some similarity of function to the Sinhala emphatic verb, as pointed out by Ramanujan (as quoted by Masica 1971: 30n). In fact, it seems plausible that it served as a model for the Sinhala emphatic in its "focus shifting" function. However, not only does the Sinhala form seem far more common in this use, but the associated emphatic structures also are part of a complex subsystem of forms and relationships involving nonverbal forms, as well. Thus, even if Dravidian influence played a role in the origin of these structures, Sinhala has developed it in a unique and interesting way. For a detailed discussion along these lines, see chapter 11, "Sinhala Focused Sentences: Naturalization of a Calque."

6. Syntactic focus can be structurally defined in Sinhala by the occurrence or potential occurrence of certain markers (Gair 1970: 49ff. and the papers on focus in this volume). Semantically, it is similar to focus in the sense of Chomsky 1971, or particularly Schachter 1973, and it raises a number of interesting questions similar to those raised in those papers.

7. It is interesting that Sinhala has the verb plus negative auxiliary cited by Southworth as a Dravidian feature shared by Marathi (Southworth 1971: 264) and that it is essentially the functional equivalent of the Tamil verb plus *illai*. However, the Sinhala emphatic form does not otherwise have a range of distribution paralleling that of the Tamil infinitive, which precedes *illai*. Unless this discrepancy is explained, one should be hesitant to conclude too firmly that there is a Tamil model involved here.

8. Involitive optatives do in fact occur with first person reference, even though the nominal involved can be considered not to be an active subject, depending on one's analysis of the sentences in which this occurs. For further discussion and references concerning the agreement characteristics of these forms, see chapter 6, "Subjects, Case and INFL in Sinhala," particularly note 23 and associated text.

9. Later note: As became clear after this paper was published, "intention" might be better than "determination" here. One aspect of the form is that it usually allows—in fact invites—assent or refusal by the hearer.

10. This is further treated in chapter 3, "Action Involvement Categories in Sinhala," as representative of an important and pervasive semantic distinction in Sinhala.

11. Later note: The *-la* participle is, in fact, the usual way of referring to a completed action the speaker does not have direct knowledge of, such as when the action and/or its agent have to be inferred to any extent from the existing situation. For further discussion and examples, see chapter 19, "Acquisition of Null subjects and Control in Some Sinhala Adverbial Clauses."

12. Only in this auxiliary function is *tiyenəwa* used with animate subjects. Otherwise, it is restricted to inanimate subjects, and *innəwa* 'be' must be used with animate ones.

This is particularly good evidence that the use with the participle constitutes functioning as a true auxiliary and not as a (higher) content verb, since the +ANIMATE feature is lacking. As we might expect, ambiguity is possible with an inanimate subject, so that *bas-ekə gihilla tiyenəwa* could possibly be interpreted as 'the bus went and is (remains)', with a conjunctive use of the participle.

13. There is also a permissive form in *-dden*, which appears to be a dialectal variant. According to Garusinghe (1962) this is used in first and third persons and both numbers. De Silva (1960) gives this form, with another variant in *-ddaawe,* and indicates a plural in *-ddella*, listing them as third person. Informants differ on their knowledge and use of these forms, but dialectal differences, as yet undetermined, are clearly involved.

14. This seems to be the simplest way to state this for present purposes to indicate the distinction between these Sinhala clauses and participial modifiers of the Hindi, and apparently more characteristically Indo-Aryan, types. In fact, there are complex restrictions that apply; for example, most case-marked nouns can be relativized, but nouns followed by postpositions or by cases in certain specific functions cannot. These are clearly of a different order from those obtaining in the Hindi case, however. For areal purposes, this is very important, since the Sinhala adjectival clauses are in virtually all respects like those in Tamil.

15. A verbal noun plus *ekə* in this nominalizing function contrasts with the same sequence in which *ekə* alone has a nominal function like English "the one" and is modified by a verbal adjective—i.e., relativized. Thus, *yanə ekə* can be 'going' or 'the one that goes', but only in the second construction can other numerals be substituted: *yanə dekə* 'the two that go'. *ekə* is also employed in Sinhala in adapting inanimate loan words, particularly from English: *bas-ekə* 'the bus', 'the car', etc.

Later note: Note that here, too, there are clear parallels in Tamil (and Malayalam), but the nominal/nominalizing form in question is the third person pronominal element *(a)tu*. Thus, Tamil *poonatu* can be 'the having gone' or 'the one that went'. In all of these languages, there is another crucial difference between the nominalizing and relativizing structures that I failed to note in this chapter, and that has sometimes been overlooked or insufficiently noted in treating these forms: The relativizing structure requires a gap coindexed with the head, whereas the nominalized structure, understandably, does not allow one, though it may, of course, include null pronouns not so indexed. Thus, *yanə ekə* may be 'the one that goes' or 'the going' (with a null pronominal subject with outside reference), but *eekə yanə eka* 'that-one go-VERBADJ *ekə*' is only possible in the nominalized reading 'that one's going'. For (Jaffna) Tamil see Gair, Suseendirarajah, and Karunatillake 1978; for Malayalam, see Madhavan 1987 and references therein.

16. The Sinhala causative has two main forms: -*wə*- and gemination. To a geminated causative verb as in *kappə*- 'cause to cut' from *kapə*- 'cut', -*wə*- may be added to form a "double causative," as in *kappəwə*-. For most speakers, however, such forms appear to be free variants with the single ones. There is some indication that some speakers may employ the double causative only when some sort of (syntactic) double causativization is involved, but even in these cases the other may substitute. In any event, this pertains to a small number of verbs, and the details are far from clear.

For some speakers at least, it is also possible to form a double causative by adding an additional -*wə*- to a stem that already includes it. The resulting -*wəwə*- is generally resolved to -*woo*-, as in *kərəwoonəwa* from *kərəwənəwa* 'cause to do'. Just how much such forms are actually used, however, is unclear, and as in the geminate+*wə* cases, it appears that the shorter form can substitute even where the sense is double causative. De Silva (1960) treats all such forms simply as mutually substitutable variants, but other speakers do appear to make the distinctions outlined here. More work is clearly needed here, including the observation of a considerable amount of natural speech.

17. Later note: For a discussion of related issues with special reference to phonology, see chapter 14, "How Dravidianized Was Sinhala Phonology."

18. Later note: Even here there is a suggestive similarity accompanied by a challenging discrepancy. The Sinhala concessive appears to include the form -*t* (literary and older *da*) in its derivation. Elsewhere, this form signifies 'also' and is essentially a functional equivalent of Tamil -*um*. However, it is not added to the conditional, as in Tamil, to form the concessive; it is added to a participial or (originally) nominal form. Furthermore, Geiger (1938: 152–54) traces the conditional to the same -*t*, but here an alternate explanation is possible. Thus the parallelism breaks down in a way that makes it difficult to account for just exactly how a Tamil model could have operated directly.

19. Later note: The range of uses of "say" quotatives differs in different languages. For a very partial account of Sinhala, see Gair 1970: 63. A general survey for South Asian languages has been given in Kachru 1979, though some of her conclusions have been challenged in other works cited and in Lowenstein 1993 for Bengali in particular. For a survey of Sanskrit uses of *iti*, with a historical account, see Hock 1982.

Chapter 16

Some of the observations made in this paper were expressed earlier in "Which Sinhalese," *U.S.E.F. Newsletter,* Colombo, June 1965, pp. 3–7. An earlier version of this paper was given at the International Conference on Ceylon held at Philadelphia in August 1967. Parts of the work reprinted here were carried out under an NDEA Fulbright–Hays grant in 1964–65, others with funds from Cornell University. During my stay in Ceylon, too many people showed characteristic Ceylon helpfulness. Without the assistance of W. S. Karunatillake, it would not have been possible to survey the amount of material this report is based on in the time involved. He has also made numerous stimulating comments, and I am indebted to him for a Sinhalese transcription of the material taken from Radio Ceylon. The kindness of Radio Ceylon in providing tapes of a number of broadcasts is also gratefully acknowledged.

1. Citation of forms involves special problems, since we are dealing with two varieties, one primarily written, the other spoken. Literary forms have been given here in a transliteration of their usual spellings. Colloquial forms are given in a transliteration of their Sinhala spellings according to the system for representing Colloquial forms in that script used in Fairbanks, Gair, and De Silva, *Colloquial Sinhalese*. This accords for the most part with usual Sinhalese practice and has the effect of reducing the contrast among [ə], [a], and [ā] to a two-way one plus some general and morpheme-specific rules. It is generally equivalent to the phonemic analysis suggested in De Silva 1963. It has the advantage, for present purposes, of allowing a single representation for many forms occurring in both varieties, and it avoids some purely graphic distinctions between forms in the two varieties such as [denə] (Colloquial, phonemic) and <dena> (Literary, graphemic), which are both pronounced the same. It does, however, mask some real pronunciation differences, for which see the section devoted to phonology. Where necessary, transliteration will be given in angled brackets and phonemic representation will be given in square brackets. For a strictly phonemic analysis of Collo-quial, see Coates and De Silva 1960 and Gair 1970.

2. There may be an exception to this statement if the *-ek* variant is used for the inanimate Literary indefinite, in which case Geiger (1938: 114) implies that the accusative (his "oblique") would still be *-ak*. How far, if at all, this is observed in current usage is still not clear.

3. At one point, Geiger says, restricting himself to animate nouns, that "the declension is confined to the formation of a Direct and an Oblique case in Sing. and Pl., the former being used as subject in the sentence, the latter as object and in conjunction with postpositions" (p. 95). Implied is a possible two-case analysis for Literary Sinhalese that has much to justify it descriptively, though inanimate nouns complicate the picture by having more inflection-ally marked cases. Later, Geiger speaks of Dative, Instrumental, and so on expressed by postfixes and postpositions. The problem is a familiar one in Indian languages and not unlike that encountered with Hindi *larkā* vs. *larke ko*, for example. Ultimately, of course, it becomes a "deep-surface" question and hinges on what we decide to call a case, but here I am con-cerned with comparing varieties rather than with theoretical questions of case and have ad-justed approach and terminology accordingly.

4. Further details for Colloquial Sinhalese are given in Gair 1970.

5. There are other present tense forms in Colloquial Sinhalese, such as the emphatic, the concessive, and so on, as set forth in De Silva 1960 and Gair 1970, but they do not mark person and number in either Literary or Colloquial Sinhala and are thus irrelevant to the present discussion.

6. The Literary Sinhalese forms generally referred to as "future tense" also show agree-ment, but these are not matched in as direct a fashion by any Colloquial forms, so that they are not given here, though they constitute another instance of person-number agreement in, for example, Literary *balannemi* 'I see', *balannemu* 'we see'.

7. As possible exceptions to nonagreement in Colloquial Sinhalese could be cited the optative forms *balannam* and *balāvi* that are restricted to first and nonfirst person respec-tively. However, these are subject also to a different interpretation, and in any event they do not affect what is said here concerning the Literary–Colloquial verb differences within the present and past tenses. (See chapter 2 on inflectional categories and parts of speech.)

8. Nonverbal predicators marked with either these person–number affixes or the asser-tion marker must be counted as "agreeing verbs" for the purpose of the accusative rule as stated earlier, since their subjects are in the nominative case, as *mama* is here.

Later note: On the basis of later work, it seems clear that the Literary assertion marker is in fact a kind of agreement. See chapter 18 and chapter 10, note 7.

9. "Functor" is used here essentially in C. F. Hockett's (1958) sense, though he also includes "pure markers" with no lexical meaning. "Functor" as used here is also essentially

an equivalent to C. C. Fries's "function word" (*The Structure of English*, New York, 1952: 87ff).

10. As long as we are dealing with written forms only, the question of adaptation to phonemic habits does not arise, and Sanskrit words are easily borrowed since there are one-to-one equivalents in Sinhalese script for the symbols in Devanagari. One important aspect of pronunciation is dealt with below in connection with the Sanskrit aspirates. In regard to inflection, it is interesting to note that while there are well-established patterns for adapting nouns and adjectives from Sanskrit, Sinhalese seldom if ever borrows verbs from any source but relies on compounding borrowings with inherited verb forms.

11. In this regard, it is interesting to note the strictures of D. Mendis Gunasekara in 1891: "But the scholar cannot but regret the disuse of the Eḷu or Sanskrit terms that might be employed, now gradually falling into oblivion. The every-day talk, particularly of natives acquainted with English, is too often a miserable conglomeration of Sinhalese, English, Portuguese, Dutch, and Tamil unintelligible in great part save to those familiar with the jargon. It should be the constant endeavor of the student, as far as practicable, to use Eḷu and Sanskrit words in writing and speaking and to dispense with the foreign importations" (Gunasekera 1891: 380–81).

12. Unlike the situation with the aspirates, even practiced and careful speakers of Literary Sinhalese do not distinguish <n> from <ṇ> or <l> from <ḷ> in pronunciation, but they are rendered by the same [n] and [l] as in Colloquial. Nor is ෂ <ṣ> distinguished from ශ <ś>, but both are [š], though they are kept distinct from ස <s> read as [s]. In Colloquial Sinhala, the contrast between [s] and [š] seems to be by now quite well established, though the [š] is as likely to be found in English borrowings as in Sanskrit. Some rural speakers, however, still have only [s].

13. Except for an occasional learned word, Colloquial Sinhalese has only one nasal, [ŋ], in final position; thus, forms that would be spelled with any of the nasals (except ඤ) ṅ, which is not generally written finally, may be rendered [ŋ]. This statement requires some qualification for Literary Sinhalese carefully read aloud, since the reader may be careful to pronounce them as written, rendering ම as [m], න as [n], and ං as [ŋ]. This affords one additional example of differences in pronunciation habits between Literary and Colloquial Sinhalese.

14. Sunil Jayawīra, *Saman Malī*, (Colombo: Saman Press, 1963), 3.

15. Sudassi Nāyaka Thero on July 6, 1965, taken from Radio Ceylon. The <ṇ> has been written and retained in transliteration where it belongs in spelling, although not distinguished in pronunciation (see note 13), and the [a]–[ə] difference is not written, though it is pronounced in the original.

16. Between two friends, graduate students abroad.

17. In an interesting recent article (De Silva 1967), which came to my attention too late to be fully taken account of in the original version of this paper, M. W. S. De Silva, after briefly characterizing the distinction between spoken and Literary Sinhala, devotes himself primarily to accounting for it historically as the product of a forced restoration of the latter variety through successive puristic movements since the late eighteenth century. Though this chapter is descriptive rather than historical in intent, the examples that De Silva gives of written Sinhalese reflecting the spoken language, particularly from the polemic literature of the nineteenth century, are worth noting, since they share many of the characteristics of our intermediate variety with a somewhat different blend of Literary and Colloquial features. If, as does not seem unlikely, they were equally distant from the common Colloquial speech of their day, the use of intermediate varieties of some kind, particularly for didactic and polemical purposes, is not an entirely recent development in Sinhalese.

18. A detailed investigation of the different formal and informal variants in Colloquial Sinhalese in Mimure, an upcountry village, was undertaken as a doctoral dissertation by Bonnie MacDougall at Cornell (see MacDougall 1973).

19. Similarly, the number of phonemically distinct nasals varies on a similar basis, and [ə] is more firmly established as distinct from [a] and [ā] in the speech of some people through English loans such as [pārsəl], [ṭikət], and [saykəl], though some have another vowel, commonly [æ] in these.

20. Differences in kinship terms are touched upon and references to previous work are given in E. R. Leach, "The Sinhalese of the Dry Zone of Northern Ceylon" in G. P. Murdock, ed., *Social Structure in Southeast Asia*, V. King Foundation Publications in Anthropology 29, 1960: 116–26, esp. 124–25. See also G. Obeyesekere, *Land Tenure in Village Ceylon*, Cambridge University Press, Cambridge, 1965: 248–53, N. Yalman, *Under the Bo Tree*, University of California Press, Berkeley, 1967: 209–24, and further references therein.

Chapter 17

1. In making revisions, I have profited by discussions with Willem Pet and Carol Rosen.

2. Later note: While agreeing generally with the conclusions in this paper, Paolillo (1992) has proposed a somewhat different view from mine concerning the structural determinants of the varieties. This topic is addressed in chapter 18 on AGR and diglossia.

3. A good overview of the reading public can be gained from the Marga Institute 1974 survey.

4. A more detailed account of these developments may be gathered from Fernando 1977 and Gair 1980 [1983c]. Since this paper was originally published, English has also been given official status.

5. De Silva (1974) has questioned Formal Spoken as a distinct level, to which I have reacted elsewhere (1978), but in any event, language with those characteristics is used by speakers for a variety of formal or relatively formal purposes, and the sharpness of its distinction from Colloquial Sinhala does not matter for present purposes. See Paolillo 1992 for further characteristics of Formal Spoken Sinhala.

6. Broadly stated, these disputes are often between a group harking back to the poetic language of the thirteenth century, with the use of inherited words, and others advocating a style allowing more Sanskrit borrowings. Interestingly, both styles have roots in the earlier literature. We thus now find sets of synonyms, often with the same ultimate source, such as *dama* vs. *dharmaya* (Colloquial *darume*) 'dharma' *hala* vs. *śālāwa* (Colloquial *saalaawa*) 'hall', *basa* vs. *bhāṣāwa* (Colloquial *baasaawa*) 'language', and *osu* vs. *auṣadhaya* (Colloquial *beet* or *behet*) 'medicine'. Ironically, as the examples show, current Colloquial forms are often closer to the Sanskritic ones.

7. Later Note: In the originally published paper, I omitted mention of the extremely striking example of the lack of the association of class or politico-economic movement with any antidiglossia movement that was provided by the writings produced by revolutionary youth. In the early 1970s, there was an insurrection by the JVP (*Janatā Vimukti Peramuṇa* 'People's Liberation Front') an extreme Marxist-oriented youth movement that was ruthlessly suppressed by the authorities. Their graffiti, including those on prison walls, were in Literary, and in fact often classicized, Sinhala. In the 1980s, there was another violent insurrection under the same name, also ruthlessly suppressed, and as John Paolillo (1992: 103ff.) noted, not only their posters, but those of the progovernment forces were in Literary Sinhala and in poetic form. As he further notes, the written output of all parties, including the Marxist and Socialist ones, adhere to the written norm, though oral presentations are for the most part in Formal Spoken, and no political party has the elimination of diglossia as part of its platform.

8. No extensive data-based study of the features actually used and their frequency has been carried out to my knowledge, but it would seem that the simplest ones to use are those

possible by making essentially one-to-one substitutions from Colloquial Sinhala, which are those that are least redundant in De Silva's (1970 and 1974) sense, such as the substitution of Literary postpositions (see Gair 1968 for details).

9. The flourishing Sinhala drama requires separate treatment, since there are different schools involving different styles.

10. Figure 17-2 has been slightly altered here from the earlier published version, which did not indicate clearly enough that the Standard for Community B was (essentially) equal to the H for Community A.

11. Diglossic bilingualism will characteristically look like Type II in Figure 17-2 except that the language of Communities A and B are different languages rather than the same language. Logically, there could be diglossic bilingualism parallel to Type I as well, in which two languages were confined to a single speech community, but I do not know of any instances.

Type I and Type II, together with diglossic bilingualism, do not exhaust the possibilities, though other situations may be reducible to combinations of them. For example, the situation regarding Latin in relation to the vernaculars in early Renaissance Europe seems to have been Type I diglossia with regard to the Romance-speaking countries, but diglossic bilingualism in relation to, say, England and the Netherlands.

12. Ferguson's observation appears to hold true in general, but there are some near counter examples. For example, it appears that in nineteenth-century Italy, only a very small proportion of the population at the time of independence could speak the variety that was to become the standard, though it was clearly a recognized literary standard (having earlier displaced Latin over a period of time). This appears to be a possible case in which a literary variety in a diglossic situation served as the basis for a later generally accepted standard. One could argue, however, that this was really a case of Type II diglossia, since that H was Tuscan-based. This and similar cases need further close study in terms of the framework proposed here. Even if they do require some revision of Ferguson's statement to make it represent the unmarked case, they do not invalidate the general statement that the fate of diglossia is affected differently in Type I and Type II situations. (I am indebted to Carol Rosen for the account of the Italian situation, for which further details may be found in Tullio De Mauro, *Storia linguistica dell' Italia Unita.* Bari: Laterza, 1970.)

Chapter 18

Thanks are due to Alice Davison and Barbara Lust for discussion, and especially to Jacqueline Toribio for much helpful criticism and editorial suggestions. An earlier version of this paper was given at a colloquium at the University of Iowa on March 13, 1992, and the participants there offered many helpful comments. Special thanks to John Paolillo are also called for. Although much of this paper is a response to him, his critique stimulated a number of refinements to my presentation, and he has contributed a great deal of valuable and open-minded discussion. Errors, are, of course, my own.

1. Sadly, Sugath, who contributed so much to the linguistic study of Sinhala, including the study of diglossia, left us in an untimely fashion. It is thus fitting that, despite the different view from his that I express here on the fundamental features of the diglossia situation, I acknowledge once more my debt to him as a colleague with and as the one who, along with Gordon Fairbanks, also sadly departed, initiated me into the intricacies of Sinhala linguistics. Without them, this paper would not exist.

2. For an extension of this view to other South Asian languages, see Gair and Wali 1988.

3. Paolillo's critique was based on a circulated version of Gair 1992a that was unpublished at the time; hence his 1991 paper deals with my 1992 one, which, however, was essentially unchanged in publication.

4. The phonological or orthographic differences in the representations are largely a function of the different media (spoken and written), and of a three-way contrast among *a*, *aa*, and *ə* in Spoken Sinhala that is unrepresented in written. Here, Spoken forms are represented phonologically, but Literary forms are given in transliteration. For discussion and examples, see Gair 1968 and Paolillo 1992.

5. The Colloquial accusative has an optional character, and, in fact, in some local dialects is used rarely if at all. Thus from a cross-dialectal perspective, there will be a surface nominative variant for every position in which the accusative occurs. In Paolillo 1992, it is referred to as the "theme marker," since it is associated with objects, which characteristically bear that thematic role, as well as with subjects of some verbs that are generally also (affected) themes. However, it can also be regarded as more of a "true" accusative than the Literary form, since its distribution is limited to direct objects or unaccusative subjects (see chapter 6 on subjects, case, and INFL), while the Literary form has a much wider distribution, which will be described later.

6. An excellent and convenient comparative summary of the verb forms, with charts, is given in Paolillo 1992. Details on the formation of the Colloquial forms can be found in Fairbanks, Gair, and De Silva 1968 and 1981, and the Literary forms are detailed in Gair and Karunatilaka 1974 and 1976.

7. Gender agreement is limited to cooccurrence with certain other categories, specifically past tense and certain nonfinite forms. This does not affect the argument here. For details, see the relevant passages of Gair and Karunatilaka 1974.

8. Since inanimate nouns lack an overt nominative–accusative distinction, they could be considered to have a single direct case, in opposition to the oblique cases. Alternatively, one could hold that there is complete homonymity between nominative and accusative in inanimate nominals. The decision between these analyses is fundamentally a theory-internal question since I know of no empirical evidence that would resolve it. The important point is the lack of both distinct nominative marking and of verbal agreement, at least for number, with inanimate nouns. Under the homonymy assumption, together with the claim made in Gair 1992a and this chapter that nominative case requires the presence of AGR surfacing as agreement, the unmarked third person singular on the verb would represent AGR. Under the "direct-only" analysis, nominative case would be relevant only for animate nouns, and nominative would require not the presence of some AGR element but coindexing with it for some specific categories. This would be equally satisfactory for our purposes, since the intimate relationship between agreement and case assignment that we will be stressing remains.

9. Here I deal only with nominal predicate equational sentences. There are also adjectival predicates, but case and agreement features are essentially the same. One qualification that must be made here is that predicate adjectives, if vowel-final, require an affix *-yi* in finite, independent sentences, but there is no reason to consider this to represent AGR agreement as we do the Literary *ya/(y)i* below. For details, see Gair and Paolillo 1988. The history of these forms is touched on in Gair 1986b, where it is also argued that there is not a null copula in Colloquial nonverbal sentences. See Gair 1970 for the range of such sentences in Colloquial Sinhala.

10. Here, of course, I except valence-changing processes such as "involitization" of various sorts, as described in Gair 1990 (chapter 6) where it is argued that they are best regarded as lexical, a notion that was adumbrated in Gair 1970).

11. Sinhala has become a strongly left-branching language, with sentence-final complementizers and subordinating affixes, as well as preposed relative clauses. See Gair 1970 and 1992b for a general description.

12. Actually, a qualification will be necessary for titles and other "freestanding" nominals, which occur in the nominative. This will be dealt with later.

13. Some can use it if forced, but has a decidedly artificial ring.

14. Examples (16) through (19) are from Paolillo 1992: 58–59, with some essentially mechanical changes in transcription and glossing of categories to accord with the system of representation used here.

15. As work by De Silva (1970) showed, these difficulties are not as great in reception, i.e., comprehension, and his conclusion that this was a function of redundancy appears to be the correct one. In turn, this led to my claim (1986a) that the difficulties in learning and coping with the Literary variety would not be a seriously threatening factor, despite the wider use of Sinhala, until there was more necessity to produce it.

16. The qualification "one kind" is necessary because not all agreement phenomena, and not even all verbal agreement, are representative of AGR. For details and specific examples, as well as a classification, see Gair and Wali 1988 and 1989. As pointed out in Gair and Wali 1987 and 1988, however, as in this chapter, Literary Sinhala agreement is to be identified with AGR. The other types, including the abstract AGR claimed for Hindi in the works cited, are irrelevant here.

17. The Chomsky quotation invokes one type of government of the subject by INFL as a crucial element. In some subsequent work, INFL has been decomposed, and the relevant relation between it and the associated NP has been differently conceived, as, for example, as a type of SPEC–HEAD agreement (Koopman and Sportiche 1988 and Toribio and Gair 1991 (this volume)). These do not seriously affect the argument here, however, since the AGR–case relation remains in one form or another, and the fractionated INFL will, in fact, be employed in the discussion of TENSE as case assigner below (see also note 22).

18. It is not necessarily the case that all morphologically represented agreement represents AGR or that AGR must necessarily surface as agreement. See note 16.

19. It also seems advantageous to add a third type, like that which Baker (1988) refers to as semantic case, to allow for adverbial uses of case, but that need not concern us here.

20. Paolillo states that another problem with my hypothesis is that "it does not differentiate between these three environments: (note 12). In the approach taken here, of course, that would be a virtue, if it entailed subsuming them under some general principle or principles.

21. Though some form of the case filter has been accepted by virtually all researchers since it was proposed by Chomsky (1981: 49, 175), there have been different versions of it in the literature, generally relating to whether structural case alone, lexical case, or some combination or disjunction of them is required or adequate to satisfy it.

22. In Pollock's presentation, TP dominates AGRP. For Sinhala at least, it appears that the opposite is the case. Without further justifying that conclusion here, I will simply note that agreement always follows tense in Sinhala, so that under the assumption of successive head raising, the correct layering follows directly from the tree suggested. Several investigators, including Claire Foley at Cornell, have done research to determine the precise configuration that characterizes these elements and negation and to relate it to other languages.

23. Or at the intersection of P(honetic) F(orm) and L(ogical) F(orm) under the version of the theory expressed in Chomsky 1992 (unpublished when this chapter was written). In any case, the account here would appear to be adaptable to that theory.

24. A footnote in Paolillo's 1991 paper states that there are also examples of constructions without agreement but with overt subjects. No examples are given, and I am unsure of what structures are referred to, but on the basis of the 1987 presentation, I assume that the reference is to sentences with essentially modal forms, often referred to in the literature on Sinhala as "quasiverbs" beginning with Gair 1970. These occur in Literary Sinhala with participial complements. If these are indeed the forms at issue, I will simply mention here that there are explanations available, some of which are in fact suggested in Paolillo 1987. I will not attempt to deal with them here, save to note that for them also, the case–AGR linkage

holds. As Paolillo states (1987: 8): "[Literary] quasi verbal sentences are of two types, agreeing and non-agreeing. Those that have agreement have nominative subjects, while those that do not typically have accusative subjects."

25. See, for example Huang 1988 for Chinese and Sūner 1984 for controlled *pro* in Spanish. Gair et al. 1989 deals with the alternation of null and overt subjects in Colloquial conjunctive participles, and Gair in prep (on control) deals with parallel phenomena for infinitive subjects in Colloquial Sinhala. See also Srikumar 1991 for similar phenomena in Malayalam.

26. In fact, Paolillo (1987) suggests an analysis along the lines that I have suggested involving head movement for assignment of accusative (allowing for subsequent developments in the theory of INFL). However, he appears to have since rejected such an approach on the basis of the kinds of evidence cited.

27. The restriction to licensed nominals in the Accusative rule eliminates "free-standing" nominals in titles or citations, which, as stated earlier, appear with nominative case inflection. Note that the Nominative rule does not prohibit such inflection on nominals that do not have structural nominative Case, but only specifies that inflection for nominals with that Case. An interesting effect of this is that both accusative (=oblique) and nominative represent default inflectional case marking, but in different domains, namely nominals that stand in syntactic relations and those that do not.

28. Aside, of course, from such hypercorrect forms as "between you and I."

29. Even this restriction may not hold, since there are sentences with the locative use of the genitive such as *ee gamee hoňday* 'that village-GEN good-PRED' = 'In that village is good.' However, these are clearly subject to another analysis involving a pleonastic null pronominal (i.e., *Ø ee gamee hoňday* or *ee gamee Ø hoňday* 'It's good in that village.' In any event, as yet I have no clear cases that would justify a decision.

30. There are, however, no accusative subjects of transitive verbs. For one proposed explanation for this, see chapter 6.

31. For details and argumentation, see chapter 6.

32. For further discussion, set in a general typological frame for South Asian languages, see Gair and Wali 1988.

33. An exception has to be made for the possessive type with existential or "become" verbs. These may have a quite different structure, with the second NP (possessed) showing more subject properties and necessarily appearing in the nominative case.

34. For a fuller account of the reasons for the scarcity of evidence on this point in Literary Sinhala, see Gair 1992a.

35. What this coindexing mechanism might be need not concern us here, but the structure of focused sentences in Sinhala has received considerable attention in the literature. See especially Gair 1983b; Gair and Paolillo 1988; Gair and Sumangala 1991; and Sumangala 1992.

36. Alternatively, its noninvolitive variant *labanavā* may be used, but that is irrelevant here.

37. This distinguishes them from the phonologically null elements that occur as subject of nonfinite clauses with controlled or abritrary interpretation, i.e., the PRO and PRO$_{arb}$ of GB theory.

38. As stated earlier, the verbs in these sentences are not being used intransitively, as the English translations might otherwise suggest. There are related intransitive verbs *wæwenəwa* 'grow' and *wæhenəwa* 'close', but these are involitive and exclude an agent, whereas the sentences under discussion not only imply an agent but *must* be used if agentivity is involved. Thus they do include, in terms of the theory employed here, a null nominal, to which the agent thematic role is assigned.

39. The results of this are somewhat attenuated by the limited marking of the nominative–accusative distinction, which applies only in the indefinite and the plural and only for animates. Since most nouns in these texts are singular, or proper nouns, or inanimate, the amount of actual overt accusative marking is limited.

40. Paolillo named this variety "Children's Literary Sinhala" (CLS), assuming that I considered it to be a variety of Literary. This was in fact not the case and his assumption was a result of my considering it a transition to Literary Sinhala in a way parallel to L2 learning, and thus using the unfortunately easily misinterpretable section heading "Literary Sinhala as L2—a Facilitating Variety," for which I had not forseen an equational reading. Instead, under the view that agreement is the defining characteristic of Literary Sinhala, these varieties would have more in common with Formal Spoken Sinhala.

41. *Hela* is one classical form for *Siŋhala* and *havula* is 'partnership', or 'association', suggesting the puristic and nativistic character of the group. See De Silva 1967, 1976.

42. As De Silva (1986: 303) states, this seems unduly restrictive when we consider the range of diglossic versus nondiglossic situations. The Sinhala case can easily be accommodated simply by relaxing one of Ferguson's eight characteristics by inserting "usually" before "formal spoken" in the phrase "is used for most written and formal spoken purposes." While it does seem advisable in general not to weaken Ferguson's original insights by including other types of situations, such as bilingual ones (for discussion, see Gair 1986a; Paolillo 1992), the Sinhala situation does clearly appear to be a true case, as De Silva suggests. Hence it seems unnecessary to postulate a new type for it and similar cases. Even the Arabic case would not fit neatly under such a strictly limited definition, at least for Tunisian Arabic and undoubtedly for others (see Belazi 1984). The actual distribution of varieties across situations is also more complex than a simple set of binary decisions on Ferguson's original criteria might suggest. Thus some instances, such as news broadcasts, are indeed in H in Sinhala. For an account, see Gair 1986a; also see the more extensive and detailed treatment in Paolillo 1992, which is in general agreement.

43. Though all of the works cited deal with parameter resetting in L2 acquisition, there are significant differences between them in approach. Thus, White holds that parameter resetting takes time and invokes persistence of the L1 setting as a factor in apparent transfer, while Flynn claims immediate resetting, with the delay being an effect in realization of the deductive consequences of the reset parameter. These differences, while important for L2 acquisition theory, need not be settled here, since all we require is the effects of different parameters and the difficulties and delays resulting therefrom.

Chapter 19

We acknowledge with love and respect the intensely precise assistance of Serena Tennakoon on the data collection and data analyses involved in the results reported in this paper. Her death is an unspeakable personal and professional loss to Sri Lankan studies.

We also acknowledge with thanks the assistance of many of our Sri Lankan collaborators: Professor W. S Karunatillake, Kalyani Karunatillake, Janaki Wijesekara, and the Sri Lankan scholarship of Nancy Goss for assistance in both data collection and analyses. We also thank Alice Davison, Peter Hook, Veneeta Srivastav, Kashi Wali, and John Paolillo for critical comments. The research reported here is partially supported by NSF BNS–8318983, 8206328, 7825115.

1. Sinhala is a diglossic language (Gair 1968), having grammatically and functionally distinct Literary and Colloquial varieties. Literary Sinhala does have a system of subject–verb agreement, which raises other problems for later language acquisition (see chapter 18 and Gair, 1992a). These properties of Sinhala are not dealt with here, since we are confining ourselves strictly to the natural acquisition of Colloquial Sinhala by children.

2. Although the English translation here is passive, this example also illustrates still another type of empty category in Sinhala, "arbitrary *pro*," which roughly equates with English unspecified "they." Thus a more literal rendering would be 'They (unspecified) have

eaten (it) all completely.' This is the usual equivalent for an English passive in Colloquial Sinhala. (For pro_{arb} in Colloquial Sinhala, see chapter 18.)

3. This is sometimes referred to as an "absolutive" participle, a usage we avoid, especially since it invites confusion with the absolutive use of -la, which will be discussed later.

4. One frequent sense is similar to that of the English verb phrase conjoinings that do not obey the conjoined structure constraint (i.e., do not impose subjacency), of the kind noted by Ross (1967): "What did you go to the store and buy?", and they commonly translate such structures. There are other definable senses as well, such as a kind of manner one: *mamə miris daala kæcmə hæduva* 'I chillies put-*la* food made' = 'I made the food (by) putting in chillies.'

5. A sentence with a dative case subject, but otherwise identical to (8a) is in fact possible, as in (8c):

(8) c. *maţə   saddæyak   æhila   diwwa.*
I-DAT   sound-INDEF   hear-*la*   ran
'I heard a sound and ran.'

However, there is a clear difference in that (8c) will allow a direct case nominal, even though coreferent with the dative one, to occur as subject of the main clause. Thus (8d) is grammatical, (though unlikely except in special circumstances, given the general sparseness in pronoun use). However, (8e), where the embedded subject is spelled out, is impossible:

(8) d. *maţə   saddəyak   æhila   mamə   diwwa.*
I-DAT   sound-INDEF   hear-la   I-NOM   ran
'I heard a sound and ran.'

e. * *mamə   maţə   saddəyak   æhila   diwwa.*
I-NOM   I-DAT   sound-INDEF   hear-*la*   ran
'I heard a sound and ran.'

6. Where precisely the -*la* clause is embedded is still an unsettled question. We have assumed an IP left-adjoined to VP, but a different analysis with the clause in SPEC, VP, and/ or CP rather than IP would not affect our argument. The crucial point is that the clause is within IP(=S) and clearly c-commanded by the higher—coreferential—subject, which seems a safe assumption.

7. For some speakers it is formed by adding it to the relativizing form based on the participial stem, hence *diipuaamə* rather than *dunnaamə,* but this is a simple variant not affecting the distribution and does not matter for our purposes. In fact, -*aamə* is historically a contracted form of *hamə* (probably ultimately < Sanskrit *samaya* 'time'), and in careful speech one can still hear *dunnə hamə* or *diipu hamə.*

8. As mentioned in note 2, the term "absolutive participle" has been used for the conjunctive participle, including the -*la* participle in Sinhala (as, for example, Reynolds 1980: 117ff.). Our use of "absolutive," however, refers not to the form itself but to its use in a construction with the specifically "nonsubject-linked" characteristic that has traditionally been referred to as "absolute," a terminological restriction that we find useful to retain.

9. The research paradigm and theoretical underpinnings for this long-term research effort, and a summary of its results, will appear in Lust forthcoming.

10. In the imitation task, 181 subjects between the ages of 2.09 and 6.04 (mean age 4.04) were tested by a native speaker in Sri Lanka in the Colombo and Kadawatha areas. All imitation data were tape recorded and transcribed in Sri Lanka, and transcript accuracy was double checked at Cornell. The results are still undergoing detailed analysis, but a preliminary report on this phase of the research, incorporating Table 19–3, was given as a conference presentation by Lust, Gair, Goss and Rodrigo in 1986.

Chapter 20

This paper was prepared with the partial support of NSF grant #BNS 8318983. An earlier version of it was presented at the annual meeting of SALA 1985 and appeared in Veneeta Srivastav, James W. Gair, and Kashi Wali (eds.), *Cornell University Working Papers in Linguistics: A special issue: Papers on South Asian Linguistics,* (8), Fall 1988. The present version, in a slightly different form, appears in Gambhir 1995. We thank Alice Davison, Vijay Gambhir, and Veneeta Srivastav for critical discussion.

1. For extension of this paradigm to the study of second language acquisition in the adult, and precise links between first and second language acquisition research with regard to this parameter, see Flynn 1987 (and later papers).

2. By "command" here we specifically intend c-command under the definition by which A c-commands B if the first branching node dominating A also dominates B, and A does not dominate B or vice versa (Reinhart 1976).

3. On this point, involving a relation between lexical and null pronouns in Hindi, see Lust, Bhatia, Gair, and Sharma 1995.

4. See Lust in preparation for full discussion of the cross-linguistic results. In point of fact, acquisition data in all languages appear to show some modulation of proform direction with structure, specifically in sentence-branching direction.

5. This question emerges crucially in second language acquisition; cf. Flynn 1987.

BIBLIOGRAPHY

Amararatna, L.S.E. 1969/1981. *Kumārodaya, palamu Śreṇiya, devena pota. (ihala bālāṇśaya). Saṇśōdhita tunvana mudraṇaya* (3rd rev. ed. Colombo: Gunasena.

Amritavalli, K. 1984. Anaphorization in Dravidian. *Central Institute of English and Foreign Languages Working Papers in Linguistics* 1: 1–31.

Anderson, Stephen R., and Edward L. Keenan. 1985. Deixis. In Timothy Shopen, ed. *Language Typology and Syntactic Description*, pp. 259–308. Cambridge: Cambridge University Press.

Andrews, Avery Delano. 1975. Studies in the Syntax of Relative and Comparative Clauses. Ph.D. dissertation, Massachusetts Institute of Technology.

Andrews, Avery Delano. 1982. The Representation of Case in Modern Icelandic. In Joan Bresnan, ed. *The Mental Representation of Grammatical Relations*, pp. 427–503. Cambridge: MIT Press.

Andrewskutty, A. P. 1971. *Malayalam: An Intensive Course*. Trivandrum, India: Dravidian Linguistic Association.

Aoun, Joseph, and Dominique Sportiche. 1983. On the Formal Theory of Government. *Linguistic Review* 2: 211–36.

Arora, H. 1985. Some aspects of Dakkhini Hindi-Urdu Syntax with special reference to convergence. Ph.D. dissertation, Delhi University, India.

Asher, R. E. 1982. Tamil. (Lingua Descriptive Studies 7.) Amsterdam: North-Holland.

Babby, Leonard. 1975. *A Transformational Grammar of Russian Adjectives*. (Janua Linguarum Series Practica 235.) The Hague: Mouton.

Baker, Mark. 1988. *Incorporation*. Chicago: University of Chicago Press.

Bedell, George, Eichi Kobayashi, and Masatake Muraki, eds. 1979. *Explorations in Linguistics: Papers in Honor of Kazuko Inoue*. Tokyo: Kenkyusha.

Belazi, Hedi. 1984. Diglossia and the Situation of Arabic in Tunisia. M.A. Thesis, Cornell University.

Belletti, Adriana. 1988. The Case of Unaccusatives. *Linguistic Inquiry* 19: 1–34.

Belletti, A., L. Brandi, and L. Rizzi, eds. 1981. *Theory of Markedness in Generative Grammar*. Pisa: Scuole Normale Superiore.

Beletti, Adriana, and Luigi Rizzi. 1988. Psych Verbs and θ Theory. *Natural Language and Linguistic Theory* 6: 291–352.

Bever, T. G., and D. T. Langendoen. 1971. A Dynamic Model of the Evolution of Language. *Linguistic Inquiry* 2: 433–63.

Bever, T. G., and D. T. Langendoen. 1972. The Interaction of Speech Perception and Grammatical Structure in the Evolution of Language. In Robert P. Stockwell and K. S. Macaulay, eds., *Linguistic Change and Grammatical Theory*, pp. 32–95. Bloomington: Indiana University Press.

Bhatia, Tej. 1974. Testing Four Hypotheses about Relative Formation and the Applicability of Ross' Constraints in Hindi. Unpublished manuscript, Champaign–Urbana: University of Illinois.

Bloch, Jules.1934. *L'Indo-Aryen du Veda aux Temps Modernes*. Paris: Maisonneuve.

Bloch, Jules. 1965. *Indo-Aryan from the Vedas to Modern Times*, trans. Alfred Master. Paris: Adrien-Maisonneuve.

Bolinger, Dwight. 1961. Syntactic Blends and Other Matters. *Language* 37,3: 366–81.

Brentari, Diane, Greg Larson, and Lynn MacLeod, eds. 1988. *Papers from the Parasession on Agreement in Linguistic Theory*. (Chicago Linguistic Society 24, 2).

Bresnan, Joan, and Sam A. Mchombo. 1987. Topic, Pronoun, and Agreement in Chicheŵa. *Language* 63,4: 685–752.

Bright, William. 1966. Dravidian Metaphony. *Language* 42,2: 311–22.

Bright, William. 1972. The Enunciative Vowel. *International Journal of Dravidian Linguistics* 1,1: 26–55.

Bright, William. 1975. The Dravidian Enunciative Vowel. In Harold F. Schiffman and Carol M. Eastman, eds. *Dravidian Phonological Systems*, pp. 11–46. Seattle: South Asian Studies Program, University of Washington. (Revised version of Bright 1972.)

Brown, Gillian, and George Yule. 1983. *Discourse Analysis*. Cambridge: Cambridge University Press.

Burzio, Luigi. 1986. *Italian Syntax: A Government-Binding Approach*. Dordrecht: Reidel.

Cardona, George. 1992. Indo-Aryan Languages. *International Encyclopedia of Linguistics* 2: 202–6. New York: Oxford University Press.

Carter, Charles. 1924/1965. *A Sinhalese–English Dictionary*. Colombo: M. D. Gunasena.

Chafe, Wallace L. 1965. Meaning in Language. In E. A. Hammel, ed. *Formal Semantic Analysis. American Anthropologist* 67,5: 23–36.

Chafe, Wallace L. 1976. Givenness, Contrastiveness, Definitiveness, Subjects, Topics, and Point of View. In Charles N. Li, ed., *Subject and Topic*, pp. 27–55. New York: Academic Press.

Choe, J. W. 1987. LF Movement and Pied Piping. *Linguistic Inquiry* 18,2: 348–53.

Chomsky, Noam. 1958/1962. A Transformational Approach to Syntax. In Archibald A. Hill, ed., *Third Texas Conference on Problems of Linguistic Analysis in English, 1958*, pp. 124–58. Austin: University of Texas.

Chomsky, Noam. 1971. Deep Structure, Surface Structure and Semantic Interpretation. In Danny D. Steinberg and Leon A. Jakobovits, eds., *Semantics*, pp. 183–216. Cambridge: Cambridge University Press.

Chomsky, Noam. 1973. Conditions on Transformations. In S. Anderson and Paul Kiparsky, eds., *A Festschrift for Morris Halle*, pp. 232–86. New York: Holt, Rinehart and Winston.

Chomsky, Noam. 1981. *Lectures on Government and Binding*. Dordrecht: Foris.

Chomsky, Noam. 1982. *Some Concepts and Consequences of the Theory of Government and Binding*. Cambridge: MIT Press.

Chomsky, Noam. 1986a. *Barriers*. Cambridge: MIT Press.

Chomsky, Noam. 1986b. *Knowledge of Language: Its Nature, Origin, and Use*. New York: Praeger.

Chomsky, Noam. 1989. Some Notes on Economy of Derivation. In I. Laka and A. Mahajan, eds., *Functional Heads and Clause Structure* (*MIT Working Papers in Linguistics 10*), pp. 43–74. Cambridge: MIT Press.

Chomsky, Noam. 1992. *A Minimalist Program for Linguistic Theory*. (MIT Occasional Papers in Linguistics 11.) Cambridge.

Coates, William A., and M. W. S. De Silva. 1960. The Segmental Phonemes of Sinhalese. *University of Ceylon Review* 18,3–4: 163–75.

Cohen, D. 1973. Hindi *apna*: A Problem in Reference Assignment. *Foundations of Language* 10,3: 399–408.

Cohen Sherman, Janet. 1983. *The Acquisition of Control in Complement Sentences*. Ph.D. dissertation, Cornell University.

Cohen Sherman, Janet, and B. C. Lust. 1986. Syntactic and Lexical Constraints on the Acquisition of Control in Complement Sentences. In Barbara Lust, ed., *Studies in the Acquisition of Anaphora* 2: 279–310. Dordrecht: Reidel.

Cohen Sherman, Janet, and B. C. Lust. 1993. Children Are in Control. *Cognition* 46: 1–51.

Comrie, Bernard. 1984. Reflections on Verb Agreement in Hindi and Related Languages. *Linguistics* 22: 857–64.

Comrie, Bernard. 1985. Reply to Saksena: Further Reflections on Verb Agreement in Hindi. *Linguistics* 23: 143–45.

Cowper, Elizabeth. 1988. What Is a Subject? Non-Nominative Subjects in Icelandic. (North Eastern Linguistic Society 18.) 1: 94–108. Amherst: GSLA, University of Massachusetts.

Davison, Alice. 1985. Experiencers and Patients as Subjects in Hindi–Urdu. In Arlene Zide, David Magier, and Eric Schiller, eds., *Proceedings of the Conference on Participant Roles: South Asia and Adjacent Areas*, pp. 168–78. Bloomington: Indiana University Linguistics Club.

Davison, Alice. 1986a. Binding Relations in Correlative Clauses. *CLS* (Chicago Linguistics Society) 22: 154–65.

Davison, Alice. 1986b. Hindi *-kar*: The Problem of Multiple Syntactic Interpretation. In Bh. Krishnamurti, Colin P. Masica, and Anjani Sinha, eds., *South Asian Languages: Structure, Convergence and Diglossia*, pp. 1–14. Delhi: Motilal Banarsidass.

Davison, Alice. 1990. Long Distance Syntactic Anaphors in Hindi–Urdu. Paper presented at the South Asian Languages Analysis Roundtable (SALA 12), Berkeley, June 1990.

Davison, Alice. In preparation. Case, Theta Roles, and Government of Finite Clauses. Iowa City: University of Iowa.

de Abrew, K. Kamal. 1963. A Syntactic Study of the Verbal Piece in Colloquial Sinhalese. M.A. thesis, University of London.

de Abrew, K. Kamal. 1981. The Syntax and Semantics of Negation in Sinhala. Ph.D. dissertation. Cornell University.

De Camp, David. 1971. Toward a Generative Analysis of a Post-Creole Speech Continuum. In Dell Hymes, ed., *Pidginization and Creolization of Languages*, pp. 349–70. Cambridge: Cambridge University Press.

De Silva, M. W. S. 1960. Verbal Categories in Spoken Sinhalese. *University of Ceylon Review* 18,1–2: 96–112.

De Silva, M. W. S. 1963. A Phonemic Statement of the Sinhalese Vowels [ə], [a], and [aa]. *University of Ceylon Review* 21: 71–75.

De Silva, M. W. S. 1967. Effects of Purism on the Evolution of the Written Language: Case History of the Situation in Sinhalese. *Linguistics* 36: 5–17.

De Silva, M. W. S. 1970. Some Thoughts on Linguistic Redundancy. *Modern Ceylon Studies* 1: 147–55.

De Silva, M. W. S. 1974. Convergence in Diglossia: The Sinhalese Situation. In Franklin Southworth and Mahadeo Apte, eds., *Contact and Convergence in South Asian Languages*, pp. 60–91. Ernakulam, India: Dravidian Linguistics Association.

De Silva, M. W. S. 1976. *Diglossia and Literacy*. Mysore: Central Institute of Indian Languages.

De Silva, M. W. S. 1979. *Sinhalese and Other Island Languages of South Asia*. Tübingen: Günther Narr Verlag.

De Silva, M. W. S. 1986. Typology of Diglossia and Its Implications for Literacy. In Bh. Krishnamurti, Colin P. Masica, and Anjani Sinha, eds., *South Asian Languages: Structure, Convergence and Diglossia*, pp. 304–11. Delhi: Motilal Banarsidass.

De Souza, A. T. A. 1969. The Teaching of English, 4. *Ceylon Observer*, April 21.

De Zoysa, A. P. 1964. *Dharmasamaya Sinhala Śabda Koṣaya*, 3 vols. Colombo: Dharmasamaya Press.

Disanayaka, J. B. 1978. In Search of a Lost Language: Some Observations on the Complex Origin of Sinhala. *Ceylon Historical Journal* 25,1–4: 51–57.

Disanayaka, J. B. 1991. *The Structure of Spoken Sinhala 1: Sounds and Their Patterns*. National Institute of Education, Maharagaura, Sri Lanka.

Donaldson, Susan. 1971. Movement in Restrictive Relative Clauses in Hindi. *Studies in the Linguistic Sciences* 1,2: 1–74.

Downing, Bruce T. 1977. Typological Regularities in Postnominal Relative Clauses. In F. R. Eckman, ed., *Current Themes in Linguistics*, pp. 163–94. New York: Wiley.

Downing, Bruce T. 1978. Some Universals of Relative Clause Structure. In Joseph H. Greenberg, ed., *Universals of Human Language*, 4: 375–418. Palo Alto: Stanford University Press.

Elizarenkova, T. 1972. Influence of Dravidian Phonological System on Sinhalese. *International Journal of Dravidian Linguistics* 1,2: 126–37.

Emeneau, Murray B. 1956. India as a Linguistic Area. *Language* 32,1: 3–16.

Emeneau, Murray. 1978. Review of Masica 1976. *Language* 54,1: 201–10.

Emonds, Joseph E. 1976. *A Transformational Approach to English Syntax*. New York: Academic Press.

Enç, M. 1989. Pronouns, Licensing and Binding. *Natural Language and Linguistic Theory* 7,1: 51–91.

Fairbanks, Gordon H., James W. Gair, and M. W. S. De Silva. 1968. *Colloquial Sinhalese*, 2 vols. (Reprinted 1981 and 1994 as *Colloquial Sinhalese (Sinhala)*. Ithaca: South Asia Program, Cornell University.

Feinstein, Mark. 1979. Prenasalization and Syllable Structure. *Linguistic Inquiry* 10,2: 243–78.

Ferguson, Charles A. 1959. Diglossia. *Word* 15: 325–40.

Ferguson, Charles A. 1978. Historical Background of Universals Research. In Joseph Greenberg, ed., *Universals of Human Language*. Vol 1, *Method and Theory*, pp. 7–31. Palo Alto: Stanford University Press.

Fernando, Chitra. 1977. English and Sinhala Bilingualism in Sri Lanka. *Language in Society* 5: 341–60.

Fernando, Madra Siromani. 1973. The Syntax of Complex Sentences in Sinhala. Ph.D. dissertation, University of London.

Fiengo, R., C. T. J. Huang, H. Lasnik, and T. Reinhart. 1988. The Syntax of Wh-in-Situ. *West Coast Conference on Formal Linguistics* 7: 81–98.

Flynn, S. 1987. *Parameter-Setting Model of L2 Acquisition: Studies in Anaphora*. Dordrecht: Reidel.

Flynn, S., and O. Brown. 1989. Three Patterns of Development in Adult Second Language Acquisition. Paper presented at Boston University Child Language Conference, October.

Flynn, Suzanne, and Wayne O'Neil. 1988. *Linguistic Theory in Second Language Acquisition*. Dordrecht: Kluwer.

Fodor, J. A., T. G. Bever, and M. F. Garrett. 1974. *The Psychology of Language*. New York: McGraw-Hill.

Foley, Claire, and James W. Gair. 1993. The Distribution of *no* in Sinhala, or, Is Subordination Necessary to Get Ahead? Paper presented at South Asia Language Analysis Roundtable (SALA 15), Iowa City, May 1993.

Freiden, Robert. 1978. Cyclicity and the Theory of Grammar. *Linguistic Inquiry* 9,4: 519–49.

Fries, Charles C. 1940. *American English Grammar*. New York: Appleton-Century-Crofts.

Fukui, Naoki. 1986. A Theory of Category Projection and Its Applications. Ph.D. dissertation, Massachusetts Institute of Theology.

Fukui, Naoki. 1987. Spec, Agreement, and the Comparative Syntax of English and Japanese. In Joyce McDonough and Bernadette Plunkett, eds., *Proceedings of the North Eastern Linguistic Society 17, 1986*, pp. 193–210. Amherst: GLSA, University of Massachusetts.

Fukui, Naoki, and M. Speas. 1986. Specifiers and Projection. In N. Fukui, T. Rapoport, and E. Sagey, eds., *Theoretical Papers in Linguistics* (MIT Working Papers in Linguistics 8), pp. 128–172. Cambridge: Department of Linguistics and Philosophy, Massachusetts Institute of Theology.

Gair, James W. 1963. Clause Structures in Spoken Colloquial Sinhalese. Ph.D. dissertation, Cornell University.

Gair, James W. 1965. Which Sinhalese. *USEF* (United States Educational Foundation) *Newsletter* (Colombo), June.

Gair, James W. 1967. Colloquial Sinhalese Inflectional Categories and Parts of Speech. *Indian Linguistics* 27: 32–45. Chapter 2, this volume.

Gair, James W. 1968. Sinhalese Diglossia. *Anthropological Linguistics* 10,8: 1–15. Chapter 16, this volume.

Gair, James W. 1970. *Colloquial Sinhalese Clause Structures*. The Hague: Mouton.

Gair, James W. 1971. Action Involvement Categories in Colloquial Sinhalese. In Mario D. Zamora, J. Michael Mahar, and Henry Orenstein, eds., *Themes in Culture: Essays in Honor of Morris E. Opler*, pp. 238–256. Manila: Kayumanggi Publishers. Chapter 3, this volume.

Gair, James W. 1976a. Is Sinhala a Subject Language, or How Restricted Is your PNP? In Manindra Verma, ed., *The Notion of Subject in South Asian Languages*, pp. 39–64. Madison: South Asia Program, University of Wisconsin.

Gair, James W. 1976b. The Verb in Sinhala, with Some Preliminary Remarks on Dravidianization. *International Journal of Dravidian Linguistics* 10,8: 259–73. Chapter 15, this volume.

Gair, James W. 1978. Review of Southworth and Apte 1974. *Language* 54: 461–65. Chapter 13, this volume.

Gair, James W. 1980. Adaptation and Naturalization in a Linguistic Area: Sinhala Focused Sentences. *Proceedings of the Annual Meeting of the Berkeley Linguistic Society*, pp. 28–43. Berkeley: Berkeley Linguistics Society.

Gair, James W. 1982. Sinhala, an Indo-Aryan Isolate. *South Asian Review* 6,3: 51–64. Chapter 1, this volume.

Gair, James W. 1983a. Ambiguity Is No Relative Matter, or How Do You Treat Your Doubtful Relatives? In F. B. Agard and G. B. Kelley, eds., *Essays in Honor of Charles F. Hockett*, pp. 128–46. Leyden: E. J. Brill.

Gair, James W. 1983b. Non-configurationality, Movement, and Sinhala Focus. Paper presented at the Linguistics Association of Great Britain, Newcastle, September. Chapter 5, this volume.

Gair, James W. 1983c. Sinhala and English in Post-Independence Sri Lanka: Effects of a Language Act. *Language Problems and Language Planning* 8,1: 43–59.

Gair, James W. 1985a. Deictic–Anaphoric Interaction in Sinhala. Paper presented at South Asian Languages Analysis Roundtable (SALA 7), Ann Arbor, University of Michigan.

Gair, James W. 1985b. How Dravidianized Was Sinhala Phonology? In Richard L. Leed and Veneeta Acson, eds., *Festschrift for Gordon H. Fairbanks*, pp. 37–55. Honolulu: Oceanic Linguistics, University of Hawaii. Chapter 14, this volume.

Gair, James W. 1986a. Sinhala Diglossia Revisited, or Diglossia Dies Hard. In Bh. Krishnamurti, Colin P. Masica, and Anjani Sinha, eds., *South Asian Languages: Structure, Convergence and Diglossia*, pp. 322–36. Delhi: Motilal Banarsidass. Chapter 17, this volume.

Gair, James W. 1986b. Sinhala Focused Sentences: Naturalization of a Calque. In Bh. Krishnamurti, Colin P. Masica, and Anjani Sinha, eds., *South Asian Languages: Structure, Convergence and Diglossia*, pp. 147–64. Delhi: Motilal Banarsidass. Chapter 11, this volume.

Gair, James W. 1990. Pronouns, Reflexives, and Anti-anaphora in Sinhala. Paper presented at the South Asian Languages Analysis Roundtable (SALA 12), Berkeley, June 1990.

Gair, James W. 1991a. Discourse and Situational Deixis in Sinhala. In B. Lakshmi Bai and R. Ramakrishna Reddy, eds., *Studies in Dravidian and General Linguistics: A Festschrift for Bh. Krishnamurti*, pp. 448–67. Hyderabad, India: Osmania University Publications in Linguistics 6.

Gair, James W. 1991b. Subjects, Case and INFL in Sinhala. In Manindra K. Verma and K. P. Mohanan, eds., *Experiencer Subjects in South Asian Languages*, pp. 13–41. Palo Alto, Calif.: Center for the Study of Language and Information. Chapter 6, this volume.

Gair, James W. 1992a. AGR, INFL, Case and Sinhala Diglossia, or, Can Linguistic Theory Find a Home in Variety. In Braj Kachru, Edward C. Dimock, and Bh. Krishnamurti, eds., *Dimensions of South Asia as a Sociolinguistic Area: Papers in Memory of Gerald B. Kelley*, pp. 179–97. Delhi: Oxford India Book House.

Gair, James W. 1992b. Sinhala. *International Encyclopedia of Linguistics* 3: 439–45. New York: Oxford University Press.

Gair, James W. 1994. Universals and the South–South Asian Language Area. Paper presented at the South Asian Languages Analysis Roundtable (SALA 16), Philadelphia, May.

Gair, James W. 1995. Linguistic Theory, L2 Acquisition Research, and Pedagogical Applications: Restoring the Link. In Vijay Gambhir, ed., *The Teaching and Acquisition of South Asian Languages*, University of Pennsylvania Press.

Gair, James W. 1997. Some Problems of Control in Sinhala. Paper presented at the Workshop on Nulls in South Asian Languages, University of Delhi, January.

Gair, James W., Suzanne Flynn, and Olga Brown. 1993. Why Japanese Object to L2 Objects. Unpublished manuscript, Cornell University and Massachusetts Institute of Technology.

Gair, James W., and W. S. Karunatilaka (Karunatillake). 1974. *Literary Sinhala*. Ithaca: South Asia Program, Cornell University.

Gair, James W., and W. S. Karunatilaka (Karunatillake). 1976. *Literary Sinhala Inflected Forms: A Synopsis*. Ithaca: South Asia Program, Cornell University.

Gair, James W., W. S. Karunatillake, and John Paolillo. 1987. *A Colloquial Sinhala Reader* (Part 3 of *Colloquial Sinhala*). Ithaca: South Asia Program, Cornell University.

Gair, James W., Barbara C. Lust, Lelwala Sumangala, and Milan Rodrigo. 1989. Acquisition of Null Subjects and Control in Sinhala Adverbial Clauses. *Papers and Reports on Child Language Development* 28: 97–106. Palo Alto: Department of Linguistics, Stanford University. Chapter 19, this volume.

Gair, James W., and John Paolillo. 1988. Sinhala Non-Verbal Sentences and Argument Structure. In Veneeta Srivastav, J. W. Gair, and Kashi Wali, eds., *Cornell Working Papers in Linguistics 8 (Special Issue on South Asian Linguistics)*, pp. 39–77. Ithaca: Cornell University. Chapter 7, this volume.

Gair, James W., and L. Sumangala. 1991. What to Focus in Sinhala. In Germán F. Westphal, Benjamin Ao, and Hee-Rahk Chase, eds., *ESCOL '91: Proceedings of the Eighth Eastern States Conference on Linguistics*, pp. 93–108. Columbus, Ohio State University Working Papers.

Gair, James W., and S. Suseendirarajah. 1981. Some Aspects of the Jaffna Tamil Verbal System. *International Journal of Dravidian Linguistics* 10,2: 370–84.

Gair, James W., S. Suseendirarajah and W.S. Karunatilaka (Karunatillake). 1978. *Introduction to Spoken [Sri Lanka Jaffna] Tamil*. Colombo: University of Sri Lanka External Services Division.

Gair, James W., and Kashi Wali. 1986. Case and Verb Agreement in Hindi and Marathi. Paper presented to the Language and Communication Conference, Syracuse University.

Gair, James W., and Kashi Wali. 1987. AGR and *agr* in Marathi. Paper presented at the South Asian Languages Analysis Roundtable (SALA 9), Ithaca, New York, June 1987.

Gair, James W., and Kashi Wali. 1988. On Distinguishing *agr* from AGR: Evidence from South Asia. In Diane Brentari, Greg Larson, and Lynn MacLeod, eds., *Papers from the Parasession on Agreement in Linguistic Theory (Chicago Linguistic Society* 24, 2), pp. 87–104. Chapter 10, this volume.

Gair, James W., and Kashi Wali. 1989. Hindi Agreement as Anaphor. *Linguistics* 27: 45–70.

Gambhir, Vijay. 1981. Syntactic Restrictions and Discourse Functions of Word Order in Standard Hindi. Ph.D. dissertation, University of Pennsylvania.

Gambhir, Vijayed, ed. 1995. *The Teaching and Acquisition of South Asian Languages*. Philadelphia: University of Pennsylvania Press.

Garusinghe, Dayaratne. 1962. *Sinhalese, the Spoken Idiom*. Munich: Max Hueber Verlag.

Geiger, Wilhelm. 1935. Sinhalese Language and Literature. In D. B. Jayatilaka, ed., *Dictionary of the Sinhalese Language*, 1: xvii–xxxviii. Colombo: Royal Asiatic Society.

Geiger, Wilhelm. 1938. *A Grammar of the Sinhalese Language*. Colombo: Royal Asiatic Society.

Geiger, Wilhelm. 1941. *An Etymological Glossary of the Sinhalese Language*. Colombo: Royal Asiatic Society, Ceylon Branch.

George, K. M. 1971. *Malayalam Grammar and Reader*. Kottayam, India: National Book Stall.

George, Leland, and Jacklin Kornfilt. 1981. Finiteness and Boundedness in Turkish. In Frank Heny, ed., *Binding and Filtering*, pp. 105–128. London: Croom Helm.

Greenberg, Joseph H. 1966. Some Universals of Grammar with Particular Reference to the Order of Meaningful Elements. In Joseph H. Greenberg, ed., *Universals of Language*, pp. 73–113. Cambridge: MIT Press.

Grierson, Sir George A. 1931–33. On the Modern Indo-Aryan Vernaculars. *The Indian Antiquary*, vols. 60 (1931), 61 (1932), and 62 (1933). Bombay: British India Press.

Gunasekara, D. Mendis. 1891/1962. *A Comprehensive Gramrnar of the Sinhalese Language.* Colombo: Sri Lanka Sahitya Mandalaya.

Gunasinghe, Khema Hemamala Himaransi. 1978. "Do" and "Happen": The Ergative in Colloquial Sinhala, A Semantic Analysis. M.A. Thesis, University of Victoria.

Gunasinghe, Khema Hemamala Himaransi. 1985. Passive Voice: A New Perspective. Some Evidence for a Reanalysis from Sinhala. Ph.D. dissertation, University of Victoria.

Gurtu, B. 1985. Anaphoric Relations in Hindi and English. Ph.D. dissertation, Central Institute of English and Foreign Languages.

Gurulugomi. ca. 1200/1967. *Amāvatura*, ed. Kōdāgoḍa Śrī Ñānālokanāyaka Sthavirayan Vahansē. Colombo: Gunasena.

Hale, Kenneth. 1978. *On the Position of Walbiri in a Typology of the Base.* Massachusetts Institute of Technology. Indiana University Linguistics Club, Bloomington.

Hale, Kenneth. 1981. Preliminary Remarks on Configurationality. In J. Pustejovsky and P. Sells, eds., *Proceedings of the North Eastern Linguistic Society* 12: 89–96.

Hale, Kenneth. 1983. Warlpiri and the Grammar of Non-configurational Languages. *Natural Language and Linguistic Theory* 1,1: 5–47.

Harbert, Wayne. 1991 (1987). Binding, SUBJECT, and Accessibility. In Robert Freidin, ed., *Principles and Parameters in Comparative Grammar.* Cambridge: MIT Press, 29–55.

Harbert, Wayne, and Veneeta Srivastav. 1988. Principle A and Accessibility. Unpublished manuscript, Cornell University.

Harbert, Wayne, and Alameida Toribio. 1991. Nominative Objects. *Cornell Working Papers in Linguistics* 9: 127–92.

Harris, Zelig S. 1957. Co-occurrence and Transformations in Linguistic Structure. *Language* 33,3: 283–345.

Herring, Susan G., and John Paolillo. 1991. Focus Position in SOV Languages. Unpublished manuscript, California State University, San Bernardino.

Hettiaratchi, D. E. 1959. The Languages of Ceylon. In Senarat Paranavitana, ed., *The History of Ceylon* 1: 33–45. Colombo: Ceylon University Press Board.

Hettiaratchi, D. E. 1974. History of the Sinhalese Verb. *Journal of the Royal Asiatic Society, Ceylon Branch, N. S.* xviii: 41–53.

Hinds, John. 1973. Anaphoric Demonstratives in Japanese. *Journal of the Association of Teachers of Japanese* 8: 1–14.

Hock, Hans Heinrich. 1982. The Sanskrit Quotative: A Historical and Comparative Study. *Studies in the Linguistic Sciences* 12,2: 39–85.

Hock, Hans Heinrich. 1991. *Principles of Historical Linguistics*, 2nd ed. Berlin: Mouton-De Gruyter.

Hockett, Charles F. 1958. *A Course in Modern Linguistics.* New York: Macmillan.

Hockett, Charles F. 1960. Grammar for the Hearer. In Roman Jakobson, ed., *The Structure of Language in Its Mathematical Aspects* (Proceedings of Symposia in Applied Mathematics, vol 12), pp. 220–36, American Mathematical Society.

Hockett, Charles F. 1968. *The State of the Art.* The Hague: Mouton.

Holmes, V. M. 1973. Order of Main and Subordinate Clauses in Sentence Perception. *Journal of Verbal Learning and Verbal Behavior* 12: 285–93.

Horvath, Julia. 1981. Aspects of Hungarian Syntax and the Theory of Grammar. Ph.D. dissertation, University of California at Los Angeles.

Horvath, Julia. 1985. *Focus in the Theory of Grammar and the Syntax of Hungarian.* Dordrecht: Foris.

Hsu, Jennifer Ryan, H. Cairns, and R. W. Fiengo. 1985. The Development of Grammars Underlying Children's Interpretation of Complex Sentences. *Cognition* 20: 25–48.

Huang, C.-T. James. 1982. *Logical Relations in Chinese and the Theory of Grammar*. Ph.D. dissertation, Massaachusetts Institute of Technology.

Huang, C.-T James. 1983. A Note on the Binding Theory. *Linguistic Inquiry* 14, 3: 554–61.

Huang, C.-T James. 1989. Pro-drop in Chinese: A Generalized Control Theory. In K. Safir and O. Jaeggli, eds., *The Null Subject Parameter*, pp. 185–214. Dordrecht: Kluwer.

Inman, Michael. 1988. Colloquial Sinhala Morphosyntax. Unpublished manuscript, Stanford University.

Inman, Michael Vincent. 1993. Semantics and Pragmatics of Colloquial Sinhala Involitive Verbs. Ph.D. dissertation, Stanford University.

Jayaseelan, K. A. 1989. Question-Word Movement in Malayalam. Unpublished manuscript. Hyderabad: Central Institute of English and Foreign Languages.

Kachru, Yamuna. 1978. On Relative Clause Formation in Hindi–Urdu. *Linguistics* 207: 5–25.

Kachru, Yamuna. 1979. The Quotative in South Asian Languages. In Braj B. Kachru, Hans Henrich Hock, and Yamuna Kachru, eds., *South Asian Language Analysis* 1: 63–77.

Kachru, Yamuna. 1980. *Aspects of Hindi Grammar*. New Delhi: Manohar.

Kachru, Yamuna. 1986. The Syntax of Dakkhini: A Study in Language Variation and Language Change. In Bh. Krishnamurti, Colin P. Masica, and Anjani Sinha, eds., *South Asian Languages: Structure, Convergence and Diglossia*, pp. 304–11. Delhi: Motilal Banarsidass.

Kachru, Yamuna. 1992. Hindi. *International Encyclopedia of Linguistics* 2: 123–27. New York: Oxford University Press.

Kachru, Yamuna, and Tej K. Bhatia. 1975. Evidence for Global Constraints: The Case of Reflexivization in Hindi–Urdu. *Studies in the Linguistic Sciences* 5,1: 42–73.

Kachru, Yamuna, and Tej K. Bhatia. 1977. On Reflexivization in Hindi–Urdu and Its Theoretical Implications. *Indian Linguistics* 38,1: 21–38.

Kachru, Yamuna, Braj Kachru, and Tej Bhatia. 1976. The Notion Subject: A Note on Hindi–Urdu, Kashmiri, and Panjabi. In Manindra Verma, ed., *The Structure of the Noun Phrase in English and Hindi*, pp. 79, 108. New Delhi: Motilal Banarsidass.

Kamio, Akio. 1979. On the Notion Speaker's Territory of Information. In George Bedell, Eichi Kobayashi, and Masatake Muraki, eds., *Explorations in Linguistics: Papers in Honor of Kazuko Inoue*, pp. 215, 231. Tokyo: Kenkyusha.

Kanapathi Pillai, M. 1952. *Poruḷoo Poruḷ*. In *Irunātakam*. Chavakachcheri: Ilaykāpimāni Publishers.

Kanapathi Pillai, M. 1958. The Jaffna Dialect of Tamil: A Phonological Study. *Indian Linguistics 19 Turner Jubilee* Volume, 219–227.

Karunatillake, W. S. 1969. Historical Phonology of Sinhalese from Old Indo-Aryan to the 14th Century A.D. Ph.D. dissertation, Cornell University.

Karunatillake, W. S. 1977. The Position of Sinhala Among the Indo-Aryan Languages. *Indian Journal of Linguistics* 4: 1–6.

Kavadi, Naresh B., and Franklin C. Southworth. 1965. *Spoken Marathi*, Book 1. Philadelphia: University of Pennsylvania Press.

Kayne, Richard. 1981. ECP Extensions. *Linguistic Inquiry* 12: 93–133.

Keenan, Edward L. 1978. Relative Clauses in the Languages of the World. Unpublished manuscript, UCLA Typology Project, University of California at Los Angeles.

Keenan, Edward L., and Bernard Comrie. 1977. Noun Phrase Accessibility and Universal Grammar. *Linguistic Inquiry* 8: 63–79. University of California at Los Angeles.

Kishimoto, Hideki. 1991. LF Pied Piping: Evidence from Sinhala. Unpublished manuscript, Tottori University, Japan.

Kiss, Katalin. 1981. Focus and Topic: The Marked Constituents of Hungarian Sentence Structure. In A. Belletti, L. Brandi, and L. Rizzi, eds., *Theory of Markedness in Generative Grammar*, pp. 347–62. Pisa: Scuole Normale Superiore.

Kitagawa, Chisato. 1979. A Note on *Sono* and *Ano*. In George Bedell, Eichi Kobayashi, and Masatake Muraki, eds., *Explorations in Linguistics: Papers in Honor of Kazuko Inoue*, pp. 212–43. Tokyo: Kenkyusha.

Klaiman, M. H. 1977. Bengali Syntax: Possible Dravidian Influence. *International Journal of Dravidian Linguistics* 3,1: 135–53.

Klaiman, M. H. 1986. Semantic Parameters and the South Asian Linguistic Area. In Bh. Krishnamurti, Colin P. Masica, and Anjani Sinha, eds., *South Asian Languages: Structure, Convergence and Diglossia*, pp. 179–94. Delhi: Motilal Banarsidass.

Kodagoda, Ñaṇaloka Sthavirayan Vahanse, ed. 1967. *Amāvatura* (Gurulugomi). Colombo: Gunasena.

Koopman, Hilda, and Dominique Sportiche. 1986. Subjects. Unpublished manuscript, University of California at Los Angeles.

Koster, Jan. 1978. *Locality Principles in Syntax*. Dordrecht: Fortis.

Krishnamurti, Bh. 1974. Topicalization/Verb Inversion Transformation. In *A Generative Grammatical Sketch of Telugu*. Hyderabad: Osmania University.

Krishnamurti, Bh. 1992a. Dravidian Languages. *International Encyclopedia of Linguistics*, 1: 373–78. New York: Oxford University Press.

Krishnamurti, Bh. 1992b. Telugu. *International Encyclopedia of Linguistics*, 4: 137–41. New York: Oxford University Press.

Krishnamurti, Bh., Colin P. Masica, and Anjani Sinha, eds. 1986. *South Asian Languages: Structure, Convergence and Diglossia*. Delhi: Motilal Banarsidass.

Kuiper, F. B. J. 1962. Notes on Old Tamil and Jaffna Tamil. *Indo-Iranian Journal* 1: 52–64.

Kuno, Susumu. 1973. *The Structure of the Japanese Language*. Cambridge: MIT Press.

Kuno, Susumu. 1974. The Position of Relative Clauses and Conjunctions. *Linguistic Inquiry* 5: 117–36.

Kuroda, S.-Y. 1986. Whether We Agree or Not: Rough Ideas about the Comparative Syntax of English and Japanese. Unpublished manuscript, University of California at San Diego.

Lakshmi Bai, B. 1985. A Note on Syntactic Convergence among Indian Languages. In Bh. Krishnamurti, Colin P. Masica, and Anjani Sinha, eds., *South Asian Languages: Structure, Convergence and Diglossia*, pp. 195–208. Delhi: Motilal Banarsidass.

Langacker, R. 1969. On Pronominalization and the Chain of Command. In D. A. Reibel and S. A Schane, eds., *Modern Studies in English*. Englewood Cliffs, N.J.: Prentice Hall.

Lasnik, Howard. 1976. Remarks on Coreference. *Linguistic Analysis* 2,1: 1–22.

Lees, Robert B. 1960. *The Grammar of English Nominalizations*. (Publication 12.) Indiana University Research Center on Anthropology, Folklore, and Linguistics. (International Journal of American Linguistics 26,3, part 2).

Lehmann, Winifred. 1973. A Structural Principle of Language and Its Implications. *Language* 49: 47–66.

Lehmann, Winifred, ed. 1978. *Syntactic Typology*. Austin: University of Texas Press.

Letterman, Rebecca. 1997. The Effects of Word-Internal Prosody in Sinhala: A Constraint-Based Analysis. Ph.D. Dissertation, Cornell University.

Lindholm, James M. 1972. Cleft Sentences in Tamil and Malayalam. In V. I. Subramoniam and Elias Valentine, eds., *Proceedings of the First All India Conference of Dravidian Linguists*, pp. 297–306. Trivandrum, India: Dravidian Linguistics Association.

Lowenstein, Joanna H. 1993. An Exploration of the Bengali Quotative. B.A. honors thesis in linguistics, Cornell University.

Lust, Barbara C. 1986. Introduction. In B. Lust, ed., *Studies in the Acquisition of Anaphora.* Vol. 1, *Defining the Constraints*, pp. 3–106. Dordrecht: Reidel.

Lust, Barbara C., ed. 1987. *Studies in the Acquisition of Anaphora.* Vol. 2. *Applying the Constraints.* Dordrecht: Reidel.

Lust, Barbara C. 1994. Functional Projection of CP and Phrase Structure Parameterization: An Argument for the "Strong Continuity Hypothesis". In B. Lust, M. Suñer, and J. Whitman, eds., *Syntactic Theory and First Language Acquisition: Cross-Linguistic Perspectives.* Vol. 1. *Heads, Projections, and Learnability*, pp. 85–118. Hillsdale, N.J.: Lawrence Erlbaum.

Lust, Barbara C. In preparation. *Universal Grammar and the Initial State: Cross-Linguistic Studies of Directionality.* Cambridge, Mass.: Bradford Books.

Lust, Barbara C., Tej K. Bhatia, James Gair, Vashini Sharma, and Jyoti Khare. 1995. Children's Acquisition of Hindi Anaphora in *jab* Clauses: A Parameter Setting Paradox. In Vijay Gambhir, ed., *The Teaching and Acquisition of South Asian Languages*, pp. 197–218. Philadelphia: University of Pennsylvania Press. Chapter 20, this volume.

Lust, Barbara C., and Y.-C Chien. 1984. The Structure of Coordination in First Language Acquisition of Mandarin Chinese: Evidence for a Universal. *Cognition* 17: 49–83.

Lust, Barbara C., Y.-C Chien, and Suzanne Flynn. 1987. What Children Know: Comparison of Experimental Methods for the Study of First Language Acquisition. In Barbara C. Lust, ed., *Studies in the Acquisition of Anaphora.* Vol. 2, *Applying the Constraints*, pp. 271–356. Dordrecht: Reidel.

Lust, Barbara C., Julie Eisele, and Reiko Mazuka. 1992. The binding theory module: Evidence from first language acquisition for Principle C. *Language* 68(12): 333–58.

Lust, Barbara C., James C. Gair, Nancy Goss, and Milan Rodrigo. 1987. Acquisition of Empty Categories in Sinhala. Paper presented at South Asian Languages Analysis Roundtable (SALA 8). Champaign-Urbana, June.

Lust, Barbara C., Gabriella Hermon, and Jaklin Kornfilt, eds. 1994. *Syntactic Theory and First Language Acquisition.* Vol. 2, *Binding, Dependencies and Learnability.* Hillsdale, N.J.: Lawrence Erlbaum.

Lust, Barbara C., and L. Mangione. 1983. The Principal Branching Direction Parameter Constraint in First Language Acquisition of Anaphora. In P. Sells and C. Jones, eds., *Proceedings of the North Eastern Linguistic Society* 13: 145–60. Amherst: GSLA, University of Massachusetts.

Lust, Barbara C., and Reiko Mazuka. 1989. Cross-linguistic Studies of Directionality in First Language Acquisition: The Japanese Data. *Journal of Child Language* 665–84.

Lust, Barbara C., L. Solan, S. Flynn, S. C. Cross, and E. Schuetz. 1986. A Comparison of Null and Pronoun Anaphora in First Language Acquisition. In Barbara C. Lust, ed., *Studies in the Acquisition of Anaphora.* Vol. 1, *Applying the Constraints*, pp. 245–77. Dordrecht: Reidel.

Lust, Barbara C., T. Wakayama, W. Snyder, R. Mazuka, and S. Oshima. 1985. Configurational Factors in Japanese Anaphora: Evidence from Acquisition. Paper presented at the Linguistic Society of America conference, Seattle, December.

Lyons, John. 1977. *Semantics.* Cambridge: Cambridge University Press.

Lyons, John. 1979. Deixis and Anaphora. In T. Myers, ed., *The Development of Conversation and Discourse*, pp. 88–103. Edinburgh: Edinburgh University Press.

MacDougall, Bonnie G. 1973. Diversity in Highland Sinhalese. Ph.D. dissertation, Cornell University.

Madhavan, P. 1987. Clefts and Pseudoclefts in English and Malayalam: A Study in Comparative Syntax. Ph.D. dissertation, Central Institute of English and Foreign Languages, Hyderabad.

Magier, David. 1983. Components of Ergativity in Marwari.*CLS* (*Chicago Linguistics Society*) 19: 244–55.

Mallinson, Graham, and Barry Blake. 1981. *Language Typology: Cross-Linguistic Studies in Syntax.* Amsterdam: North Holland.

Marantz, Alec C. 1984. *On the Nature of Grammatical Relations.* Cambridge: MIT Press.

Marga Institute. 1974. *The Sinhala Reading Public.* (Marga Research Studies 4.) Colombo: Marga Institute.

Martohardjono, Gita, and James W. Gair. 1991. Apparent UG Inaccessibility in Second Language Acquisition: Misapplied Principles or Principled Misapplications? In Fred Eckman, ed., *Linguistics, L2 Acquisition, Speech Pathology*, pp. 79–103. Amsterdam: John Benjamins.

Masica, Colin P. 1971. A Study of the Distribution of Certain Syntactic and Semantic Features in Relation to the Definability of an Indian Linguistic Area. Ph.D. dissertation, University of Chicago.

Masica, Colin P. 1972. Relative Clauses in South Asia. In Paul M. Peranteau, Judith N. Levi, and Gloria C. Phares, eds., *The Chicago Which Hunt: Papers from the Relative Clause Festival*, pp. 198–204. Chicago: Chicago Linguistic Society.

Masica, Colin P. 1976. *Defining a Linguistic Area: South Asia.* Chicago: University of Chicago Press.

Masica, Colin P. 1991. *The Indo-Aryan Languages.* New York: Cambridge University Press.

Masica, Colin P. 1992. South Asian Languages. *International Encyclopedia of Linguistics* 4: 38–41. New York: Oxford University Press.

McCawley, James. 1972. Japanese Relative Clauses. In Paul M. Peranteau, Judith N. Levi, and Gloria C. Phares, eds., *The Chicago Which Hunt: Papers from the Relative Clause Festival*, pp. 205–14. Chicago: Chicago Linguistic Society.

McGregor, R. 1972. *Outline of Hindi Grammar.* Delhi: Oxford University Press.

Meenakshi, K. 1986. The Quotative in Indo-Aryan. In Bh. Krishnamurti, Colin P. Masica, and Anjani Sinha, eds., *South Asian Languages: Structure, Convergence and Diglossia*, pp. 209–18. Delhi: Motilal Banarsidass.

Moag, Rodney F. 1986. *Malayalam: A University Course and Reference Grammar* (rev. ed.). Ann Arbor: Center for South and Southeast Asian Studies, University of Michigan.

Mohanan, K. P. 1981a. Grammatical Relations and Anaphora in Malayalam. M.S. thesis, Massachusetts Institute of Technology.

Mohanan, K. P. 1981b. Pronouns in Malayalam. *Studies in the Linguistic Sciences* 11,2: 67–75.

Mohanan, K. P. 1982. Grammatical Relations and Anaphora in Malayalam. In Alec Marantz and Tim Stowell, eds., *Papers in Syntax: MIT Working Papers in Linguistics* 4: 163–90.

Mohanan, K. P. 1983. Grammatical Relations and Clause Structure in Malayalam. In Joan Bresnan, ed., *The Mental Representation of Grammatical Relations*, pp. 504–89. Cambridge: MIT Press.

Mohanan, K. P. 1992. Malayalam. *International Encyclopedia of Linguistics* 2: 270–374. New York: Oxford University Press.

Moulton, William G. 1962. What Standard for Diglossia? The Case of German Switzerland. *Report of the 13th Annual Roundtable on Languages and Linguistic Studies*, pp. 133–44. Washington, D.C.: Georgetown University.

Nishigauchi, Taisuke. 1990. *Quantification in Syntax.* Dordrecht: Kluwer.

Nuñez, Del Prado, Zelmira, and James W. Gair. 1994. The Position of Negation in Bengali: An Account of Synchronic and Diachronic Variation. In Alice Davison and Frederick M. Smith, eds., *Papers from the Fifteenth South Asian Language Analysis Roundtable* (SALA 15), pp. 234–50. Iowa City: South Asia Studies Program, University of Iowa.

Ortiz de Urbina, Juan. 1983. Empty Categories and Focus in Basque. *Studies in the Linguistic Sciences* 13,1: 133–56.

Ostler, N. 1979. Case-Linking: A Theory of Case and Verb Diathesis Applied to Sanskrit. Ph.D. dissertation, Massachusetts Institute of Technology.

Pandharipande, Rajeshwari. 1992. Marathi. *International Encyclopedia of Linguistics* 2: 386–89. New York: Oxford University Press

Paolillo, John C. 1986. The Syntax and Semantics of Predication in Sinhala. B.A honors thesis, Cornell University.

Paolillo, John. 1989a. A Brief Look at Factors in the Development of the Literary Sinhala Passive. Unpublished manuscript, Stanford University.

Paolillo, John. 1989b. Literary Sinhala—A Syntactic Sketch of Clause Types. Unpublished manuscript, University of Kelaniya, Sri Lanka.

Paolillo, J. 1990. Why Agreement Is a Marker of H in Sinhala. Paper presented at the 12th Annual South Asian Language Analysis Workshop, Berkeley, June.

Paolillo, John. 1991. Sinhala Diglossia and the Theory of Government and Binding. *Southwest Journal of Linguistics* 10,1: 41–59.

Paolillo, John. 1992. Functional Articulation in Diglossia: A Case Study of Grammatical and Social Correspondences in Sinhala. Ph.D. dissertation, Stanford University.

Paolillo, John. 1994. The Co-Development of Finiteness and Focus in Sinhala. In William Paglia, ed., *Perspectives on Grammaticalization*, pp. 151–70. Amsterdam: John Benjamins.

Paranavitana, Senarat. 1956. *Sigiri Graffiti*. 2 vols. Oxford: Oxford University Press.

Pattanayak, D.P. 1966. *A Controlled Historical Reconstruction of Oriya, Assamese, Bengali and Hindi*. The Hague: Mouton.

Peranteau, Paul M., Judith N. Levi, and Gloria C. Pharos, eds. 1972. *The Chicago Which Hunt: Papers from the Relative Clause Festival*. Chicago: Chicago Linguistic Society.

Perera, Heloise Marie Charmaigne. 1976. Adjective–Substantive Relationships in Sinhala. M.A. thesis, Cornell University.

Perlmutter, David M. 1978. Impersonal Passives and the Unaccusative Hypothesis. *BLS* (Berkeley Linguistic Society) 4: 157–89.

Pesetsky, David. 1987. Wh-in-situ: Movement and Unselective Binding. In E. Reuland and A. G. B. ter Meulen, eds., *The Representation of (In)definiteness*, pp. 98–129. Cambridge: MIT Press

Pollock, Jean-Yves. 1989. Verb Movement, Universal Grammar, and the Structure of IP. *Linguistic Inquiry* 20,3: 365–424.

Ramunajan, A. K., and Colin P. Masica. 1969. Towards a Phonological Typology of the Indian Linguistic Area. In Thomas A. Sebeok, ed., *Linguistics in South Asia* (Current Trends in Linguistics, vol. 5), pp. 543–577. The Hague: Mouton.

Ratanajoti, Hundirapola. 1975. The Syntactic Structure of Sinhalese and Its Relation to that of the Other Indo-Aryan Dialects. Ph.D. dissertation, University of Texas.

Reinhart, Tanya. 1976. The Syntactic Domain of Anaphora. Ph.D. dissertation, MIT.

Reinhart, Tanya. 1981. A Second COMP Position. In A. Belletti, L. Brandi, and L. Rizzi, eds. *Theory of Markedness in Generative Grammar*, pp. 517–58. Pisa: Scuole Normale Superiore.

Reinhart, Tanya. 1983. *Anaphora and Semantic Interpretation*. London: Croom Helm.

Reynolds, C. H. B. 1980/1995. *Sinhalese: An Introductory Course*. 2nd ed. London: School of Oriental and African Studies.

Reynolds, C. H. B., ed. 1970. *An Anthology of Sinhalese Literature up to 1815*. London: George Allen and Unwin.

Rhys-Davis, T. W., and William Stede. 1921–1925/1966. 5th ptg. *The Pali Text Society's Pali-English Dictionary*. London: Luzac.

Rochemont, Michael S. 1986. *Focus in Generative Grammar*. Amsterdam: Benjamins.

Ross, John R. 1967. Constraints on Variables in Syntax. Ph.D. dissertation, MIT.

Saito, M. 1984. On the Definition of C-Command and Government. In Charles Jones and Peter Sells, eds., *Near Eastern Linguistics Society* 14: 402–17. GLSA: Amherst, Mass.

Saksena, Anuradha. 1981. Verb Agreement in Hindi. *Linguistics* 19: 467–74.

Saksena, Anuradha. 1985. Verb Agreement in Hindi, Part 2. *Linguistics* 23: 137–42.

Saxon, Leslie. 1984. Disjoint Anaphora and the Binding Theory. In Cobler et al., eds., *Proceedings of the West Coast Conference on Formal Linguistics*, pp. 242–62. Stanford.

Schachter, Paul. 1973. Focus and Relativization. *Language* 49,1: 19–46.

Schiffman, Harold. 1979. *A Reference Grammar of Kannada*. Washington D.C.: Office of Education Report, Department of Health, Education and Welfare.

Schiffman, Harold. 1980. The Role of the Tamil Film in Language Change and Political Change. Paper presented at the Association for Asian Studies meeting, Washington, D.C.

Schiffman, Harold. 1992. Kannada. *International Encyclopedia of Linguistics* 2: 266–78. New York: Oxford University Press.

Shanmugam Pillai, M. 1962. A Tamil Dialect in Ceylon. *Indian Linguistics* 23: 90–98.

Shapiro, Michael C., and Harold E. Schiffman. *Language and Society in South Asia*. Delhi: Motilal Banarsidass.

Silva, M. H. P. 1961. Influence of Dravidian on Sinhalese. Ph.D. dissertation, University of Oxford.

Singh, Rajendra. 1975. Hindi: COMP-initial or COMP-Final? *Montreal Working Papers in Linguistics* 9: 203–7.

Southworth, Franklin. 1971. Detecting Prior Creolization: An Analysis of the Historical Origins of Marathi. In Dell Hymes, ed., *Pidginization and Creolization of Languages*, pp. 255–73. Cambridge: Cambridge University Press.

Southworth, Franklin, and Mahadeo Apte, eds. 1974. *Contact and Convergence in South Asian Languages*. Special issue of the *International Journal of Dravidian Linguistics*. Ernakulam, India: Dravidian Linguistics Association.

Srikumar, K. 1991. Control in Malayalam. *International Journal of Dravidian Linguistics* 20: 104–16.

Srikumar, K. 1992. Question-Word Movement in Malayalam and GB Theory. Ph.D. dissertation, Osmania University. Hyderbad, India.

Srivastav, V. 1991. WH Dependencies in Hindi and the Theory of Grammar. Ph.D. dissertation, Cornell University.

Stahlke, Herbert F. W. 1976. Which That. *Language* 52: 584–610.

Steever, Sanford B. 1988. *The Serial Verb Formation in the Dravidian Languages*. Delhi: Motilal Banarsidass

Steever, Sanford B. 1992. Tamil. *International Encyclopedia of Linguistics* 4: 131–36. New York: Oxford University Press.

Stowell, T. 1981. Origins of Phrase Structure. Ph.D. dissertation, MIT.

Subbarao, K. V. 1974. Phrase Structure Rule for Noun Phrase in Hindi. *Indian Linguistics* 35: 173–84.

Subbarao, K. V. 1984. *Complementation in Hindi Syntax*. New Delhi: Academic Publishers.

Sumangala, Lelwala. 1988a. Pro-drop and Control in Sinhala. Unpublished manuscript, Cornell University.

Sumangala, Lelwala. 1988b. Subjects in Sinhala. Unpublished manuscript, Cornell University.

Sumangala, Lelwala. 1989a. Binding Theory and Sinhala *taman*. Unpublished manuscript, Cornell University.

Sumangala, Lelwala. 1989b. Sinhala Focus and Predication. Unpublished manuscript, Cornell University.

Sumangala, Lelwala. 1991. Case and Agreement in Sinhala. Paper presented at the Symposium on Agreement in South Asian Languages, Madison, Wisconsin, November.

Sumangala, Lelwala. 1992. Long-Distance Dependencies in Sinhala: The Syntax of Focus and WH Questions. Ph.D. dissertation, Cornell University.

Suñer, Magui. 1984. Controlled *pro*. In Philip Baldi, ed. *Papers from the 12th Linguistics Symposium in Romance Languages*. (Current Issues in Linguistic Theory 26), pp. 253–273. Amsterdam: John Benjamins.

Suseendirarajah, S. 1966. Contrastive Study of Ceylon Tamil and English. *Proceedings of the First International Conference-Seminar of Tamil Studies*, 2: 751–56. Kuala Lumpur, Malaysia: International Association of Tamil Research.

Suseendirarajah, S. 1967. A Descriptive Study of Ceylon Tamil (with Special Reference to Jaffna Tamil). Ph.D. dissertation, Annamali University.

Suseendirarajah, S. 1970. Reflections of Certain Social Differences in Jaffna Tamil. *Anthropological Linguistics* 12,7: 239–45.

Suseendirarajah, S. 1973a. Phonology of Sri Lanka Tamil and Indian Tamil Contrasted. *Indian Linguistics* 34,3: 171–179.

Suseendirarajah, S. 1973b. A Study of Pronouns in Batticaloa Tamil. *Anthropological Linguistics* 15,4: 172–182.

Suseendirarajah, S. 1978. Caste and Language in Jaffna Society. *Anthropological Linguistics* 20,7: 312–319.

Thananjayarajasingham, S. 1962. Some Phonological Features of the Jaffna Dialect of Tamil. *University of Ceylon Review* 20,2: 292–302.

Thananjayarajasingham, S. 1966. The Phoneme /k/ in the Jaffna Dialect of Tamil. *Prof. Suryakumara bhuyan Commemoration Volume, 82nd All India Oriental Conference*, pp. 196–98. Gauhati, India:

Thananjayarajasingham, S. 1973. Bilingualism and Acculturation in the Kuravar Community of Ceylon. *Anthropological Linguistics* 15,6: 276–90.

Toribio, Almeida, and James W. Gair. 1991. In Case There Is Agreement. Paper presented at the Symposium on Agreement in South Asian Languages, Madison, Wisconsin, November.

Ullrich-Baylis, Helen. 1974. Morphological Coexistence: A Key to Linguistic Convergence. In Franklin C. Southworth and Mahadeo Apte, eds., *Contact and Convergence in South Asian Languages*. Special issue of the *International Journal of Dravidian Linguistics*, pp. 224–30. Ernakulam: Dravidian Linguistics Association.

Verma, Manindra. 1971. *The Structure of the Noun Phrase in English and Hindi*. New Delhi: Motilal Banarsidass.

Verma, Manindra, ed. 1976. *The Notion of Subject in South Asian Languages*. Madison: South Asia Program, University of Wisconsin.

Wali, Kashi. 1979. Two Marathi Reflexives and the Causative Structure. *Studies in Language* 3, 3: 405–38.

Watanabe, A. 1992. Wh-in-situ, Subjacency, and Chain Formation. Unpublished manuscript, Massachusetts Institute of Technology.

Wexler, Paul. 1971. Diglossia, Language Standardization and Purism: Parameters for a Typology of Literary Languages. *Lingua* 27: 330–54.

White, Lydia. 1989. *Universal Grammar and Second Language Acquisition*. Amsterdam: John Benjamins.

White, Lydia. 1991. Adverb Placement in Second Language Acquisition: Some Effects of Positive and Negative Effects in the Classroom. *Second Language Research* 7: 133–61.

Wijeratne, P. B. F. 1945–57. Phonology of the Sinhalese Inscriptions up to the End of the 10th Century A.D. *BSOAS* (Bulletin of the School of Oriental and African Studies) 11.3:

580–94; 11.4: 823–36; 12.1: 163–83; 13.1: 166–81; 14.2: 263–98; and 19.3: 479–514.

Williams, Edwin. 1980. Predication. *Linguistic Inquiry* 11,1: 203–38.

Williams, Edwin. 1981. Argument Structure and Morphology. *Linguistic Review* 1,1: 81–114.

Williams, Edwin. 1983. Against Small Clauses. *Linguistic Inquiry* 14,2: 287–308.

Williams, Edwin. 1984. Grammatical Relations. *Linguistic Inquiry* 15,4: 639–73.

Williams, Edwin, and Lisa Travis. 1982. Externalization of Arguments in Malayo-Polynesian Languages. *Linguistic Review*: 2,1: 57–77.

Yadurajan, K.S. 1988. Binding Theory and Reflexives in Dravidian. *Cornell Working Papers in Linguistics* 8: 181–203.

Zaenen, Annie, Joan Maling, and Hoskuldur Thrainsson. 1985. Case and Grammatical Functions: The Icelandic Passive. *Natural Language and Linguistic Theory* 3: 441–84.

Zvelibil, Kamil V. 1959. Dialects of Temil. *Archiv Orientalni* 28: 272–317.

Zvelibil, Kamil V. 1959–60. Notes on Two Dialects of Ceylon Tamil. *Transactions of the Linguistic Circle of Delhi, Dr. Siddheswara Varma Jubilee Volume*, pp. 28–36.

Zvelibil, Kamil V. 1960. Dialects of Tamil, II. *Archiv Orientalni* 28: 414–56.

Zvelibil, Kamil V. 1966. Some Features of Ceylon Tamil. *Indo Iranian Journal* 9,2: 113–38.

Zvelibil, Kamil V. 1990. *Dravidian Linguistics: An Introduction*. Pondicherry: Pondicherry Institute of Linguistics and Culture.

Index